# Adventure
# Guide
# to
# the
# Triangle

JOHN F. BLAIR, PUBLISHER WINSTON-SALEM, NORTH CAROLINA

# ADVENTURE GUIDE TO THE TRIANGLE

## MAIA DERY

Maps by Brent Abbey / Abbey Digital Graphics

*The paper in this book meets the guidelines
for permanence and durability of the Committee on
Production Guidelines for Book Longevity
of the Council on Library Resources.*

*Cover Images by the author*
*Background - The Neuse River*
*Insets on right, top to bottom - NC Bicycling Highway 2  /  Orange County Trail  /  Cane Creek Reservoir*

Library of Congress Cataloging-in-Publication Data
Dery, Maia.
Adventure Guide to the Triangle / by Maia Dery.
p.        cm.
Includes index.
ISBN-10: 0-89587-312-5 (alk. paper)
ISBN-13: 978-0-89587-312-5
1. Outdoor recreation—North Carolina—Guidebooks. 2. North Carolina—
Guidebooks.  I. Title.
GV191.42.N72D47 2005
917.5604'44—dc22                    2005005225

*Maps by Brent Abbey of Abbey Digital Graphics, unless otherwise noted*
*Design by Debra Long Hampton*

# Contents

# State and Locally Designated Road Biking Routes

# Triangle Paddling

# Preface

In the three and a half decades I've lived in the Triangle, this area has seen tremendous change. Some of it has been wonderful. Economic development has meant remarkably low unemployment rates, a delightful proliferation of ethnic and organic food, and many interesting people to share it with. Of course, the good times have come at a price. For one, suburban sprawl and highways have replaced the wooded and agricultural open spaces that drew many of us from cities without such aesthetic amenities. As the influx has continued, small but committed groups of people have joined forces with local governments to develop the recreational potential of the natural areas that remain. The promise of communities in which everyone has access to a quiet path for walking, a safe lane for cycling, and a clean river for paddling seems great. If the promise can be realized, it will increase our quality of life in ways too great to measure. Recent bonds passed in many Triangle communities attest to the citizenry's commitment to this promise.

I grew up in the Triangle and have benefited greatly from all this area has to offer. When I took up road biking and hiking in college, I began to understand how lucky I was to live someplace where I could easily pursue both avocations.

For more than a decade after graduating from college, I worked in local outdoor shops. Scores of customers came in asking for a comprehensive guide to outdoor recreation in the Triangle. Although North Carolina hiking guru Allen DeHart's *Trails of the Triangle*, *Raleigh News and Observer* columnist Joe Miller's *Take It Outside*, and Paul Ferguson's *Paddling Eastern North Carolina* are all must-have guides for any outdoor-minded Triangle resident, there wasn't one book that newcomers could read to acquaint themselves with the variety of things to see and do outside. So I finally set about the task of researching and writing this guide.

In the years it took me to paddle every river, walk or mountain-bike every trail and greenway, and cycle every designated bike route, I came to know and appreciate my community in ways I'd never anticipated. Although much work remains to be done, the committed citizens of the Triangle have made a tremendous start in preserving some of our most beautiful and unique natural areas and in developing the recreational potential of these places. Preservation and recreation don't always go hand in hand in urban communities such as this one, but if people don't use and appreciate natural areas, they're apt to disappear in the ongoing effort to make way for housing developments and shopping centers. It is my humble hope that this guide will serve to introduce newcomers and old-timers alike to the great potential afforded by what remains of our natural environment in and around the Triangle.

Unlike landscapes where the topography is more dramatic, the gentle terrain of the Triangle is easily plowed under, paved over, or otherwise harmed by human activities. Perhaps this guide will help more people get out and find the delights that are ours to enjoy because a few committed citizens have begun the hard work it takes to ensure the survival of these special places. You'll find enough hikes, bike rides, and paddling routes to keep your weekends occupied for years. I wish you many happy hours of exploration. Be safe, appreciate the quiet beauty of North Carolina's Piedmont, and, above all, have fun!

# What is the Triangle?

According to the Triangle J Council of Governments, the area includes the counties of Chatham, Durham, Johnston, Lee, Orange, and Wake. For the purposes of this guide, I have also included limited information about Alamance, Franklin, Granville, Harnett, and Person Counties because of their easy accessibility to many Triangle residents, or because bike rides or paddling routes in Triangle counties continue into these outlying areas.

# How to Use This Guide

This guide is organized first according to activity, then according to geography. All of the hiking and mountain biking trails are in one section and are grouped together by county. Since road biking and paddling routes rarely fall within the boundaries of a single county, these are described in separate sections.

# Hiking and Mountain Biking Trails

The guide includes descriptions of most of the trails and greenways that were completed at the time the manuscript went to press. Each trail is described according to length, difficulty, and surface. Blazes, if any, are noted, as is the permissibility of bikes.

The lengths of the trails and the "Mileposts," where included, come from measurements I made with a wheel that counts off feet as it is pushed along the ground. These wheels tend to be much more accurate on smooth surfaces than on uneven ones, but in most cases, my measured distances differed only slightly from those of the parks and recreation departments. If there was a discrepancy, I used my own measurements. My original intent was to include only overall distances for the trails, but as I pushed my wheel along, many people asked me the distance between one point and another, so I decided to include the measurements as "Mileposts" for all trails except urban greenways, where the municipalities often display trail lengths on signs. Likewise, I have not listed blazes for urban greenways. The length listed for each trail is the distance from one end to the other and does not include that required to return to the starting point, unless the trail is a loop. If it is a loop, it will be apparent on the map and is also mentioned in the description.

Most of the trails included here are easily followed, particularly if you can read a map. Use the maps in this guide or those provided by the parks or recreation departments. An even better option is get a USGS topographic map to supplement your trail map. These inexpensive maps contain a wealth of information. Many technically minded people have begun carrying Global Positioning System units that often include topographic software. As this guide was going to press, many parks were in the process of using this technology to update and refine their maps.

Each section about a specific park or trail system begins with an overview, after which each individual trail is briefly described. Be aware that conditions can change due to storms and that trails are occasionally closed due to flooding, tree fall, or other damage. Always check with the park or town office to make sure you won't be disappointed by a closing.

Each section includes directions to get you from a nearby interstate or major highway to the park. The route listed is usually only one of many possible approaches. Although I have tried to make it possible to reach the various destinations without the use of a map, you will have an easier time finding these sites if you consult a city map or atlas to ascertain the most convenient route from your location.

In the time I was researching this guide, several roads were substantially altered to make way for more cars, new developments, or other changes, and some sections of trails or river were closed due to damage by development or storms. Be aware that things in the Triangle have been changing in a hurry for quite some time, and that the pace shows no sign of slowing. Not only roads but city and county boundaries, traffic patterns, parks, trails, and natural features are sometimes altered dramatically. Even if you have thoroughly researched your outing using this or another guide, it is recommended that you call the relevant contact before finalizing your plans, to be certain your destination is currently open and accessible. A growing number of websites are devoted to providing up-to-the-minute information about local recreation areas.

# A Word about Mountain Bike Safety

When the risk of motor vehicle traffic is absent, the troubles faced by mountain bikers are often well within their power to avoid. As with road biking, a helmet is a necessity. Some of the trails described in this book are also open to horses. Mountain bikers should always yield to any other type of trail user, especially equestrians. Attempting to speed past an unsuspecting horse might result in serious injury to you, the horse, or the rider. The best course of action is to stop your bike and get off the trail. If in doubt, quietly ask the rider for advice. Be on the lookout for other trail users, particularly on blind curves, and always let others know when you are approaching. Never lose control of your bike. Proceed at a safe speed that will allow you time to react to other trail users and unexpected obstacles. Be self-sufficient. Know how to make minor repairs that mountain bikes are liable to need—tire changes, adjustments after broken spokes, etc.

Fairly or not, mountain bikers have a reputation for being a destructive force. This need not be the case. Confine your riding to open, dry trails where you will cause no lasting impact. If you have any doubts about what shape a trail is in, call the park and ask for current conditions. Always pack out your trash, and be courteous to others.

# Triangle Road Biking

While the mountains and the coast certainly have the edge in some recreational pursuits, the rolling hills of the Piedmont are ideal for a long bicycle ride along quiet country roads. Although development has spread to many places that were once rural, there are still outlying areas within reach of city-dwelling cyclists. Many serious recreational and competitive cyclists know the secret: Peddle north out of Raleigh and surprisingly soon you are in the bucolic country north of Falls Lake. Once you cross into Granville County, the traffic slackens further. South of Cary, north of Durham, and west of Chapel Hill, you can ride away from the urban bustle and set your own pace among the green hills. The best seasons to ride are spring and fall, but summer and winter are never without their beautiful days.

Where you live, how much traffic you can stand, how many miles you're comfortable riding, and other personal considerations will determine the best places for you to ride. Listed in Appendix 2 are several local clubs that sponsor group rides. Bike shops are usually staffed by fellow cyclists who will be happy to share information about the best and safest routes from your home or office. In a few instances, officials have done your homework for you and laid out routes. The city of Raleigh has 13 numbered bike routes. It also has some bike lanes and is in the process of developing a greenways system that will provide a great place for cyclists to ride free of auto traffic. Durham has published a bike map that rates all city streets in terms of their suitability for cyclists. Chapel Hill and Carrboro have an extensive system of bike lanes that provides some of the least hair-raising urban riding in the Triangle.

If a signed route outside the urban centers is more to your liking, you'll be glad to learn that the North Carolina Department of Transportation's Office of Bicycle and Pedestrian Transportation has developed bicycle routes all over the state. These routes use back roads whenever possible. Routes laid out under this program are officially known as the North Carolina Bicycling Highways, and three of these "highways"—the Carolina Connection (part of an interstate route), the North Line Trace, and the Mountains-to-Sea Route—pass through or near the Triangle. As interest in cycling has grown, counties have begun working with the state to develop their own signed routes. Chatham County and Alamance County (which is beyond the scope of this guide) have mapped out excellent routes for cyclists. As this book went to press, a map was also being developed for Orange County.

I have limited coverage of designated bike routes to the counties included in this guide, even though some of them extend beyond those boundaries.

Most of the terrain in our area consists of gently rolling hills. The difficulty ratings included in this guide are necessarily subjective but, I hope, consistent relative to one another. Use your own judgment. If I have described a 35-mile route as *easy* and you've never ridden more than 10 miles at one time, that *easy* rating won't apply in your case. It means that particular ride is easy relative to other 35-mile rides in the area. If you have doubts, get a copy of the relevant USGS topographic map or the DeLorme *North Carolina Atlas and Gazetteer*, which has topographic maps of the entire state. You can check out the elevation gains and losses for yourself.

Although most of the routes are described complete, I have broken up multi-county state bicycling highways into smaller sections for the purpose of description.

The turns along the routes are marked by signs put up by the DOT, but signs are occasionally missing, so it's wise to bring a map. Mileages for some geographical, historical, and recreational features and for stores and other services are listed in the "Highlights and Services" section for each route.

While maps are included for all of these routes, I strongly recommend that you use these only to get an idea of the routes, and that you acquire an updated road map from the North Carolina Department of Transportation or the relevant county. In the few years I took to research this guide, several roads were moved or renamed. As development continues apace, so will road construction and changes to existing routes.

A word about road biking safety: Cyclists do not usually fare too well when they get into a tussle with a motor vehicle of any description. Sharing the road with cars and trucks is an inherently dangerous activity. While many of North Carolina's country roads are a feast for the cyclist's senses, they are narrow and often have no shoulders, and they are driven by motorists who frequently travel at high speeds and do not always look for bikes. Most of the same can be said for cycling in the cities, but urban riding comes with a host of added hazards. Parallel parking creates a slew of potential dangers, from doors opening suddenly to drivers nudging their cars out of a space to see. A driver will sometimes speed past a cyclist, only to slam on the brakes and make a right turn directly in the rider's path.

On the other hand, some cyclists refuse to follow the rules of the road and to adhere to common courtesy. They pass lines of waiting traffic on the right, dart in and out among moving or stopped vehicles, stubbornly persist in riding two or more abreast when a car is attempting to pass, and flagrantly run red lights. A little education, common sense, and decency will go a long way toward keeping you safe on the roads. Wear a helmet. Make sure you and your bike are equipped with all of the required safety equipment, including reflectors and lights if you will be riding at dawn or dusk. If you have any doubt about the rules of the road, the North Carolina Department of Motor Vehicles will gladly answer your questions.

Although carrying a cell phone in case you need help is a good idea, it's best to be self-sufficient. Know how to change a tire, and have all of the necessary equipment to do it. Bring plenty of water in the summer, extra clothes if inclement weather threatens, and emergency snacks in case a store you were counting on happens to be closed.

# Lakes and Rivers

This guide provides an introduction to the lakes and rivers of the Triangle. Of all the activities described herein, paddling is perhaps the one that is most often underestimated in its potential for risk of injury or death. It seems that every time local rivers reach flood stage, some person who has no business being on the river gets into trouble. This kind of foolishness puts both the boater and rescue personnel in unnecessary danger. It also gives the responsible paddling community a bad reputation it doesn't deserve. If you are not an experienced paddler who has been trained by an accredited instructor, you should not use this guide to do anything other than locate a club or professional guide service that can teach you the skills necessary to safely paddle flat or moving water. Consult Appendix 2 for listings. Start your search with the Carolina Canoe Club, an extremely active and committed group that can provide you with all the information you need about preparing yourself to safely enjoy an outing on our local rivers.

Experienced paddlers will be pleased to learn that the Triangle has some good, albeit inconsistent, spots where they can work on their play-boating or chase a heron across a quiet lake. The rivers are broken down by section. I have provided general descriptions of each section, listings of major rapids, and information on classes and levels when it was available.

I myself am a terrified class-2+ paddler. Most of the descriptions in this guide owe their existence to the generosity of members of the paddling community who helped me make sense of the rapids and rock gardens of our rivers.

## Camping

Campgrounds are noted in the relevant chapters. If camping is your primary goal, see Appendix 1, where you'll find a list of Triangle campgrounds.

## Know How to Take Care of Yourself Outdoors

This guide is in no way intended to teach you how to conduct yourself safely in the places it describes. Most of the land routes are no farther than a few miles from a road or from a ranger who might offer help if you get into trouble. Take a cell phone. Of course, it's best to know how to avoid trouble in the first place. Always tell someone at home where you're going and when to expect you back. Anytime you plan an outdoor adventure, you should take these essentials:

    a compass
    water
    extra food

rain gear and extra clothing
a fire starter
matches
a first-aid kit
an army knife or other multipurpose tool
a flashlight and extra batteries
sunscreen and sunglasses

Although it's not on the list, don't forget the most essential ingredient in any successful outing: common sense. Be sure to follow the rules of the park or responsible agency. Pay attention to signs and brochures alerting you to rules and warnings.

Finally, the most sensible precaution anyone can take when entering an isolated area is to travel with a partner. In addition to providing a disincentive to anyone with nefarious intentions, a partner can help in the event of injury. If you're thinking about undertaking any activity for the first time, do some reading and get instruction from a qualified teacher. Beginners can also try a guided trip.

## Local Hazards

Tick season in the Triangle extends through the warm months. Anyone who enters the woods is likely to find a tick now and then. When you return from the woods, check yourself thoroughly. Ticks cause diseases such as Rocky Mountain spotted fever and Lyme disease. If you experience symptoms after removing a tick, see your doctor.

Mosquitoes can ruin what would otherwise be an idyllic outing. In recent years, concern has grown over the mosquito-borne West Nile virus. Mosquitoes tend to be worst at dawn and dusk and around standing water. The safest prevention is to wear long pants, a long-sleeve shirt, and a hat. Of course, wearing such a costume in the heat of summer carries its own risks. If you choose to wear insect repellent, the most effective contain Deet (diethyltoluamide). Many herbal products are also available, most of which contain citronella. These repellents work well for some people and not at all for others. Experiment in your backyard before a big trip.

While mosquitoes might ruin a special day, chiggers can spoil a whole week. They are red arachnids so small they usually can't be seen. Chiggers are plentiful throughout our region, particularly in grassy areas and woodlands. Once they've climbed onto you, they dig into your skin, often close to wherever elastic you're wearing—socks, underwear, waistbands—where they raise large red welts after half a day or so. Insect repellent provides some protection. Also, a good, harsh scouring with soap and water after a trip can sometimes dislodge them before they tunnel into your skin.

Poison ivy is abundant throughout our region. It can grow almost anywhere. Every resident or visitor should learn to recognize and avoid it. The plant has three shiny green leaves and sometimes grows up the trunks of trees in a thick, fuzzy vine. If you come into contact with it, wash the exposed area repeatedly with warm water and soap.

If you're planning to participate in outdoor activities in the Triangle, you should learn to recognize the symptoms of heat exhaustion and the potentially fatal condition of heat stroke. You should also be familiar with first-aid treatment for these conditions.

A tragic result of the Triangle's economic and population boom is the dramatic decline in local air quality. Although children, the elderly, and those with respiratory conditions are most at risk, even healthy lungs can be damaged by exposure to toxic levels of ozone. To protect yourself, be aware of the ozone alerts broadcast on local media in the warm months. Limit outdoor exertion to mornings during ozone-alert days. Also, do your part to reverse this disturbing threat to our quality of life. Carpool whenever possible. Always drive the most efficient car you can to your outing—or, even better, take the bus. All of the area's urban buses have bike racks, and some of the most visited parks are accessible by bus. Numbers for the three major bus systems are provided in Appendix 2. If you believe in public transportation to recreational areas, let your government representatives and park officials know.

# Get Involved

I assume that folks who take the time to paddle a river, peddle across the county, or hike deep into the woods are not responsible for the cigarette butts, beer cans, soda bottles, and other litter that finds its way into our natural areas. The shores of area lakes are particularly abused. It's a good idea to stick a trash bag in your pack and help the effort to clean up after the less responsible members of our species. Environmental organizations that offer information on clean-up efforts are listed in Appendix 2.

Almost all of the places described in this book have either benefited from or owe their existence to some organization or individual who volunteered time and skills in the service of the community. See Appendix 2 for a list of the organizations you can contact to make a contribution to help ensure a better, safer, more fun Triangle for yourself and others.

# The Counties

## Chatham County

Although Chatham County is growing rapidly, many farms remain, and the landscape is more open and rural than in some other Triangle counties. This pastoral character is particularly evident once you get past the suburbs of northern Chatham that blend with Chapel Hill. The Haw and Deep Rivers attracted settlers as early as the 1740s and are still drawing visitors today. The Haw is one of few rivers in the Triangle where expert whitewater paddling is possible, while the Deep offers one of the most scenic canoe trips in the area.

Chatham County's outdoor recreational opportunities are many. Its most visited attraction, Jordan Lake State Recreation Area, is popular with powerboaters but also has appeal for those who prefer human-powered recreation. The recreation area includes hiking trails, campgrounds, and canoe and kayak access. Although it's a tiny town, Pittsboro has begun to develop a local trail program. The Chatham bike routes are another wonderful way to explore the county. As this guide was going to press, government representatives were working with citizens to find funding to open American Tobacco Trail through Chatham. Finally, White Pines Nature Preserve is one of the most scenic and rewarding places to hike in the Triangle.

## Durham County

Like booming Orange County to its west and Wake County to its east, Durham County has seen much of its rural character disappear in the last decades. Efforts to protect the remaining natural areas have taken on urgency. Durham County has joined Orange County and the cities of Durham and Chapel Hill to create a master plan that, if realized, will result in a continuous corridor of protected green space. Under this plan, Eno River State Park, Duke Forest, the New Hope Creek Valley, and the Army Corps of Engineers land surrounding Jordan Lake would be connected by a network of trails. Upon completion, this plan will make Durham one of the most hiker-friendly urban counties anywhere.

Durham County currently has some exceptional recreational opportunities. Eno River State Park, which Durham shares with Orange County, is one of the Piedmont's best hiking parks. The Durham Division of Duke Forest, also shared with Orange, offers many miles of trails and roads for hikers and mountain bikers. As this guide was going to press, Little River Regional Park was about to open; miles of hiking and mountain biking trails will be available in the near future. As for cycling, northern Durham County still has a few quiet back roads, but serious cyclists in search of light traffic may wish to continue north into Person County.

## City of Durham

Like other Triangle cities, Durham has experienced explosive growth in the last few decades. Between 1990 and 1999, its population increased by 30 percent. Fortunately, Durham's population isn't the only thing that's grown rapidly. In 1999, the city had 4 miles of greenways. As this guide was going to press, 16 miles of greenways were completed and another 4 were under construction. Most notably, the first section of American Tobacco Trail was opened in 2000.

Good opportunities for recreational cycling are scarce within the city. Durham has no designated bike routes, bike lanes outside the Duke University campus are scant, and traffic is heavy. The city has posted Share the Road signs and publishes the *Durham Bike Map*, a complete city map that color-codes roads based on traffic volume and safety for cyclists. Free copies of the map are available from the city or the DOT's Office of Pedestrian and Bicycle Transportation. The map is particularly useful for commuters looking for a reasonably safe ride to and from work.

Hikers in Durham are lucky, as West Point on the Eno is possibly the most appealing city park in the Triangle.

## Harnett County

Harnett County lies south of Wake County, within an easy drive for most Triangle residents. Harnett is far enough from the Triangle to have retained much of its rural character. Most of its communities are nestled close to the Cape Fear River. The river is one of several reasons Triangle residents should not overlook Harnett County. Cape Fear Canoe Trail and Raven Rock State Park together provide the region's only opportunity for canoe camping. The state park is also a good destination for hikers, equestrians, and family campers. Raven Rock is what many hope will be the southern anchor for a long swath of protected lands. The Triangle Land Conservancy is working to protect one of the Cape Fear's major tributaries, the Deep River, from Moore County all the way downstream to Raven Rock.

A designated state bike route called the Cape Fear Run passes through Harnett. The fall zone that separates the Piedmont from the coastal plain runs through the county. Because much of Harnett is in the coastal plain, this bike route is significantly flatter than those to the north and west. The fall zone is also responsible for the rapids on the upper Cape Fear River. The eastern two-thirds of the county are noticeably flatter than the rolling hills of the western third. Some of the county lies on what is known as the Raleigh Belt. Raven Rock State Park is on the southern end of the belt. The 150-foot-tall Raven Rock is the most dramatic of several outcroppings along the Cape Fear in Harnett County.

## Johnston County

Johnston County borders Wake County. This proximity to one of the fastest-growing metropolitan regions in the country is rapidly changing the character of Johnston County.

Johnston includes sections of the Deep River Triassic Basin, the rockier Carolina Slate Belt, and the flat, sandy coastal plain. The fall line that separates the Piedmont from the coastal plain runs through Johnston, so the county has a great variety of landscapes. On Flower Hill, a rocky section in the northwestern part of the county where the elevation is above 300 feet, Catawba rhododendron, mountain laurel, and other highland plants grow. By contrast, the southeastern section of the county has elevations as low as 80 feet.

Johnston is home to Clemmons State Educational Forest, Legend Park, and Bentonville Battleground. The educational forest is a good destination for families looking for an easy hike in the woods. Legend Park and the neighboring private lands hold miles of rolling mountain bike trails. Bentonville Battleground Loop makes for a nice, easy road ride, as well as a fascinating history lesson.

# Lee County

Lee County, a small county south of Chatham, forms the southern corner of the Triangle. The Deep River, the Carolina Connection (US Bike Route 1), and San-Lee Environmental Education and Recreation Park are the county's major outdoor draws. The Deep is one of the few local rivers that has enough water for year-round paddling. San-Lee Park has well-designed hiking trails and a mountain bike trail.

# Orange County

Orange County has much to recommend it to outdoor enthusiasts. Its miles of open country roads attract cyclists. Paddlers can take advantage of the Eno and Little Rivers, as well as two reservoirs—Cane Creek and University Lake. Hikers and mountain bikers can select from four divisions of Duke Forest and the Johnston Mill Nature Preserve. Although it's listed in the Durham County section for the purposes of this book, the majority of Eno River State Park's acreage lies in Orange County. Occoneechee Mountain offers great hiking and a hill with a view, a rare occurrence in the Piedmont. Finally, the development of Little River Regional Park on the border with Durham County promises to further increase options for adventure. At present, there are no camping opportunities in the county, but Jordan Lake State Recreation Area and the Few's Ford Section of Eno River State Park are within an easy drive for most Orange County residents.

## Town of Chapel Hill

From the perspective of outdoor enthusiasts, Chapel Hill is a friendlier city than most. Many of its busy streets have designated bike lanes or paths, and all city buses are equipped with bike racks and are fare-free. Also, the town is developing a greenways system that promises to further increase transportation and recreation alternatives with each passing year.

Chapel Hill has a good variety of trails and is well situated for easy access to some of the Triangle's finest outdoor adventures. The Chapel Hill Parks and Recreation Department offers rock-climbing lessons on the town's indoor climbing wall.

## Town of Carrboro

Carrboro, being a small place, has just a few greenways (the town calls them "bikeways") and parks. Its network of bike lanes has almost turned it into a bicycle commuter's paradise—I say *almost* because vehicle exhaust and air quality are as much an issue in Carrboro as elsewhere in the Triangle. Easy access to the many rural rides north of town makes Carrboro a favorite for road riders as well.

## Wake County

Wake is the most densely populated county in the Triangle, encompassing over 627,000 residents and 12 municipalities, including Raleigh, the state capital. Although Wake is no longer the bucolic place it once was, it still offers plenty of opportunities for hiking, biking, and paddling. Extensive trail systems form the heart of the county's two state parks. Hikers are more fortunate than road cyclists, since finding a stretch of Wake County road with few cars has become increasingly difficult over the last decade. Mountain bikers, however, can enjoy one of the best assortments of rides this side of the Blue Ridge Parkway. Crabtree County Park, William B. Umstead State Park, and the trails at Falls Lake State Recreation Area offer the off-road set an unusual variety of well-maintained trails. Wake County also has the Neuse River. Officials have begun to work harder at protecting this special resource while developing its recreational potential. The choices for flat-water paddlers include Falls Lake, Lake Crabtree, and Harris Lake.

# City of Raleigh

In 2000, *Money* magazine named Raleigh "the best place to live in the South." At that time, the city's population was upward of 280,000, a figure that represented a 30 percent increase over the previous decade. Projections forecast that by 2025, the population will be 520,000. If you talk about this explosive growth with local residents, you'll get either a gleeful discussion of new jobs and rising property values or a groaning tale of traffic and plowed-under fields. It is fortunate for current residents that, during the mid-1970s, city administrators looked at the rapid rate of growth and realized it wasn't going to stop. If nothing was done, Raleigh's remaining natural beauty would be lost. City officials and citizens decided to take what was then the revolutionary step of developing an interconnected system of linear parks. The impressive Raleigh Greenways system is the result.

The greenways link parks and offer an opportunity to see the Neuse River, Crabtree Creek, and Walnut Creek—Raleigh's three major waterways—along with many of their tributaries. One of the program's long-term goals is a closed network of trails that will allow residents to walk or bicycle around town without encountering the trouble and danger of busy roadways.

Thanks for this program are due to the citizens of the Capital City. Their representatives in municipal government have prioritized funding for the planning, construction, and maintenance of greenways. In addition, many private citizens have donated land and time to make them a reality. It is to be hoped that committed and generous citizens will enable the program to continue growing into the future.

Raleigh has published a map of city bike routes and marked each route with directional signs.

# Town of Cary

From a recreational standpoint, Cary includes some of the best and worst the Triangle has to offer. The town is still characterized by car-congested roads where pedestrians and cyclists take their lives into their hands. On the other hand, it also boasts a remarkable parks and greenways system with many interesting attractions, including Swift Creek Trail, a greenway made entirely of recycled materials, and the impressive Stevens Nature Center. Just outside the city limits is the delightful, though beleaguered, William B. Umstead State Park.

As for the future, Cary has a bold vision that is beginning to have a real, positive impact on the town's character. This vision has been incorporated into the town's master plan, available for review at www.townofcary.org. This plan specifies how the town intends to continue developing its greenways system, including a crucial link to American Tobacco Trail. Cary also has an exemplary Comprehensive Transportation Plan that recognizes bicycles as a legitimate means of transportation on a par with motor vehicles. What the town terms "the bicycle element" of its plan includes bike lanes, bike paths, connections to greenways, a map of Cary bike routes, and the larger goal of making bicycling safe, fun, and practical. If Cary sticks to its plan, it will indeed change its status from a leading example of runaway growth to one of sensible progress that encourages human-powered pursuits and the enjoyment of our natural resources.

# Acknowledgments

It is impossible for me to offer adequate thanks to the many people who helped me research this guide.

I would have never begun the project without the suggestion and enthusiasm of Isabel Dickson, who left the Triangle for new adventures in the mountains of North Carolina and, later, South America.

I owe thanks to all of those who accompanied me on trails, roads, lakes, and rivers while I was getting to know the places I thought I already knew. In no particular order, they are Diane Amato, Craig Armstrong, Michelle Bellanger, John Bemis, Laura Billings, Nancy Brayson, Matt Chenet, Jerry Covington, Nicole Dery, Meg Dolan, Haven Kimmel, Ben Levenson, Mary Sugden, Leigh Sweet, Lindsay Stoecker, John Svara, Audrey Townsend, Karl Wetter, Alyssa Wittenborn, and Mike and DeeAnna VanReken. Carolyn Allmendinger gave me sensible editorial advice as well as kind hand-holding. Before I ultimately went to John F. Blair, Publisher, Bill Webster contributed immeasurably to the text.

I owe an enormous debt of gratitude to the administrators and rangers at the parks and government agencies who provided the information and assistance that made this guide possible. These people were generous with their time and are working tirelessly to meet the growing demands for local recreation.

The paddling section of this book would not exist but for the kind and generous help of three men. First, Le Scott gave me detailed firsthand accounts of rapids I wouldn't dare run; most of the descriptions of the whitewater sections are his careful work. Second, Joe Greiner generously reviewed the text for accuracy. Finally, Banks Dixon of Frog Hollow Boat Rentals supplied me with canoes to paddle the lakes and sections of river my skills allowed.

My family and friends deserve medals for putting up with me during this seemingly endless effort. In particular, Carolyn Allmendinger, Diane Amato, Nicole Dery, Steve Hoover, Haven Kimmel, Gretchen Longenecker, Paula Sims, John Svara, Karl Wetter, and Alyssa Wittenborn were kind beyond my powers of description. Above all, I owe thanks for this project as well as everything else in my life to my partner, Senga Carroll, who walked, peddled, and paddled almost as much as I, who made hundreds of lunches for the road, and who generally kept me from losing my mind.

While this project could not have been completed without the assistance of many others, the inevitable mistakes are the sole responsibility of the author. An e-mail account (guidebook@maiadery.com) has been set up to receive any suggestions or corrections for possible future editions.

# Adventure Guide to the Triangle

# Hiking
# and
# Mountain Biking Trails

# Chatham County

## Pittsboro Trails

This small town has just begun to develop a system of trails. As this guide was going to press, THANKS Trail was complete and Town Lake Park Trail was being cleared.

### THANKS Trail

**Length:** 0.9 mile
**Difficulty:** Easy
**Blazes:** None
**Surface:** Asphalt
**Bicycles:** Cyclists should ride slowly and beware of pedestrians.
**Directions:** The trail is located on the grounds of Central Carolina Community College. From the intersection of US 15/US 501 and US 64 at the traffic circle in Pittsboro, take US 64 west for 0.8 mile to the CCCC entrance on the right. The trailhead is near the farthest parking lot.

This trail's name is an acronym for Trail for Health, Art, and Nature for Kids to Seniors. Fitness stations and a picnic table are located next to a bridge that used to be part of US 64.

### Mileposts

**0.0 mile:** Begin at the signboard beside the garden. Head left to follow the exercise stations in order.

**0.1 mile:** The right fork goes to a bridge and picnic table. Continue straight.
**0.9 mile:** You'll return to the parking lot. The right fork crosses a bridge to the Senior Center.

# Jordan Lake State Educational Forest

**Address:** 2832 Big Woods Road, Chapel Hill, NC 27514
**Telephone:** 919-542-1154
**Hours:** 9 A.M. to 5 P.M. on weekdays, 11 A.M. to 8 P.M. on weekends during daylight savings time and from 11A.M. to 5 P.M. the rest of the year.
**Maps:** USGS Farrington; a free trail map is available from the forest.
**Directions:** From the intersection of US 64 and Big Woods Road (SR 1716), take Big Woods north for 2.8 miles. The state forest entrance is on the right.

This section of Jordan Lake is operated by the North Carolina Forest Service. It includes Talking Tree Trail, which has recorded interpretive messages, the 1.5-mile Forest Demonstration Trail, a new wetland trail, a pond, an amphitheater, and a picnic area where rangers conduct educational programs for schoolchildren.

## Forest Demonstration Trail

**Length:** 1.5 miles
**Difficulty:** Easy
**Blazes:** Green
**Surface:** Natural
**Bicycles:** No

This wooded interpretive trail offers a glimpse of the lake within the first 0.5 mile. An interesting and informative display describes a meadow planted with food for local fauna.

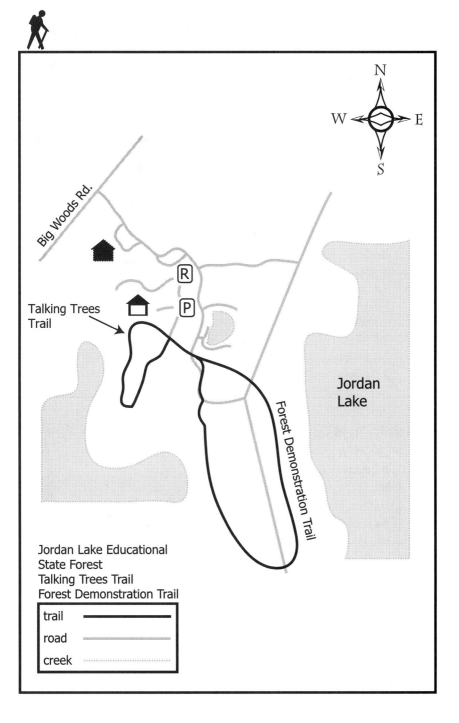

### Mileposts

**0.0 mile:** Begin from the parking lot at the trailhead. Turn left before the log building. Within 100 yards, you'll reach a T intersection. Head right.

**0.2 mile:** You'll pass two forks. Go right at the first fork and left at the second.

**0.3 mile:** You'll cross a bridge.

**0.7 mile:** You'll cross another bridge. Continue straight across the gravel road.

**1.2 miles:** You'll cross a bridge.

**1.3 miles:** You'll cross another bridge.

**1.4 miles:** You'll return to the first fork. Go right. At the next intersection, turn left to return to the parking lot.

**1.5 miles:** You'll return to the parking lot.

*Jordan Lake*

## Talking Trees Trail

**Length:** 0.75 mile
**Difficulty:** Easy
**Blazes:** None
**Surface:** Natural
**Bicycles:** No

The recorded messages are the highlight of this trail. For scenic appeal, Forest Demonstration Trail is a better choice.

### Mileposts

**0.0 mile:** Begin the loop by walking straight past the log building.

**0.75 mile:** You'll return to the parking lot.

# Jordan Lake State Recreation Area

**Address:** Route 2, Box 179, Apex, NC 27502
**Telephone:** 919-362-0586
**Hours:** (unless otherwise posted) November through February, 8 A.M. to
6 P.M.; March and October, 8 A.M. to 7 P.M.; April and September,
8 A.M. to 8 P.M.; May and August, 8 A.M. to 9 P.M.
**Maps:** Free large-scale maps are available from the park office, which
is a good place to begin your visit.
**Directions:** To reach the park office, take US 64 West for 1 mile past
Wilsonville. The park office is on the left.

Although the lake is the primary draw at this recreation area, there
are several trails and some fine campgrounds (see Appendix 1). For a
more detailed introduction to Jordan Lake, see pages 422-27 .

## Wildlife Observation Trail

**Length:** 1.6 miles
**Difficulty:** Easy
**Blazes:** White
**Surface:** Natural
**Bicycles:** No
**Map:** USGS Green Level
**Directions:** From the intersection of NC 751 and I-40, drive
south on NC 751 for 6.5 miles. The parking lot is on the
right and is marked by a brown sign.

This is an easy loop trail with more variety than you
might expect in such a short distance. The trail passes
through a former tobacco farm. Some fields remain, but a
mixed forest surrounds most of the trail. The New Hope
Audubon Society has printed an excellent brochure
describing different habitats and animals you might
encounter; the brochure is available at the trailhead.

The stars of the show here are the bald eagles. The
eagles draw many visitors to the wildlife observation

platform, located on a point of land where Indian Creek and the New Hope Creek run into Jordan Lake. Ospreys are sometimes spotted in the area as well.

## Mileposts

**0.0 mile:** Begin at the far right corner of the second parking area.

**0.1 mile:** Where the trail forks, take the right fork if you want to follow the numbered stations in order. You'll return via the left fork.

**0.7 mile:** You'll arrive at the observation deck. After several yards, the trail forks. The left fork loops back to join the trail you took on the way in. The right fork heads into the woods.

**1.25 miles:** Continue left at the fork.

**1.4 miles:** You'll emerge from the woods.

**1.5 miles:** You'll rejoin the path from the parking lot.

**1.6 miles:** You'll reach the parking lot.

# Ebenezer Church Recreation Area (fee area) _____

**Maps:** USGS New Hill, Merry Oaks

**Directions:** Take US 64 to Wilsonville, turn south on Beaver Creek Road (SR 1008), and drive 2.2 miles to reach the recreation area, on the right. To reach the trailhead, pass the gate, then take the first right to reach the large parking lot.

## Old Oak Trail

**Length:** 0.8 mile

**Difficulty:** Easy

**Blazes:** Red

**Surface:** Natural

**Bicycles:** No

**Directions:** The trailhead for Old Oak Trail is on the east side of the driveway where it intersects the parking lot. A map and information sign are located at the trailhead.

The two ponds on Old Oak Trail make this short walk interesting. Move quietly and you may spot a turtle basking on a log.

## Mileposts

**100 yards:** The trail intersects the return loop.
**0.2 mile:** You'll pass a pond.
**0.4 mile:** You'll pass a second pond and an informational sign.
**0.8 mile:** You'll reach the boardwalk near the first intersection, then the intersection itself. Turn right to return to the parking lot.

# Trail to the Beach

**Length:** 0.4 mile
**Difficulty:** Easy
**Blazes:** None
**Surface:** Natural
**Bicycles:** No

This short, easy trail parallels the road between parking areas. The trailhead is on the west side of same parking lot as the Old Oak trailhead. The beach parking lot is also the location of the Ebenezer Church trailhead, so you can walk Old Oak, this trail, and Ebenezer Church Trail and spend most of your time in the woods.

## Mileposts

**0.2 mile:** You'll arrive at the second parking lot.
**0.3 mile:** You'll cross two driveways, reenter the woods, and pass a picnic area.
**0.4 mile:** The trail forks. The right fork goes to shelters. The left fork continues toward the beach and Ebenezer Church Trail. In less than 100 yards, you'll emerge at the beach parking lot. The beach is straight ahead. The trailhead for Ebenezer Church Trail is in the far left corner of the

parking lot and is marked with a large informational sign.

## Ebenezer Church Trail

**Length:** 1 mile
**Difficulty:** Easy
**Blazes:** None
**Surface:** Natural
**Bicycles:** No
**Directions:** Begin at the south corner of the beach parking lot. The trailhead is marked with a large sign.

This flat, shaded trail offers a look at a pond and a historical site. A historical marker at the site gives a brief description of the history of the church, which was built in the late 1700s at a different location.

### Mileposts

**30 yards:** Take the right fork at the T intersection. In another 70 yards, you'll cross a wooden bridge.
**0.1 mile:** You'll intersect the return loop on the left and arrive at the former site of Ebenezer Church.
**0.2 mile:** You'll cross a bridge.
**0.4 mile:** You'll cross the road before passing a pond.
**0.8 mile:** You'll reach the intersection with the trail from the parking lot. The parking lot is to the right.
**0.9 mile:** You'll arrive back at the first intersection. Either direction will take you out of the woods and into the beach parking lot and driveway.
**0.1 mile:** You'll arrive at the parking lot.

# Vista Point (fee area)

**Map:** USGS Merry Oaks
**Directions:** To reach Vista Point, follow US 64 West for 3.4 miles past Wilsonville to Griffins Crossroads, then turn left on North Pea

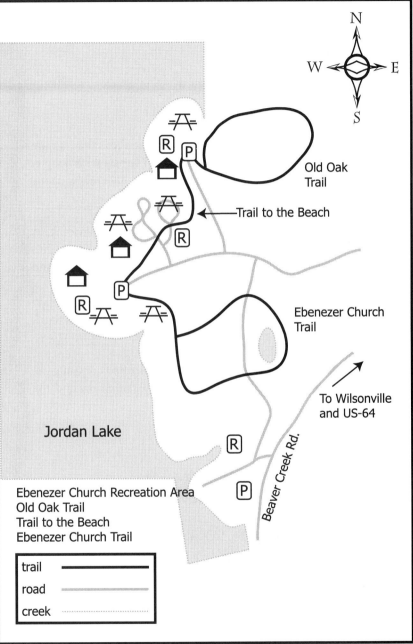

N

W ✦ E

S

Old Oak
Trail

Trail to the Beach

Ebenezer Church
Trail

To Wilsonville
and US-64

Jordan Lake

Beaver Creek Rd.

Ebenezer Church Recreation Area
Old Oak Trail
Trail to the Beach
Ebenezer Church Trail

| | |
|---|---|
| trail | ——————— |
| road | ~~~~~~~~~ |
| creek | ········· |

Ridge Road (SR 1700). Drive 2.5 miles to reach Vista Point.

## View Point Trail

**Length:** 2.7 miles
**Difficulty:** Easy
**Blazes:** Red
**Surface:** Natural
**Bicycles:** No

View Point Trail is true to its name. Less than a mile into the walk, you'll reach a delightful bench with a view.

### Mileposts

**0.0 mile:** Begin at the trailhead near the bathrooms. A crosswalk crosses the driveway just before it widens into the parking lot. After 100 yards, you'll cross a bridge and then a field before returning to the woods.
**0.8 mile:** A short trail to the left leads to a bench.
**2.5 miles:** The trail forks shortly before the picnic shelter. A map is posted at the shelter. The trail turns right and crosses the road.
**2.6 miles:** The trail forks. Take the right fork to continue the trail. The left fork heads to the group camp area and the beach.
**2.7 miles:** You'll return to the trailhead.

# Seaforth Recreation Area (fee area) _____

**Map:** USGS Merry Oaks
**Directions:** From Wilsonville, follow US 64 West for 2.4 miles, then turn left. The trailhead is directly across the parking lot from the second set of restrooms.

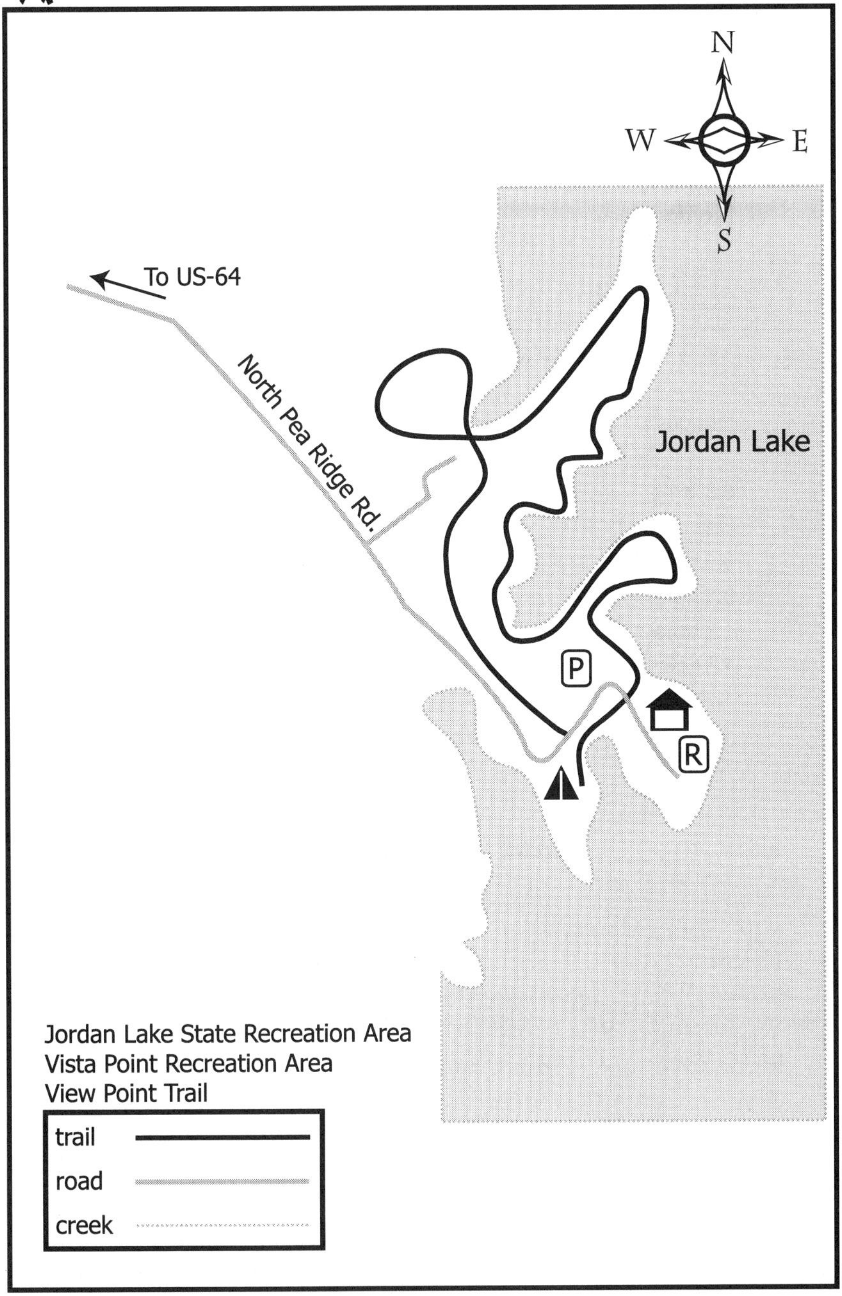

N

W &harr; E

S

To US-64

North Pea Ridge Rd.

Jordan Lake

P

R

Jordan Lake State Recreation Area
Vista Point Recreation Area
View Point Trail

| trail | ———— |
| road | |
| creek | |

## Pond Trail

**Length:** 1.4 miles, plus a 0.2-mile walk back to the parking lot
**Difficulty:** Easy
**Blazes:** Red and white
**Surface:** Natural
**Bicycles:** No

This trail offers a look at three marshy ponds and a lake. It also features a series of boardwalks, one of which has a particularly appealing view.

### Mileposts

**0.3 mile:** After negotiating the boardwalk, you'll pass a pond.
**0.6 mile:** You'll pass a second pond.
**0.9 mile:** You'll cross a driveway.
**1.3 miles:** You'll reach a third pond.
**1.4 miles:** You'll reach a signboard and the edge of the picnic area. Look to the left to see the lake through the woods. The parking lot is beyond the picnic shelter to the right.

# New Hope Overlook Recreation Area (fee area)

**Map:** USGS Merry Oaks
**Directions:** From Raleigh, take US 1 South to the Pea Ridge Road exit (Exit 81). Turn right on Pea Ridge Road (SR 1972), drive 3 miles to W. H. Jones Road (SR 1974), turn left, and drive into New Hope Overlook. From Chapel Hill, take US 15/US 501 South (South Columbia Street) out of town. After crossing the overpass over NC 54, turn left on Mount Carmel Church Road (SR 1008). After 12.5 miles, you'll intersect US 64 at Wilsonville. Continue straight across US 64 to Beaver Dam Road. After 3.3 miles, turn right on Pea Ridge Road (SR 1972) and go 2.3 miles to W. H. Jones Road, on the right. W. H. Jones Road leads to the New Hope Overlook driveway.

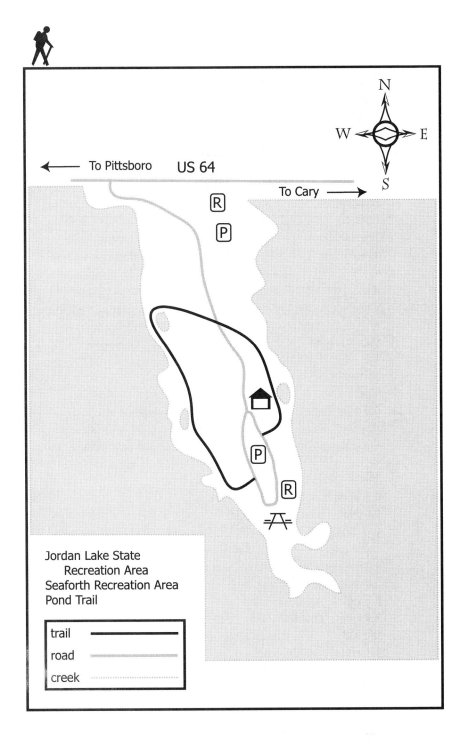

To Pittsboro    US 64

To Cary →

Ⓡ

Ⓟ

Ⓟ

Ⓡ

Jordan Lake State
Recreation Area
Seaforth Recreation Area
Pond Trail

| | |
|---|---|
| trail | ─────── |
| road | ─────── |
| creek | ·········· |

# New Hope Overlook Trail

**Length:** 2.7 miles
**Difficulty:** Easy to moderate
**Blazes:** Red (loops) and blue (connector)
**Surface:** Natural
**Bicycles:** No

As this guide was going to press, 2.7 miles of this trail were open for use and another 2.5 were planned for the near future. The open section is a loop that goes from the parking lot uphill to the gravel road near Camping Area A, then returns via a pleasant lakeside trail. A spur trail leads to a bench with a view of a small island in the lake. The second section will be a loop that extends toward Camping Area B. The completed trail will be of particular interest to campers, since there is a fee for day use during late spring and summer. If you are interested in a free hike with lake views, check out Falls Lake Trail.

## Mileposts

**0.0 mile:** Begin at the trailhead near the signboard, located to your left as you enter the near parking lot. After less than 100 yards, the trail forks. The right fork leads directly to the lake side of the trail. The left fork heads uphill and to the far loop before returning. Go left.

**0.3 mile:** You'll cross a gravel road.

**0.6 mile:** You'll reach a fork. When completed, the left fork will lead to Camping Area B before returning to the near loop and the parking lot. Take the right fork. After 130 yards, you'll cross a small seasonal creek.

**1.8 miles:** You'll cross a creek, then a gravel road near Camping Area A.

**2.0 miles:** The trail forks. The left fork goes directly to a lakeside bench. Take the right fork.

**2.2 miles:** You'll cross a bridge.

**2.5 miles:** You'll cross another bridge.

**2.7 miles:** You'll return to the first fork, then exit left in less than 100 yards.

# White Pines Nature Preserve

**Address:** Triangle Land Conservancy, 1101 Haynes Street, Suite 205, Raleigh, NC 27604
**Telephone:** 919-833-3662
**Hours:** Sunrise to sunset
**Map:** USGS Colon
**Directions:** From Chapel Hill, take US 15/US 501 South to Pittsboro. From Raleigh, take US 64 West to the intersection with US 15/US 501 South at the traffic circle in Pittsboro. From Pittsboro, head south on US 15/US 501 for 8 miles from the traffic circle. Turn left on River Fork Road (SR 1958), the first left after the Rocky River Bridge. Make an immediate right, drive 1.7 miles, turn right at the stop sign, and go 0.5 mile to the Triangle Land Conservancy sign. Turn left and proceed to the parking area on the right. The trail is a thinner continuation of the driveway you rode in on.

Insulated from the hustle of the Triangle's cities, White Pines Nature Preserve offers one of the most beautiful and rewarding hikes in the area. The Triangle Land Conservancy owns this 258-acre piece of land—and thank goodness that it does. The area was of particular interest to TLC because it supports a significant number of white pines and other plants more common in cooler mountain climates.

Ten thousand years ago, at the end of the last glacial period, the ancestors of today's trees were part of a population of white pines that stretched from the mountains across the Piedmont and into the coastal plain. When the climate warmed, only those trees in relatively cool microclimates were able to survive and reproduce in the Piedmont. The north-facing slopes at the confluence of the Rocky and Deep Rivers provided a place where white pines could grow alongside other montane species such as mountain laurel, rhododendron, and hemlock. The largest of the white pines in the preserve are 20 inches in diameter and are estimated to be 180 years old.

In addition to providing a haven for rare trees, this land has contributed to the survival of one of North Carolina's endangered species, a small fish called the Cape Fear shiner. The confluence of the Rocky and Deep Rivers has been identified as the best breeding ground for this rare fish, which has an extremely limited range.

Rivaling the botanical appeal of this place is the access it provides to the two rivers. There are four hiking trails in White Pines. White Pines Trail leaves the parking lot and runs down the spine of the preserve, leading to an overlook of the Rocky with good winter views. Schoolkid Trail loops upstream off Overlook Trail. River Trail leads to the Rocky River, follows it downstream to its confluence with the Deep River, then heads upstream before looping back to White Pines Trail. Comet Trail connects River Trail to White Pines Trail, offering a quick tour of the descent from upland to bottomland.

## White Pines Trail

**Length:** 0.6 mile
**Difficulty:** Easy to moderate
**Blazes:** White
**Surface:** Natural
**Bicycles:** No

This wide trail is easy to follow and gives access to the three other trails in the preserve.

### Mileposts

**0.1 mile:** You'll pass the remains of old buildings on the right side of trail.
**0.2 mile:** You'll reach a fork. The left fork heads down to River Trail. Keep right to remain on White Pines Trail.
**0.4 mile:** The trail forks. The left fork is Comet Trail. White Pines Trail continues to the right.
**0.5 mile:** You'll arrive at a loop. A short, blazed spur leads to an overlook and a memorial plaque honoring David Hewes Howells (1920-95), an engineer and conservationist who made invaluable contributions to water-pollution control.

# Comet Trail

**Length:** 0.2 mile
**Difficulty:** Easy to moderate
**Blazes:** Maroon
**Surface:** Natural
**Bicycles:** No

Comet Trail offers hikers a look at the changing flora as they walk from upland to bottomland forest.

## Mileposts

**0.2 mile:** You'll reach the river and the end of Comet Trail at the intersection with River Trail.

# Schoolkid Trail

**Length:** 0.2 mile
**Difficulty:** Easy to moderate
**Blazes:** Yellow
**Surface:** Natural
**Bicycles:** No

Schoolkid Trail begins on the left about 60 yards before River Trail reaches the Rocky River. Schoolkid Trail winds through the bottomland to the edge of a rocky bluff where the remnants of an old cable bridge are visible; this is easiest to find in winter. The children of families that used to live in the area would cross the cable bridge to get to school on the north side of the river. From this point, the trail turns to meet the Rocky River, then heads downstream back to River Trail. Schoolkid Trail is the only one in the park than can be difficult to follow, especially in summer. It is well blazed, so be sure to look for the blazes if the trail is overgrown. If you find yourself beside the river heading upstream and crawling over difficult rock outcroppings, go back, since you are off the trail.

## Mileposts

**0.1 mile:** You'll reach a bluff and an old cable bridge. The trail turns to meet the Rocky River and follows it downstream.

**0.2 mile:** You'll reach an intersection with River Trail. Turn right on River Trail to head back to White Pines Trail and the parking lot. Straight ahead, River Trail goes downstream to the confluence with the Deep River, follows the Deep upstream, then heads back up to White Pines Trail.

## River Trail

**Length:** 0.7 mile
**Difficulty:** Easy
**Blazes:** Blue
**Surface:** Natural
**Bicycles:** No

The most spectacular of the hikes at White Pines Nature Preserve, this trail offers many views of the Deep River.

## Mileposts

**0.0 mile:** River Trail begins at the 0.2-mile mark on White Pines Trail. After 60 yards, you'll come to a T intersection. River Trail follows the river downstream to the right, while Schoolkid Trail follows it upstream to the left.

**0.2 mile:** River Trail intersects Comet Trail, which heads uphill to the right. River Trail continues straight ahead.

**0.5 mile:** After passing the confluence of the Rocky and Deep Rivers, River Trail heads to the right upstream along the Deep.

**0.7 mile:** The trail ends at the intersection with White Pines Trail, which goes left toward the parking area and right toward the overlook.

# Durham County

## Duke Forest

**Address:** Office of Duke Forest, School of the Environment, Box 90332, Duke University, Durham, NC 27708
**Telephone:** 919-613-8013
**Hours:** Dawn to dusk
**Maps:** See division listings below
**Directions:** See division listings below

Duke Forest is one of the happiest accidents to ever happen to Durham. In the mid-1920s, when the Duke University administration began to purchase small farms to provide the campus with a buffer, no one envisioned the well-loved and well-used aesthetic and recreational retreat that exists today. As Durham has grown, so has the importance of this island of woods where Duke welcomes the public. Visitors can walk and bicycle for miles without fear of trespassing. The primary purpose of the forest is still research; some of the original forestry experiments are still under way. But the public is welcome to hike the trails, to ride horses and bicycles on graded roads, to fish, and to picnic.

Duke Forest consists of 8,300 acres of land in five divisions (Durham, Korstian, Blackwood, Eno, and Hillsboro) and two tracts (Dailey and Dodsons Crossroads). Recreational trails and other facilities are located in all divisions. Shortly before this guide was completed Duke sold one of tis former divisions (Haw River) to the state, thereby ensuring its preservation for the future.

Like the rest of the Piedmont, Duke Forest consists of gentle,

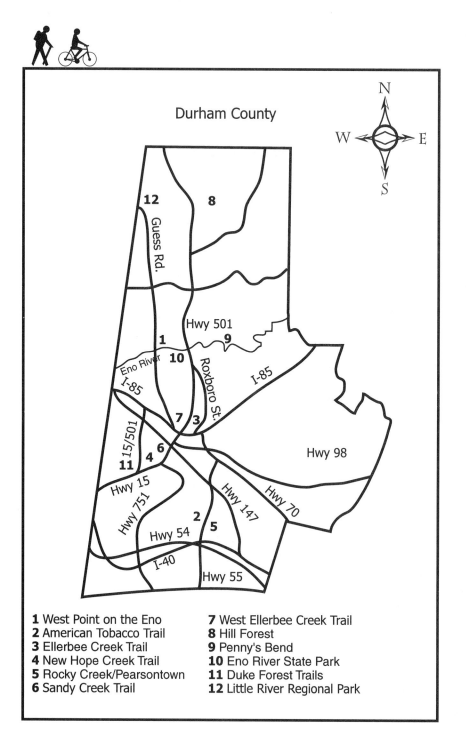

Durham County

N
W — E
S

12　　　8

Guess Rd.

Hwy 501

1　　　9
10
Eno River
I-85

Roxboro St.
I-85

7　3

Hwy 98

6
11　4

Hwy 15
Hwy 751
Hwy 147
Hwy 70

2　5
Hwy 54
I-40
Hwy 55

115/501

**1** West Point on the Eno
**2** American Tobacco Trail
**3** Ellerbee Creek Trail
**4** New Hope Creek Trail
**5** Rocky Creek/Pearsontown
**6** Sandy Creek Trail

**7** West Ellerbee Creek Trail
**8** Hill Forest
**9** Penny's Bend
**10** Eno River State Park
**11** Duke Forest Trails
**12** Little River Regional Park

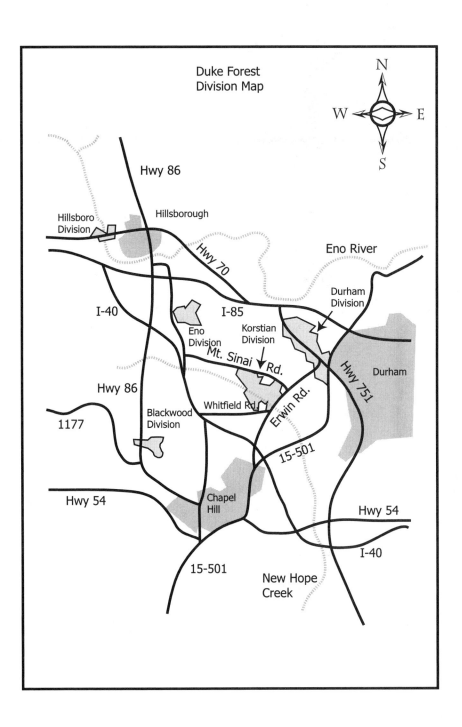

Duke Forest
Division Map

N
W E
S

Hwy 86

Hillsborough

Hillsboro
Division

Eno River

Hwy 70

Durham
Division

I-40

I-85

Eno
Division

Korstian
Division

Mt. Sinai Rd.

Durham

Hwy 86

Whitfield Rd.

Erwin Rd.

Hwy 751

1177

Blackwood
Division

15-501

Hwy 54

Chapel
Hill

Hwy 54

I-40

15-501

New Hope
Creek

*Duke Forest*

rolling hills. They range from a low point of 260 feet on the golf course to 760 feet at the top of Bald Mountain in the Blackwood Division.

Over 100 species of trees have been identified in Duke Forest. It boasts natural stands of hardwoods over 200 years old. The Korstian Division has the largest known black walnut tree in the state, measuring 113 feet tall. You'll also find plenty of wildflowers, especially in the spring. Among them are crested dwarf iris, phlox, and rhododendron.

Birds, salamanders, beavers, and deer can be found in the forests. Perhaps the most unlikely fauna are several species of lemurs that live at the Duke Primate Center and use portions of Duke Forest to swing, forage, call, and do everything lemurs do in their native habitat. The Duke Primate Center is a research facility, not a zoo, but tours can be arranged by calling 919-489-3364.

Many of the place names in Duke Forest hint at the history of the land. Couch Mountain, for instance, takes its name from the family of Thomas Couch, who acquired 300 acres north of New Hope Creek in 1754. Couch lived in a true wilderness with poor transportation to the growing village of Hillsborough, which had a population of 30 to 40 residents by 1764. The Couches grew corn, a crop that soon exhausted the land, forcing them to clear more and more acreage.

By 1822, Thomas Couch, Jr., owned 25 slaves. Many of their names have been lost, but a few were noted in his will. Their names were Old Jenny, Abram, Caleb, and Gabriel. The land was eventually leased to tenant farmers, who had trouble with soil exhaustion and, as a result, tax collectors. In 1947, the land was purchased by the university and added to the growing acreage of Duke Forest.

Visitors to the forest must abide by the following rules:

•Enter only at gated roads, marked by chains between green and white posts.

•Access is not permitted after sunset, except at established picnic sites.

•Do not block gates for any reason. Roads are used in emergencies as well as for normal access.

•Cars, motorcycles, and motorized trail bikes are not allowed except at designated picnic sites.

•Horses and mountain bikes must stay on graded and mowed roads and fire trails.

•No fires of any kind are allowed except in the grills at the designated picnic sites.

•No hunting or shooting of firearms or rifles is allowed.

•Overnight camping is not permitted.

•No vegetation may be cut, picked, scarred, or damaged in any way.

•Dogs should be leashed in accordance with Durham and Orange County animal control ordinances.

Note that picnic sites are located at Gates C, D, and 8 off NC 751. You can reserve these sites by contacting the School of the Environment. The R. L. Rigsbee Picnic Shelter at Gate F can also be reserved. All reservations require a deposit.

## Duke Cross Country Trail

**Length:** 2.9 miles, plus a 0.9-mile fitness loop and a 0.2-mile spur trail

**Difficulty:** Easy

**Blazes:** None

**Surface:** Fine gravel

**Bicycles:** Yes

**Directions:** Take US 15/US 501 Bypass to the NC 751 exit (Exit 107). Turn east on Cameron Boulevard and drive 0.4 mile to the parking lot for Gate 1, on the right.

Definitely not a wilderness experience, this trail is

perfect for anyone who wants a walk in the woods but doesn't like a back-country feeling. Emergency phones are located every 0.5 mile or so, which means visitors never feel far from help. The trail includes a fitness trail, where intermittent signs suggest various calisthenics. The trail winds through a thin strip of woods bordered at various points by US15/US 501, Cameron Boulevard, and the Washington Duke Golf Course. Traffic noise is loud enough to interfere with conversation at several points, and you're often an easy chip shot away from a green. That said, the convenient location of this trail and the fact that it is much more pedestrian- and biker-friendly than any road in the vicinity make it deservedly popular among after-work athletes.

## Mileposts

**0.0 mile:** Begin from the parking lot in front of Gate 1.

**0.1 mile:** You'll pass an emergency phone, cross a bridge, and pass a thin trail that forks right at the phone. This secondary trail emerges on Cameron Avenue.

**1.3 miles:** You'll pass another emergency phone. The trail forks left and right. Continue left. After 0.1 mile, the right fork emerges on Cornwallis Road across the street from the Judea Reform Congregation.

**1.8 miles:** You'll pass an emergency phone. The trail forks. Head straight to remain on Duke property.

**1.9 miles:** You'll cross a bridge.

**2.0 miles:** The trail forks left and right. To the right are a 0.9-mile fitness trail loop and a 0.2-mile spur trail leading to the intersection of NC 751 and Academy Road. Take the left fork.

**2.3 miles:** You'll pass an emergency phone and a water fountain.

**2.4 miles:** You'll pass through the entrance to the Washington Duke Inn, walking parallel to Cameron Avenue.

**2.6 miles:** You'll cross the driveways for the Washington Duke Inn and the Duke Faculty Club.

**2.9 miles:** You'll return to the parking lot at Gate 1.

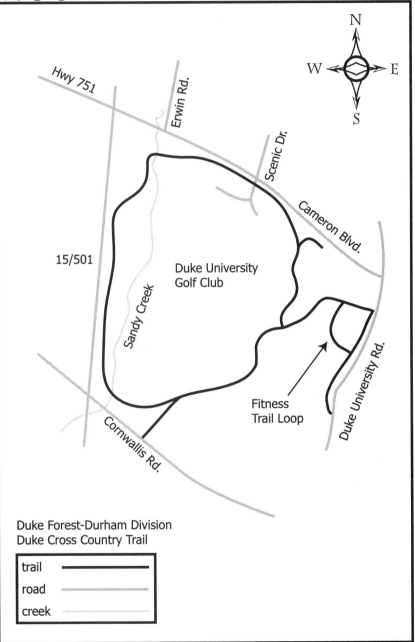

N

W ←✦→ E

S

Hwy 751

Erwin Rd.

Scenic Dr.

Cameron Blvd.

15/501

Duke University
Golf Club

Sandy Creek

Fitness
Trail Loop

Duke University Rd.

Cornwallis Rd.

Duke Forest-Durham Division
Duke Cross Country Trail

| trail | ——————— |
| road | ————————— |
| creek | ·············· |

# Durham Division _____

**Maps:** USGS Northwest Durham; Duke Forest maps are available from the director's office for a small fee.
**Directions:** Take US 15/US 501 Bypass to the NC 751 exit (Exit 107). Turn west onto NC 751 North (Cameron Boulevard). All gates except Gate 14 are in numerical order on either side of NC 751.

## Gate 2/Gate 4 Road, Old Oxford Road, Cotton Mill Fire Trail, and Mud Creek Fire Trail

**Directions:** Take US 15/US 501 Bypass to the NC 751 exit (Exit 107). Turn west onto NC 751 North (Cameron Boulevard). Gate 2 is 0.2 mile ahead on the right, directly across NC 751 from the intersection with Erwin Road.

This section of trails totals 2 miles in length. You will most likely hear the sounds of traffic from nearby US 15/US 501, particularly on the easternmost sections of trail during the winter months. You can walk all the trails out and back or return to your car at Gate 2 by turning left on NC 751. The distance from Gate 4 to Gate 2 via the highway is 0.6 mile.

### Gate 2/Gate 4 Road
**Length:** 1.1 miles
**Difficulty:** Easy
**Blazes:** None
**Surface:** Gravel
**Bicycles:** Yes

Gate 2/Gate 4 Road is a wide gravel road. On the eastern half of the trail is a longleaf pine forest. Duke Forest has posted signs with information about the past management of these trees. The western half of Gate 2/

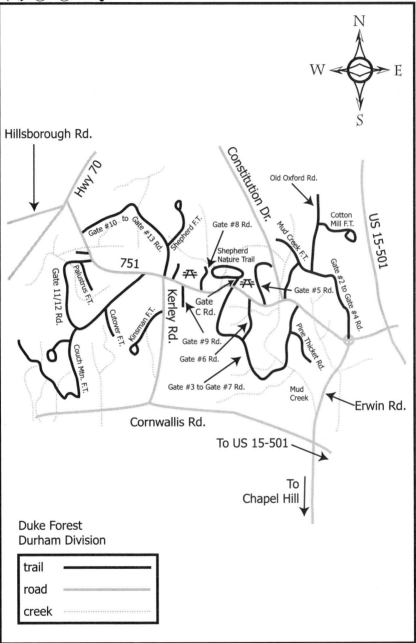

Duke Forest
Durham Division

| trail | ——— |
| road | ——— |
| creek | ········· |

Gate 4 Road passes through a stand of loblollies planted in 1932.

## Mileposts

**0.0 mile:** Begin at Gate 2.

**0.1 mile:** Follow the sign instructing all hikers to leave the gravel road (which bends to the left) and instead walk the trail straight ahead.

**0.2 mile:** A still-narrower trail branches off to the left. Follow this trail toward Gate 2/Gate 4 Road. The trail straight ahead dead-ends just off the shoulder of US 15/US 501.

**0.4 mile:** You'll emerge onto Gate 2/Gate 4 Road. Head right.

**0.7 mile:** You'll reach an intersection with Old Oxford Road, on the right.

**0.9 mile:** You'll reach an intersection with Mud Creek Fire Trail, to the right.

**1.1 miles:** You'll reach Gate 4 and NC 751.

## Old Oxford Road

**Length:** 0.4 mile
**Difficulty:** Easy
**Blazes:** None
**Surface:** Gravel, natural, and cobblestone
**Bicycles:** Yes

Old Oxford Road is still laid with cobblestones dating from the years when it was a major thoroughfare linking Chapel Hill and Oxford.

## Mileposts

**0.0 mile:** Begin at the intersection with Gate 2/Gate 4 Road.

**0.2 mile:** You'll reach an intersection with Cotton Mill Fire Trail.

**0.4 mile:** You'll reach the end of Old Oxford Road and

the boundary of the Duke Forest property.

## Cotton Mill Fire Trail

**Length:** 0.3 mile
**Difficulty:** Easy
**Blazes:** None
**Surface:** Natural
**Bicycles:** Yes

Cotton Mill Fire Trail is the most attractive trail in this section. Its surface is grass and dirt, rather than gravel, and it is lined with mature hardwoods. In winter, only the sounds of traffic from US 15/US 501 disturb the peace. There is less noise when the trees are in leaf. Spring and fall find wildflowers sprinkled along the trail.

### Mileposts

**0.0 mile:** Begin at the intersection with Old Oxford Road.
**0.3 mile:** The trail ends in a cul-de-sac.

## Mud Creek Fire Trail

**Length:** 0.2 mile
**Difficulty:** Easy
**Blazes:** None
**Surface:** Gravel
**Bicycles:** Yes

Mud Creek Fire Trail crosses the creek of the same name and passes through a splendid stand of bottomland hardwoods.

### Mileposts

**0.0 mile:** Begin at the intersection with Gate 2/Gate 4 Road.
**0.2 mile:** You'll cross Mud Creek. Within 100 yards, you'll reach the end of the fire trail and the boundary of the Duke Forest property.

# Gate 3/Gate 7 Road,
# Pine Thicket Fire Trail, and Gate 6 Road

**Directions:** Take US 15/US 501 Bypass to the NC 751 exit (Exit 107). Turn west on NC 751 (Cameron Boulevard). Gate 3 is 0.7 mile ahead on the left.

## Gate 3/Gate 7 Road

**Length:** 1.6 miles
**Difficulty:** Easy to moderate
**Blazes:** None
**Surface:** Gravel
**Bicycles:** Yes

From Gate 3 to the intersection with Pine Thicket Fire Trail, Gate 3/Gate 7 Road passes through a mixed forest of hardwoods and pines. This section of road is a bit narrower than the other fire trails in Duke Forest, so hikers get a nice in-the-woods feel.

Beyond Pine Thicket Fire Trail, the road crosses a small tributary of Mud Creek. Located near Gate 7 is a Southern pine beetle salvage area, where Duke students study the effects of this pest.

### Mileposts

**0.0 mile:** Begin at Gate 3 on NC 751.
**0.2 mile:** You'll reach an intersection with Pine Thicket Fire Trail, to your right.
**0.4 mile:** You'll cross a bridge over Mud Creek.
**0.8 mile:** You'll cross a tributary of Mud Creek.
**1.0 mile:** You'll reach an intersection with Gate 6 Road, on your right.
**1.6 miles:** You'll reach Gate 7 and NC 751.

## Pine Thicket Fire Trail

**Length:** 0.3 mile
**Difficulty:** Easy
**Blazes:** None
**Surface:** Natural
**Bicycles:** Yes

Pine Thicket Fire Trail is one of Duke Forest's finest. The forest floor is thickly carpeted with pine needles from the tall pines, still thriving amid the encroaching hardwoods.

### Mileposts

**0.0 mile:** Begin at the intersection with Gate 3/Gate 7 Road.
**0.3 mile:** You'll reach the end of the trail and the Duke Forest boundary.

## Gate 6 Road

**Length:** 0.3 mile
**Difficulty:** Easy
**Blazes:** None
**Surface:** Gravel
**Bicycles:** Yes

Gate 6 Road has many thinly forested areas and many downed trees on either side of the trail. It boasts some very tall loblollies.

### Mileposts

**0.0 mile:** Begin at the intersection with Gate 3/Gate 7 Road.
**0.3 mile:** You'll reach NC 751. From Gate 6, you can walk on NC 751 to return to your car at Gate 3. The distance is 0.4 mile.

# Gate 5 Road and Shepherd Nature Trail

**Directions:** Take US 15/US 501 Bypass to the NC 751 exit (Exit 107). Turn west on NC 751 (Cameron Boulevard). Gate 5 is 0.8 mile ahead on the right.

## Gate 5 Road

**Length:** 0.4 mile
**Difficulty:** Easy
**Blazes:** None
**Surface:** Gravel
**Bicycles:** Yes

This short road's chief draw is access to Shepherd Nature Trail.

### Mileposts

**0.0 mile:** Begin at Gate 5.
**0.2 mile:** You'll reach an intersection with Shepherd Nature Trail on the left. Shepherd Nature Trail follows Gate 5 Road for about 70 yards, then leaves the road to the left.
**0.4 mile:** Gate 5 Road ends at the Duke Forest boundary and the edge of an apartment complex.

## Shepherd Nature Trail

**Length:** 0.9 mile
**Difficulty:** Easy
**Blazes:** Wooden signs with a painted tree
**Surface:** Gravel and natural
**Bicycles:** No

Shepherd Nature Trail began as an Eagle Scout project in 1995. The interpretive signs provide a good introduction to local flora and the effects of prior land use. This nature trail can be accessed from Gate C Road as well as Gate 5. A walk on Shepherd Nature Trail is enhanced by the interpretive signs offering information about Duke's research and the human and natural history of the forest.

From Gate 5 Road, Shepherd Nature Trail goes left and leads to Gate C Road directly across from the Bobby Hunter Ross, Jr., Memorial Shelter, a gift made in August 1995. The shelter offers picnic tables and a grill but no running water or restrooms. The nature trail continues in a loop that can be accessed on either side of the shelter. As you walk back toward NC 751 on Gate C Road (to the left if you're facing the shelter), the nature trail begins again near a picnic table and grill.

### Mileposts

**0.0 mile:** Begin at the picnic shelter.
**0.5 mile:** You'll reach an intersection with a spur trail to Gate C Road on the right. Keep left to return to Gate 5 Road.
**0.9 mile:** You'll return to Gate 5 Road. Walk left to complete the loop.

# Gate 11/Gate 12 Road, Cutover Fire Trail, Palustrus Fire Trail, and Couch Mountain Fire Trail

**Directions:** Take US 15/US 501 Bypass to the NC 751 exit (Exit 107). Turn west on NC 751 (Cameron Boulevard). Gate 11 is 2 miles ahead on the right.

## Gate 11/Gate 12 Road

**Length:** 1.5 miles
**Difficulty:** Easy
**Blazes:** None
**Surface:** Gravel
**Bicycles:** Yes

Gate 11/Gate12 Road is a wide gravel road that is neither particularly beautiful nor interesting. But the side roads that emerge from it are worth exploring.

## Mileposts

**0.0 mile:** Begin at Gate 11.

**0.1 mile:** Two restricted private roads branch off to the left.

**0.5 mile:** You'll reach an intersection with Cutover Fire Trail on the left.

**0.8 mile:** Couch Mountain Fire Trail heads to the left.

**1.2 miles:** You'll reach a power cut and a service road to your left. The trail makes a sharp turn to the right.

**1.3 miles:** A private road forks off to the right.

**1.4 miles:** You'll reach an intersection with Palustrus Fire Trail to your right.

**1.5 miles:** You'll reach Gate 12 and an intersection with NC 751. It is 0.5 mile to the right on NC 751 to Gate 11.

## Palustrus Fire Trail

**Length:** 0.2 mile
**Difficulty:** Easy
**Blazes:** None
**Surface:** Natural
**Bicycles:** Yes

Palustrus is a piney paradise where the thick layer of pine straw carpeting the forest floor makes naturalist John Muir's habit of sleeping on similar ground seem more luxurious than hardy.

## Cutover Fire Trail

**Length:** 0.4 mile
**Difficulty:** Easy
**Blazes:** None
**Surface:** Natural
**Bicycles:** Bikes are allowed on the first 0.1 mile only.

Cutover Fire Trail is a pleasant, shady trail that passes through a mixed forest of hardwoods and pines before ending at the Duke Forest boundary.

## Mileposts

**0.0 mile:** Begin at the intersection with Gate 11/Gate 12 Road.
**0.4 mile:** You'll reach the end of the trail.

# Couch Mountain Fire Trail

**Length:** 1 mile
**Difficulty:** Easy
**Blazes:** None
**Surface:** Natural
**Bicycles:** Yes

Couch Mountain Fire Trail has the feel of a true mountain trail as it skirts the side of Couch Mountain. The relatively clear understory of the mature hardwood forest offers brief but beautiful views of the valley below.

## Mileposts

**0.0 mile:** Begin at the intersection with Gate 11/Gate 12 Road. The trail forks after 100 yards. The right fork goes 0.2 mile to a cul-de-sac at the top of Couch Mountain. Take the left fork.
**1.0 mile:** The trail ends at a clearing.

# Gate 8 Road

**Length:** 0.1 mile
**Difficulty:** Easy
**Blazes:** None
**Surface:** Gravel
**Bicycles:** Yes

This is a short gravel road with a picnic table.

## Gate 10/Gate 13 Road and Shepherd Fire Trail

**Directions:** Take US 15/US 501 Bypass to the NC 751 exit (Exit 107). Turn west on NC 751 (Cameron Boulevard). Gate 10 is 1.9 miles ahead on the right.

### Gate 10/Gate 13 Road

**Length:** 1.1 miles
**Difficulty:** Easy
**Blazes:** None
**Surface:** Gravel and natural
**Bicycles:** Yes

This road leads to the Global Climate Research site, which is restricted. Close to Gate 13, it parallels the tracks of a Southern Railroad line.

#### Mileposts

**0.0 mile:** Begin at Gate 10.
**0.1 mile:** You'll reach an intersection with Shepherd Fire Trail.
**1.1 mile:** You'll reach Gate 13.

### Shepherd Fire Trail

**Length:** 0.3 mile
**Difficulty:** Easy
**Blazes:** None
**Surface:** Natural
**Bicycles:** Yes

This short road will lead you to an unnamed, beautiful 0.1-mile fire trail with many towering oaks and hickories offering plentiful shade.

**0.0 mile:** Begin at the intersection with Gate 10/Gate 13 Road.
**0.1 mile:** You'll reach an intersection with an unnamed fire trail.
**0.3 mile:** You'll reach the end of the trail.

## Kinsman Fire Trail/Gate 14 Road

**Length:** 0.2 mile
**Difficulty:** Easy
**Blazes:** None
**Surface:** Natural
**Bicycles:** Yes
**Directions:** Gate 14 is the only gate on Kerley Road. From the intersection of Kerley Road and NC 751, take Kerley Road 0.1 mile south to the gate on the right.

This is a nice grassy trail.

**Mileposts**

**0.0 mile:** Begin at Gate 14.
**0.2 mile:** You'll reach a cul-de-sac at the end of the trail.

# Durham Greenways

**Address:** Durham Parks and Recreation Department, 403 Blackwell Street, Durham, NC 27701
**Telephone:** 919-560-4355
**Maps:** USGS NW Durham, NE Durham, SW Durham, and SE Durham; free greenway maps are available from the Parks and Recreation Department.

## Ellerbee Creek Trail

**Length:** 1.1 miles
**Difficulty:** Easy
**Surface:** Asphalt
**Bicycles:** Yes
**Directions:** The greenway entrance is at the corner of Stadium Drive and the National Guard Armory driveway.

This greenway passes some pretty spots as it winds south from Stadium Drive. The northern end of the creek is particularly attractive; there's even a small, rocky outcropping. After passing the North Carolina Museum of Life and Science, the trail winds through Jaycee Field Park and then Northgate Park before ending on Club Boulevard at the spot where South Ellerbee Creek Trail picks up. Near the north end of this greenway is Stadium Drive Trail.

## South Ellerbee Creek Trail

**Length:** 1.4 miles
**Difficulty:** Easy
**Surface:** Sidewalk and asphalt
**Bicycles:** Yes
**Directions:** South Ellerbee Creek Trail begins as a sidewalk that connects the previous paved trail with one that starts at the intersection of Washington Street and Club Boulevard and ends on Trinity Avenue beside the Duke Diet Center. You can also begin at Northgate Park on Club Boulevard. The greenway follows the sidewalk of Club heading west.

South Ellerbee Creek Trail is less scenic than Ellerbee Creek Trail. It winds past neighborhoods along the banks of South Ellerbee Creek, which joins with Ellerbee Creek just southeast of the beginning of this greenway. Its chief appeal is to those who live nearby and anyone looking to link greenways for a longer trip.

## West Ellerbee Creek Trail

**Length:** 0.5 mile
**Difficulty:** Easy
**Surface:** Asphalt
**Bicycles:** Yes
**Directions:** Westover Park is 0.5 mile south of the Guess Road exit (Exit 175) off I-85.

At the time of this writing, West Ellerbee Creek Trail was a short, easy path leading from Westover Park on Guess Road through Indian Trail Park and Albany Street. After road work on I-85 is completed, this greenway will be extended to the North-South Greenway (also incomplete as of this writing), making it a boon to human-powered commuters. For the time being, creek views make this path worthwhile for local residents.

## Stadium Drive Trail

**Length:** 1 mile
**Difficulty:** Easy
**Surface:** Sidewalk and asphalt
**Bicycles:** Yes
**Directions:** The easiest access is from Warren Creek Trail in Whippoorwill Park, where parking is available. The entrance to Whippoorwill Park is off Rowemont Drive near the intersection with Glasgow Street. The greenway entrance is between the tennis courts.

As this guide was going to press, construction was under way to complete Stadium Drive Trail, which will connect the Warren Creek greenway to the Ellerbee Creek greenway. Once completed, this link will create a 5.75-mile greenway from Horton Road to Trinity Avenue.

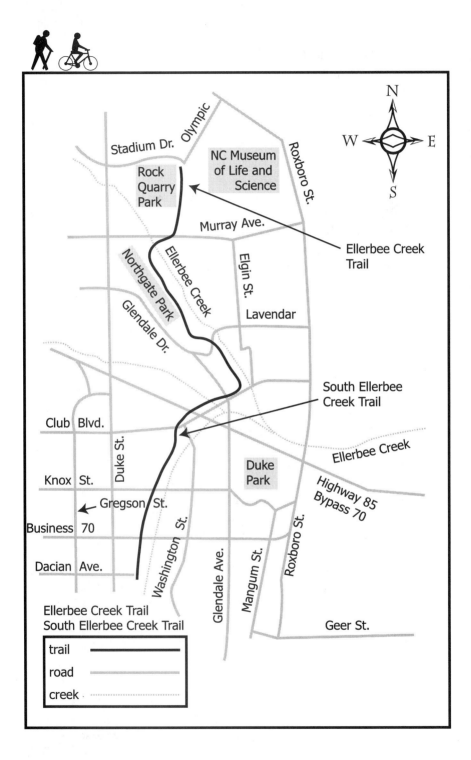

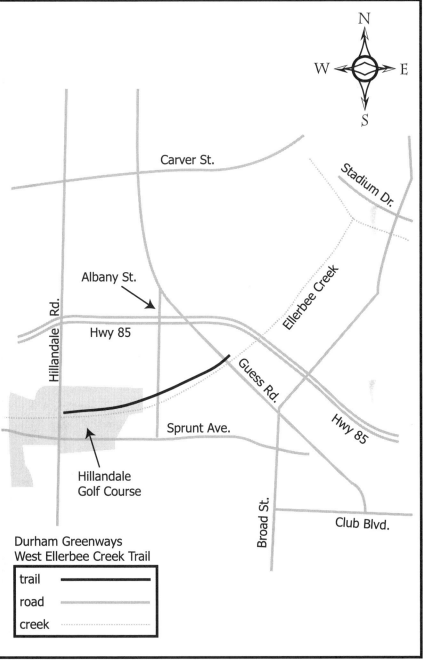

Carver St.

Stadium Dr.

N

W   E

S

Albany St.

Ellerbee Creek

Hillandale Rd.

Hwy 85

Guess Rd.

Hwy 85

Sprunt Ave.

Hillandale
Golf Course

Broad St.

Club Blvd.

Durham Greenways
West Ellerbee Creek Trail

| trail | ——— |
| road | ——— |
| creek | ········ |

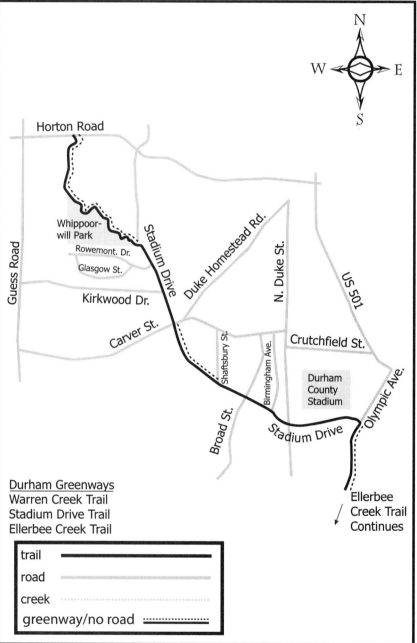

Horton Road

Whippoor-
will Park

Rowemont. Dr.

Glasgow St.

Guess Road

Stadium Drive

Kirkwood Dr.

Carver St.

Duke Homestead Rd.

N. Duke St.

US 501

Crutchfield St.

Shaftsbury St.

Birmingham Ave.

Durham
County
Stadium

Broad St.

Stadium Drive

Olympic Ave.

Ellerbee
Creek Trail
Continues

N
W &harr; E
S

<u>Durham Greenways</u>
Warren Creek Trail
Stadium Drive Trail
Ellerbee Creek Trail

| | |
|---|---|
| trail | ——— |
| road | ——— |
| creek | ········· |
| greenway/no road | ············ |

## Warren Creek Trail

**Length:** 0.75 mile
**Difficulty:** Easy
**Surface:** Asphalt and cement
**Bicycles:** Yes
**Directions:** See Stadium Drive Trail above.

As this guide was going to press, Phase 1 of Warren Creek Trail was complete. This pleasant, tree-lined greenway goes from Stadium Drive through Whippoorwill Park to Horton Road. When completed, it will extend north to West Point on the Eno City Park, where trail users will be able to access Eno Greenway.

## Eno Greenway

Eno Greenway should be under construction by the time this guide is available. It will link West Point on the Eno Park to River Forest Park.

## New Hope Creek Nature Trail

**Length:** 2.2 miles
**Difficulty:** Easy
**Blazes:** Yellow
**Surface:** Natural
**Bicycles:** No
**Directions:** From the NC 751 exit off I-40, turn north on NC 751 and drive 1.1 miles. Immediately after the intersection with NC 54, turn left on Garrett Road. Drive 2 miles, then turn left on Old Chapel Hill Road. Githens Middle School is 0.8 mile ahead on your right. Park on the east side of the school (the right side, if you're facing the front entrance). You'll see the track and playing fields to the far right. As you look down the length of the track, the trailhead is in the far right corner.

The terrain through which this trail passes is mostly

rich bottom land in the New Hope Creek flood plain. If you are familiar with the creek as it winds through Duke Forest, note how different it is here. There are no rock outcroppings or bluffs along the New Hope in this part of Durham. Instead, the creek is broad, slow, and swampy. On the second half of this trail, you can hear the traffic on US 15/US 501.

An extension of the trail will be built when the North Carolina Department of Transportation constructs a new bridge for Durham-Chapel Hill Boulevard. The trail will continue under the bridge on the same side of the creek.

## Rocky Creek and Pearsontown Trails

**Length:** 2 miles
**Difficulty:** Easy
**Surface:** Natural and sidewalk
**Bicycles:** Yes
**Directions:** At present, the easiest access is from Elmira Park off Elmira Avenue. Once the trail is completed, Burton Park will also provide access and parking.

Rocky Creek Trail has exceptional scenic appeal as it follows the course of lovely Rocky Creek through Elmira Park to American Tobacco Trail. Future construction will include a spur that extends to Burton Park.

## Sandy Creek Trail

**Length:** 1 mile
**Difficulty:** Easy
**Surface:** Natural
**Bicycles:** Yes
**Directions:** From US 15/US 501 Business, turn north on Tower Boulevard. When Tower ends at Pickett Road, turn left. After crossing US 15/US 501 Bypass, take the first left onto Sandy Creek Road and drive to the parking area.

This trail runs from Sandy Creek Drive north to

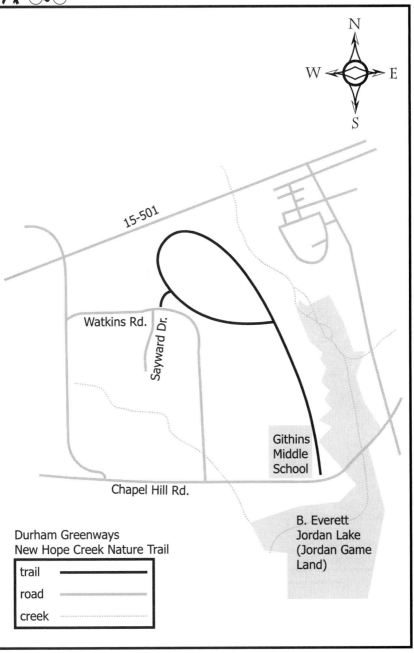

N

W ← → E

S

15-501

Watkins Rd.

Sayward Dr.

Githins
Middle
School

Chapel Hill Rd.

Durham Greenways
New Hope Creek Nature Trail

| trail | ——— |
| road | ~~~~~ |
| creek | ········· |

B. Everett
Jordan Lake
(Jordan Game
Land)

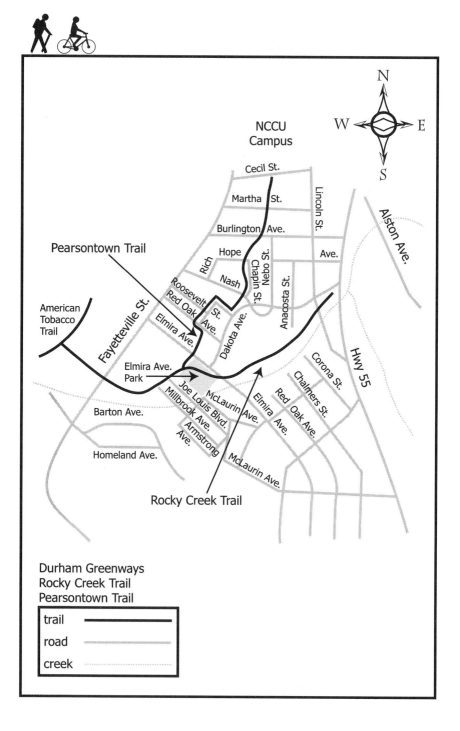

Pearsontown Trail

NCCU
Campus

Cecil St.

Martha St.

Burlington Ave.

Lincoln St.

Alston Ave.

Hope

Ave.

Rich

Nash

Open St.

Chapin St.

Anacosta St.

American
Tobacco
Trail

Roosevelt
St.

Red Oak
Ave.

Fayetteville St.

Elmira Ave.

Dakota Ave.

Hwy 55

Elmira Ave.
Park

Corona St.

Chalmers St.

McLaurin Ave.

Joe Louis Blvd.

Millbrook Ave.

Elmira Ave.

Red Oak Ave.

Barton Ave.

Armstrong
Ave.

Homeland Ave.

McLaurin Ave.

Rocky Creek Trail

Durham Greenways
Rocky Creek Trail
Pearsontown Trail

| trail | ——————— |
| road | ~~~~~~~~~ |
| creek | ········· |

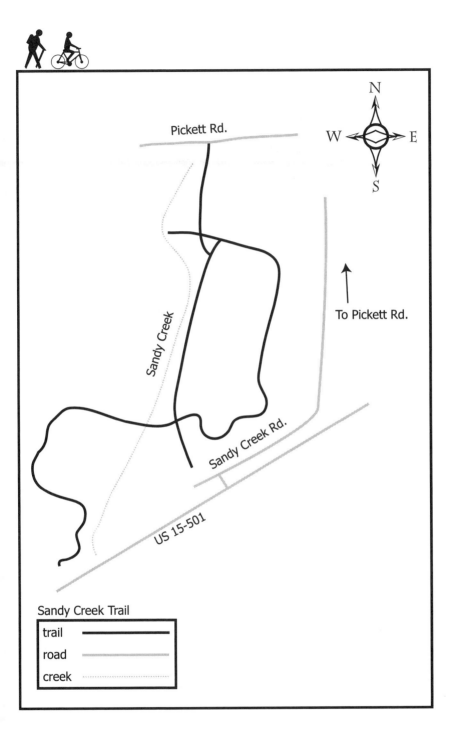

Pickett Rd.

N
W    E
S

To Pickett Rd.

Sandy Creek

Sandy Creek Rd.

US 15-501

Sandy Creek Trail

| trail | ———— |
| road | ░░░░░ |
| creek | ········· |

*Durham Greenways*

Pickett Road. A loop trail is planned for the south end. A future extension of the trail will cross Pickett Road and go north to Cornwallis Road, where a connection with the Duke Forest trails may be possible.

## American Tobacco Trail

**Length:** 7.1 miles, including the 1.5-mile Riddle Road Spur
**Difficulty:** Easy
**Surface:** Asphalt
**Bicycles:** Yes
**Directions:** To travel the entire trail, begin in downtown Durham south of Durham Bulls Athletic Park at the intersection of Willard and Blackwell Streets. Parking is available under the NC 147 overpass. The trail extends south. Other convenient access points include Elmira Park, Solite Park, and the ATT parking area on Fayetteville Road. To reach this parking area, take the Fayetteville Road exit (Exit 276) off I-40 and turn north on Fayetteville Road. Cross NC 54, take the first left into the Southpointe Crossing shopping center, and take the first left into the gravel parking lot. A signboard provides information and a map of ATT.

American Tobacco Trail (ATT) is part of the national rails-to-trails movement. Volunteers in many states have worked to convert abandoned railway corridors into linear recreational parks and safe routes for alternative transportation. These parks also preserve the corridors for possible future public transportation, such as light rail.

Although most of ATT is included in the Durham section of this guide, the trail already has a segment in Wake County. The master plan calls for a 30-mile trail extending south of I-40 through Durham, Chatham, and Wake Counties before ending near Bonsal. The towns of Cary and Apex plan to connect their own parks and greenways systems to ATT. If all of the proposed trail systems connected with ATT come into being, the Triangle will have a 70-mile network of interconnected urban, suburban, and rural greenways.

The paved sections of ATT are largely straight and flat, making them good places for roller blading and stroller pushing, as well as for walking and cycling. The trail's location means that it is also a potential route for self-propelled commuters. ATT provides access to downtown Durham and North Carolina Central University and crosses Cornwallis Road west of Research Triangle Park. By the time this guide is available, construction will be under way to extend the trail across NC 54 and I-40 to provide access to the Southpointe Mall area.

Scenery on ATT varies widely. As you head south out of downtown, the urban landscape gives way to residential areas. Some stretches have a pleasant, natural feel. The most scenic spot is probably the crossing of Rocky Creek; if you have a taste for creek views, take the Rocky Creek Greenway off ATT.

Extra caution is required at all street crossings.

The railroad line that is now ATT has been owned by several companies over the course of its nearly 100 years of history. The line began in 1906, although the section that reaches the north terminus of the trail near the ballpark was not completed until 1925. This railroad line was valuable because it reached into the heart of Durham's textile and tobacco industries. It was moved to higher ground in the early 1970s to make way for Jordan Lake. A subsequent merger between two railroad companies rendered the stretch of track that is now ATT redundant, so it was abandoned. A concerted effort by local citizens including members of the Triangle Rails to Trails Conservancy and the Triangle Greenways Commission led to the creation of this invaluable local resource. The first section of ATT was dedicated in June 2000.

## American Tobacco Trail (south)

**Length:** 3.1 miles
**Difficulty:** Easy
**Blazes:** None
**Surface:** Natural and gravel
**Bicycles:** Yes
**Directions:** To reach this section of ATT, take the Fayetteville Road exit (Exit 276) off I-40 and turn south on Fayetteville Road (SR 1118). Drive 2.5 miles south to Scott King Road (SR 1103). Turn left and drive 0.8 mile to Herndon Park, on the left. ATT crosses Scott King Road 0.1 mile ahead. Limited parking and an informational sign are located at this intersection.

This section of ATT is kept open entirely through volunteer labor. Lined with a young mixed forest, it goes from Massey Chapel Road to Crooked Creek.

## Eagle Spur Trail

**Length:** 2.2 miles
**Difficulty:** Easy
**Blazes:** None
**Surface:** Natural
**Bicycles:** Yes
**Directions:** From I-40, take the NC 751 South exit (Exit 274). After 1.2 miles on NC 751 South, turn right on Stagecoach Road (SR 1107). Drive 0.2 mile to the gate at the trailhead, on the left. Limited space is available along the road. Do not block the gate.

Although Eagle Spur Trail passes through an extensive

wetland area, you won't have to worry about getting your shoes wet. It follows an elevated railroad bed through the woods between Stagecoach Road and one of the northernmost fingers of Jordan Lake. The trail is on land owned by the Army Corps of Engineers and managed by the North Carolina Wildlife Resources Commission. Translation for hikers and mountain bikers: This land is used by hunters. During hunting season, avoid using Eagle Spur Trail except on Sundays, when hunting is not permitted. Wear orange if there is any chance hunters might be using the land adjacent to the trail.

As for the trail itself, it is not clearly labeled and is sporadically maintained by volunteer labor. It may become overgrown during the summer months, but from autumn through spring, it is easy to follow and provides a unique opportunity for birders. If you make it all the way to Jordan Lake, you'll be rewarded with an avian feast for the eyes. Ducks, geese, herons, and egrets frequent this section of the lake, and patient observation might be rewarded with a glimpse of an eagle or osprey.

Eagle Spur Trail is of historical interest beyond its role as an early-20th-century rail line. According to the Triangle Rails to Trails Conservancy, the Civil War's final skirmish resulting in casualties took place just west of this trail. At a site called New Hope Battleground, Confederate troops suffered their final casualties in the days prior to the meeting of Generals Joseph Johnston and William T. Sherman at Bennett Place in Durham on April 17, 1865. During that meeting, the generals began the process that concluded on April 26 with the surrender of 90,000 Confederate troops to Sherman, effectively ending the war in the Carolinas, Georgia, and Florida.

## Mileposts

**1.3 miles:** You'll reach a fork. Keep right to remain on Eagle Spur Trail.
**2.0 miles:** You'll reach a second fork. Keep right again.
**2.2 miles:** You'll reach Jordan Lake.

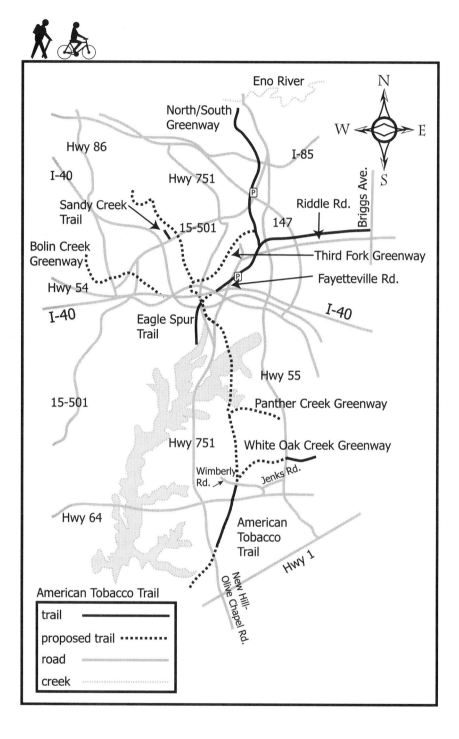

*West Point on the Eno River*

# West Point on the Eno

**Address:** Park Office, 5101 North Roxboro Road, Durham, NC 27704
**Telephone:** 919-471-1623
**Hours:** The park is open from 8 A.M. until dark. The buildings are open Saturday and Sunday from 1 P.M. to 5 P.M.
**Maps:** USGS NW Durham. A map is carved into a sign in the parking lot just up the hill from the mill. It shows the layout of the entire park, including the buildings and trails. It's worth a look to get your bearings.
**Directions:** From I-85, take the US 501 North/Duke Street exit (Exit 176). Note that the name will change to Roxboro Road before you reach the park. After 3.3 miles, turn left at Seven Oaks Road to reach the main parking area and the exhibits. To reach the north-bank entrance, amphitheater, and field, continue north on Roxboro Road for 0.2 mile and turn left.

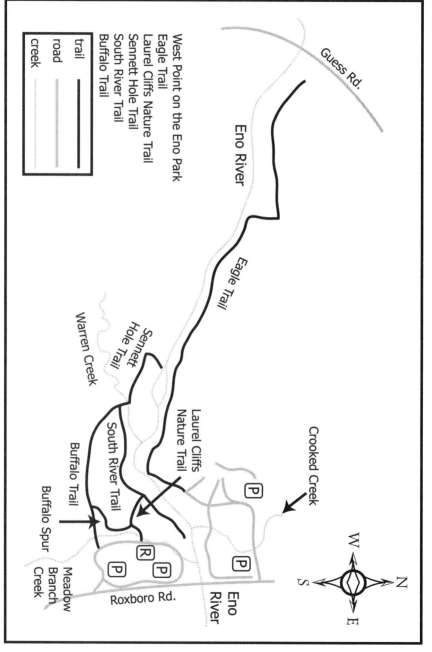

Guess Rd.

Eno River

Eagle Trail

Crooked Creek

Warren Creek

Sennett Hole Trail

Laurel Cliffs Nature Trail

South River Trail

Buffalo Trail

Buffalo Spur

P

R

P

P

Meadow Branch Creek

Roxboro Rd.

Eno River

West Point on the Eno Park
Eagle Trail
Laurel Cliffs Nature Trail
Sennett Hole Trail
South River Trail
Buffalo Trail

trail
road
creek

W
N
S
E

It's difficult to imagine a city park with better hiking than West Point on the Eno. While you walk the trails along the riverbank, it's easy to forget the rush of traffic just beyond the park's border. The fully restored 19th-century McCown-Mangum farmhouse, a restored 18th-century gristmill, and the Hugh Mangum Museum of Photography are also in the park. Each merits a visit.

The gristmill is like many that once dotted the Eno and most other local rivers. It offers a look back into Triangle history. The old mill wheel still turns for several hours each weekend, so you can watch the gears and belts work and then take home a bag of meal or flour ground on the premises. The West Point mill operated from 1778 to 1942, longer than any other mill on the Eno. Because of its location at a good ford and the junction of important roads, it was prosperous. By the early 19th century, the mill had become the center of a business community that included a blacksmith shop, a general store, and a post office. The name West Point comes from the community's location at the most westerly point on the mail route between Roxboro and Raleigh.

The Greek Revival farmhouse was built in the 1840s by John Cabe McCown. It was sold to the Presly Mangum family in 1891. Presly's son Hugh sketched an appealing likeness of his sister, which now hangs on a downstairs wall in the restored house. Hugh's real love was photography. His photographs decorate the walls of the house and the former pack house in the backyard. A tiny room in the top of the pack house served as Hugh's darkroom. The discovery of 500 of his original glass negatives in the 1970s inspired the renovation of the pack house into the Hugh Mangum Museum of Photography. Prints from the negatives and some of Hugh's cameras are on display. The museum also has a new wing where visitors can see the work of contemporary artists.

In the 1970s, all of the buildings at West Point were in ruins. An effort lead by the Eno River Association and the Junior League of Durham saved the buildings and ensured their restoration. The city of Durham now manages the property. The McCown-Mangum House and the picnic shelters are available for rent to the public.

Geologically speaking, West Point on the Eno sits precisely

where the Carolina Slate Belt gives way to the Durham Triassic Basin. If you were to go upstream from West Point, you would see rocky bluffs, rapids, and a narrower, faster-moving Eno River. Downstream from West Point, the soil become sandier and the river is slower and wider.

Once your hike or museum tour is complete, be sure to take the short walk to the old dam, where there's an overlook. Below the dam is a spot where families gather for picnics and toe dipping when the temperature is high and the water is low.

West Point is the location of the annual Festival for the Eno, held for three days each year around the Fourth of July. The music, crafts, and demonstrations attract visitors from all over the Triangle, who enjoy a great time for an even greater cause. Funds raised during the festival enable the Eno River Association to continue its work to protect lands along the river and add to the acreage of Eno River State Park, just upstream from West Point.

## Buffalo Trail/Sennett Hole Trail

**Length:** 0.6 mile
**Difficulty:** Easy
**Blazes:** White, then red
**Surface:** Natural
**Bicycles:** No

These two trails are really one. The route is called Buffalo Trail before the Warren Creek crossing and Sennett Hole Trail after it. These trails can be combined with South River Trail to form a scenic loop leading through an upland forest and bottomland. Note that the trail is not maintained past Sennett Hole, although a thin path continues down the bank. Beyond the maintained trail lies more poison ivy than you can shake a stick at.

In the 19th century, Buffalo Trail was a farm road. Sennett Hole derives its name from Michael Synnott, the first miller on this stretch of the Eno. Synnott's mill began operations in 1752 but was eventually run out of business by the more favorably located West Point Mill.

**0.0 mile:** Begin at the trailhead across the main driveway from the small picnic shelter nearest the main entrance. You'll cross Meadow Branch Creek almost immediately.

**0.1 mile:** You'll reach a fork. To the right is Buffalo Spur, a 0.2-mile trail that leads to Laurel Cliffs Nature Trail. Take the left fork.

**0.4 mile:** You'll reach another fork. To the right is the western terminus of South River Trail. Take the left fork. You'll soon cross Warren Creek.

**0.6 mile:** The trail ends at Sennett Hole.

## South River Trail

**Length:** 0.5 mile
**Difficulty:** Easy
**Blazes:** Yellow
**Surface:** Natural
**Bicycles:** No

This trail leads upstream from the dam. Much of it is situated above the river on bluffs and high banks. For the first 0.2 mile, you'll see numbered posts for Laurel Cliffs Nature Trail.

**Mileposts**

**0.0 mile:** Begin near the dam, which may be reached by crossing the bridge beside the mill or the one just south of it.

**0.2 mile:** You'll reach a fork. To the left is Laurel Cliffs Nature Trail, which leads back to the driveway. Continue straight.

**0.5 mile:** South River Trail ends at Buffalo Trail. Head left to return to the driveway or right to reach Sennett Hole.

# Eagle Trail

**Length:** 1.8 miles
**Difficulty:** Easy
**Blazes:** Blue
**Surface:** Natural
**Bicycles:** No

The best trail in the park, Eagle Trail gets you close to the water and offers great views of the dramatic south bank of the Eno. The trail was named in honor of the Eagle Scouts who have worked on projects in West Point. To reach the trailhead, cross the Eno below the mill. Turn left on the main driveway and follow it to the trail. You can also reach the trailhead from the parking area on the north bank.

## Mileposts

**1.2 miles:** The trail turns away from the river.
**1.3 miles:** You'll reach a fork. The right fork leads 100 yards to the Lockhaven Hills entrance. Take the left fork.
**1.8 miles:** Eagle Trail ends at the Guess Road entrance.

# Laurel Cliffs Nature Trail

**Length:** 0.4 mile
**Difficulty:** Easy
**Blazes:** Yellow
**Surface:** Natural
**Bicycles:** No

This trail has numbered interpretive stations. A free trail guide is provided at the trailhead. For the last half of its length, this trail runs conjunctively with South River Trail.

## Mileposts

**0.0 mile:** Begin across the driveway from the large picnic shelter with the restrooms.

**0.1 mile:** You'll reach a fork. To the left is Buffalo Spur Trail, which leads 0.2 mile to Buffalo Trail. Take the right fork.

**0.2 mile:** You'll reach a T intersection. Laurel Cliffs Nature Trail continues to the right, where it runs conjunctively with South River Trail.

**0.3 mile:** You'll reach the first of two right turns. Either of these turns will take you back to the driveway.

# Eno River State Park

**Address:** Park Office, 6101 Cole Mill Road, Durham, NC 27705-9275
**Telephone:** 919-383-1686
**Hours:** From November to February, the park is open from 8 A.M. to 6 P.M. During March and October, it is open from 8 A.M. to 7 P.M. During April and September, it is open from 8 A.M. to 8 P.M. From May to August, it is open from 8 A.M. to 9 P.M.
**Maps:** USGS NW Durham; a free map is available at the park office.
**Directions:** See the individual sections below.

Rangers here describe Eno River State Park as a hiker's park. Indeed, it offers some of the best hiking in the Piedmont, as well as opportunities for solitude. The trails that see the most use are those that connect the parking areas and the river. The longer, upland trails are where one can escape the crowds.

All the trails in the park are marked with blazes, and most are easy to follow. Trail maps are available at the park office in the Few's Ford section. Occasionally, there are a few at the trailheads.

The river begins as a spring in Orange County and gathers size as it flows along its 40-mile course before joining the Flat River to form the Neuse. The Eno River and the park surrounding it epitomize the kind of adventure the Triangle has to offer. The forests along the banks have been cut and the trails traveled many times. These are not rugged lands with endless views, and you are not likely to feel as though you're the only person on the planet. Instead, Eno River State Park offers a quiet, intimate beauty peopled by the ghosts of those who have walked these woods for hundreds, perhaps thousands, of years. It's still possible to discover an arrowhead left by a member of the Native American tribe whose name this river has taken—although you should be aware that removing or tampering with any artifact is a violation of state law. The ruins of mills dot the shoreline and invite careful exploration. You may recognize the names of the mills from streets in Durham and Hillsborough. The history of the river is the history of these towns. They exist because the river was here over two centuries ago when European settlers began to push into the Piedmont.

The timber in this area has been harvested repeatedly over the years, but within the park, the forests reign once again. The fields cleared and farmed in the recent past offer an opportunity to study what is called old field succession. During succession, pine forests grow first. Many areas of the park still have short, young pines taking advantage of the unfiltered sunshine. Eventually, young hardwoods will grow, and a mixed forest of pines and hardwoods will prevail for a time. Many of the upland trails in Eno River State Park pass through such forests. The species of pine that tends to dominate in this area is the loblolly. The most common hardwoods are hickories and oaks. In time, the hardwoods will tower above the pines, blocking the sunlight. A mature hardwood forest will then emerge. The Eno River Valley has many mature oak-hickory forests, but there are also plenty of other hardwoods. Poplars, sweet gum, river birches, and the beautiful, towering sycamores grow plentifully in the bottom land near the river. In some places, these trees shade much of the river's breadth.

Eno River State Park is also home to a profusion of wildflowers, many of them rare. Spring offers by far the best flower show, although you won't be disappointed in summer and fall. Please leave these wonderful blooms for all to enjoy. Rhododendrons and mountain laurel are here, as are a variety of wild orchids, lilies, rare ferns, trillium, crested iris, galax, blood root, Dutchman's breeches, spring and closed gentian, and many others.

The varied plant communities in Eno River State Park provide homes for an equally wide variety of animals. Down on the river, beavers are royalty, and evidence of their reign is abundant. You can find plenty of chewed stumps and logs. Careful observation of the small streams running into the Eno often reveals beaver dams and ponds. Adult beavers weigh in around 60 pounds. They live with their families in lodges or dens along the riverbank. The entrances to these homes are safely underwater. Spotting a beaver isn't easy, but if you quietly sit on the shore near a den as the sun goes down, you may glimpse a dark, furry head gliding through the water. If you move or make the slightest sound, the beaver will be aware of your presence and slap its tail on the water in a loud warning before it dives out of sight. Some of the other mammals in the park are more easily spotted than others. The river otters are elusive. Easier to find are gray squirrels, eastern cottontails, raccoons, white-tailed deer, and chipmunks.

Among the many birds seen and heard in the forests are wild turkeys, owls, and woodpeckers. You may also spot bobwhites, nuthatches, titmice, and chickadees. Along the water, you may even see a blue heron or an egret.

To the delight of Triangle anglers, the Eno River has exceptionally clean water. Bluegill and largemouth bass populate the waters. The Eno is also home to the Roanoke bass, a game species that inhabits only three of North Carolina's rivers—the Eno, the Tar, and the Roanoke. Few's Ford, Holden's Mill, and Cole Mill are reputed to be good spots to land redeyes. Be advised that a North Carolina fishing license is required to fish in the park.

Signs of the Eno's health are readily evident to hikers in the form of freshwater mussel shells strewn on the trails by muskrats finished with a hearty snack. The presence of freshwater mussels indicates that the river water is clean, as the species cannot tolerate much pollution. But the Eno has not been entirely free of impact. Another indicator species resides in the water—the Virginia Panhandle pebble snail. By the 1950s, this river snail, once common as far north as Virginia and Maryland, could only be found in two rivers, one of them the Eno. Currently, the Eno has the only known remaining population of the pebble snail. In 1997, a study found thriving populations of the snail in the river. But the intense development near the banks of the Eno threatens water quality and thus the snails. Construction of new homes and roads loosens the soil, after which rainfall washes sediment into the Eno and its tributaries. Due to increased sedimentation, riffle weed is unable to survive. Riffle weed is the green plant you see growing among the boulders of the river. It also happens to be the home of the Virginia Panhandle pebble snail.

From the late 1990s past the turn of the millennium, a controversy raged over whether the North Carolina Department of Transportation would complete construction of a four-lane highway called Eno Drive. This road would parallel the park for its entire length, shattering the silence and causing enormous impact on the park's plant and animal life. At the time this book went to press, the Department of Transportation was responding to concern from citizens' groups like the Eno River Association by considering an alternate route.

The Eno River flows through two different geological regions. In Orange County and west Durham County, it makes its way through a region known as the Carolina Slate Belt or the Piedmont Upland, which consists primarily of volcanic and igneous rock about 600 million years old. The river valley in this region of relatively high elevation is deep and V-shaped. The banks of the river are almost mountainous. Granite bluffs, mountain laurel, and rhododendron frequently line the shores. An abrupt transition occurs between the Piedmont Upland and the region known as the Durham Basin. The river encounters this transition precisely at West Point on the Eno. The basin, lower in elevation, is comprised primarily of 200-million-year-old sedimentary rocks, mostly sandstone and shale. These rocks are softer than those upstream. As a result, the river becomes broad and slow as it winds toward the Neuse.

Families of Scots-Irish immigrants settled on the river in the 1750s. One of the first English explorers to write about the river was John Lawson, who was exploring the Great Indian Trading Path in 1701 when he came to the Native American town of Achonechy on the Eno. Lawson's party met a man named Enoe-Will from the town of Adshusheer, a sizable community whose ruins lie buried near Durham. Enoe-Will, the king of the combined tribes of the Eno, the Shakori, and the Adshusheer, became a guide and a friend to Lawson. After feeding the party a feast of bear and venison, Enoe-Will guided Lawson until his expedition ended near Washington, N.C. Lawson remembered the Eno as "the Flower of the Carolina."

Although the towering chestnut trees that shaded Lawson's journey are gone, Eno River State Park offers a unique opportunity to walk a trail that was once a wagon road, to poke around the ruins of a 100-year-old mill site, and, above all, to surround yourself with natural beauty. The park, like the growing cities that surround it, is a work in progress. As of this writing, it consists of 2,738 acres divided into five separate access areas and a total of 12 miles of river. Since 1972, when local resident Margaret Nygard and the Eno River Association successfully thwarted a plan to dam the river for a reservoir and instead won a state park, the association has never ceased its efforts to acquire more land for the public. Its future goals include protecting more of the Eno and linking it to protected lands along New Hope Creek in Orange County.

## Few's Ford Access Area _____

**Directions:** From I-85, take the Cole Mill Road exit (Exit 173). Drive North on Cole Mill Road (SR 1569) for 5.1 miles to the Few's Ford Access Area. Once you're inside the park, you'll find the office on the first driveway to the right. To get to the Cox's Mountain trailhead, drive to where the park road dead-ends. To reach Buckquarter Creek Trail, drive past the park office to the second parking area on the right. Beside the parking lot is a picnic area. Trails leave both the picnic area and the parking lot and join just before the river's edge.

Few's Ford is named after some of the early residents of the area. The Few family first owned land on the Eno in the 1750s. William Few became a United States senator and signer of the Constitution. His brother was a bit less lucky. He was hanged after participating in the Battle of Alamance prior to the Revolutionary War. A later Few served as the first president of Duke University. Some descendants of this old Eno family still live around Durham today.

The trails that wind through this section of the park total

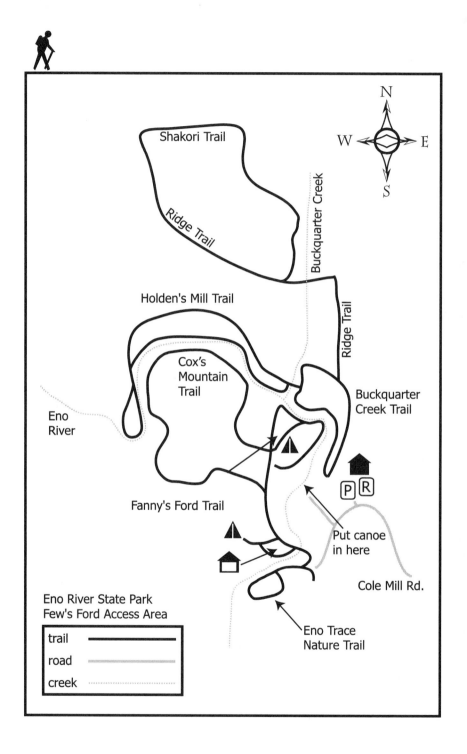

Shakori Trail

Ridge Trail

Buckquarter Creek

Holden's Mill Trail

Cox's Mountain Trail

Ridge Trail

Buckquarter Creek Trail

Eno River

P R

Fanny's Ford Trail

Put canoe in here

Cole Mill Rd.

Eno River State Park
Few's Ford Access Area

| trail | |
| road | |
| creek | |

Eno Trace Nature Trail

about 11 miles in length. There are actually two separate sets of connecting trails. Eno Trace Nature Trail, Cox's Mountain Trail, and Fanny's Ford Trail connect for a 5-mile walk. Buckquarter Creek, Holden's Mill, Ridge, and Shakori Trails combine to form a set of loops of approximately 6 miles. It's difficult to get lost in this park, but not impossible. Most of the trails are well maintained and blazed.

## Eno Trace Nature Trail

**Length:** 0.3 mile
**Difficulty:** Easy
**Blazes:** Yellow
**Surface:** Natural
**Bicycles:** No

Both ends of this short loop trail intersect Cox's Mountain Trail, the main trail here. If you take the right fork of Eno Trace Nature Trail, you'll begin at Station 1, where you can start to work your way through the explanations of the various environments you'll encounter on your travels in the park. This trail can serve as either an introduction or a beautiful but brief complete route. For the elderly, those with small children, and those who just appreciate a good sit in the woods, there is a bench between Stations 9 and 10. Just across from Station 10, be on the lookout for hollow tulip poplars that look like they could comfortably house a woodland fairy or two.

## Cox's Mountain Trail

**Length:** 3.7 miles
**Difficulty:** Moderate
**Blazes:** Blue
**Surface:** Natural
**Bicycles:** No

If you come off Eno Trace Nature Trail and follow the path down to the river, you'll see a log structure on the other side of the water. This is a shelter next to a

*Eno River*

group campsite. If you walk upstream a few yards, you'll see a swinging footbridge. Even if you haven't planned a long hike, this bridge is definitely worth experiencing. Beautiful sycamores arch over the river here. Those ready for a couple hours of hiking can decide between the north and south sides of the river. For the south-side trails, head across the footbridge and go up the hill. The two trails that fork off to the left go to the group campsite and the shelter.

After you've passed these trails, Cox's Mountain Trail loops off to the left. It has the steepest climb, so if you tackle it first, you'll be well rewarded for your efforts later in the hike. From the top, you'll begin to head back down to the river. At the bottom of the hill, the trail bears right and follows a creek back to the Eno. After a short distance alongside the river, the trail makes a right and follows an old road. Be on the lookout for the 1-mile Fanny's Ford Trail. A few unmaintained trails skirt the river's edge and offer an opportunity to perch on a slab of granite and watch the water move.

## Mileposts

**0.0 mile:** Begin in the last parking lot in Few's Ford Access Area. The trailhead is in the far right corner of the parking lot, beside the picnic area.

**0.1 mile:** The trail forks. The left fork heads to Eno Trace Nature Trail. Cox's Mountain Trail continues to the right.

**0.2 mile:** The trail reaches the riverbank and heads upstream. After 50 yards, it reaches the swinging bridge. Cross the bridge to continue on Cox's Mountain Trail. On the far bank, a trail branches off to the left (downstream) and heads 0.1 mile to the cabin.

**0.3 mile:** The trail splits into three. The left forks go to the group camp and the cabin. Cox's Mountain Trail continues to the right.

**0.7 mile:** The trail forks. The right fork goes to the individual campsites and Fanny's Ford Trail. Take the left fork, which goes up Cox's Mountain and intersects Fanny's Ford Trail.

**0.9 mile:** You'll cross a power cut.

**1.6 miles:** You'll reach the river. Turn right and head downstream.

**1.7 miles:** You'll cross the ruins of a mill dam.

**2.0 miles:** Head right up the hill.

**2.2 miles:** You'll cross a power cut.

**2.7 miles:** You'll reach an intersection with Fanny's Ford Trail and the end of the short trail to the campsites.

**2.8 miles:** You'll reach the intersection with the other end of the Fanny's Ford loop.

**3.0 miles:** Head left at the fork to return to the parking lot.

**3.4 miles:** You'll reach the intersection with the trail to the group campsite. The site is about 100 yards to the right. Almost immediately after that, you'll intersect the short trail to the cabin just before the bridge. To reach the parking lot, cross the bridge and turn right.

**3.6 miles:** You'll reach the intersection with the trail to the parking lot and Eno Trace Nature Trail. The parking lot is to the left. Eno Trace is straight ahead.

**3.7 miles:** You'll return to the parking lot.

# Fanny's Ford Trail

**Length:** 0.9 mile
**Difficulty:** Easy
**Blazes:** Purple
**Surface:** Natural
**Bicycles:** No

This trail offers another bench in a beautiful spot. You'll come upon a sharp drop to the river, but look for a more gentle slope just past the bench. If you head down to the water's edge, you'll see where Buckquarter Creek empties into the Eno. You'll know you've arrived at a scenic spot when you begin to hear rushing water to your left. Soon, you'll find short waterfalls and fabulous rocks for sunning.

A short, unnamed secondary trail branches off Fanny's Ford Trail. It leads to the five backpack-camping sites.

When you reach the end of Fanny's Ford Trail, you'll join the old Hillsborough Coach Road, which dates from the 1750s. It was once a major thoroughfare that saw many a horse-drawn vehicle on its way to and from the riverside mills. From here, you can see the ford—the place where horses crossed the river with their loads. You're only a few minutes and an easy hike from the footbridge, from which you can head back to the parking lot or press on to the north-side trails.

## Mileposts

**0.0 mile:** Begin at the intersection at the 2.7-mile mark on Cox's Mountain Trail.
**0.3 mile:** Fanny's Ford Trail reaches the river.
**0.5 mile:** You'll reach a trail that leads 0.3 mile past the walk-in campsites and rejoins Fanny's Ford Trail.
**0.8 mile:** The trail reaches Fanny's Ford and turns right, heading away from the river.
**0.9 mile:** You'll reach an intersection. To the right, the trail continues 100 yards, then returns to the three-way

intersection where Cox's Mountain Trail, Fanny's Ford Trail, and the campsite trail meet. The fork leading straight ahead goes back to the swinging bridge.

## Buckquarter Creek Trail

**Length:** 1.7 miles
**Difficulty:** Easy
**Blazes:** Red
**Surface:** Natural
**Bicycles:** No

Of the set of trails that includes Buckquarter Creek, Holden's Mill, Ridge, and Shakori Trails, only Buckquarter Creek is accessible from the parking areas. The rest of the trails branch off Buckquarter Creek. To reach the trailhead, go past the park office to the next parking area on the right. If you set out from there, you can follow the loop in either direction by taking the old road to the right or the trail to the left. The old road, once known as the Knight-Fire Road, was one of the major routes between Durham and Hillsborough.

The riverside section of Buckquarter Creek Trail is distinguished by its rock outcrops. Numerous flat rocks in the river are suitable for picnicking and toe-dipping. You'll note a few respectable boulders as you make your way downstream. In the summer, you can easily rock-hop from one bank to the other. After you cross the power cut, you'll head up a set of steps to return to the parking lot.

### Mileposts

**0.0 mile:** Begin from the second parking lot in the Few's Ford Access Area. The lot is located near the Piper-Cox House. After 100 yards, you'll reach the river and the official start of Buckquarter Creek Trail. The trail heads upstream to the right. In less than 50 yards, it forks. The right fork heads to the park office and the first parking lot. Take the left fork.

**0.6 mile:** You'll reach the confluence of Buckquarter Creek and the Eno. The trail turns right and follows Buckquarter Creek upstream.

**0.7 mile:** The trail reaches a bridge across Buckquarter Creek. You can cross and walk Holden's Mill Trail (see the description below) or continue on Buckquarter Creek Trail as it loops back toward the parking lot.

**1.0 mile:** You'll cross a creek.

**1.2 miles:** You'll cross another creek.

**1.4 miles:** The trail forks. The left fork leads to the park office at 1.6 miles. Take the right fork.

**1.7 miles:** You'll return to the trailhead at the second parking lot.

## Holden's Mill Trail

**Length:** 2.6 miles
**Difficulty:** Easy to moderate
**Blazes:** Red
**Surface:** Natural
**Bicycles:** No

This loop trail is accessible only via Buckquarter Creek Trail. If you begin by hiking right from the intersection with Buckquarter Creek, you'll have a moderate climb through a mixed-hardwood forest before descending to the river's edge.

If you walk upstream, look to your right for the ruins of Holden's Mill, established in 1811. This public mill operated for almost 100 years until 1908, when a major flood shut it down for good. At one time, it boasted enough employees that a schoolhouse was constructed for their children. The remains of the schoolhouse chimney are still in the park. The daffodils and daylilies that were planted around its yard still bloom.

**0.0 mile:** Begin at the trailhead on Buckquarter Creek Trail.

**0.7 mile:** You'll reach a ridge and cross a power cut.

**1.0 mile:** The trail forks. The left fork returns to the trailhead. To complete Holden's Mill Trail and reach the mill ruins, follow the right fork across the tributary and continue upstream.

**1.2 miles:** The trail forks into two halves of the loop trail to the mill. Follow the right fork. You'll return via the riverside trail.

**1.3 miles:** The trail loops back and follows the river downstream.

**1.5 miles:** You'll reach the mill ruins. The remnants of the dam are visible on both sides of the river.

**1.7 miles:** You'll return to the beginning of the mill loop.

**1.9 miles:** The trail crosses a power cut.

**2.6 miles:** Holden's Mill Trail ends at the bridge over Buckquarter Creek.

## Ridge Trail

**Length:** 1.3 miles
**Difficulty:** Moderate
**Blazes:** Inverted blue U's
**Surface:** Natural
**Bicycles:** No

Ridge Trail is accessible via Buckquarter Creek Trail. You won't find a bridge where Ridge Trail crosses Buckquarter Creek, so be prepared to rock-hop or wade. The trail follows the old Ridge Road, which went from Durham to Roxboro. It begins at an elevation slightly above the Eno and climbs gently but steadily to the northern boundary of the park, ending at the intersection with Shakori Trail. At the top of the climb, you'll be rewarded with scenery that includes a wintertime glimpse of ridges to the west and a few rock outcrops. Ridge Trail also provides access to Knight Trail.

The mature hardwood forest that lines part of Ridge Trail owes its existence in part to a man named Grover Cleveland Shaw, who owned 300 acres here. Despite financial hardship, Shaw held onto his beloved land until 1975, when he finally sold it to the state for Eno River State Park. Large Christmas ferns and extensive running cedar add to the appeal of the trail.

## Mileposts

**0.0 mile:** Begin at the trailhead on Buckquarter Creek Trail.
**0.3 mile:** You'll pass Knight Trail to the right. Follow Ridge Trail to the left.
**0.4 mile:** The trail crosses Buckquarter Creek.
**0.5 mile:** The southern trailhead of Shakori Trail is to the right. Continue left on Ridge Trail.
**1.3 miles:** Ridge Trail ends at a gate at the park boundary. Shakori Trail continues to the right.

## Shakori Trail

**Length:** 1 mile
**Difficulty:** Moderate
**Blazes:** Inverted Yellow U's
**Surface:** Natural
**Bicycles:** No

The trailheads for Shakori Trail are on Buckquarter Creek Trail and Ridge Trail. You can combine Shakori Trail with Ridge Trail for a loop. If you walk down Shakori Trail from the trailhead at the far north end of Ridge Trail, you'll descend about 200 feet to an old roadbed that follows Buckquarter Creek back to Ridge Trail.

## Mileposts

**0.0 mile:** Begin at the north end of Ridge Trail.
**0.5 mile:** The trail reaches Buckquarter Creek.
**1.0 mile:** Shakori Trail ends at the intersection with Ridge Trail.

N
W     E
S

canoe put-in

Dunnagan's Trail

Pea Creek Trail
Cole Mill Trail

Pump
Station
Trail

Bobbit's Hole
Trail

P

Eno River

Rivermont Rd.

P

Nancy Rhoades Creek

Valley Springs

Sparger Rd.

Cole Mill Rd.

Rose of Sharon Rd.

Eno River State Park
Trails in Cole Mill/Pump Station Access Areas

| trail | ——————— |
| road | ≈≈≈≈≈≈≈ |
| creek | ·············· |

# Cole Mill Road Access Area _____

**Directions:** Take the Cole Mill Road exit (Exit 173) off I-85 and follow the signs for Eno River State Park. Drive north for 3.3 miles, then turn left on Old Cole Mill Road just after the Eno River Bridge and the brown sign for Eno River State Park. After 0.3 mile, Old Cole Mill Road passes through the park gate.

The trails in this section include Cole Mill Trail, Bobbit's Hole Trail, Pea Creek Trail, and Dunnagan's Trail.

## Cole Mill Trail

**Length:** 1.2 miles
**Difficulty:** Easy
**Blazes:** Yellow
**Surface:** Natural
**Bicycles:** No

Cole Mill Trail and Bobbit's Hole Trail are two adjoining loops. Cole Mill Trail is the loop that leaves from and returns to the parking lot. You can begin it either by passing through the picnic area or by leaving from the end of the parking lot next to the information sign. If you start at the trailhead beside the first parking lot (just left of the restroom), you'll enjoy a forest hike for the first half of the loop before returning via a riverside trail. A hike on this trail can serve as a brief prelude to a shaded picnic at one of several well-placed tables between the first parking lot and the river. Drinking water and restrooms are close by.

### Mileposts

**0.0 mile:** Begin at the trailhead beside the first parking lot. Cole Mill Trail starts just left of the restrooms. In just under 100 yards, you'll reach a T intersection. Cole Mill Trail goes to the right.
**0.1 mile:** You'll cross under a power line.

**0.3 mile:** You'll cross a small creek via a wooden bridge. After 100 yards, the trail forks. The right fork is the beginning of Bobbit's Hole Trail. Continue straight on Cole Mill Trail.

**0.5 mile:** You'll cross under a power line just before reaching the river.

**0.7 mile:** You'll cross a bridge.

**1.0 mile:** The trail forks. The yellow-blazed Cole Mill Trail heads left up the hill, then parallels the river.

**1.1 miles:** The trail forks again. The left fork heads past several picnic tables before ending at 1.2 miles near the restroom where it began. The right fork emerges at 1.2 miles beside the second parking lot near the trailhead of Pea Creek Trail.

## Bobbit's Hole Trail

**Length:** 1.4 miles
**Difficulty:** Easy
**Blazes:** Orange
**Surface:** Natural
**Bicycles:** No

Bobbit's Hole Trail is a loop trail that can be reached only from Cole Mill Trail. If you hike upstream on Cole Mill Trail, you can turn right at the junction with Bobbit's Hole Trail and follow Cole Mill for a shorter walk. You'll pass the other end of Bobbit's Hole Trail before heading back to the parking area.

If you follow Bobbit's Hole Trail from the riverside intersection with Cole Mill Trail, watch for a short side trail to the left that leads to Bobbit's Hole, named for a man named Bobbit who drowned here. Bobbit's Hole is one of the nicest spots in the park. It's located at the base of a small group of rapids and a sharp bend in the river. In the fall, colorful leaves blanket the still pool.

**0.0 mile:** Both trailheads for Bobbit's Hole Trail are on Cole Mill Trail. Cole Mill Trail can be accessed behind the picnic tables off the first parking lot or beside the second parking lot.

**0.3 mile:** You'll cross a bridge.

**0.6 mile:** The trail crosses a power cut.

**0.7 mile:** You'll cross a bridge.

**0.8 mile:** You'll cross another bridge.

**0.9 mile:** You'll arrive at a T intersection. The right fork is a short spur trail leading to Bobbit's Hole. (Note: The trail that forks up the hill near the end of Bobbit's Hole Trail is not a state park trail. It ends on private property.) Take the left fork to continue on Bobbit's Hole Trail.

**1.0 mile:** You'll cross a wooden bridge. The trail goes both left and right. The left fork ends at the creek. Follow the right fork downstream along the bank of the Eno.

**1.3 miles:** The trail crosses a bridge.

**1.4 miles:** The trail rejoins Cole Mill Trail. The fork to the left (under the power lines) is the higher-elevation, woodland half of the Cole Mill loop. Follow the lower-elevation, riverside fork straight ahead along the bank. Either direction will take you back to the parking lot.

## Pea Creek Trail

**Length:** 1.3 miles
**Difficulty:** Easy to Moderate
**Blazes:** Blue
**Surface:** Natural
**Bicycles:** No

Pea Creek Trail and Dunnagan's Trail are loop trails that combine to form one of the most beautiful and interesting hikes in the area, especially during spring and fall, when the wildflowers bloom. Pea Creek Trail is awash in color at those times.

**0.0 mile:** Begin just beyond the far end of the parking lot. A signboard with maps is located at the trailhead. Pea Creek Trail forks after 50 yards. The left fork is a short trail to a picnic table with a grill. Take the right fork. Pea Creek Trail forks at the bank of the Eno after 140 yards. Take the left fork, which heads upstream on the north bank.

**0.2 mile:** You'll pass under the Cole Mill Road bridge. Seventy yards later, the trail crosses a tributary via a wooden bridge.

**0.3 mile:** Pea Creek Trail forks. The riverside half of the loop goes straight ahead. To the left, the trail heads uphill. Take the left fork.

**0.4 mile:** You'll cross a power cut.

**0.6 mile:** The trail reaches the bridge over Pea Creek. Dunnagan's Trail begins on the opposite side of the creek. Follow Pea Creek along the river.

**1.3 miles:** You'll return to the trailhead.

## Dunnagan's Trail

**Length:** 1.8 miles
**Difficulty:** Easy
**Blazes:** Red
**Surface:** Natural
**Bicycles:** No

Dunnagan's Trail is worth your while, as it is a path rich in both natural and human history. You can perch atop a boulder and look across the river at the remains of the pump station that provided water to Durham from 1887 until the late 1920s. The pump station was frequented by Victorian-era picnickers and swimmers. It was managed by Captain John Michie until the lake that bears his name was created to meet the thirst of a growing population.

You can pay your respects at the graveyard of the

Dunnagan family. The writing on P. Catherine Dunnagan's headstone indicates that she was born March 7, 1826, and died January 6, 1914. The grave is particularly beautiful in late April, when the dogwood that shades the sunken ground drops its white blossoms.

## Mileposts

**0.0 mile:** The trail begins at Pea Creek. It forks after 40 yards. The riverside section of the loop heads right. Take the left fork to hike the upland section of the loop.

**0.5 mile:** The Dunnagan gravestones are on the right side of the trail.

**0.6 mile:** You'll cross a bridge.

**0.7 mile:** The trail forks. Follow the orange-blazed fork to the right. The left fork is not an official park trail. It provides park access to residents of the Continental Drive neighborhood.

**1.0 mile:** You'll arrive at the bank of the Eno. When you reach the large boulder, you'll see the old pump station on the opposite bank.

**1.2 miles:** You'll cross a bridge.

**1.8 miles:** Dunnagan's Trail ends at the bridge over Pea Creek. Either fork of Pea Creek Trail will take you to the parking area.

# Pump Station Access Area

**Directions:** From I-85, take the Cole Mill Road exit (Exit 173). Drive North on Cole Mill Road (SR 1569) for 2.4 miles to Rivermont Road, turn right, and go 0.6 mile to the bridge over Nancy Rhoades Creek. Park in one of the gravel pull-outs.

## Pump Station Trail
**Length:** 1.4 miles
**Difficulty:** Easy to moderate

**Blazes:** Signs with arrows
**Surface:** Natural
**Bicycles:** No

The sign at the trailhead and the small trail signs will point you in the right direction. Follow the arrows to avoid wandering onto private property. This trail crosses Nancy Rhoades Creek and leads past the ruins of the old Durham Pump Station, which was likely the site of a mill that may have been in operation by 1752. You can explore the remaining rock walls and foundation of the pump station, but be careful! The building is in the process of falling apart, so enter at your own risk. And beware of the poison ivy that covers the area during the warm months.

The trail passes through uplands and bottom lands and offers views of the Eno. Ferns, laurel, and wildflowers grow along the slopes that ascend from the river.

## Mileposts

**0.2 mile:** You'll cross a power cut.
**0.3 mile:** The trail crosses a bridge. Thirty yards later, it joins a road and goes left. After 20 yards, the trail forks again. Take the left fork. The fork leading straight ahead is the yellow-blazed Laurel Bluffs Trail (see next page). As you approach the river, Pump Station Trail forks once more. The right fork goes to the ruins of the pump station. The trail continues straight ahead and over the bridge.
**0.4 mile:** You'll cross the bridge.
**0.5 mile:** The trail reaches the bank of the Eno and heads upstream.
**1.0 mile:** The trail forks. Follow the left fork away from the river.
**1.1 miles:** You'll cross a power cut.
**1.2 miles:** The trail forks. Follow the left fork.
**1.4 miles:** The trail emerges at the bridge.

# Laurel Bluffs Trail

**Length:** 2.4 miles
**Difficulty:** Moderate to strenuous
**Blazes:** Yellow
**Surface:** Natural with some gravel
**Bicycles:** No

Laurel Bluffs Trail was still under construction as this guide went to press. From the trailhead in Pump Station Access Area, the trail parallels the Eno as far as the Guess Road bridge. The park plans to continue the trail to Cabe Lands Access Area at some future date. In addition to many fine views of the Eno, the trail offers access to a handful of creeks and, true to its name, a rocky bluff. It will one day be a section of North Carolina Mountains-to-Sea Trail.

## Mileposts

**0.0 mile:** Begin at the trailhead 0.3 mile down Pump Station Trail (see page 82).
**0.1 mile:** Keep right when the trail forks. Follow the gravel path for 100 yards, then go left at the bottom of the steps. You'll cross a small seasonal creek.
**0.2 mile:** The trail forks again. Keep left and head uphill.
**0.3 mile:** You'll emerge into a clearing. Turn right, follow the buried-cable signs for 100 yards, then reenter the woods to your left.
**0.7 mile:** You'll cross a creek.
**0.8 mile:** You'll again cross a creek.
**0.9 mile:** The trail turns left and crosses a small creek.
**1.3 miles:** You'll cross a creek twice.
**1.5 miles:** The trail crosses a small creek, then another. You'll reach a trail intersection at the second creek. Continue uphill.
**1.7 miles:** Continue straight at the fork.
**1.9 miles:** The trail heads right before the creek, then turns left across the creek and heads uphill to the right.
**2.4 miles:** You'll cross a creek and reach the steps leading up to Guess Road in less than 100 yards.

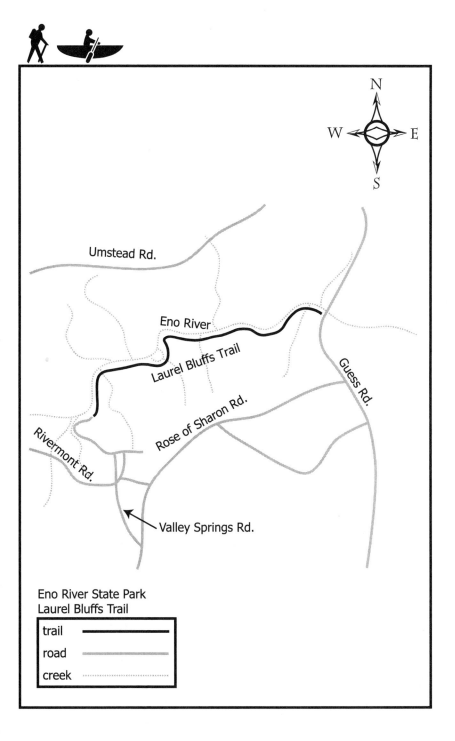

N
W E
S

Umstead Rd.

Eno River

Laurel Bluffs Trail

Guess Rd.

Rose of Sharon Rd.

Rivermont Rd.

Valley Springs Rd.

Eno River State Park
Laurel Bluffs Trail

| trail | ——— |
| road | |
| creek | ········ |

# Cabe Lands Access Area ─────────────────────

**Directions:** From I-85, take the Cole Mill Road exit (Exit 173). Drive north on Cole Mill Road (SR 1569) for 2.4 miles to the intersection with Sparger Road. Turn left (south) on Sparger Road, go 1.3 miles, turn right on Howe Street, and drive 0.5 mile to the parking lot on the right.

## Cabe Lands Trail

**Length:** 1.2 miles
**Difficulty:** Moderate
**Blazes:** Orange
**Surface:** Natural
**Bicycles:** No

The relatively unpopulated Cabe Lands Trail passes through a place where the promise of and the threat to this urban nature park are both readily apparent. The relatively short loop begins with an old service road you can follow down to the river; on the left, you'll pass the footpath leading back to the parking lot. About the time you reach the water's edge, you'll begin to lose the sounds of traffic from nearby I-85 and enter another world.

The trail follows a section of the river that is at first deep and slow, then rockier with small rapids. You'll have easy access to the bank, so you can search out that perfect secluded spot for sunning or fishing. As the river gets rockier, look on the left side of the trail for the remains of Cabe's Mill, which began operating in 1779 and continued on and off until the end of the 19th century. Although the site is hidden by dense brush and leaves during the summer, the foundation is visible in winter. You can walk right up the former millrace.

### Mileposts
─────────────────────────────────────────────

**0.1 mile:** The trail forks. Take the right fork.
**0.4 mile:** The trail reaches the Eno and heads left (upstream)

Eno River State Park
Cabe Lands Trail

| trail | ——————— |
|-------|----------|
| road  | ········· |
| creek | ········· |

across a small wooden bridge over a tributary.

**0.5 mile:** You'll pass the ruins of the stone wall of Cabe's Mill on the left.

**0.7 mile:** You'll reach a T intersection with another trail. Turn left to stay on Cabe Lands Trail.

**1.0 mile:** You'll cross a bridge.

**1.1 miles:** You'll return to the intersection where the loop splits. Go right.

**1.2 miles:** You'll arrive at the parking lot.

# Hill Forest

**Address:** NCSU Forestry Camp, P.O. Box 71, Rougemont, NC 27572
**Telephone:** 919-477-1125
**Hours:** Sunrise to sunset, year-round
**Maps:** USGS Rougemont, Lake Michie
**Directions:** From I-85, take the US 501 exit (Exit 176). Drive north on US 501 for 13 miles, turn right on Moores Mill Road, and make an immediate right on SR 1614. You'll find a signboard, a map, and limited parking 0.7 mile ahead on the left. Slocum Forestry Camp is 0.2 mile farther on the left.

Owned by North Carolina State University, the 2,401 acres of Hill Forest offer more than most of us dare hope for in our Triangle parks: trails for hiking, biking, and horseback riding, and a river to look at and float on. Hill Forest, bisected by the Flat River, is just far enough off the beaten path that you may even have a stretch of trail or river to yourself. There are many places where you can picnic beside the river. The most accessible of these is the bridge just below Slocum Camp.

The forest is managed by NCSU to serve as an outdoor classroom and laboratory for the benefit of its forestry and wildlife biology program. The unnamed trails within the forest consist of a combination of gravel roads and narrow dirt trails. All of them are open to equestrian use, which brings up a special concern for mountain bikers: Always give horses the right of way. That means get off of your bike, get off of the trail, and wait for the horse and rider to pass.

This is one of the few Triangle natural areas open to the public where there are no signs and where no maps are available. Only general descriptions of the narrow, single-track trails are included in this guide. For more information about the Flat River and threats to this valuable local resource, see pages 400-401.

In 1929, George Watts Hill made his initial gift of 378 acres to NCSU. Part of the land that now comprises Hill Forest was once the home of one of the area's most prominent early citizens, William Person Mangum (1792-1861). Mangum was a United States congressman for two terms, a United States senator for three

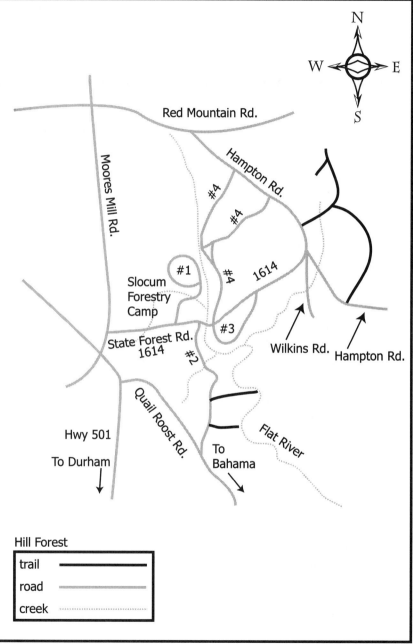

Red Mountain Rd.

N

W E

S

Moores Mill Rd.

Hampton Rd.

#4

#4

#1

#4

1614

Slocum
Forestry
Camp

#3

State Forest Rd.
1614

Wilkins Rd.

Hampton Rd.

#2

Quail Roost Rd.

Flat River

Hwy 501

To Durham

To
Bahama

Hill Forest

| trail | ——————— |
| road | ~~~~~~~~~ |
| creek | ·········· |

terms, and president *pro tempore* of the Senate from 1842 to 1845. Mangum's Federal-style home was called Walnut Hall, so named for two large walnut trees that stood until the middle of the 20th century. Mangum, his wife, and four children lived on the plantation, as did a number of slaves. Records show that Mangum owned 20 slaves in 1850 and 12 in 1860, on the eve of the Civil War. He opposed the dissolution of the Union, but when war broke out, he resigned himself to the Confederate cause. He sent his youngest child and only son, William Preston Mangum, to fight for the Confederacy. William, a member of an infantry company know as the Flat River Guards, was mortally wounded at First Manassas in July 1861.

## SR 1614

**Length:** 1.6 miles
**Difficulty:** Easy
**Blazes:** None
**Surface:** Gravel
**Bicycles:** Yes

### Mileposts

**0.0 mile:** Begin at the Slocum Forestry Camp gate and head across the Flat River.
**0.5 mile:** A dirt road (Road 3 to the right, Road 4 to the left) crosses SR 1614.
**1.0 mile:** The right leg of Road 3 ends at SR 1614.
**1.6 miles:** SR 1614 ends at the intersection with Wilkins Road (SR 1613) 0.2 mile south of the intersection of Wilkins Road and Hampton Road (SR 1603).

## Road 1

**Length:** 1.7 miles
**Difficulty:** Easy
**Blazes:** None
**Surface:** Gravel
**Bicycles:** Yes

Numerous narrow trails go north from the northern-most point on this road. Most head to the river or to the edge of the Hill Forest property.

## Mileposts

**0.0 mile:** Begin at the intersection with SR 1614 some 0.7 mile from the junction of SR 1614 and Moores Mill Road.
**0.3 mile:** You'll pass buildings associated with Slocum Forestry Camp.
**0.5 mile:** You'll reach a fork. To the left is the return loop. Take the right fork.
**1.0 mile:** The trail reaches a T intersection. The left fork heads downhill. Take the right fork uphill.
**1.3 miles:** You'll return to the fork you passed at 0.5 mile.
**1.7 miles:** The trail returns to the signboard.

# Road 2

**Length:** 1.8 miles
**Difficulty:** Easy
**Blazes:** None
**Surface:** Gravel
**Bicycles:** Yes

This road extends south (right, if you're headed downhill from Moores Mill Road) from Slocum Forestry Camp.

## Mileposts

**0.0 mile:** Begin at Slocum Forestry Camp.
**0.7 mile:** A trail forks right after you cross an unnamed creek. Continue straight.
**1.3 miles:** You'll reach a fork. The dirt road to the left goes a little over 0.6 mile to a great spot on the river with a sandy shore and bluffs on the opposite bank. Take the right fork.
**1.6 miles:** You'll reach another fork. The dirt road that forks left goes a little over 0.5 mile to end above the river. Take

the right fork.
**1.8 miles:** Road 2 ends on SR 1516.

## Road 3

**Length:** 1.4 miles
**Difficulty:** Easy
**Blazes:** None
**Surface:** Gravel
**Bicycles:** Yes

On the east side of the Flat River, Road 3 is the loop road that crosses SR 1614 headed south. Numerous trails branch off this road. The ones heading right generally end at the Hill Forest property line or continue east to SR 1613.

### Mileposts

**0.6 mile:** A thin trail heads right to the river.
**1.4 miles:** Road 3 ends at the intersection with SR 1614.

## Road 4 Loop

**Length:** 3.8 miles
**Difficulty:** Easy
**Blazes:** None
**Surface:** Gravel and asphalt
**Bicycles:** Yes

Road 4 Loop is one of the longest routes you can take without backtracking. To reach Road 4, follow SR 1614 to the east side of the Flat River. Walk uphill until you see Road 4, which heads north (left).

### Mileposts

**0.8 mile:** You'll pass an intersection. The return loop is to the left.
**1.5 miles:** You'll reach the Hill Forest property boundary.

Backtrack or keep straight to get to Hampton Road (SR 1603) to complete the loop. Be careful to stay on the gravel road here to avoid trespassing.

**1.6 miles:** You'll reach Hampton Road (SR 1603). Turn left.

**1.8 miles:** The trail crosses an unnamed creek.

**2.0 miles:** Turn left on the gravel road and reenter Hill Forest. Note: You cannot clearly see the Hill Forest sign from SR 1603 at this intersection.

**3.0 miles:** You'll arrive at the intersection you passed at 0.8 mile. Head right to return to Slocum Forestry Camp.

**3.8 miles:** You'll reach SR 1614. Turn right to return to Slocum Forestry Camp.

# Little River Regional Park and Natural Area

**Address:** This park is managed jointly by Durham and Orange Counties. For information, contact Durham County Open Space Land Manager, 101 City Hall Plaza, Durham, NC 27701 (919-560-7956) or Orange County Recreation and Parks Department, Central Recreation Center, 300 West Tryon Street, P.O. Box 8181, Hillsborough, NC 27278 (919-245-2660).

**Directions:** From I-85, take the Guess Road Exit (Exit 175). Turn north onto Guess Road and drive approximately 12 miles to Little River Park Way. Note: the entrance is about 1 mile past the bridge over the south fork of the Little River. Turn right to enter the park.

**Hours:** November through March, 8 A.M. to 5 P.M.; April and May, 8 A.M. to 6 P.M.; June through Augues, 7 A.M. to 8 P.M.; September and October, 8 A.M. to 6 P.M.

**Maps:** USGS Rougemont

**Telephone:** 919-245-2660

At the time this guide went to press, Little River Regional Park and Natural Area was preparing to host its grand-opening celebration. The counties of Durham and Orange, the Triangle Land Conservancy, and the Eno River Association worked to fund the purchase of land for this 391-acre park on the border between the counties. The park's forests are in various stages of succession. You can see everything from young pine stands to mature oaks. The area includes 1.25 miles of frontage on the North Fork of the Little River and a small gorge with scenery that's exceptionally dramatic for the Piedmont. By the time this guide is available, the park will have two picnic shelters, about 7 miles of hiking trails, a 0.25-mile wheelchair-accessible loop trail, and 7 miles of mountain bike trails constructed with volunteer help from the Durham-Orange Mountain Bike Organization. By the summer of 2005, some 4 to 5 miles of equestrian trails should be nearing completion.

# Penny's Bend Nature Preserve

**Address:** North Carolina Botanical Garden, CB Box 3375, Totten Center, Chapel Hill, NC 27599
**Telephone:** 919-962-0522
**Hours:** Open during daylight hours
**Maps:** USGS NE Durham; free trail maps are available from the Totten Center (see page 161).
**Directions:** From I-85 in Durham, take Exit 177 and turn north on Roxboro Road. Drive 1.3 miles, turn right on Old Oxford Road (SR 1004), go 3.2 miles, and turn left on Snow Hill Road (SR 1631). Turn left immediately into the parking area for Penny's Bend.

Penny's Bend lies in Durham County just upstream from the confluence of the Eno and Little Rivers and Falls Lake. In addition to being a great place to take a walk, the 84 acres of the nature preserve lie atop a unique geological feature called a diabase sill. The rock underlying this bend in the river is harder than the surrounding rock. When the waters of the Eno couldn't erode the hard diabase, they went around it, eroding the softer adjacent rock and twisting the river's course into an oxbow shape.

In addition to determining the course of the Eno, the diabase affected the soil and, in turn, the plants within this pronounced bend in the river. The plants at Penny's Bend are common in prairie states such as Illinois but are rare in the Southeast. In fact, there

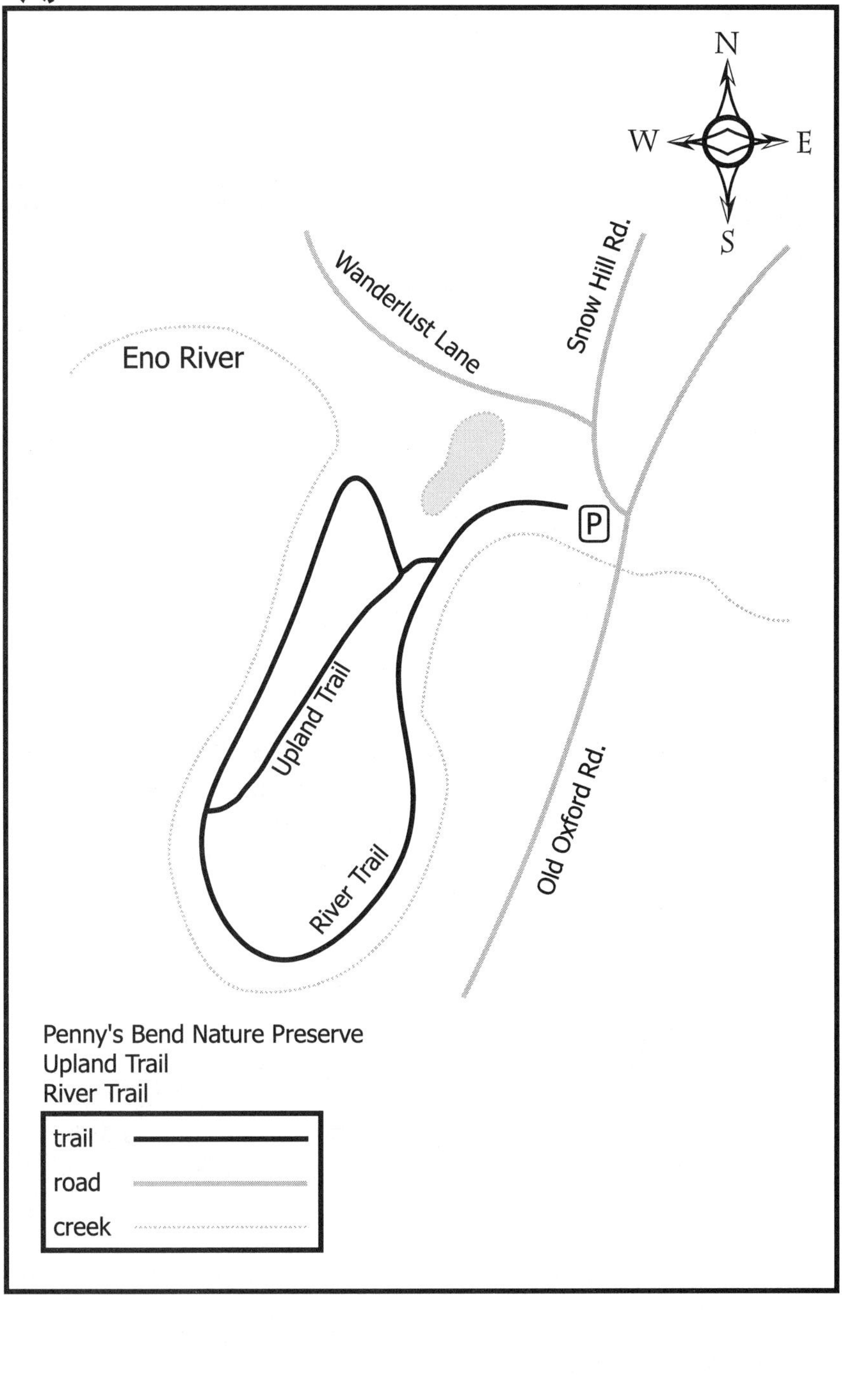

N
W ⟷ E
S

Eno River

Wanderlust Lane

Snow Hill Rd.

P

Upland Trail

River Trail

Old Oxford Rd.

Penny's Bend Nature Preserve
Upland Trail
River Trail

| trail | ———— |
| road | ≈≈≈≈≈ |
| creek | ·····|

are more prairie species here than at any other site in North Carolina. This is most dramatically illustrated in late spring, when the spectacular wild blue indigo blooms. The profusion of wildflowers attracts an equally spectacular array of butterflies, making spring the ideal time to visit.

In the decades leading up to the Civil War, the Penny's Bend area was the home of one of the Triangle's prominent early citizens, Duncan Cameron. Cameron's Federal-style home, Fairntosh, served as the model for his friend and neighbor, William Mangum, who built his house on land now part of Hill Forest (see page 88). The gristmill and sawmill Cameron owned were located along the river very close to the trailhead.

## River Trail

**Length:** 1.9 miles
**Difficulty:** Easy to moderate
**Blazes:** White
**Surface:** Natural
**Bicycles:** No

This scenic loop trail follows the river as it winds around the diabase. Although there is little elevation change, this is not a particularly easy trial. Hikers should watch their step, as they'll encounter a few drop-offs adjacent to the trail, as well as some uneven ground. Wear long pants, and be on the lookout for poison ivy in the warm months.

### Mileposts

**0.0 mile:** Begin at the trailhead on the west side of the parking lot (to the right, if you're facing the river). The trail forks a few feet beyond the parking lot. The right fork goes past some interpretive signs. Follow the left fork to the river. At 130 yards, you'll cross a bridge.

**0.2 mile:** The trail forks at the trailhead to the Upland Trail loop. Continue to the left.

**1.5 miles:** The trail turns sharply upward and away from the river.

**1.7 miles:** The path straight ahead completes the Upland Trail loop. Go left into the woods at the signpost to continue on River Trail.

**1.8 miles:** Back at the river, head left (downstream) to return to the parking lot.

**1.9 miles:** You'll reach the parking lot.

## Upland Trail

**Length:** 0.6 mile
**Difficulty:** Easy
**Blazes:** Pale yellow
**Surface:** Natural
**Bicycles:** No

### Mileposts

**0.0 mile:** Begin at the Upland Trail trailhead 0.2 mile down River Trail. You'll climb away from River Trail. After 130 yards, you'll reach a clearing. Turn left and follow the path.

**0.4 mile:** You'll pass a pond.

**0.5 mile:** You'll return to the intersection above.

**0.6 mile:** You'll return to the trailhead. The parking lot is 0.2 mile to the left.

*Raven Rock State Park*

# Harnett County

## Raven Rock State Park

**Address:** Superintendent, 3009 Raven Rock Road, Lillington, NC 27546
**Telephone:** 910-893-4888
**Hours:** From November to February, the park is open from 8 A.M. to 6 P.M. During March and October, it is open from 8 A.M. to 7 P.M. During April, May, and September, it is open from 8 A.M. to 8 P.M. From June to August, it is open from 8 A.M. to 9 P.M. The park is closed on Christmas.
**Maps:** USGS Mamers; free state park maps are available in the park.
**Directions:** To reach the hiking trails in the southern section of the park from Chapel Hill and the western Triangle, take US 15/US 501 South to US 421 in Sanford, then follow US 421 South for 18.2 miles to Raven Rock Road. Turn left on Raven Rock Road, which will take you through the park gate. The park office is on the left as you drive to the parking lot. Campers must stop here to register and pay for campsites.

To reach the northern section of the park from the parking lot in the southern section, return on Raven Rock Road to US 421 and turn left. Drive 6.4 miles into Lillington and turn left on US 401. Drive 1.6 miles and turn left to stay on US 401. Drive 3.3 miles, turn left on Christian Light Road (SR 1412), go 3.9 miles, and turn left on River Road (SR 1418). Drive 1.6 miles and turn left into the parking lot.

Of all the parks in and around the Triangle, Raven Rock has the most dramatic scenery. The cliffs, an easy mile walk from the parking lot, were carved by the park's other principal attraction, the Cape Fear River. The Cape Fear divides the park into two sections. The seven hiking trails, the campsites, and Raven Rock itself are in the southern part. The northern section has two equestrian trails totaling 7 miles. Those trails are also open to hikers.

Visitors with an interest in topography and geology will love this park. Raven Rock is only the largest of the many interesting rocks along the park's river and creeks. Raven Rock and the other large outcrops are made of a hard, layered rock known as mica schist. In the distant past, Raven Rock was a small outcrop. The rock was exposed as the Cape Fear River eroded the more recently deposited gravel layers and the softer metamorphic rocks.

Significant rapids are located in the vicinity of the state park, which make this an appealing spot for whitewater boaters. The rapids occur on the fall line, where the hard rocks under the Piedmont meet the softer underlayer of the coastal plain.

The variety of geological features in the park yields an equally diverse array of plant life. The north-facing slopes of Raven Rock, the bottom-land forests, former fields undergoing the process of succession—all provide habitat for different plants and animals. The mountain laurel and Catawba rhododendron in the park are about as far as they get from their central range in the Blue Ridge. And they are not alone. A great profusion of wildflowers covers the ground in early spring before the leaves block the passage of sunlight to the forest floor. Tons of Dutchman's breeches, Solomon's seal and Atamasco lilies greet spring explorers. You'll find mature oak-hickory forests at many of the higher elevations, but most of the impressively large trees are near the creeks and river and are easily spotted from the trails.

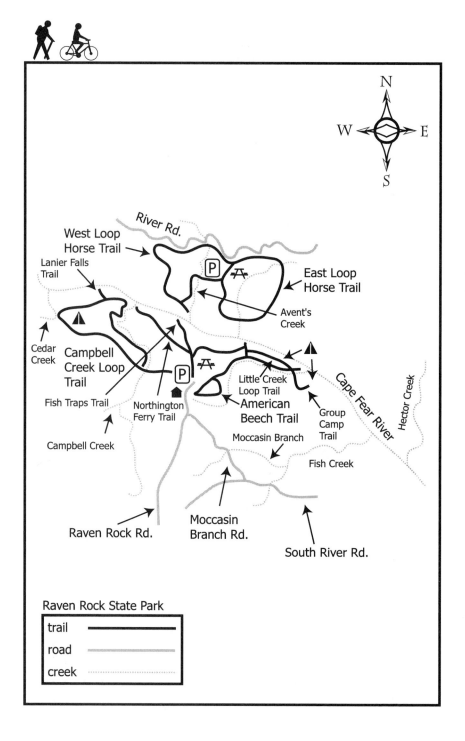

Raven Rock State Park

| trail | ——————— |
| road | ——————— |
| creek | ·············· |

Many animals live in Raven Rock State Park. Anglers generally have the best luck at the mouths of the park's major creeks. The creeks provide an ideal spot for salamanders and other amphibians. Spring is an amazing time in Raven Rock, and not just because of the wildflowers. Many migratory birds pass through the park as they head north, and the woods are full of their songs. Winter also offers great birding opportunities, as mallards and other waterfowl wait out the cold months. As for mammals, the park's gray squirrels, raccoons, and opossums are relatively easy to spot. More difficult to see are the Southern flying squirrels, which leave their nests only at night. The flying squirrels are the smallest squirrels in the Piedmont. The largest, fox squirrels, also live in the park. White-tailed deer live here as well.

Long before the land around Raven Rock was a state park, Sioux and Tuscarora Indians hunted and fished here. European settlers first arrived in the middle of the 18th century. They began to alter the character of the land as they built farms, roads, and mills. Around the turn of the 19th century, the Northington family owned much of the land in and around what is now the park. Northington Road was a major thoroughfare in its day, providing a route from Fayetteville to Raleigh. It crossed the Cape Fear by ferry near the mouth of Campbell Creek and the end of Northington Trail. In one of the many attempts to tame the Upper Cape Fear, the Northington (or Norrington) lock and dam were completed in 1855. This dam was located immediately below Fish Traps Falls. Its remains are still visible at the end of Fish Traps Trail. The lock and dam were destroyed by a hurricane in 1858.

Raven Rock got its name in 1854 when ravens were seen nesting on the rock. That same year, locks and dams were put in along the river to aid in transportation. Although the summer canoeists bottoming out here might find it hard to believe, river steamers once used the Cape Fear River to move goods and people.

Some of what is now park acreage began the 20th century as farmland. In the 1960s, Dr. Robert Soots led concerned residents of the surrounding counties in an effort to preserve the area around Raven Rock. Finally, in 1969, Raven Rock State Park was created.

# Southern Section Trails _____

## American Beech Trail

**Length:** 0.7 mile
**Difficulty:** Easy
**Blazes:** White
**Surface:** Natural
**Bicycles:** No

American Beech is a short, wooded loop trail with benches and numbered posts indicating interpretive stations. An interpretive trail guide is available at the trailhead.

### Mileposts _____

**0.0 mile:** To reach the trailhead, follow Raven Rock Loop Trail from the northwest corner of the parking lot. The turnoff to American Beech Trail is just a few yards ahead on the right.

**0.2 mile:** You'll cross a wooden bridge over a stream.

**0.3 mile:** You'll pass an interpretive wheel on the right, then cross a bridge.

**0.5 mile:** You'll reach a junction with Raven Rock Loop Trail. Head left to return to the parking lot.

**0.7 mile:** You'll reach the parking lot.

## Raven Rock Loop Trail

**Length:** 2.1 miles, including the spurs to the base of Raven Rock and the overlook
**Difficulty:** Easy, except for the 10 flights of stairs leading down to the base of Raven Rock
**Blazes:** Red
**Surface:** Natural
**Bicycles:** No

The most popular trail in the park, this wooded loop

trail leads along Little Creek to Raven Rock, the overlook, Little Creek Loop Trail, the group camp, the canoe camp, Fish Traps Trail, and Northington Ferry Trail. If you walk only one trail in the park and don't mind some company, this is the one for you.

## Mileposts

**0.0 mile:** Begin at the trailhead in the northwest corner of the parking lot.

**0.2 mile:** You'll pass the American Beech trailhead.

**0.5 mile:** The trail reaches the first of four creek crossings via bridges.

**0.9 mile:** You'll reach the Little Creek Loop trailhead. Turn left to remain on Raven Rock Loop Trail.

**1.0 mile:** You'll reach the second Little Creek Loop trailhead. The steps down to Raven Rock are a few yards ahead. The fork leading to the rest of Raven Rock Loop Trail and the overlook is 100 yards ahead on the left. At the bottom of the steps to Raven Rock is a short, sandy trail that runs between the base of the rock and the Cape Fear River.

**1.5 miles:** The trail reaches a fork. The right fork goes directly to the overlook. Head left to return to the parking lot.

**1.6 miles:** The Fish Traps trailhead is on the right. (Note that the Northington Ferry's trailhead is off Fish Traps.) Continue left toward the parking lot.

**2.0 miles:** You'll pass the Campbell Creek Loop trailhead before reaching the parking lot.

## Little Creek Loop Trail

**Length:** 1.5 miles
**Difficulty:** Easy
**Blazes:** Yellow
**Surface:** Natural
**Bicycles:** No

If Raven Rock offers one of the most dramatic sights in the Piedmont, Little Creek Loop Trail is a wonderful example of the smaller, more subtle beauty this region has to offer. The creek has tiny falls and boulders worn flat and smooth by its water. In late April, the fallen flowers of laurel bushes ride these rapids and cover the boulders. Most hikers pass this trail by in favor of more time at Raven Rock, which gives Little Creek Loop Trail an added attraction: solitude.

### Mileposts

**0.0 mile:** Begin at the first trailhead off Raven Rock Trail.
**0.8 mile:** The trail forks. To the right is the orange-blazed Group Camp Trail, which goes over the bridge to the group campsites. (To reach the group camping area, go 0.3 mile, then head left at the dirt road for another 0.2 mile.) To continue on Little Creek Loop Trail, take the left fork, which leads past the turnoff to the canoe campsites, then back to Raven Rock Loop Trail.
**1.5 miles:** You'll return to Raven Rock Loop Trail. From this point, you can head left to the parking lot or right past Raven Rock to complete Raven Rock Loop Trail.

## Fish Traps Trail

**Length:** 0.7 mile
**Difficulty:** Easy
**Blazes:** Orange
**Surface:** Natural
**Bicycles:** No

This easy out-and-back trail leads to the Cape Fear River. Much of it is an old roadbed. At the trail's end is a series of river rapids where Native Americans set traps to catch fish migrating upstream.

**0.0 mile:** Begin at the trailhead off Raven Rock Loop Trail. The Northington Ferry trailhead is on the left after 100 yards.
**0.6 mile:** You'll reach the Cape Fear River at the Fish Traps rapids. The end of the trail is 0.1 mile downstream near the remains of the Northington lock and dam.

## Northington Ferry Trail

**Length:** 1 mile
**Difficulty:** Easy
**Blazes:** Yellow
**Surface:** Natural
**Bicycles:** No

This out-and-back trail follows another wooded old roadbed. It leads to the former site of the Northington Ferry. This was once a major crossing point of the Cape Fear River.

**Mileposts**

**0.0 mile:** Begin at the trailhead off Fishtraps Trail.
**1.0 mile:** After crossing a wooden bridge, the trail ends along the river.

## Campbell Creek Loop Trail

**Length:** 5.1 miles
**Difficulty:** Easy to moderate
**Blazes:** Blue
**Surface:** Natural
**Bicycles:** No

This trail leads across and down Campbell Creek to the Lanier Falls trailhead. It then passes the family campsites and loops back to the creek and the parking lot. The many rocks and small rapids make the section along Campbell Creek appealing. Much of the other half of the trail is a dirt road that passes through what appear to be very young forests just regaining a foothold. In fact, the mature forest here has been subjected to natural disturbances such as hurricanes and pine beetles, resulting in the openings in the forest canopy. This part of the trail is a good place to see the early stages of succession.

## Mileposts

**0.0 mile:** Begin at the trailhead in the northwest corner of the parking lot.
**0.7 mile:** You'll cross a wooden bridge over Campbell Creek. The trail divides, going both straight and right along creek. Take the right fork.
**0.9 mile:** You'll cross a tributary of Campbell Creek.
**1.1 miles:** You'll cross another tributary.
**1.3 miles:** You'll cross another tributary.
**1.6 miles:** The trail crosses two bridges.
**2.0 miles:** The trail crosses another bridge.
**2.1 miles:** You'll reach the mouth of Campbell Creek, where you'll have a great view of the river. To the left is the remainder of Campbell Creek Loop Trail.
**2.5 miles:** You'll reach the Lanier Falls trailhead.
**3.4 miles:** The trail crosses a stream.
**3.7 miles:**: The trail crosses a bridge.
**4.3 miles:** The trail crosses another bridge.
**4.4 miles:** You'll return to the first bridge over Campbell Creek. Cross the bridge to return to the parking lot.
**5.1 miles:** You'll reach the parking lot.

## Lanier Falls Trail

**Length:** 0.3 mile
**Difficulty:** Moderate
**Blazes:** Orange
**Surface:** Natural
**Bicycles:** No

This short trail consists mostly of steps down to the riverbank, a wonderful place from which to watch the river and catch a glimpse of some of its inhabitants.

## Mileposts

**0.0 mile:** Begin at the trailhead, located 2.5 miles from the parking lot on Campbell Creek Loop Trail.
**0.3 mile:** You'll arrive at the Cape Fear River.

# Northern Section Trails _____

The northern section of the park offers bridle trails intended for equestrian use. However, if you don't mind dodging a few droppings, they're also a great place to hike.

## West Loop Horse Trail
**Length:** 3.4 miles
**Difficulty:** Easy
**Blazes:** White
**Surface:** Natural
**Bicycles:** No

West Loop Horse Trail offers several views of Avents Creek, as well as access to the Cape Fear River and the remains of the Northington lock and dam. The spot on the river where the trail deposits visitors is one of the prettiest in the park. The confluence of Avents Creek and the Cape Fear lends the feeling that you're surrounded by water.

Since this trail is meant for horses, be sure to give equestrians the right of way at all times. Also, be aware that there are no wooden footbridges, so you'll have to cross the small streams and brooks. At least one ankle-deep (in dry weather) crossing of Avents Creek is required. The trail has many boot-sucking mud patches in wet weather.

Two trailheads are in the parking lot. The directions below describe the hike beginning at the trailhead in the northwest corner.

*Raven Rock State Park*

## Mileposts

**0.0 mile:** Begin at the trailhead in the northwest corner of the parking lot. (The other trailhead, in the center of the parking lot, leads past the picnic area. It offers the shortest route to the creek and the river.)

**0.5 mile:** After traveling within sight of the road, the trail joins it to cross Avents Creek, then heads left back into the woods.

**2.1 miles:** After passing through a lush bottom-land forest, you'll arrive at a fork. Straight ahead is a 0.2-mile spur leading to the river and the remains of the Northington lock and dam. Take the left fork to continue on West Loop Horse Trail.

**2.3 miles:** You'll cross a small tributary of Avents Creek.

**2.6 miles:** You'll cross a small tributary of Avents Creek just before coming to a shallow crossing. In high water, you'll have to get your feet wet to continue.

**2.9 miles:** You'll reach a junction with East Loop Horse Trail. Go left toward the parking lot. East Loop Horse Trail goes to the right.

**3.4 miles:** You'll pass a picnic area and arrive at the parking lot.

# East Loop Horse Trail

**Length:** 3.6 miles
**Difficulty:** Easy
**Blazes:** White
**Surface:** Natural
**Bicycles:** No

In contrast to West Loop Horse Trail, which provides a tour of the bottomlands, this loop winds through higher-elevation forests.

## Mileposts

**0.0 mile:** Begin at the trailhead in the center of the parking lot.

**0.5 mile:** The turnoff to West Loop Horse Trail is on the right.

**1.8 miles:** After crossing a couple of brooks, you'll cross a larger stream.

**2.9 miles:** The trail crosses a power cut.

**3.2 miles:** You'll cross a small brook.

**3.3 miles:** You'll cross a muddy little brook.

**3.5 miles:** You'll cross the power cut again.

**3.6 miles:** You'll reach the parking lot.

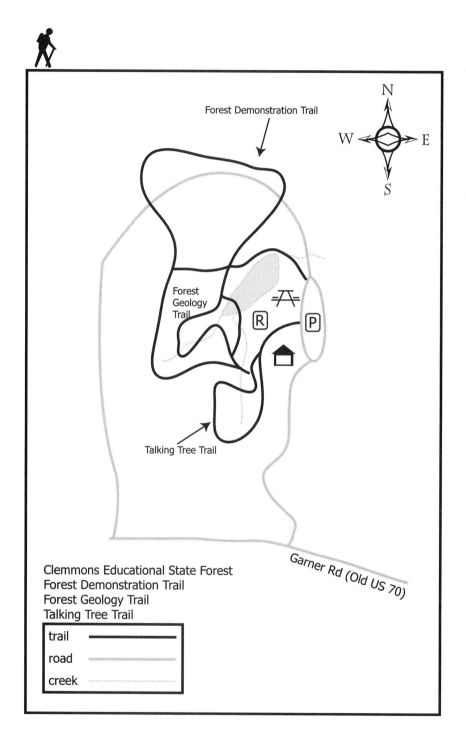

Forest Demonstration Trail

N
W ◄──◆──► E
S

Forest
Geology
Trail

R    P

Talking Tree Trail

Garner Rd (Old US 70)

Clemmons Educational State Forest
Forest Demonstration Trail
Forest Geology Trail
Talking Tree Trail

| trail | ━━━━━━ |
| road | ▬▬▬▬▬ |
| creek | ········· |

# Johnston County

## Clemmons State Educational Forest

**Address:** 2411 Old US 70 West, Clayton, NC 27520
**Telephone:** 919-553-5651
**Hours:** Guests can visit the forest from mid-March through mid-November; call for details. It is open Tuesday through Friday from 9 A.M. to 5 P.M. and Saturday and Sunday from 11 A.M. to 8 P.M. during daylight saving time and from 11 A.M. to 5 P.M. the rest of the year.
**Maps:** USGS Clayton; free maps are available at the park office.
**Directions:** Follow I-40 to the US 70 East exit (Exit 306) east of Garner. Drive about 3.5 miles on US 70 East to the intersection with Guy Road (SR 2558). Turn left, drive 0.4 mile, turn right on Garner Road (SR 1004), go 2 miles, and turn left into the Clemmons State Educational Forest driveway. The park office is just ahead on the right.

Clemmons is one of two state forests in the Triangle that serve as living outdoor classrooms; the other is Jordan Lake State Educational Forest (see page 6). The interpretive displays at Clemmons include Talking Tree Trail and the Forestry Exhibit Center. The exhibits here are geared toward a young audience, but the forest itself and many of the artifacts on display will engage the interest of all ages. The well-maintained, easily followed trails pass through a variety of habitats. A beautiful spring is within easy walking distance of the parking lot. Rangers at Clemmons give classes to groups of 10 or more, and educational materials are available for teachers. Call the forest office for details.

If you visit Clemmons, pack a lunch to take advantage of the shaded picnic tables—and don't miss the pond, where you can easily spot birds and reptiles from the shore.

## Forest Demonstration Trail

**Length:** 2.2 miles
**Difficulty:** Easy
**Blazes:** Red
**Surface:** Natural and wood-chip mulch
**Bicycles:** No

This trail will take you through most of the environments in Clemmons, including an open field maintained with controlled burns.

### Mileposts

**0.0 mile:** Begin at the parking lot near the fire observation tower. If you're facing the picnic tables, follow the trail farthest to your left.
**0.1 mile:** You'll reach the Forestry Exhibit Center. Forest Demonstration Trail begins behind the building.
**0.2 mile:** Follow the red blazes up the hill to the boardwalk and the spring. Take the red-blazed trail up the hill to your right, then take an immediate left at the next fork.
**0.4 mile:** To complete the trail, continue straight at the intersection. To the left is a shortcut trail to the backside of Forest Demonstration Trail. A right turn leads past the pond and the parking lot.
**0.5 mile:** Turn left on the dirt road.
**0.9 mile:** You'll reach an intersection. Turn left to continue on Forest Demonstration Trail.
**1.3 miles:** You'll pass the shortcut trail on your left.
**2.1 miles:** You'll return to the Forestry Exhibit Center. Follow the trail around the building to return to the parking lot.
**2.2 miles:** You'll arrive at the parking lot.

## Talking Tree Trail

**Length:** 0.6 mile
**Difficulty:** Easy
**Blazes:** Green
**Surface:** Natural
**Bicycles:** No

This short, easy walk offers recorded messages about the trees and habitats along the trail.

### Mileposts

**0.0 mile:** Begin behind the Forestry Exhibit Center (see the Mileposts for Forest Demonstration Trail on page 112).
**0.4 mile:** You'll cross a small wooden bridge over a gully.
**0.6 mile:** You'll return to the Forestry Exhibit Center.

## Forest Geology Trail

**Length:** 0.4 mile
**Difficulty:** Easy
**Blazes:** Yellow
**Surface:** Natural
**Bicycles:** No

This short trail offers a view of the spring and its small waterfall. Adding interest to the hike are the large boulders identified by signs and recorded messages.

### Mileposts

**0.0 mile:** Begin behind the Forestry Exhibit Center (see the Mileposts for Forest Demonstration Trail on page 112).
**0.1 mile:** Follow the yellow blazes left at the boardwalk to continue on Forest Geology Trail.
**0.4 mile:** You'll reach the end of Forest Geology Trail at the red-blazed Forest Demonstration Trail. To see the pond, head right and follow the mowed path back to the parking lot.

# Legend Park

**Address:** Clayton Parks and Recreation Department, 340 McCullers Street, Clayton, NC 27520
**Telephone:** 919-553-1550
**Hours:** Sunrise to sunset, year-round
**Maps:** USGS Clayton; maps are posted at the trailhead and at intervals along the trails; you can also find a map at TriangleMTB.com.
**Directions:** Take I-40 east of Raleigh to the US 70 East/Garner exit (Exit 306). Follow US 70 East for about 6.5 miles to Robertson Road, on the left. Go 0.5 mile on Robertson Road to West Stalling Street. Turn left on Stalling, then take the second right onto City Road. The entrance to Legend Park is 0.4 mile ahead on the right.

The Legend Park trails were developed for mountain bikers. In an earlier manifestation, the park offered just a couple miles of flat trails through the flood plain of Sams Creek. Thanks to an agreement with park neighbor Mildred Gordon, a challenging set of paths collectively known as the Upper Trails was constructed. It added enough mileage to make Legend Park a much more interesting destination for eastern Triangle mountain bikers. The Upper Trails include Harvey's Pond, Magnolia's Run, Larry's Loop, and Little Big Horn Trails. Riders enjoy tackling the significant elevation changes and the constructed obstacles. The trail builders were thoughtful of neophytes; most of the difficult obstacles have a ride-around option. Many of these are clearly labeled with signs. Two particular challenges—one on Allen's Trail and one called Hucksville—make this park unique. In general, the trails are well marked and easy to follow. Though a few of the rides rated as *moderate* do not boast serious obstacles, they'll certainly raise your heart rate as much as those rated *strenuous*.

## Main Trail

**Length:** 1.1 miles
**Difficulty:** Easy to moderate
**Blazes:** None, though there are signs at the intersections

**Surface:** Natural
**Bicycles:** Yes

This trail leads to the others and to the most difficult obstacles in the park. When you're returning from the Upper Trails to the exit via Main Trail, don't be confused by the power cut that veers right as Main Trail continues left.

## Mileposts

**0.0 mile:** To begin at the signboard, go left around the ball field. You'll enter the woods and come to the first fork with Allen's Trail. Continue to the right.
**0.1 mile:** You'll reach a second junction with Allen's Trail.
**0.3 mile:** You'll reach another fork. The short, difficult Allen's Trail rejoins Main Trail immediately ahead.
**0.5 mile:** The trail passes the ball field.
**0.6 mile:** You'll reach a fork. The left fork leads less than 0.1 mile to the Lower Trails. Take the right fork, which heads to the Upper Trails. You'll immediately come to a wide dirt road on the left leading to Hucksville. Continue to the right. In a few yards, you'll turn left into the woods to remain on Main Trail.
**0.7 mile:** You'll reach the Harvey's Pond trailhead on the left. Continue right.
**0.8 mile:** The Magnolia's Run trailhead is on the left. Immediately ahead on the left is the return loop of Magnolia's Run. Directly across Main Trail is the first Little Big Horn trailhead. Continue straight on Main Trail.
**1.1 miles:** You'll reach the end of Main Trail and the second Little Big Horn trailhead.

## Allen's Trail

**Length:** 0.2 mile
**Difficulty:** Strenuous
**Blazes:** None, though there are signs at the intersections
**Surface:** Natural and wood
**Bicycles:** Yes

The first loop off Main Trail, Allen's Trail is short but both difficult and interesting. It leads to a set of narrow, elevated obstacles called "the Skinnies." Nonexperts should stay off them. If you're not the type who thinks falling off a bridge is an acceptable risk, there's room to stand and watch those who feel otherwise.

### Mileposts

**0.0 mile:** Begin at the first trailhead off Main Trail.
**0.1 mile:** You'll reach the obstacles.
**0.2 mile:** You'll return to Main Trail. The parking lot is to the left.

# Upper Trails

## Harvey's Pond Trail

**Length:** 0.2 mile
**Difficulty:** Strenuous
**Blazes:** None, though there are signs at the intersections
**Surface:** Natural
**Bicycles:** Yes

This trail leads down to a pleasant, scenic pond, then back up to Main Trail.

### Mileposts

**0.0 mile:** Begin at the first trailhead off Main Trail.
**0.1 mile:** You'll reach the shore of a pond.
**0.2 mile:** You'll return to Main Trail. The parking lot is to the right.

## Magnolia's Run

**Length:** 1 mile
**Difficulty:** Moderate to strenuous
**Blazes:** None, though there are signs at the intersections
**Surface:** Natural
**Bicycles:** Yes

This fine trail boasts some hair-raising descents. For the fastest ride, start at the second trailhead off Main Trail.

### Mileposts

**0.0 mile:** Begin at the second trailhead off Main Trail.
**0.3 mile:** A short loop goes to an obstacle before rejoining the trail.
**1.0 mile:** You'll emerge on Main Trail. The parking lot is to the right.

## Little Big Horn Trail

**Length:** 0.8 mile
**Difficulty:** Moderate
**Blazes:** None, though there are signs at the intersections
**Surface:** Natural
**Bicycles:** Yes

This scenic trail offers many elevation changes, a deep, fern-lined creek valley, and two log obstacles with ride-around options.

### Mileposts

**0.0 mile:** Begin at the second trailhead off Main Trail.
**0.3 mile:** You'll reach the Larry's Loop trailhead. Take the far right fork to continue on Little Big Horn Trail.
**0.8 mile:** You'll return to Main Trail.

## Larry's Loop

**Length:** 0.4 mile
**Difficulty:** Strenuous
**Blazes:** None, though there are signs at the intersections
**Surface:** Natural
**Bicycles:** Yes

Aerobically speaking, this is the most difficult trail in the park. If that isn't enough to intrigue you, there are a few significant obstacles to add interest.

### Mileposts

**0.0 mile:** Begin at the trailhead at the far end of Main Trail.
**0.4 mile:** You'll return to Main Trail.

# Lower Trails

At a couple of places on the Lower Trails, you might lose your bearings because of short, unsigned loops off Main Trail. Signs are located at the major intersections, and a map is posted at the Long Loop trailhead, so it's not necessary to keep track of where you are. As long as you stay on the trail and don't ride in circles, you'll eventually return to Main Trail or the map. Beware of the bumper crop of poison ivy growing beside these two trails. Be sure to wear long pants in the warm months.

## Short Loop

**Length:** 0.5 mile
**Difficulty:** Easy
**Blazes:** None, though there are signs at the intersections
**Surface:** Natural
**Bicycles:** Yes

This is the nearest of the Lower Trails. Whereas the Upper Trails are technically challenging because of all the roots, the Lower Trails have plenty of rocks to keep you engaged. Short Loop is a flat, easy trail that offers glimpses of Sam's Creek.

## Mileposts

---

**0.0 mile:** Begin at the trailhead off Main Trail. Head left around the loop.

**0.2 mile:** You'll reach a fork. To the left is Long Loop. Continue right on Short Loop.

**0.3 mile:** You'll reach another fork. To the left is a short connector to Long Loop. Short Loop continues to the right.

**0.4 mile:** You'll reach a fork. To the left is the second Long Loop trailhead. Short Loop continues right, then crosses a gravel road.

**0.5 mile:** You'll reach the trailhead on Main Trail.

## Long Loop

**Length:** 0.3 mile
**Difficulty:** Easy
**Blazes:** None, though there are signs at the intersections
**Surface:** Natural
**Bicycles:** Yes

This trail is very similar to Short Loop.

## Mileposts

---

**0.0 mile:** Begin at the first trailhead on Short Loop.

**0.2 mile:** You'll reach a fork. To the right is a short connector. Long Loop continues left.

**0.3 mile:** You'll reach the end of Long Loop. To return to the parking lot, keep left on Short Loop to return to Main Trail, then take a right.

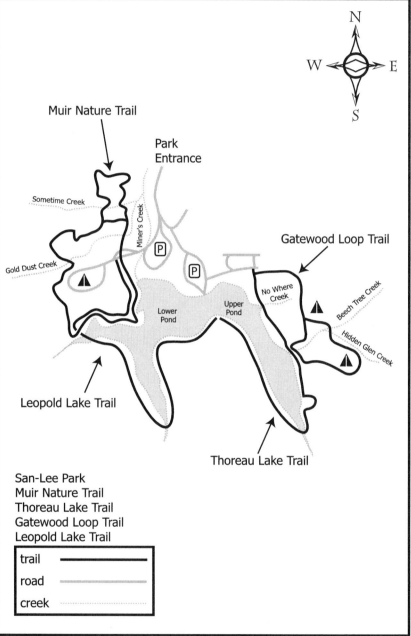

Muir Nature Trail

Park Entrance

N
W — E
S

Gatewood Loop Trail

Sometime Creek

Miner's Creek

Gold Dust Creek

P

P

No Where Creek

Beech Tree Creek

Hidden Glen Creek

Lower Pond

Upper Pond

Leopold Lake Trail

Thoreau Lake Trail

San-Lee Park
Muir Nature Trail
Thoreau Lake Trail
Gatewood Loop Trail
Leopold Lake Trail

| trail | ——— |
| road | ～～～ |
| creek | ········ |

# Lee County

## San-Lee Environmental Education and Recreation Park

**Address:** Park Office, 512 Pumping Station Road, Sanford, NC 27330
**Telephone:** 919-776-6221
**Hours:** Hours vary seasonally. Check with the park office.
**Maps:** USGS Sanford; free hiking trail maps are available at the park office.
**Directions:** From Chapel Hill, take US 15/US 501 South to US 1 Business South to reach downtown Sanford. From Raleigh, take US 1 South to US 1 Business South to reach the downtown. From downtown Sanford, take US 1 Business South until it turns into Hawkins Avenue and ends on Charlotte Avenue. Turn left on Charlotte Avenue, drive 1.1 miles to San-Lee Drive (SR 1509), turn right, and go 2.1 miles to Pumping Station Road (SR 1510). Turn right and drive 0.5 mile to San-Lee Park, on the right.

San-Lee has a lot to offer for a relatively small park. Because its mission includes a strong emphasis on environmental education, interpretive programs are scheduled year-round.

The best place to begin a visit to San-Lee is the nature center, where you can get a close look at some of North Carolina's native wildlife. You might see a red-tailed hawk, a turkey vulture, or whatever animal happens to currently be under the care of the Wildlife Rescue Center. The rescue center's volunteers rehabilitate injured or orphaned animals before releasing them back into the wild.

San-Lee's most prominent features are two adjoining 10-acre ponds stocked with catfish. For anglers who like to travel light, the park participates in the Rod and Reel program, which offers members fishing equipment on loan. San-Lee has a tent campground and a separate set of sites for RVs. Both campgrounds are well shaded and have restrooms with flush toilets.

The park has two trail systems, one for mountain biking and one for hiking. If you like both activities, you'll find San-Lee well worth the drive from the Triangle proper. You can bring your bike and your boots and follow up an exciting ride with a peaceful walk in the woods. Three trails—Thoreau Lake Trail, Leopold Lake Trail, and part of Muir Nature Trail—combine to form the park's most rewarding hike. When combined, these trails will take you around both ponds and across all the park's significant creeks. The trails are easy to follow. The intersections are generally marked with signs and sporadic blazes. Numerous squirrels frolic in the woods, and turtles sun themselves in the ponds.

San-Lee Park sees its heaviest use on weekends. If you plan to spend the night in the tent campground during the middle of the week, you might have the place to yourself.

Note that the sign on the wall of the nature center says 1933, the year Sanford built a new waterworks on Pumping Station Road. The plant provided Sanford with water until 1972, when the city constructed a new plant and closed the old one. In 1975, the city donated 90 acres to Lee County with the understanding that it would be turned into a public park. The donation included both ponds and the building that now houses the nature center. Subsequent acquisitions brought the park to nearly 144 acres—plenty of room for a day in the woods.

## Thoreau Lake Trail

**Length:** 0.9 mile
**Difficulty:** Easy
**Blazes:** None
**Surface:** Natural
**Bicycles:** No

This trail begins the circumnavigation of the ponds.

Or you can cross the bridge at the end of Thoreau Trail and return to the boat-launch area off the upper parking lot. The trail is mostly flat but has a few gentle hills at the beginning as you descend to the pond. It's easy to follow, although it's not blazed. You'll enjoy views of Upper Pond and a crossing of lovely Crawdad Creek as it runs into Upper Pond.

## Mileposts

**0.0 mile:** Begin in the upper parking lot at the gated gravel driveway to the RV camping area.

**0.1 mile:** The trailhead is on the right just past the Colter Amphitheater. Head right for Thoreau Trail. Note that this section runs conjunctively with Gatewood Loop Trail.

**0.2 mile:** You'll cross Nowhere Creek before reaching a fork. Gatewood Loop Trail heads left. Continue right across Beech Tree Creek.

**0.3 mile:** You'll reach a second fork. Gatewood Loop Trail heads left. Thoreau Trail continues right.

**0.5 mile:** You'll cross a wooden bridge over Crawdad Creek. Turn right after the bridge.

**0.8 mile:** You'll reach the end of Thoreau Trail. You can walk 0.1 mile across the bridge to the right and return to the parking lot or continue on Leopold Lake Trail.

## Leopold Lake Trail

**Length:** 0.8 mile
**Difficulty:** Easy
**Blazes:** None
**Surface:** Natural
**Bicycles:** No

This trail is very similar to Thoreau Trail. Its highlights include views of Lower Pond and the bridges across Turtle Creek and Placer Creek. After crossing Placer Creek, the trail joins the lower leg of the Muir Nature Trail loop.

Note that there are two trailheads. The Mileposts listed below begin at the far end of the dam. Follow the driveway from the upper parking lot toward the boat-launch area. To reach the second trailhead, follow the driveway to the tent camping area. It's on the left as you head up the hill.

## Mileposts

**0.0 mile:** Begin at the far end of the dam between Upper Pond and Lower Pond.

**0.3 mile:** You'll cross a bridge over Turtle Creek. Head right.

**0.4 mile:** The trail crosses a power cut.

**0.5 mile:** You'll cross a bridge over Placer Creek and reach a fork. Muir Nature Trail heads straight up the hill and joins Leopold Lake Trail along the shore. Continue right over the wooden steps.

**0.7 mile:** You'll cross a power cut.

**0.8 mile:** You'll reach the end of Leopold Lake Trail and Muir Nature Trail on the driveway to the tent camping area. Future work on Muir will extend it through the woods across the driveway. To return to the upper parking lot, turn right down the hill at the beginning of Thoreau Trail and walk past the nature center and up the wooden steps.

## Muir Nature Trail

**Length:** 1 mile
**Difficulty:** Easy to moderate
**Blazes:** Blue
**Surface:** Natural
**Bicycles:** No

This loop trail offers interpretive stations and a few more hills than the lake trails. It will give you a good look at the difference between upland forests and the fern-covered flood plains.

Muir Nature Trail has two trailheads. The Mileposts listed below begin at the trailhead on the grassy area across the creek from the main park driveway. If you cross Miner's Creek on the driveway near the nature center, this trailhead is to your right. If you cross the creek on the large wood-and-steel bridge to San-Lee Mountain Bike Trail, the Muir trailhead is to your left. The second trailhead is off the driveway leading to the tent campground.

## Mileposts

**0.0 mile:** Begin at the trailhead on the far side of Miner's Creek. After 100 yards, you'll cross a bridge over a gully.
**0.1 mile:** You'll reach an intersection with San-Lee Mountain Bike Trail. Muir Nature Trail makes a hairpin turn to the left.
**0.2 mile:** You'll cross a bridge over Sometime Creek.
**0.5 mile:** You'll cross a bridge over Gold Dust Creek. After 100 yards, you'll pass the first of two short spur trails to the tent camping area, located on the left.
**0.7 mile:** You'll reach a fork at the bottom of a steep hill. Leopold Lake Trail goes right across Placer Creek, then east around Lower Pond. To continue on Muir Nature Trail (and the northern leg of Leopold Lake Trail), head left over the wooden steps.
**0.8 mile:** You'll cross a power cut.
**1.0 mile:** You'll reach the end of Muir Nature Trail at the driveway to the tent camping area. Head right down the hill to return to the parking lot.

## Gatewood Loop Trail

At the time this book went to press, Gatewood Loop Trail was not being maintained due to a question about the boundary between the park and the adjacent private property. Please check with the park office for the current status.

## San-Lee Mountain Bike Trail

**Length:** 4.5 miles
**Difficulty:** Moderate to strenuous
**Blazes:** None
**Surface:** Natural
**Bicycles:** Yes

This wonderfully designed, well-maintained trail was built by members of the Sanford Area Mountain Biking Association, in cooperation with San-Lee Park. It takes full advantage of the elevation changes within the park's 144 acres, offering enough ups and downs to keep advanced riders happy. The trail is predominantly single-track and technical. It has rocks and roots along much of its length. Although difficult in spots, the trail is a worthwhile destination for beginners as long as they're in reasonably good condition. For those who enjoy scenery as well as adrenaline, the trail boasts picturesque stream crossings (some via bridges, some not) and views of the park's two ponds. At the time of this writing, the park's trail maps did not show San-Lee Mountain Bike Trail.

### Mileposts

**0.0 mile:** Begin at the gated gravel road leading from the upper parking lot to the RV campground.
**0.1 mile:** After passing the Colter Amphitheater and the Gatewood Loop and Thoreau trailheads, you'll reach the San-Lee Mountain Bike trailhead on the right. Please sign in at the mailbox.
**0.3 mile:** You'll cross a bridge over a creek bed.
**0.4 mile:** You'll cross a bridge over a creek.
**1.4 miles:** You'll cross a bridge over a tributary of Crawdad Creek.
**2.0 miles:** After descending on switchbacks, the trail crosses Turtle Creek.
**2.5 miles:** You'll pass an old, dilapidated ropes course. Going near this structure is strictly forbidden.

**2.9 miles:** The trail crosses Placer Creek.

**3.4 miles:** You'll reach an intersection with a large trailhead to the right. Keep right as the trail forks again.

**3.6 miles:** You'll cross Gold Dust Creek.

**4.0 miles:** You'll cross a bridge over Sometime Creek.

**4.3 miles:** You'll cross a large bridge over Miner's Creek before crossing the park driveway and heading back to the upper lot.

**4.5 miles:** You'll return to the upper parking lot.

*Occoneechee Mountain State Natural Area*

# Orange County

## Occoneechee Mountain State Natural Area

**Address:** Eno River State Park, 6101 Cole Mill Road, Durham, NC 27705-9275
**Telephone:** 919-383-1686
**Hours:** From November to February, the natural area is open from 8 A.M. to 6 P.M. During March and October, it is open from 8 A.M. to 7 P.M. During April, May, and September, it is open from 8 A.M. to 8 P.M. From June to August, it is open from 8 A.M. to 9 P.M.
**Map:** USGS Hillsborough
**Directions:** From I-85 outside Hillsborough, take Exit 164 and turn north on Churton Street. Drive 0.2 mile from the I-85 overpass to Mayo Street (SR 1192), located just after Hillsborough Commons Shopping Center. Turn left on Mayo Street, drive 0.3 mile to Orange Grove Road (SR 1006), turn left, and drive 0.4 mile to Virginia Cates Road (SR 1183). Turn right on Virginia Cates Road and drive 0.4 mile past the ponds to the parking area on the left.

This state natural area consists of about 130 acres in northern

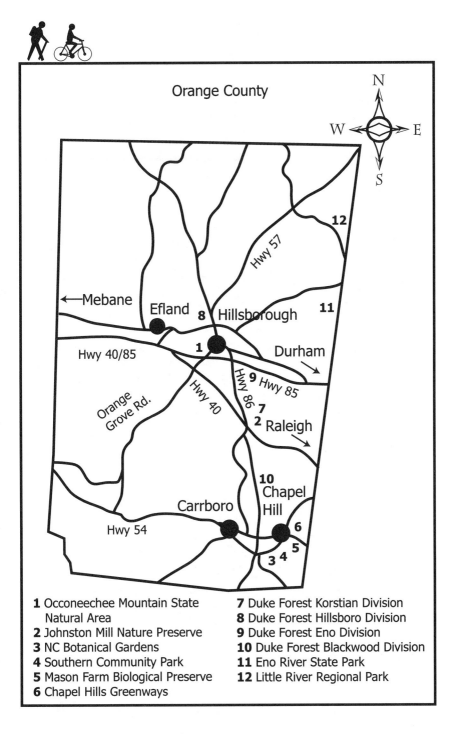

## Orange County

N
W ← → E
S

Hwy 57

← Mebane

Efland

**8** Hillsborough

**12**

**11**

Durham

Hwy 40/85

**1**

Orange Grove Rd.

Hwy 40

Hwy 86

Hwy 85

**9** Hwy 85

**7**

**2** Raleigh

**10** Chapel Hill

Carrboro

Hwy 54

**6**

**5**

**3** **4**

**1** Occoneechee Mountain State Natural Area
**2** Johnston Mill Nature Preserve
**3** NC Botanical Gardens
**4** Southern Community Park
**5** Mason Farm Biological Preserve
**6** Chapel Hills Greenways

**7** Duke Forest Korstian Division
**8** Duke Forest Hillsboro Division
**9** Duke Forest Eno Division
**10** Duke Forest Blackwood Division
**11** Eno River State Park
**12** Little River Regional Park

Orange County immediately south of West Hillsborough. Occoneechee Mountain is one of the few spots in the Triangle that offers an expansive view. From the high points along the park trails, you can see the Eno River and West Hillsborough. Visitors should be aware that landslides resulted in the closure of the overlooks atop the quarry's cliffs. Contact the park for updates.

The loftiest of the three peaks comprising Occoneechee Mountain measures 867 feet, making it the highest spot in Orange County. The top of the mountain is adorned with transmission towers and is accessible by a gravel road. The peak is technically outside of the natural area's boundaries, and trees obscure the view from the top.

Near the parking area and entrance gate are two ponds that are open to fishing and boating. Only human- and electric-powered boats are allowed.

As with so many preserved areas in the Triangle, this park owes its existence to a group of dedicated volunteers. The Eno River Association purchased the timber rights to Occoneechee Mountain in 1993 to avoid the imminent possibility of clear-cutting. Occoneechee Mountain was operated as a park by the town of Hillsborough until the state dedicated the natural area in 1999.

Occoneechee Mountain has three trails—Occoneechee Mountain Trail, Brown Elfin Knob Trail (which can be accessed from Occoneechee Mountain Trail), and a brief, unnamed riverside trail that dead-ends at the park boundary.

Although these trails make Occoneechee worth a visit, this area's designation as a state natural area, as opposed to a state park, means that human recreational activities take a backseat to preservation of natural resources. Occoneechee Mountain supports several species rare in the Piedmont. The high elevations and dry soil are home to a population of Virginia pines, the small, short-needle trees that line the cliff's edge and grow up next to its face. A relatively mature chestnut oak forest stands at the summit. Down by the Eno, the trail passes beside a small cliff with Catawba rhododendron growing among the rocks and galax. Mountain witch alder, a rare plant in this part of the state, has also been found here.

The animals in the park include squirrels, muskrats, red bats, foxes, black rat snakes, and rough green snakes. Spotted salamanders, fence lizards, and skinks are numerous. The pond has a resident family of beavers that are the stars of evening programs run by the rangers. In addition to human anglers, both green and great blue herons fish in the ponds. Perhaps the most exciting discovery made by naturalists studying Occoneechee's inhabitants is the brown elfin butterfly. One of the park trails is named after this butterfly, which emerges in March and flies for only a brief period. Occoneechee Mountain is believed to be its easternmost habitat. The closest brown elfin neighbors reside in Hanging Rock State Park near Winston-Salem.

The land that comprises Occoneechee Mountain Natural Area has a rich human history. The cliff was the site of a pre-Civil War quarry. Stones from the quarry were used in the construction of North Carolina railroads. Although the tracks on the south side of the Eno River were removed, trains still pass through this railroad corridor a few times each day. The quarry operated into the 1900s. On land adjacent to the park was a thriving mill village associated with the Eno Cotton Mill. The mill, built in 1889, operated into the 20th century. Its village included 30 homes and a general store. Some Hillsborough old-timers have memories of living in the village. The houses, moved across the Eno to West Hillsborough in the 1950s, are still visible on the hillsides facing Occoneechee Mountain. Also visible, especially in winter, is a brick building with two chimneys that served as a military academy.

Geologists attribute the height of Occoneechee Mountain to a process called differential erosion. The mountain is composed of substances that are harder and slower to erode than the surrounding land. Over time, Occoneechee Mountain retained more of its height as the land around it lost elevation. The face of the cliff owes its pink hue to pyrophyllite, a mineral that may have been mined from the hillside for commercial use. Once upon a time, pyrophyllite was used to make talcum powder and tombstones. Nowadays, it's used in ceramics and as a base for insecticides. A modern, working pyrophyllite quarry is visible east of the power cut near the overlooks.

## Occoneechee Mountain Trail

**Length:** 1.4 miles
**Difficulty:**: Moderate to strenuous
**Blazes:** Orange
**Surface:** Natural
**Bicycles:** No

This trail, the longest in the park, will take you to both of the other trails. It begins as a continuation of the driveway, then offers a look at the ponds before heading into the woods and beginning the climb. The edge of the field and woods here is a great place to see two of the stages of old-field succession. Small pines and cedars are coming up in the field, and the tallest trees in the woods for the first part of the hike are young pines.

The south side of the trail—the portions near the beginning and end—is plagued by the sound of traffic from I-85. But once you crest the first hill and make your way to the north side of the mountain, the noise dwindles and you enter another world. Here, the familiar plants and topography of the Piedmont give way to a rocky laurel- and rhododendron-dotted taste of the mountains. Along the power cut, be on the lookout for wildflowers in spring and fall and a carpet of moss year-round.

You'll reach an interesting stop 0.9 mile along the trail. At the top of the knoll is a rectangular hole that was dug to find out which way the grain of the rock runs. Also, don't miss the short trail down to the Eno River. On one side is a 15-foot rock that slightly overhangs the trail. Although this trail dead-ends at the park boundary after only 0.4 mile, it includes one of the most scenic little spots in the Triangle.

### Mileposts

**100 yards:** Turn right at the signboard and head across the field. Turn left as you reach the first pond.
**0.2 mile:** The trail turns left into the woods.
**0.5 mile:** Near the top of the hill, you'll reach a junction

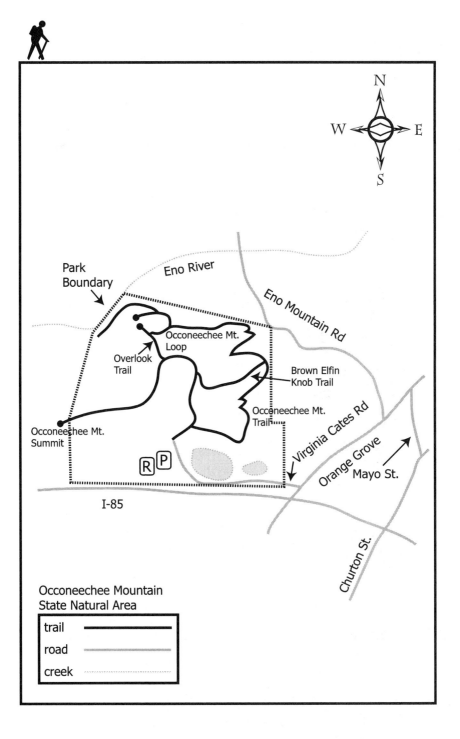

N
W E
S

Park
Boundary

Eno River

Eno Mountain Rd

Occoneechee Mt.
Loop

Overlook
Trail

Brown Elfin
Knob Trail

Occoneechee Mt.
Trail

Occoneechee Mt.
Summit

Virginia Cates Rd

Orange Grove
Mayo St.

R P

I-85

Churton St.

Occoneechee Mountain
State Natural Area

| trail | ——————— |
| road | ~~~~~~~ |
| creek | ·········· |

with Brown Elfin Knob Trail to the left. Continue straight.

**0.7 mile:** The trail emerges into a power cut and turns left.

**0.8 mile:** Just after the trail bottoms out, it turns left into the woods.

**0.9 mile:** You'll reach a fork. Occoneechee Mountain Trail continues left up the hill. The right fork goes to a low overlook that offers a view of the cliff to the left; after 100 yards, it forks left and reaches the bank of the Eno after 0.4 mile.

**1.0 mile:** The trail loops past the overlooks, then heads back uphill. The overlooks are currently closed; call the ranger for updates.

**1.1 miles:** You'll reach a gravel road. The highest point on Occoneechee Mountain is to the right. The trail continues left.

**1.2 miles:** On the left is the western terminus of Brown Elfin Knob Trail.

**1.4 miles:** You'll return to the trailhead.

## Brown Elfin Knob Trail

**Length:** 0.2 mile
**Difficulty:** Easy
**Blazes:** Blue
**Surface:** Natural
**Bicycles:** No

This short trail, named after a butterfly (see the introductory section on page 131), can be used to trim some distance off the loop trail. The feel of this rocky trail is high and dry. It offers limited wintertime views. Interstate traffic is audible throughout.

### Mileposts

**0.0 mile:** Begin at the 0.5-mile mark on Occoneechee Mountain Trail.

**0.2 mile:** The trail ends on Occoneechee Mountain Trail. The parking area is 0.2 mile to your left.

# Duke Forest

For contact information and an overview, see the Durham County section on page 23.

## Blackwood Division _____

**Maps:** USGS Hillsborough; Duke Forest maps are available from the director's office for a small fee.
**Directions:** From I-40, take the NC 86 exit (Exit 266), drive south for 0.1 mile, then take a right on Eubanks Road (SR1727). Go about 3 miles to the T intersection with Old NC 86 and turn right. The gate is on the left after 0.9 mile.

There are several roads in this division, but only one is open to the public. Still, it's a great route. You'll get a look at a swamp and at the forest's highest point, 762-foot Bald Mountain.

### Bald Mountain Fire Trail
**Length:** 1.1 miles
**Difficulty:** Easy
**Blazes:** None
**Surface:** Natural and gravel
**Bicycles:** Yes

One of Duke Forest's finest trails, Bald Mountain Fire Trail is home to some exceptionally large trees and a lovely assortment of spring wildflowers. The elevation affords some winter views. It's often possible to have the trail to yourself.

## Eno Division _____

**Maps:** USGS Hillsborough; Duke Forest maps are available from the director's office for a small fee.

**Directions:** Take I-40 to the New Hope Church Road exit (Exit 263). Drive north on New Hope Church Road for 0.8 mile to NC 86, turn left, and go 1.2 miles to the entrance to the North Carolina Forest Service's Hillsborough District Headquarters. Park outside the main gate to avoid being locked in. To reach Gate 21, head through the main gate and straight down the driveway to Eno Road.

Although small, this section of Duke Forest is scenic and, best of all, little used. Eno Road, which runs from one end of the division to the other, provides access to all the other trails. Eno Division's main topographic feature is Stony Creek, a tributary of the Eno River.

## Eno Road

**Length:** 1.4 miles
**Difficulty:** Easy
**Blazes:** None
**Surface:** Gravel
**Bicycles:** Yes

### Mileposts

**0.0 mile:** Begin at Gate 29.

**0.3 mile:** An intersection with Bivens Fire Trail is to the left.

**0.8 mile:** You'll reach an intersection with Stone Wall Fire Trail to the right and Flat Rock Fire Trail to the left.

**1.4 miles:** Eno Road ends at Gate 28 on New Hope Church Road. New Hope Church Road intersects NC 86 some 1.4 miles to the right.

## Bivens Fire Trail

**Length:** 0.4 mile
**Difficulty:** Easy
**Blazes:** None

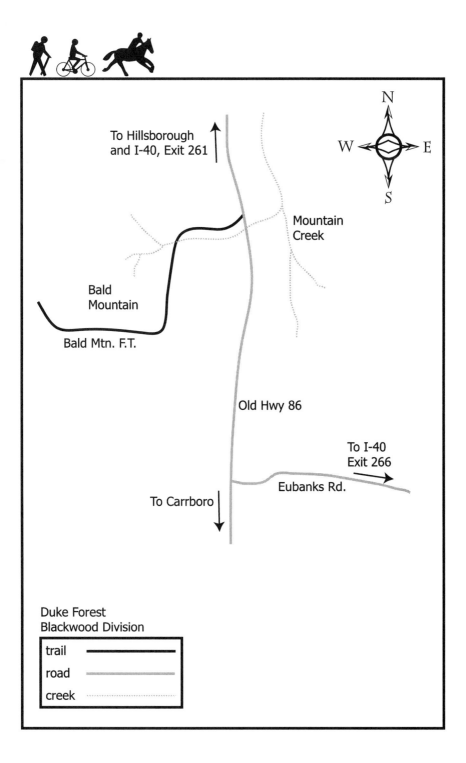

To Hillsborough
and I-40, Exit 261

Mountain
Creek

N

W ← → E

S

Bald
Mountain

Bald Mtn. F.T.

Old Hwy 86

To I-40
Exit 266

Eubanks Rd.

To Carrboro

Duke Forest
Blackwood Division

| trail | |
|-------|---|
| road | |
| creek | |

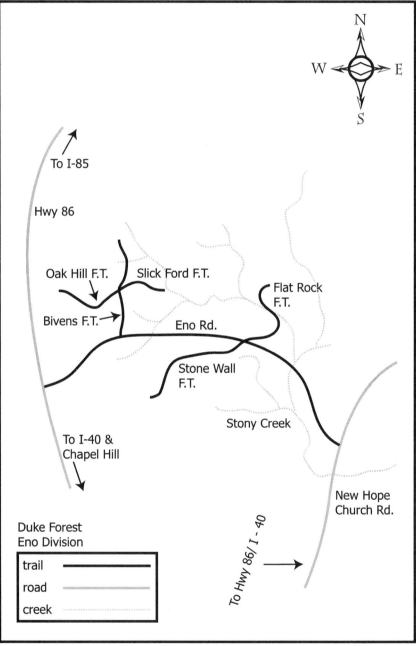

N
W — E
S

To I-85

Hwy 86

Oak Hill F.T.    Slick Ford F.T.

Flat Rock
F.T.

Bivens F.T.

Eno Rd.

Stone Wall
F.T.

Stony Creek

To I-40 &
Chapel Hill

New Hope
Church Rd.

To Hwy 86/ I - 40

Duke Forest
Eno Division

| trail | |
|---|---|
| road | |
| creek | |

**Surface:** Gravel and natural
**Bicycles:** Yes

### Mileposts

**0.0 mile:** Begin at the intersection with Eno Road.
**0.2 mile:** You'll reach an intersection with Oak Hill Fire Trail, to the left, then Slick Ford Fire Trail, to the right.
**0.4 mile:** Bivens Fire Trail ends at the edge of the Duke Forest property.

## Stone Wall Fire Trail

**Length:** 0.8 mile
**Difficulty:** Easy
**Blazes:** None
**Surface:** Natural
**Bicycles:** Yes

True to its name, Stone Wall Fire Trail has ruins of, you guessed it . . .

### Mileposts

**0.0 mile:** Begin at the intersection with Eno Road.
**0.8 mile:** You'll reach the end of the trail near a small creek.

## Flat Rock Fire Trail

**Length:** 0.5 mile
**Difficulty:** Easy
**Blazes:** None
**Surface:** Natural
**Bicycles:** Yes

Hardwoods and running cedar add to the character of this trail. The flat rock beside an attractive creek crossing makes this a hike worth taking. Pack a picnic and plan to stay awhile.

**0.0 mile:** Begin at the intersection with Eno Road.
**0.2 mile:** You'll cross a bridge over Stony Creek.
**0.5 mile:** You'll reach the end of the trail.

## Oak Hill Fire Trail

**Length:** 0.3 mile
**Difficulty:** Easy
**Blazes:** None
**Surface:** Natural
**Bicycles:** Yes

Pines and then hardwoods line this road.

**Mileposts**

**0.0 mile:** Begin at the intersection with Bivens Fire Trail.
**0.3 mile:** You'll reach the end of the trail.

## Slick Ford Fire Trail

**Length:** 0.2 mile
**Difficulty:** Easy
**Blazes:** None
**Surface:** Natural
**Bicycles:** Yes

This short trail ends just above a small creek.

**Mileposts**

**0.0 mile:** Begin at the intersection with Bivens Fire Trail.
**0.2 mile:** You'll reach the end of the trail.

# Hillsboro Division _____

**Maps:** USGS Hillsborough; Duke Forest maps are available from the director's office for a small fee.
**Directions:** From I-85, take the Hillsborough exit (Exit 161), go 1 mile to US 70, turn east, and drive 1 mile to the gate, on the left.

Only Wagon Fire Trail (Gate 31 Road) is open to the public.

## Wagon Fire Trail
**Length:** 0.6 mile
**Difficulty:** Easy
**Blazes:** None
**Surface:** Natural
**Bicycles:** Yes

Although the evidence is no longer obvious, sites along this trail incurred significant damage in a tornado that passed through the Hillsborough area in 1992. Otherwise, this is a lovely trail with a couple of creeks to explore.

### Mileposts

**0.2 mile:** You'll cross a tributary of the Eno River.
**0.6 mile:** You'll reach a second tributary and the end of the trail.

# Korstian Division _____

**Maps:** USGS Chapel Hill and Hillsborough; maps are available from the Duke Forest director's office for a small fee; a hand-drawn map by the late, great William Nealy is available from local outdoor stores.
**Directions:** You can reach the Korstian Division by taking I-40 to the NC 86 exit (Exit 266). Turn south on NC 86. Whitfield Road

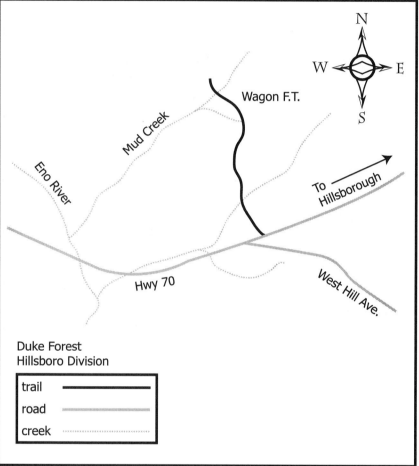

Wagon F.T.

Mud Creek

Eno River

To Hillsborough

Hwy 70

West Hill Ave.

Duke Forest
Hillsboro Division

| trail | ———— |
| road | ░░░░░ |
| creek | ·········· |

(SR 1731) is 0.2 mile ahead on the right, and Mount Sinai Road (SR 1718) is 1.7 miles ahead on the right. Or you can take US 15/US 501 Bypass to the NC 751 exit (Exit 107) and turn south on NC 751 (Cameron Boulevard). Erwin Road is 0.3 mile ahead on the left. The turns are to the right off Erwin Road.

The Korstian Division is sandwiched between Mount Sinai Road to the north and Whitfield Road to the south. It boasts

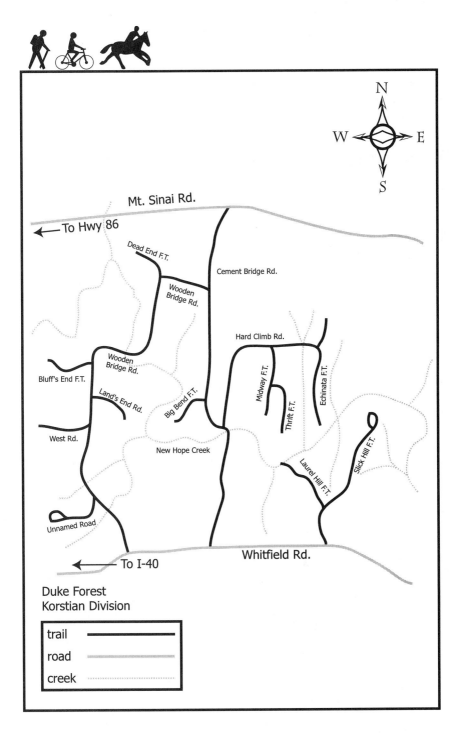

Duke Forest
Korstian Division

| trail | ――――― |
| road | ........... |
| creek | ............ |

some of the most beautiful scenery the Piedmont has to offer. What makes this 1,950-acre parcel so special is New Hope Creek, which winds past rhododendron, granite bluffs, and some of the best foot-dangling, picnicking boulders anywhere.

## Slick Hill Fire Trail and Laurel Hill Fire Trail

**Directions:** Take I-40 to the NC 86 exit (Exit 266). Drive 0.2 mile north on NC 86 to Whitfield Road (SR1731), turn right, and go 2.9 miles to Gate 26, on the left. Roadside parking is available, but be sure not to block the gate.

### Slick Hill Fire Trail

**Length:** 0.8 mile
**Difficulty:** Moderate
**Blazes:** None
**Surface:** Gravel
**Bicycles:** Yes

Slick Hill Fire Trail, like most fire trails in Duke Forest, is an easy, level gravel road. Following a gentle downhill slope, you'll pass through a forest of mixed hardwoods and come to a cul-de-sac that signals the end of this road. The area around the cul-de-sac was cleared in 1998.

#### Mileposts

**0.0 mile:** Begin at Gate 26 on Whitfield Road.
**0.2 mile:** You'll reach a fork where Laurel Hill Fire Trail heads left.
**0.8 mile:** You'll reach the cul-de-sac at the end of Slick Hill Fire Trail.

## Laurel Hill Fire Trail

**Length:** 0.8 mile
**Difficulty:** Easy to moderate
**Blazes:** None
**Surface:** Gravel and natural
**Bicycles:** Yes; please note that no bicycles are allowed off the fire trails in Duke Forest.

This is one of the more popular trails in Duke Forest. It holds this distinction because it leads to some of the Triangle's most beautiful spots. The most scenic areas include the boulder-strewn creek and the bluffs lying between the end of the trail and New Hope Creek. Signs warn visitors away from the bluffs, as people have been known to get themselves killed by falling to the rocks below. Luckily, the bluffs are even more beautiful from below, where the danger factor is considerably less.

Laurel Hill Fire Trail also provides access to two primitive foot trails, one connecting to New Hope Creek Trail to the east and the other to Concrete Bridge Road to the west.

### Mileposts

**0.0 mile:** Begin at the intersection of Laurel Hill and Slick Hill Fire Trails.
**0.1 mile:** You'll pass the first foot trail on your right and, 50 yards later, the second foot trail on your left.
**0.8 mile:** You'll reach the cul-de-sac at the end of Laurel Hill Fire Trail. To the right is a foot trail leading 0.1 mile down to the creek. It is marked with a yellow sign.

# Cement Bridge Road, Big Bend Fire Trail, Hard Climb Road, Midway Fire Trail, and an unnamed foot trail

**Directions:** From I-40, take the NC 86 Exit (Exit 266). Drive on NC 86 north for 1.7 miles to Mount Sinai Road (SR 1718). Take a right on Mount Sinai Road and go 3 miles to the Gate 23 parking area, located on the right at Cement Bridge Road.

## Cement Bridge Road

**Length:** 1.8 miles
**Difficulty:** Easy
**Blazes:** None
**Surface:** Gravel
**Bicycles:** Yes

Cement Bridge Road includes a few sites where the forest's managers have conducted prescribed burns of trees and vegetation.

### Mileposts

**0.0 mile:** Begin at Gate 23.
**0.3 mile:** You'll pass Wooden Bridge Road on the right.
**0.8 mile:** You'll pass Big Bend Fire Trail on the right.
**1.1 miles:** You'll pass Hard Climb Road on the left.
**1.2 miles:** You'll arrive at the Cement Bridge. Continue toward Gate 25.
**1.6 miles:** The foot trail on the left leads to Laurel Hill Fire Trail.
**1.8 miles:** You'll reach Gate 25 on Whitfield Road.

## Big Bend Fire Trail

**Length:** 0.2 mile
**Difficulty:** Easy
**Blazes:** None
**Surface:** Gravel and natural
**Bicycles:** Yes

This short fire trail ends in a thin foot trail. The foot trail winds down to the creek and passes an old stone wall before ending at the Cement Bridge.

### Mileposts

**0.0 mile:** Begin at the intersection of Cement Bridge Road and Big Bend Fire Trail.
**0.2 mile:** The fire trail ends and the foot trail begins.

## Hard Climb Road

**Length:** 0.7 mile
**Difficulty:** Moderate
**Blazes:** None
**Surface:** Gravel and natural
**Bicycles:** Yes

True to its name, this fire road boasts some elevation change. Hard Climb Road will take you to Midway and Echinata Fire Trails.

### Mileposts

**0.0 mile:** Begin at the intersection with Cement Bridge Road.
**0.5 mile:** You'll pass Midway Fire Trail on the right.
**0.7 mile:** Hard Climb Road ends at the T intersection with Echinata Fire Trail, which dead-ends 0.1 mile to the left and 0.3 mile to the right.

## Midway Fire Trail

**Length:** 0.3 mile
**Difficulty:** Easy
**Blazes:** None
**Surface:** Natural
**Bicycles:** Yes

**0.0 mile:** Begin at the intersection with Hard Climb Road.
**0.1 mile:** On the left is Trice Trail, which dead-ends after 0.25 mile.
**0.3 mile:** Midway Fire Trail ends.

# Wooden Bridge Road, Unknown Road, West Road, Land's End Road, Bluff's End Fire Trail, and Dead End Fire Trail

**Directions:** Wooden Bridge Road begins at Gate 24 just off Whitfield Road and ends at an intersection with Concrete Bridge Road 0.3 mile south of Mount Sinai Road.

## Wooden Bridge Road

**Length:** 2.2 miles
**Difficulty:** Easy to moderate
**Blazes:** None
**Surface:** Gravel
**Bicycles:** Yes

Wooden Bridge Road is one of the longer trails in Duke Forest. Between its towering poplars and young pines, it offers a look at Piedmont forests in many different stages of succession. The wooden bridge itself is a sight worth seeing. Five separate fire trails run off Wooden Bridge Road. Visitors can combine them to make a substantial hike.

### Mileposts

**0.0 mile:** Begin at the Whitfield Road entrance.
**0.1 mile:** You'll cross the gate onto Duke Forest property.
**0.4 mile:** You'll pass Unknown Road on the left.
**0.9 mile:** West Road is on the left.
**1.0 mile:** Land's End Road is on the right.

**1.2 miles:** Bluff's End Fire Trail is on the left. After this intersection, the trail bends sharply to the right.

**1.5 miles:** You'll cross the wooden bridge over New Hope Creek and intersect with the creek-side foot trail.

**2.0 miles:** You'll reach a fork. Wooden Bridge Road continues to the right. Dead End Fire Trail is just ahead on the left.

**2.2 miles:** You'll reach the end of Wooden Bridge Road and the intersection with Concrete Bridge Road.

## Bluff's End Fire Trail

**Length:** 0.3 mile
**Difficulty:** Easy
**Blazes:** None
**Surface:** Gravel and natural
**Bicycles:** Yes

This road dead-ends above New Hope Creek near the Duke Forest boundary.

## Unknown Road

**Length:** 0.2 mile
**Difficulty:** Easy
**Blazes:** None
**Surface:** Gravel and natural
**Bicycles:** Yes

This short trail ends in a cul-de-sac.

## West Road

**Length:** 0.3 mile
**Difficulty:** Easy
**Blazes:** None
**Surface:** Natural
**Bicycles:** Yes

This road dead-ends at the Duke Forest boundary.

## Land's End Road

**Length:** 0.3 mile
**Difficulty:** Easy
**Blazes:** None
**Surface:** Natural
**Bicycles:** Yes

This road ends above New Hope Creek.

## Dead End Fire Trail

**Length:** 0.4 mile
**Difficulty:** Easy
**Blazes:** None
**Surface:** Natural
**Bicycles:** Yes

This pleasant path features a small creek.

### Mileposts

**0.0 mile:** Begin at the intersection with Wooden Bridge Road.
**0.4 mile:** The trail ends in a cul-de-sac.

# Johnston Mill Nature Preserve

**Address:** Triangle Land Conservancy, 1101 Haynes Street, Suite 205, Raleigh, NC 27604
**Telephone:** 919-833-3662
**Hours:** Sunrise to sunset
**Maps:** USGS Northwest Durham, Southwest Durham, Chapel Hill; trail maps are available from the Triangle Land Conservancy.
**Directions:** From I-40, take Exit 266 and turn right on NC 86 North. After 1.7 miles, turn right on Mount Sinai Road (SR 1718). The Mount Sinai Road parking area is a mile ahead on the right, just before the road crosses New Hope Creek. To reach the Turkey

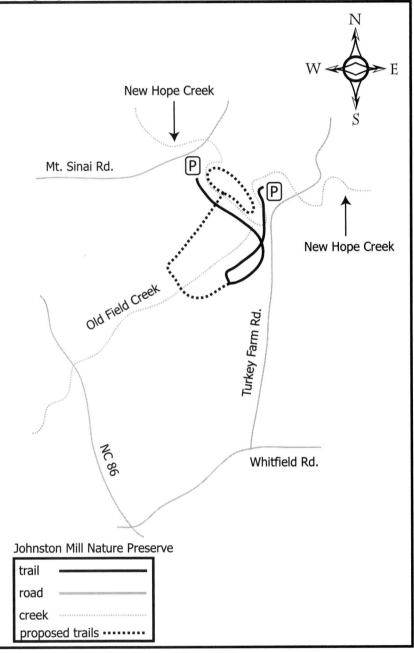

New Hope Creek

N
W E
S

Mt. Sinai Rd.

P

P

New Hope Creek

Old Field Creek

Turkey Farm Rd.

NC 86

Whitfield Rd.

Johnston Mill Nature Preserve

| | |
|---|---|
| trail | ▬▬▬ |
| road | ▬▬▬ |
| creek | ·········· |
| proposed trails | ▪▪▪▪▪▪▪▪ |

Farm Road parking area, continue 0.8 mile to the intersection with Turkey Farm Road (SR 1730). Turn right, go 0.8 mile, cross New Hope Creek, and look for the parking area on the right.

This 296-acre parcel is the Triangle Land Conservancy's largest developed preserve. In addition to being a great place to hike, Johnston Mill is a critical connection between the Oosting Natural Area and the Korstian Division of Duke Forest. The preserve protects a 0.75-mile stretch of New Hope Creek and sections of two important tributaries, Johnston Branch and Old Field Creek. If Chapel Hill and Durham, along with Orange and Durham Counties, can meet the goals set out in their open-space master plan, Johnston Mill Nature Preserve will be a small piece of a green corridor that runs unbroken from the Army Corps of Engineers' land surrounding Jordan Lake to Eno River State Park.

Just under 2 miles of trails had been completed in the preserve as this guide was being researched. The trails afford opportunities to explore Old Field and New Hope Creeks, as well as the upland forests and two historic mill sites. Although the trails are not blazed, they are easy to follow. There are plans for another mile of trail that will parallel the power cut, cross Old Field Creek, and join the upland loop.

The creeks of this area were a magnet for early settlers, who used the water for themselves and their livestock and to turn the wheels that powered their mills. Two mill sites are within the preserve. The Johnston Mill site has an intact stone foundation and is within an easy 0.5-mile walk of the Turkey Farm Road parking area. Hogan's Mill, the other site, is located 0.3 mile from the Mount Sinai Road parking area. It has a ford for crossing the creek.

Although development has taken much of the forests surrounding New Hope Creek, the creek itself remained relatively unmolested through the 1990s. Realizing that this oasis of green would not survive without both public and private effort, the Triangle Land Conservancy led a campaign in 1998-99 to raise the funds necessary to protect this vulnerable section of New Hope Creek. A grant from the North Carolina Clean Water Management Trust Fund, combined with the efforts of many local residents, made the preserve a reality. The first trails were constructed in 2000.

## Johnston Mill Trails

**Length:** 1.3 miles, plus a 0.6-mile loop
**Difficulty:** Easy to moderate
**Blazes:** None
**Surface:** Natural
**Bicycles:** No

## Mileposts

**0.0 mile:** Begin at the Turkey Farm Road parking area.
**0.4 mile:** The trail emerges alongside Turkey Farm Road and parallels the road before reentering the woods. When you reach the creek, you'll pass the first mill site.
**0.5 mile:** You'll reach a bridge.
**0.6 mile:** You'll reach an intersection with the 0.6-mile upland trail loop. Walking straight or left leads to the upland trail. Continue right and across the bridge.
**0.9 mile:** You'll cross a power cut and descend to the second mill site.
**1.3 miles:** You'll reach the Mount Sinai Road parking area.

# Town of Chapel Hill

**Address:** Chapel Hill Parks and Recreation Department, 200 Plant Road, Chapel Hill, NC 27514
**Telephone:** 919-968-2784

# Cedar Falls Park

**Map::** USGS Chapel Hill
**Hours:** Sunrise to sunset
**Directions:** From the intersection of US 15/US 501 and Erwin Road, follow Erwin Road for 0.5 mile to Weaver Dairy Road, turn left (north), and go 1.5 miles. The park entrance is on the left. From the intersection of NC 86 (Airport Road) and Weaver Dairy Road,

turn southeast onto Weaver Dairy and drive 1.5 miles to the park entrance, on the right.

Located in northern Chapel Hill, Cedar Falls Park provides an opportunity for local walkers and runners to get into the woods for a short but scenic trip. Three blazed loop trails circle through the park's mixed forest of hardwoods and pines. The park's trails are too limited for all but novice mountain bikers. However, if you're a cyclist pressed for time, Blue Trail does have one good hill and plenty of rocks and roots for honing your technical skills.

## Blue Trail

**Length:** 0.8 mile
**Difficulty:** Easy
**Blazes:** Blue
**Surface:** Natural
**Bicycles:** Yes

This loop trail will take you to the high, southern edge of the park before returning you to the parking area. During wet winter weather, it's possible to get a partial view of the small rapids on Cedar Fork from above. Listen for the water as you approach the junction with Lakeshore Lane.

### Mileposts

**0.0 mile:** Begin at the trailhead beside the signboard on the paved path. Continue up the pavement and follow the blue blazes into the woods.
**0.1 mile:** You'll reach Jo Peeler Nature Trail. Continue left.
**0.2 mile:** A spur trail goes left to the tennis courts. Continue right.
**0.25 mile:** You'll pass Jo Peeler Nature Trail again. Continue straight. Immediately, White Trail branches off to the right. Continue straight to follow Blue Trail. If you want to shorten the loop, follow White Trail; after 0.2 mile, it rejoins Blue Trail at the 0.6-mile mark.

**0.4 mile:** Continue right up the hill at the T intersection.
**0.6 mile:** You'll rejoin White Trail, then reach the short spur to the end of Lakeshore Lane. After 100 yards, you'll reach a fork. Keep right and join Jo Peeler Nature Trail to complete the loop. The left fork goes to the ballfields.
**0.8 mile:** You'll return to the signboard.

## Joe Peeler Nature Trail

**Length:** 0.6 mile
**Difficulty:** Easy
**Blazes:** Yellow
**Surface:** Natural
**Bicycles:** Yes

This short nature trail was jointly developed by the Chapel Hill Parks and Recreation Department and the Lake Forest Garden Club. It's flatter and easier than Blue Trail. Its many interpretive stations offer an excellent chance for nature study.

### Mileposts

**0.0 mile:** Begin at the signboard.
**0.2 mile:** You'll reach a fork where the blue and white trails branch off to the right. Jo Peeler Nature Trail continues left.
**0.4 mile:** You'll intersect the blue and white trails again. Continue straight.
**0.6 mile:** You'll return to the signboard.

# Southern Community Park

**Maps:** USGS Chapel Hill, Farrington; a free photocopied map is available from the Chapel Hill Parks and Recreation Department. See map on page 159.
**Hours:** Sunrise to sunset

**Directions:** From the point south of downtown Chapel Hill where US 15/ US 501 and NC 54 separate, drive 1.1 miles south on US 15/US 501 to Main Street in A Southern Village. Turn right onto Main Street and go left around the circle to the Park and Ride lot on the far side of the church. The trailhead is straight ahead at the far side of the parking lot. It is marked by a sign.

This natural area is slated to be developed into a city park in 2005. In the meantime, the Chapel Hill Parks and Recreation Department has allowed a group of volunteers to develop a 1.5-mile natural-surface loop trail open to hikers and mountain bikers. The trail never gets quite out of earshot of the traffic on US 15/US 501. Despite the noise, it's a nice walk or ride through mixed forests. There are plenty of rocks and roots and a few obstacles to keep mountain bikers happy.

## Southern Community Park Trail

**Length:** 1.5 miles
**Difficulty:** Easy to moderate
**Blazes:** None
**Surface:** Natural
**Bicycles:** No

### Mileposts

**0.0 mile:** The trail forks immediately after the trailhead. Head left.
**0.4 mile:** The trail crosses Dogwood Acres Road, then crosses a power cut.
**0.7 mile:** Go left at the fork. To the right is a short spur to Merritt Drive.
**1.0 mile:** You'll cross the power cut, then cross Dogwood Acres Road.
**1.5 miles:** You'll return to the parking lot.

*Mason Farm Biological Preserve*

# Mason Farm Biological Preserve

**Address:** North Carolina Botanical Garden, CB 3375, Totten Center, University of North Carolina, Chapel Hill, NC 27599-3375
**Telephone:** 919-962-0522
**Map:** USGS Chapel Hill
**Hours:** Open daylight hours
**Directions:** See the directions for the North Carolina Botanical Garden on page 161. From the Totten Center, drive Old Mason Farm Road for 0.7 mile to the stop sign next to the Finley Golf Course clubhouse. Take a right, drive 0.2 mile on the gravel road to the gate, and continue to the first right. Turn right and cross the cement ford. *Do not attempt to cross if the water is so high that you can't see the concrete.* Park in the gravel lot on the other side of Morgan Creek.

This nature preserve is owned by the University of North Carolina. It is open to the public, but you must first stop by the Totten Center at the North Carolina Botanical Gardens to get a user's permit. The permit is free and good for the calendar year. The Totten Center is worth a visit in itself, so this requirement is not too onerous. And it helps the university keep track of who is using the preserve.

The preserve is located just downstream from the point at which Chapel Creek and Waters Creek join Morgan Creek. You'll get a great view of Morgan Creek as you drive over the only old-style ford still open to cars in the Triangle.

The trails through Mason Farm are actually fire roads, so they're easy to follow. The subtle beauty of this place is particularly suited to those who appreciate peace and quiet and have enough patience to wait for an encounter with the animals that live among the preserve's trees, banks, and bogs. You can watch a vulture soar over acres of open field or sit quietly beside a beaver pond and see if one of its residents will grace you with her presence.

Mason Farm abuts the Army Corps of Engineers' land at Jordan Lake, so the wild animals here have access to the lake's acreage as well. Deer, beavers, foxes, rabbits, and a tremendous variety of salamanders and birds are all frequent sights at Mason Farm. Parts of the preserve are wooded, while other parts are mowed periodically to maintain a meadow habitat.

Anyone interested in the joys of Mason Farm or Piedmont flora and fauna in general should get a copy of *From Laurel Hill to Siler's Bald*. This award-winning book was written by renown naturalist John Terres while he lived in Chapel Hill. It's a great read that enhances enjoyment of all the local natural areas.

**Length:** 1.7 miles
**Difficulty:** Easy
**Blazes:** None
**Surface:** Natural and gravel
**Bicycles:** No

**Mileposts**

**0.0 mile:** The trails form a large loop that can be followed in either direction. The directions below go counter-clockwise. Follow the gravel path that leads from the southwest corner of the parking lot.
**0.1 mile:** You'll reach a fork. Go right.
**0.5 mile:** You'll reach a second fork. Go left. To the right is a pleasant 0.3-mile spur that ends at the park boundary.
**1.6 miles:** You'll reach an intersection with a grassy trail.

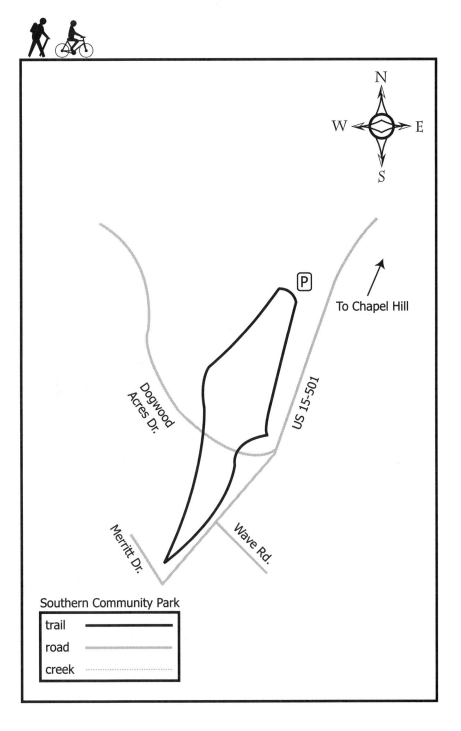

N

W E

S

P

To Chapel Hill

Dogwood
Acres Dr.

US 15-501

Merritt Dr.

Wave Rd.

Southern Community Park

| trail | |
| road | |
| creek | |

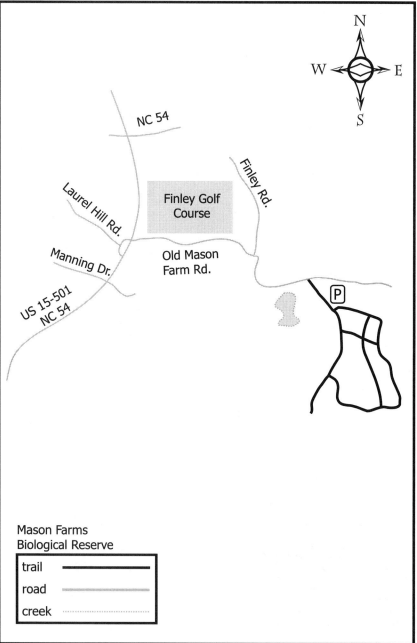

N
W &#8596; E
S

NC 54

Finley Rd.

Laurel Hill Rd.

Finley Golf Course

Manning Dr.

Old Mason Farm Rd.

US 15-501 NC 54

P

Mason Farms Biological Reserve

| trail | —— |
| road | ▨▨▨▨▨ |
| creek | ·············· |

After 100 yards, this trail requires bushwhacking. Continue on the main trail.

**1.7 miles:** You'll return to the first fork. The parking area is to your right.

# North Carolina Botanical Gardens

**Address:** University of North Carolina, CB 3375, Totten Center, Chapel Hill, NC 27599-3375
**Telephone:** 919-962-0522
**Hours:** Dawn to dusk
**Map:** USGS Chapel Hill
**Directions:** The entrance to the gardens is off US 15/US 501 Bypass a mile from the University of North Carolina campus between Manning Drive and the NC 54 East exit. A large brown sign for the gardens is on the highway.

These gardens are well worth the couple of hours it takes for an introductory visit. If you're from a region that doesn't share North Carolina's flora and fauna, the self-guided nature trails will provide you a wealth of information about the habitats and ecosystems you'll encounter in all of the areas described in this book. While you won't feel like you're in the middle of the wilderness, this is a good place to stretch your legs and get to know the state's natural heritage. The two adjoining nature trails total about 1.5 miles of walking. If you walk from the lowest point to the highest, you'll gain 146 feet of elevation, so the trails can provide a decent workout. The self-guided tour points out several enormous trees felled by hurricanes Hazel (1954) and Fran (1996) and describes the growth that takes place in the wake of such events. While visiting the gardens, you can see the cabin once used by North Carolina poet laureate Paul Green. Prior to the building of University Lake, the spring that feeds Meeting-of-the-Waters Creek provided the university campus with water.

If you have only a few minutes for a quick picnic, you'll be pleased to learn that the gardens boast one of the most idyllic benches of any urban park in the area. Stop at the information

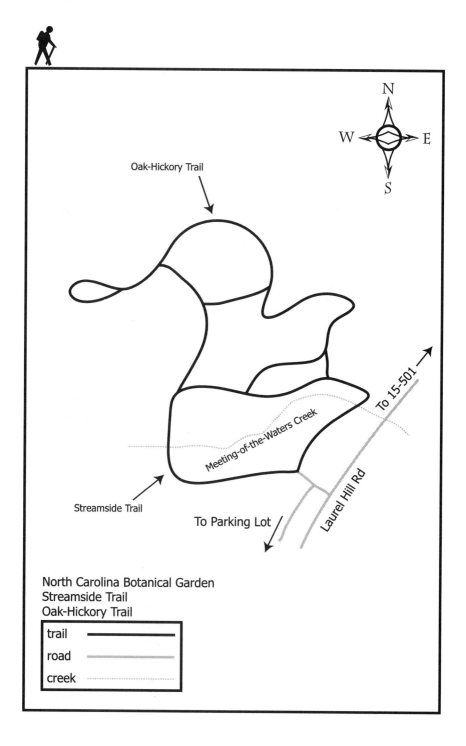

Oak-Hickory Trail

N
W · E
S

Meeting-of-the-Waters Creek

To 15-501 →

Laurel Hill Rd

Streamside Trail

To Parking Lot

North Carolina Botanical Garden
Streamside Trail
Oak-Hickory Trail

| trail | ———— |
| road | ⸺⸺ |
| creek | ········· |

board near the parking lot or run across Old Mason Farm Road to the Totten Center and pick up a trail map. If you begin walking Streamside Trail, you'll find this bench in the grassy bottom land next to Meeting-of-the-Waters Creek about 0.2 mile down the hill.

The displays outside the Totten Center include examples of several different ecosystems within reach of wheelchairs and small children. Among the offerings is a poisonous-plants garden marked by a gate with a large spider carved into it. The paved pathways of the garden are a good place to learn the various poisonous plants that grow around the Triangle. If you get to know poison ivy here, maybe you won't become intimately familiar with its effects later. Other attractions include additional plant collections, sculptures, tours, lectures, and a group of shaded picnic tables between the two parking lots.

## Streamside Trail

**Length:** 0.7 mile
**Difficulty:** Easy
**Blazes:** Yellow
**Surface:** Natural
**Bicycles:** No

From the parking lot, Streamside Trail descends to cross Meeting-of-the-Waters Creek. It then goes uphill and eventually connects with Oak-Hickory Trail. Streamside and Oak-Hickory Trails provide an excellent hike for the directionally impaired. All of the intersections are marked with arrows. Or you can simply follow the numbers and letters on your map and match them to the signposts you'll encounter at regular intervals.

### Mileposts

**0.0 mile:** Begin at the trailhead beside the signboard in the farthest parking lot.
**0.1 mile:** Go left at the first fork.
**0.2 mile:** You'll cross Meeting-of-the-Waters Creek.

**0.3 mile:** You'll pass Oak-Hickory Trail to the left. Continue right. In just over 100 yards, you reach the end of Oak-Hickory Trail on the left. Continue straight.

**0.4 mile:** You'll reach the first of two closely spaced forks. Keep right at both to continue on Streamside Trail. The left trail at the first fork is a short spur to Oak-Hickory Trail. The left trail at the second fork goes less than 100 yards to Laurel Hill Road. Immediately after the second fork, you'll cross a bridge over Meeting-of-the-Waters Creek.

**0.6 mile:** You'll return to the first fork. The parking lot and the Totten Center are to the left. To reach the Totten Center, bear left at the next fork. To reach the parking lot, bear right.

**0.7 mile:** You'll return to the parking lot.

## Oak-Hickory Trail

**Length:** 0.8 mile
**Difficulty:** Moderate
**Blazes:** Red
**Surface:** Natural
**Bicycles:** No

This trail ascends to the climax hardwood forest at the highest point in the gardens. In winter, it's possible to get a glimpse of the more famous and slightly higher hill that lies just to the northeast—Chapel Hill.

### Mileposts

**0.0 mile:** Begin at the first (easternmost) trailhead off Streamside Trail.

**0.1 mile:** You'll reach a fork. The right fork heads 100 yards to connect with the last stretch of Oak-Hickory Trail. Taking this shortcut reduces the length of Oak-Hickory Trail to 0.4 mile. Go left at the fork.

**0.2 mile:** You'll reach another fork. The left fork is a pleasant spur with a short loop at the end that adds 0.2 mile to the walk. Take the right fork. Before you arrive at the next official fork, you'll pass an intersection with a clearly marked unofficial trail that leads off the botanical gardens property. Please stay on the designated trails.

**0.4 mile:** You'll reach a fork. To the right is the 100-yard spur leading back to the first fork and then the beginning of Oak-Hickory Trail. Follow the red arrows straight. You'll pass another intersection with another unofficial trail. Follow the red arrows to stay on the designated trail.

**0.5 mile:** You'll reach a fork. Straight down the hill is a short spur to Streamside Trail. Take the right fork.

**0.6 mile:** You'll reach the end of Oak-Hickory Trail at the intersection with Streamside Trail. To the right, it is 0.3 mile back to the parking lot. To the left, it is 0.4 mile back.

# Chapel Hill Greenways

**Address:** Chapel Hill Parks and Recreation Department, 200 Plant Road, Chapel Hill, NC 27514
**Telephone:** 919-968-2784
**Maps:** USGS Chapel Hill; free maps are available from the Chapel Hill Parks and Recreation office.

Chapel Hill is a small town with a big plan for its greenways system. The Chapel Hill Parks and Recreation Department and the Greenways Commission are committed to developing over 28 miles of trails. When the plan is completed, the greenways will offer a great alternative to the increasingly busy roads. At present, 11.4 miles of greenways are finished. Two of the most interesting routes are Bolin Creek Trail and Battle Branch Trail. Because of its significant length, Bolin Creek Trail draws people from around the town in search of a place to be outside and get some exercise away from traffic. Battle Branch is one of the few trails in Chapel Hill where mountain bikers can get a taste of the woods. (Mountain bikers should also see the section on Southern Community Park, pages 155-56.)

The paved trails are designed to be as wheelchair-accessible as possible for the terrain. They are shared by people using a variety of wheeled conveyances, from cyclists to roller bladers to parents pushing baby strollers to elderly citizens using walkers. The natural-surface paths are open to both pedestrians and mountain bikers. These trails are generally less crowded and more physically challenging.

## Battle Branch Trail

**Length:** 1.5 miles, including spurs and loops
**Difficulty:** Easy to moderate
**Surface:** Natural
**Bicycles:** Yes
**Directions:** From Fordham Boulevard (US 15/US 501 Bypass), follow South Estes Drive for 0.4 mile to the entrance to the Chapel Hill Community Center, on the left. The trailhead is behind the community center; follow the boardwalk to the sidewalk. Less than 200 yards from the trailhead, the trail crosses the creek and turns right into the woods.

Battle Branch Trail roughly parallels Franklin Street as it descends from the university's Forest Theater to the valley containing the shopping centers, businesses, and apartments in Chapel Hill's lower-elevation business district. It offers a peaceful commute by foot or mountain bike for those willing to exchange a few extra minutes for a dose of natural beauty. The trail closely follows Battle Branch, crossing back and forth over small wooden bridges. As befits a university town, ivy grows abundantly along the hillsides. Houses are visible along most of the lower half of the trail, so lone walkers needn't feel entirely isolated. As this guide was going to press, the University of North Carolina had committed funds to add bridges and remove downed trees from the section of Battle Branch Trail on university property.

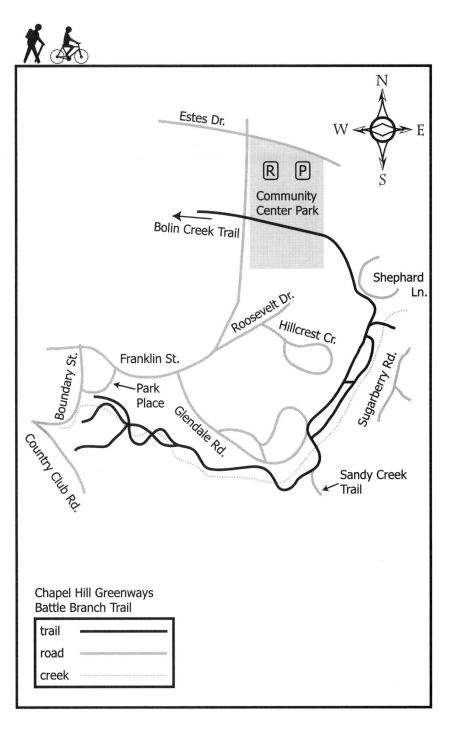

Estes Dr.

R  P

Community
Center Park

Bolin Creek Trail

Shephard
Ln.

Roosevelt Dr.

Hillcrest Cr.

Franklin St.

Boundary St.

Park
Place

Sugarberry Rd.

Country Club Rd.

Glendale Rd.

Sandy Creek
Trail

Chapel Hill Greenways
Battle Branch Trail

| trail | ━━━━ |
| road | ··········· |
| creek | ············· |

## Bolin Creek Trail

**Length:** 1.5 miles
**Difficulty:** Easy
**Surface:** Asphalt          *Bolin Creek Trail*
**Bicycles:** Yes
**Directions:** From Fordham Boulevard (US 15/US 501 By-pass), follow South Estes Drive for 0.4 mile to the entrance to the Chapel Hill Community Center, on the left.

This paved greenway takes you from the end of Battle Branch Trail at the Chapel Hill Community Center Park to Airport Road. It passes within easy sight of scenic Bolin Creek for almost all of its length.

Although it's short, Bolin Creek Trail is great for walking, skating, and cycling. Cyclists and skaters should be prepared to control their speed and share the space.

## Lower Booker Creek Trail

**Length:** 0.8 mile
**Difficulty:** Easy
**Surface:** Cement
**Bicycles:** Yes
**Directions:** From the intersection of US 15/US 501 and Erwin Road, take Erwin Road north for 0.3 mile, then turn left on Old Oxford Road East. Go 0.3 mile, then turn right on Booker Creek Road. The entrance to the greenway is 0.2 mile ahead on the left.

This trail follows Booker Creek. It has no hills to speak of. Aside from the seams in the concrete, this is a dream greenway for the baby-jogger set. The limited parking means that this greenway is of most interest to those living nearby.

## Tanyard Branch Trail

**Length:** 0.4 mile
**Difficulty:** Moderate to strenuous
**Surface:** Natural
**Bicycles:** Yes
**Directions:** The eastern terminus of the trail intersects the driveway at Community Center Park and takes you by the park's rose garden. The western terminus is 0.9 mile north of the intersection of Franklin Street and Airport Road/Columbia Street. The trail may be accessed at Elizabeth Street 0.25 mile after it intersects Franklin Street.

This short trail connects Caldwell Street and the Northside neighborhood with Umstead Park. If you travel it by bike, you'll have a rocky, rooty ride that's either all uphill (if you start at Umstead) or all downhill (if you start on Caldwell). You'll negotiate some steep stretches and enjoy plenty of views of the creek. The south end of the trail, which goes through cutover areas, isn't as scenic as the forested north end.

## Fan Branch Trail

**Length:** 1 mile
**Difficulty:** Easy
**Surface:** Asphalt
**Bicycles:** Yes
**Directions:** The greenway entrance is at the intersection of Culbreth Drive and US 15/US 501 South just south of where US 15/US 501 separates from Fordham Boulevard.

The houses of A Southern Village, rather than the creek, dominate the scenery along this greenway. If Fan

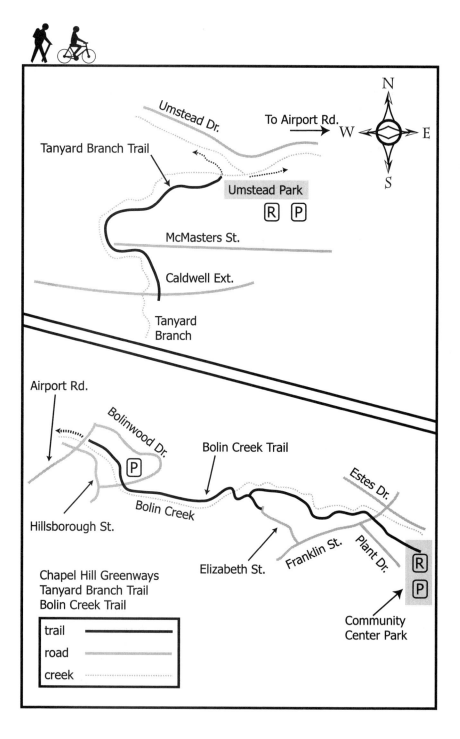

Umstead Dr.

To Airport Rd.

N

W  E

S

Tanyard Branch Trail

Umstead Park

R  P

McMasters St.

Caldwell Ext.

Tanyard
Branch

Airport Rd.

Bolinwood Dr.

Bolin Creek Trail

P

Estes Dr.

Bolin Creek

Hillsborough St.

Elizabeth St.

Franklin St.

Plant Dr.

R

P

Community
Center Park

Chapel Hill Greenways
Tanyard Branch Trail
Bolin Creek Trail

| trail | ——— |
| road | ——— |
| creek | ········· |

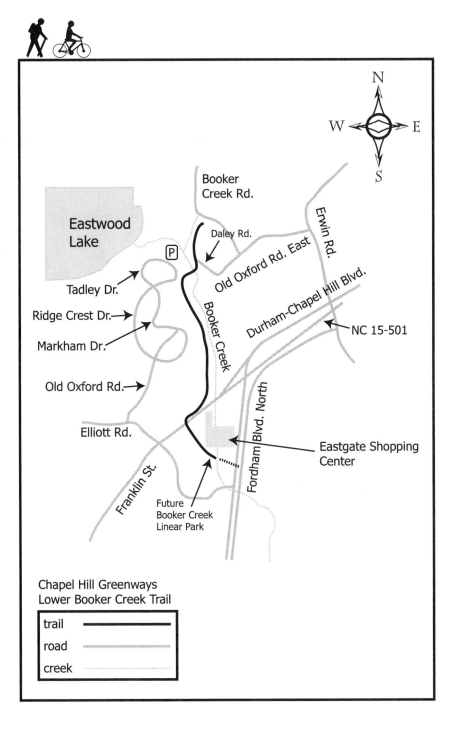

N
W ← → E
S

Booker
Creek Rd.

Erwin Rd.

Eastwood
Lake

Daley Rd.

P

Old Oxford Rd. East

Tadley Dr.

Durham-Chapel Hill Blvd.

Ridge Crest Dr.→

NC 15-501

Markham Dr.

Booker Creek

Old Oxford Rd.→

Elliott Rd.

Fordham Blvd. North

Eastgate Shopping
Center

Franklin St.

Future
Booker Creek
Linear Park

Chapel Hill Greenways
Lower Booker Creek Trail

| trail | ——— |
|-------|------|
| road | |
| creek | |

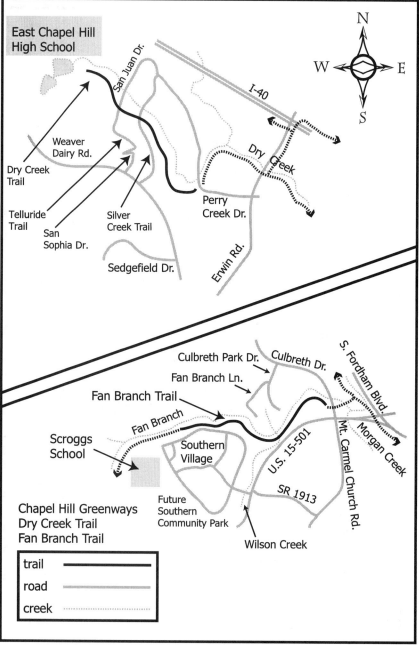

East Chapel Hill
High School

San Juan Dr.

I-40

N

W        E

S

Weaver
Dairy Rd.

Dry Creek
Trail

Dry Creek

Telluride
Trail

Silver
Creek Trail

San
Sophia Dr.

Perry
Creek Dr.

Sedgefield Dr.

Erwin Rd.

Culbreth Park Dr.        Culbreth Dr.

Fan Branch Ln.

Fan Branch Trail

S. Fordham Blvd.

Fan Branch

Scroggs
School

Southern
Village

U.S. 15-501

Mt. Carmel Church Rd.

Morgan Creek

Chapel Hill Greenways
Dry Creek Trail
Fan Branch Trail

Future
Southern
Community Park

SR 1913

Wilson Creek

| trail | ▬▬▬▬▬ |
| road | ▬▬▬▬▬ |
| creek | ·········· |

Branch Trail is extended as planned, local residents and cyclists will have a means of avoiding US 15/US 501 on a traffic-free path from Culbreth to Southern Community Park.

## Dry Creek Trail

**Length:** 1.2 miles
**Difficulty:** Easy to moderate
**Surface:** Natural
**Bicycles:** Yes

Dry Creek Trail links East Chapel Hill High School and Cedar Falls Park with the Silver Creek and Springcrest neighborhoods. This is Chapel Hill's most dramatic greenway, thanks to the field of large boulders and the small waterfall on Dry Creek on the west side of Silver Creek Trail. The greenway passes through dry upland forests and a flood plain along a narrow strip of woods between houses. Access is off San Juan Road, Silver Creek Trail, and Perry Creek Road. Chapel Hill plans to extend Dry Creek Trail to Erwin Road in late 2005.

# Carrboro Bikeways

**Address:** Recreation and Parks Department, Carrboro Century Center, 100 North Greensboro Street, Carrboro, NC 27510
**Telephone:** 919-918-7364

## Libba Cotton Bikeway

**Length:** 0.4 mile
**Difficulty:** Easy
**Blazes:** None
**Surface:** Asphalt and cement
**Bicycles:** Yes
**Directions:** From Main Street in Carrboro (in front of Carr Mill Mall), turn south on Roberson Street. The bikeway is 0.1 mile ahead on the left.

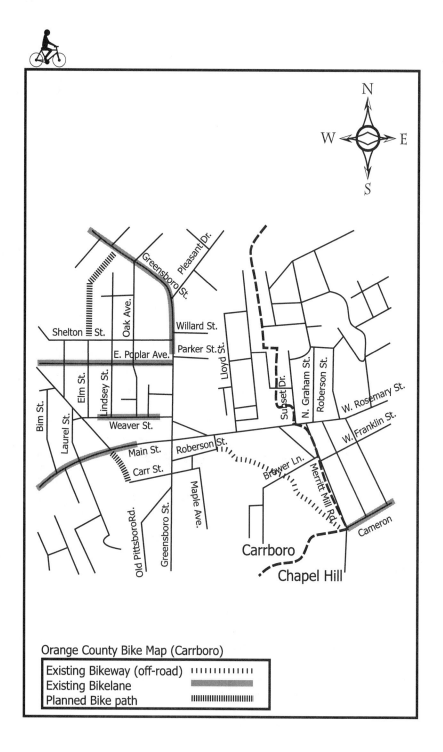

N
W — E
S

Pleasant Dr.
Greensboro St.
Oak Ave.
Shelton St.
Willard St.
E. Poplar Ave.
Parker St. St.
Lloyd St.
Sunset Dr.
N. Graham St.
Roberson St.
W. Rosemary St.
Elm St.
Lindsey St.
Bim St.
Laurel St.
Weaver St.
W. Franklin St.
Main St.
Roberson St.
Carr St.
Brewer Ln.
Merritt Mill Rd.
Cameron
Old Pittsboro Rd.
Greensboro St.
Maple Ave.
Carrboro
Chapel Hill

**Orange County Bike Map (Carrboro)**

| Existing Bikeway (off-road) | IIIIIIIIIIIII |
| Existing Bikelane | ▬▬▬▬▬ |
| Planned Bike path | IIIIIIIIIIIIIIIIIIIIIIIIII |

*Libba Cotton Bikeway*

This paved mini-road open to pedestrians and cyclists amounts to a major thoroughfare, complete with traffic buildups during rush hour. It provides a safer alternative to Main Street, a critical connection among many residential areas in Carrboro, and a bike route leading to the UNC campus. Lanes are marked for pedestrians, as well as for east- and west-bound cyclists. Since the bikeway sees constant use, it's important to stay in your lane to avoid accidents.

The bikeway is named for Elizabeth "Libba" Cotton, who was born in Chapel Hill in 1895 and lived in North Carolina until she married as a teenager. At age 12, Cotton wrote the now-famous folk song "Freight Train," about the train that followed the tracks along what would one day become the bikeway. Libba Cotton died in 1987.

## Bikeway between Jones Ferry Road and Carr Street

**Length:** 0.1 mile
**Difficulty:** Easy
**Blazes:** None
**Surface:** Asphalt
**Bicycles:** Yes
**Directions:** The bikeway begins at the intersection of Main Street and Jones Ferry Road, beside the PTA Thrift Shop.

This short bikeway gives cyclists a means of avoiding a busy section of road but is otherwise uninteresting.

## Frances Lloyd Shetley Bikeway

**Length:** 0.3 mile
**Difficulty:** Easy
**Blazes:** None
**Surface:** Asphalt
**Bicycles:** Yes
**Directions:** The bikeway goes from the intersection of Greensboro Street and Estes Drive to the intersection of Elm and Shelton Streets.

This short bikeway is the most scenic in Carrboro.

# Wake County

## American Tobacco Trail, Wake County Section

**Maps:** See map on page 56.
**Directions:** From the intersection of US 64 and NC 751, drive south on New Hill-Olive Chapel Road (SR 1141) for 2 miles to the main parking area, located on the left immediately after the bridge over Beaver Creek. This parking area is the only one large enough to accommodate equestrian trailers. To reach it from US 1, take Exit 89 and go north on New Hill-Olive Chapel Road for 4 miles. The smaller parking area is off Wimberly Road. To reach it, take US 64 to Jenks Road (SR1601), turn right, and go 0.5 mile to Wimberly Road (SR1603). It is 1 mile to the parking area, located on the right after the bridge over White Oak Creek.

For a complete introduction to American Tobacco Trail, see page 52. The 5.5-mile section in Wake County officially opened in July 2003. It provides a crucial link in a rail-trail route that will run from downtown Durham south through Wake and Chatham Counties to its southern terminus near Bonsal. This trail is particularly scenic as it passes through boggy wetlands.

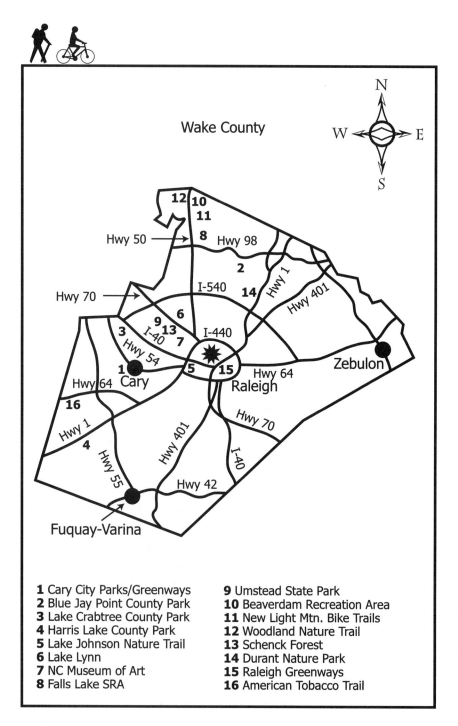

**Wake County**

Hwy 50
Hwy 98
Hwy 70
I-540
I-440
I-40
Hwy 54
Hwy 64
Hwy 1
Hwy 401
Cary
Raleigh
Hwy 64
Zebulon
Hwy 1
Hwy 401
Hwy 70
Hwy 55
I-40
Hwy 42
Fuquay-Varina

**1** Cary City Parks/Greenways
**2** Blue Jay Point County Park
**3** Lake Crabtree County Park
**4** Harris Lake County Park
**5** Lake Johnson Nature Trail
**6** Lake Lynn
**7** NC Museum of Art
**8** Falls Lake SRA

**9** Umstead State Park
**10** Beaverdam Recreation Area
**11** New Light Mtn. Bike Trails
**12** Woodland Nature Trail
**13** Schenck Forest
**14** Durant Nature Park
**15** Raleigh Greenways
**16** American Tobacco Trail

*Lake Crabtree County Park*

# Lake Crabtree County Park

**Address:** Crabtree Park Office, 1400 Aviation Parkway, Morrisville, NC 27560
**Telephone:** 919-460-3390
**Hours:** The park is open from 8 A.M. to sunset every day except Thanksgiving, Christmas Eve, Christmas, and New Year's.
**Maps:** USGS Cary; a free park map is available in the park.
**Fees:** No fee is charged for hiking, but there is a small charge for launching or renting a boat.
**Directions:** Take I-40 to the Aviation Parkway exit (Exit 285) and head south on Aviation Parkway. The park entrance is on the left after less than a mile. A series of parking lots is on the right after you enter the park. You can park in any of them and not be too far from the trails.

The central feature of this park is the 520-acre Lake Crabtree. Its official duty is flood control, but it also serves as a stocked fishing and boating lake. Created by the damming of Crabtree, Black, Brier, and Stirrup Iron Creeks, Lake Crabtree provides a great spot for paddling or small-craft sailing. Boats are available for rent, or you can pay a fee to launch your own non-gas-powered craft.

Another exceptional feature of the park is the fishing pier built out over the lakeshore. Its picnic tables and benches are set in one of the most scenic spots in the Triangle.

The park's 200 acres of land offer an exceptional variety of recreational opportunities, especially considering the location. This park is far from the back country. The view includes several corporate office buildings, and you can watch planes that have just left RDU climbing skyward; the best view of the planes is from Black Creek Trail as it crosses the dam. The proximity of urban life is a bonus. Thousands of people who work in RTP or live in Cary are near a trail that meanders for miles with woods on one side and a gently lapping lake on the other.

Lake Crabtree County Park offers trails for mountain bikers, hikers, and those with limited mobility. The proximity of the airport makes this a great park for business travelers who have a few free hours before catching a flight home.

## Lake Crabtree Trail

**Length:** 5.5 miles
**Difficulty:** Moderate
**Blazes:** Blue
**Surface:** Natural
**Bicycles:** Only the first 0.2 mile open to bicycles

This trail circumnavigates Lake Crabtree. It shares some of its distance with the Cary greenways system. On the north shore, the trail is flat and scenic. On the south shore, you'll have a few hills to climb. But the wetlands provide the biggest challenge. Wear boots, since the mud may suck the sneakers right off your feet. And be prepared to get a little wet and very dirty.

Of note along the trail are two observation towers. One of these is the Heather Lee Carr Memorial Observation Tower, built in honor of a young woman who died in 1989. The second tower, just past the dam, offers a panoramic view of the lake.

**0.0 mile:** Begin at the trailhead located off the third parking lot near the main driveway. You'll cross three paved driveways within the first 300 yards.

**0.2 mile:** The trail forks after crossing a bridge. Continue right. From this point, Lake Crabtree Trail is closed to bikes. The left fork is Highland Trail, which is open to bikes.

**0.4 mile:** You'll pass the Heather Lee Carr Memorial Observation Tower.

**0.9 mile:** You'll emerge from the woods just below I-40. Highland Trail is on the left. Continue to the right.

**1.0 mile:** After walking along the eastern shore of the lake, you'll pass through a chain-link gate.

**1.1 miles:** You'll reach an intersection with the paved Black Creek Trail, part of the Cary greenways system. Black Creek Trail is open to bikes. The trail turns 90 degrees to the right and crosses the grassy dam. A map and some interpretive information are posted here.

**1.5 miles:** You'll pass through a second chain-link gate.

**1.6 miles:** The trail passes the second observation tower.

**1.7 miles:** You'll pass a private, gated dirt trail to the left, then cross a bridge.

**1.9 miles:** Lake Crabtree Trail and Black Creek Trail separate. Lake Crabtree Trail is the 90-degree right turn. Black Creek Trail continues ahead as a paved trail, while Crabtree heads uphill and over a series of small wooden bridges before passing behind some corporate offices.

**3.0 miles:** You'll cross a bridge.

**4.0 miles:** The trail follows Evans Road to the right.

**4.5 miles:** You'll cross a bridge over Crabtree Creek.

**4.9 miles:** You'll reach Aviation Parkway. Walk right along the roadside.

**5.4 miles:** Upon reaching the end of the guardrail, turn right toward the lake and proceed through the woods.

**5.5 miles:** You'll emerge from the woods into a wide, grassy field. The boathouse and parking area are visible ahead.

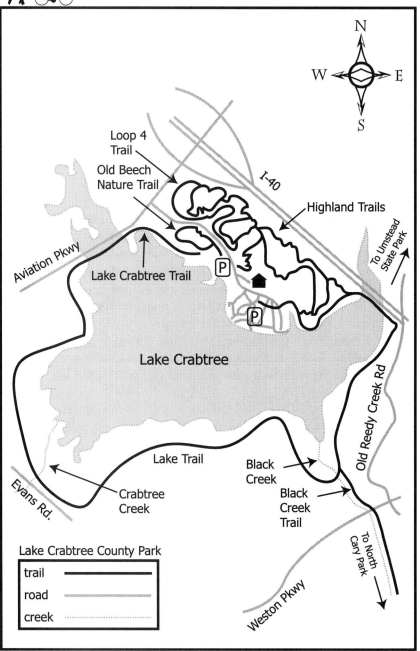

N
W — E
S

Loop 4
Trail

Old Beech
Nature Trail

I-40

Highland Trails

To Umstead State Park

Aviation Pkwy

P

P

Lake Crabtree Trail

Lake Crabtree

Old Reedy Creek Rd.

Lake Trail

Black
Creek

Black
Creek
Trail

Crabtree
Creek

Evans Rd.

To North Cary Park

Weston Pkwy

Lake Crabtree County Park

| trail | ——————— |
| road | ――――――― |
| creek | ·············· |

# Old Beech Nature Trail

**Length:** 0.6 mile
**Difficulty:** Easy
**Blazes:** White
**Surface:** Screenings (fine mulch)
**Bicycles:** No

This trail is a good one for young children. In addition to the tree for which the trail is named—an American beech over 100 years old—it offers a tree identification wheel and old sawmill sites.

## Mileposts

**0.1 mile:** The trail forks. Head right. The tree identification wheel is less than 100 yards away.
**0.5 mile:** You'll return to the trail you came in on. Turn right.
**0.6 mile:** You'll return to the parking lot.

# Highland Trail

**Length:** 5.7 miles, or 6.1 miles if you go to Old Reedy Creek Road and back
**Difficulty:** Moderate
**Blazes:** The loops have yellow blazes; the connectors have red blazes.
**Surface:** Natural
**Bicycles:** Yes
**Directions:** The entrance to Highland Trail is on the left across the street from the first parking lot. If you're riding to the trail, there is also access from Old Reedy Creek Road just before the bridge over I-40.

Highland Trail was designed by and for mountain bikers. It was built by the N.C. Fats Mountain Bike Club in cooperation with the Wake County Parks Department. N.C. Fats continually works on the trails to keep them in good shape, and the park staff oversees use. Highland Trail is closed if it's wet or likely to become wet. The trail sees some use by hikers, so it's important to remain alert.

The trail consists of four loops and four connector trails. The trails vary in difficulty, but all are appropriate for beginning to intermediate riders. All are wooded. Riders have to contend with a few spots of rocks and roots. This trail provides easy access to the Bike and Bridle Trail in William B. Umstead State Park, so it's possible to piece together a longer ride. Given Highland Trail's location—close to RTP and much of Cary—it is a great place to try mountain biking or to practice your skills.

## Mileposts

**Note:** This set of loop trails has maps posted at nearly every intersection. The Mileposts below describe one possible route. Most first-time riders won't have any trouble figuring out where they are in the trail network.

**0.0 mile:** Begin on the access trail off the park's driveway and ride the trails clockwise. The trail forks immediately. Go right to a second fork. This time, follow the connector left. To the right is a 0.15-mile trail to Loop 1 and the Old Home Site.

**0.3 mile:** You'll reach Loop 1. Go left.

**0.5 mile:** Loop 1 continues right. The short connector to Loop 2 is to the left. Go left here, then left again in 20 yards when the connector ends at Loop 2.

**0.9 mile:** The connector to Loop 3 is to the left. Loop 2 continues right for less than 0.1 mile. Go left.

**1.3 miles:** You'll reach Loop 3. Head right.

**1.6 miles:** Loop 4 is to the right. Continue left on Loop 3. (Note: At this point, you could follow the 1.5-mile Loop 4 back to the main trailhead.)

**1.8 miles:** You'll pass the connector to Loop 4 to the left.

**1.9 miles:** You'll return to the beginning of Loop 3. Continue ahead on the connector.

**2.3 miles:** You'll return to Loop 2. Continue left.

**2.4 miles:** You'll reach Loop 1. Continue left.

**2.8 miles:** You'll reach a connector on the right that shortens Route 1. Continue left.

**2.9 miles:** You'll reach a fork. To the left is a connector that goes 0.2 mile to Old Reedy Creek Road. Continue right on Loop 1. (Note: To reach William B. Umstead State Park, turn left on Old Reedy Creek Road and ride to the gate.)

**3.1 miles:** You'll reach a fork. To the left is a 0.3-mile connector that crosses several driveways and ends at the trailhead near the boat rental complex. Continue right on Loop 1.

**3.3 miles:** You'll reach the other end of the short connector you passed at 2.8 miles. Continue left.

**3.7 miles:** You'll reach the end of the first connector from the parking lot. Turn left to return to the entrance trailhead.

**4.0 miles:** You'll reach the trailhead.

# Harris Lake County Park

**Address:** Park Office, 2112 County Park Drive, New Hill, NC 27562

**Telephone:** 919-387-4342

**Hours:** The park is open from 8 A.M. to sunset.

**Map:** A free brochure is available from the park office.

**Directions:** From Raleigh, take US 1 South to New Hill Holleman Road (SR 1127). Turn left and drive about 2.5 miles to the Progress Energy visitor center on the right or 3 miles to the County Park Road entrance, also on the right. Once on the main drive in the county park, turn right at the first driveway to reach the park office, where you can pick up a brochure. To reach the lakeside facilities, continue straight on the main driveway.

From Durham and Chapel Hill, take I-40 to the NC 751 exit (Exit 274). Follow NC 751 South to US 64. Cross US 64 and continue south on New Hill Olive Chapel Road (SR 1141). On the other side of Old US 1, the name of the road changes to New Hill Holleman Road (SR 1127). Cross US 1 and follow the directions in the preceding paragraph.

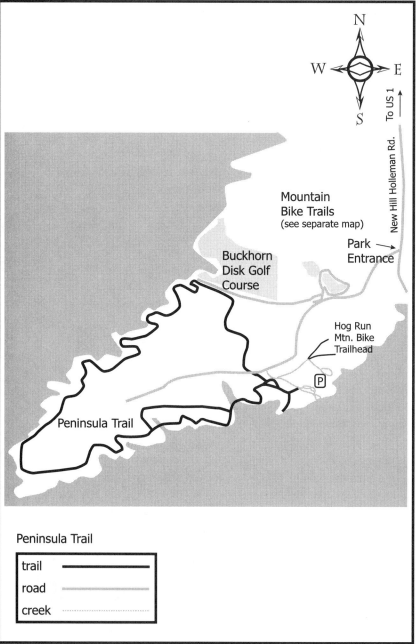

N

W ← → E

S

To US 1

New Hill Holleman Rd.

Mountain
Bike Trails
(see separate map)

Park →
Entrance →

Buckhorn
Disk Golf
Course

Hog Run
Mtn. Bike
Trailhead

P

Peninsula Trail

Peninsula Trail

| | |
|---|---|
| trail | ━━━━━━ |
| road | ─────── |
| creek | ·········· |

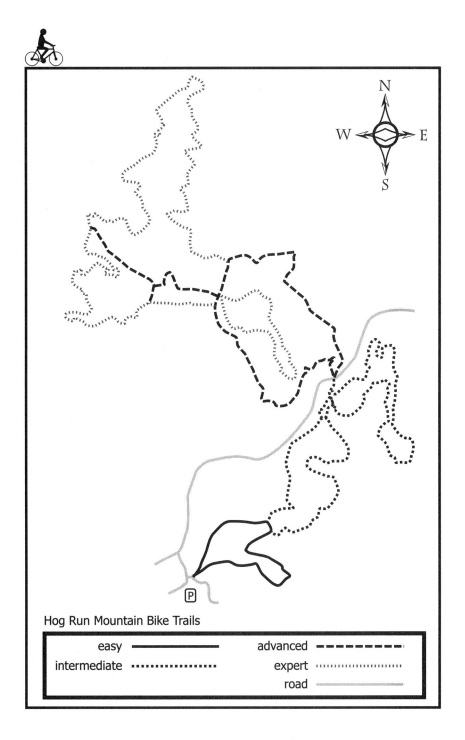

Hog Run Mountain Bike Trails

| easy | ———————— | advanced | – – – – – – |
|------|----------|----------|-------------|
| intermediate | •••••••••••••• | expert | ⋯⋯⋯⋯⋯⋯ |
| | | road | ▨▨▨▨▨▨▨ |

Harris Lake straddles the border between Chatham and Wake Counties near Harnett County. Its land is provided by Progress Energy, formerly Carolina Power & Light. The lake was created by damming Buckhorn Creek about 2 miles above the Cape Fear River. The area encompasses about 7,000 acres of land and the 4,000-acre lake. About 5,000 of those acres are managed by the North Carolina Wildlife Resources Commission's Game Lands Program. Much of the land is open to hunters. No hunting is allowed on Progress Energy property that is not posted as game lands. Hunting is also prohibited on county park land.

The distinguishing feature of this area is the Harris Nuclear Power Plant's massive cooling tower, plainly visible from many points in the park. Regardless of how you feel about nuclear power, the tower with its huge cloud of steam is an amazing sight. If a view of the power plant is what you are after, Peninsula Trail crosses a power cut that gives the most unobstructed view of the tower.

Aside from the power plant, the park has much to recommend it. A 680-acre peninsula of land on Harris Lake was leased from CP&L in 1985 and opened to citizens as a park in 1999. The Progress Energy Visitor Center offers White Oak Nature Trail and displays and exhibits that provide information about local plants. Peninsula Trail gives fine views of the lake at sunset. In addition to playgrounds and picnic facilities, the park offers several small farm ponds managed and stocked for anglers.

A cautionary note: Park officials are clearing away debris left from the land's former life as a farm. Many hazards remain, including barbed wire and broken glass. Please exercise extra caution and keep an eye on youngsters at all times.

## Peninsula Trail

**Length:** 5 miles
**Difficulty:** Easy
**Blazes:** Red
**Surface:** Natural
**Bicycles:** No

This trail offers a variety of sights, from farm ponds

to pine forests to the lakeshore itself. It also provides access to a car-top boat launch.

## Hog Run Trail

The bike trails collectively known as Hog Run Trail include three loops accurately called the Beginner Loop, the Intermediate Loop, and the Advanced Loop. Since the builders had a few hundred acres to work with, the trails feel more spread out than those at Crabtree County Park. All in all, they're a good place for a moderate workout or an introduction to the sport.

## Beginner Loop

**Length:** 1 mile
**Difficulty:** Easy
**Blazes:** Green
**Surface:** Natural
**Bicycles:** Yes

This loop is flat and has no significant obstacles. It offers a lake view.

### Mileposts

0.4 mile: Go left at this fork and the next fork.
1.0 mile: You'll return to the trailhead.

## Intermediate Loop

**Length:** 2.5 miles, not including the Beginner Loop
**Difficulty:** Easy to moderate
**Blazes:** Blue
**Surface:** Natural
**Bicycles:** Yes

This loop has a few small hills and obstacles that can be avoided by taking ride-around trails.

---

**0.0 mile:** The loop begins 0.4 mile down the Beginner Loop.

**1.4 miles:** You'll cross a bridge.

**1.7 miles:** You'll reach a fork. The Advanced Loop is on the right. Continue left. Keep right at the next two forks, then reenter the woods on the left.

**2.5 miles:** The loop ends on the Beginner Loop. Continue right to the parking lot.

## Advanced Loop

**Length:** 3.3 miles, not including the small loops off the larger trail
**Difficulty:** Moderate to strenuous
**Blazes:** Black
**Surface:** Natural
**Bicycles:** Yes

This loop offers a couple of moderate hills, several obstacles—some of which you must ride or walk over—a set of great gully drops, and lake views. As this guide went to press, work was under way to develop smaller loops off the main route. The map provided here is accurate, according to a new survey of the park. The Mileposts listed below do not include the small loops or the distance to and from the trailhead on the Beginner Loop and the Intermediate Loop.

**Mileposts**

---

**0.0 mile:** Begin at the trailhead on the Intermediate Loop, then cross the park driveway.

**0.5 mile:** Keep right at the fork. To the left is a short loop that rejoins the trail just ahead.

**0.6 mile:** Keep right at the fork. Going left will shorten the loop.

**1.2 miles:** Take either fork.

**1.8 miles:** Keep right at the fork to complete the loop. Going left adds smaller loops.
**2.8 miles:** You'll reach an intersection with the road. Keep left.
**2.9 miles:** Keep right at the fork.
**3.3 miles:** You'll emerge at the road. Continue straight, then follow Intermediate Loop and then Beginner Loop to reach your car.

# Falls Lake State Recreation Area

## Falls Lake Trail State Park _____

**Address:** 13304 Creedmoor Road, Wake Forest, NC 27587
**Telephone:** 919-676-1027
**Maps:** USGS Wake Forest, Bayleaf, Creedmoor; a free large-scale map is available from the park office.

For a complete introduction to Falls Lake State Recreation Area, see page 428.

Measuring approximately 27 miles, Falls Lake Trail is the Triangle's longest hiking trail. Most of it winds through woodlands along the shores of Falls Lake. The gentle terrain consists mostly of small, rolling hills. In winter, lake views abound. In summer, leaves sometimes obscure the sight of the water, but they also provide hikers with a welcome break from the sun. The secluded sections of the trail offer many opportunities to see small wildlife. Turtles bask on logs, and frogs hide along the banks of the lake and the creeks feeding into it. Beaver may be spotted at sunset, and deer are plentiful. Other sections of the trail skirt residential backyards. For this reason, it is important to stay on the marked trail and respect private property. The best season to hike the trail is spring, when wildflowers bloom and a remarkable number of flowering rhododendron and laurel bushes dot the hillsides. Autumn is also delightful, as the clear skies reflect on the water and the trees along the lakeshore flame into color.

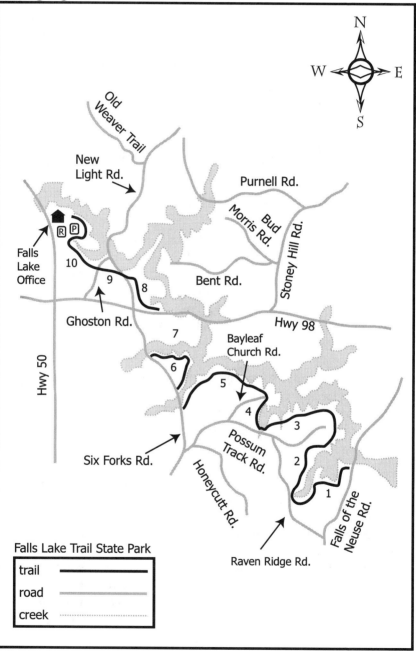

N
W E
S

Old Weaver Trail

New Light Rd.

Purnell Rd.

Bud Morris Rd.

Stoney Hill Rd.

Falls Lake Office

R P

10

9

8

Bent Rd.

Ghoston Rd.

Hwy 98

7

Bayleaf Church Rd.

6

5

4

3

Hwy 50

Six Forks Rd.

Possum Track Rd.

2

Honeycutt Rd.

1

Falls of the Neuse Rd.

Raven Ridge Rd.

**Falls Lake Trail State Park**

| trail | ——— |
| road | ~~~~~ |
| creek | ········ |

Hikers on Falls Lake Trail will notice the Mountains-to-Sea (MST) signs marking the trailheads. MST is an approximately 1,000-mile trail that stretches from Clingmans Dome in the Blue Ridge Mountains to Jockey's Ridge on the Outer Banks. Falls Lake Trail State Park provides a crucial link in this cross-state route currently comprised of roughly 500 miles of trails and 500 miles of rural roads. For further information, contact the Friends of the Mountains-to-Sea Trail by visiting www.ncmst.org or pick up a copy of *Hiking North Carolina's Mountains-to-Sea Trail* by MST mastermind Allen DeHart.

If you hike Falls Lake Trail during hunting season, be cautious. Deer season in North Carolina runs from September through December, and small-game season runs from September through mid-May. No hunting is allowed on Falls Lake Trail, but note that the park is actually a 200-yard swath that cuts through North Carolina Wildlife Resources Commission game lands in many places. Hunting is allowed on the lands adjacent to the trail. Park officials strongly encourage hikers to wear blaze orange while hiking the trail during hunting season. Currently, Falls Lake Trail has 10 named sections divided by road crossings. The sections vary greatly in length and appeal.

A general note about directions: Falls Lake Trail crosses roads at different trailheads. Only one small loop is on Falls Lake Trail proper, in the Falls of the Neuse section. A loop can be hiked in Blue Jay County Park using the county park's trails. The rest of Falls Lake Trail can be hiked or run as out-and-back by using two vehicles, or it can be combined with a walk or run along the roadways to make a loop. All distances given are from one trailhead to the next and do not include mileage for a return trip.

## Honeycutt Creek, East Section (1)

**Length:** 3.4 miles to the next trailhead; you can backtrack or loop back on Raven Ridge and Falls of the Neuse Roads.
**Difficulty:** Easy
**Blazes:** White
**Surface:** Natural
**Bicycles:** No
**Directions:** From Raleigh take Falls of the Neuse Road (SR

2000) north to the Neuse River (approximately 2 miles north of the intersection with Raven Ridge Road). Just before the bridge turn right into the Tailrace Fishing Access Area. A large paved parking lot is near the dam. The trailhead is directly across the parking lot from the restrooms. White blazes mark the way, although they are a bit scarce during the first 0.5 mile. The trail follows an old road.

This section begins at the Tailrace Fishing Access Area beside the Falls of the Neuse Dam and extends to Raven Ridge Road. A few creeks and lake views lend it character. Some private homes are visible from the trail. Much of the walk is through bottom lands, so the trail can be messy if it has rained recently.

## Mileposts

**100 yards:** Turn left off the old road onto a foot trail.
**0.2 mile:** Go right at the fork. The blue-blazed spur trail that veers left rejoins the main trail and can be used to make a small loop hike.
**0.3 mile:** You'll cross a paved road. The trail continues on the opposite side through trees bordering a cleared area. You'll see an Army Corps of Engineers maintenance building ahead. This building has restrooms, a water fountain, maps, and exhibits.
**0.4 mile:** You'll reach the driveway of the maintenance facility. Turn right and follow the paved drive behind the building.
**0.6 mile:** Turn right off the pavement back onto the trail.
**0.9 mile:** You'll cross a paved service road. Follow the white-blazed trail when it forks right.
**2.6 miles:** You'll descend to and cross a rocky creek via a wooden bridge. The trail continues behind some homes.
**3.3 miles:** You'll emerge onto Raven Ridge Road. To continue on Falls Lake Trail, turn right and walk across the bridge. The trail resumes just past the bridge on the same side of the road.

# Honeycutt Creek, West Section (2)

**Length:** 2.6 miles
**Difficulty:** Easy
**Blazes:** White
**Surface:** Natural
**Bicycles:** No
**Directions:** To reach the trailheads on Raven Ridge Road from Raleigh, take Falls of the Neuse Road north to Raven Ridge Road and turn left. After 1 mile, the trailheads are on the right. The trailhead before the bridge leads east to Falls of the Neuse. The one after the bridge heads west toward the Possum Track Road trailhead.

From Durham, take NC 98 east for 1.6 miles from the intersection with NC 50. Turn right on Six Forks Road (SR 1005), drive 3.1 miles to Possum Track Road (SR 2002), turn left (east), and go 2.4 miles to Raven Ridge Road. (Here, Raven Ridge Road is designated SR 2002 and Possum Track Road is SR 2062.) Turn right (south) on Raven Ridge Road and drive 1.5 miles to the trailhead on the left just before the bridge across the lake. The next trailhead is also on the left, 0.2 mile farther down Raven Ridge. The trailhead on the near side of the bridge will take you to the dead end of Possum Track Road. The trailhead on the far end will take you to the Tailrace Fishing Access Area.

This section of trail goes from Raven Ridge Road to the dead end of Possum Track Road. The west section has fewer lake views than the east section. You'll see many private homes and a lengthy chain-link fence marking the edge of private property. This is an easy-to-follow length of trail featuring an exceptionally pretty creek, a small waterfall in wet seasons, and a delightful grove of American holly and dogwood trees.

## Mileposts

**0.4 mile:** You'll cross a bridge.

**1.3 miles:** You'll cross a trail that veers right to the lake; to the left, it runs into private property.

**1.5 miles:** You'll cross a dam between the pond on the left and the lake on the right.

**1.7 miles:** A trail to the lake branches off to the right.

**1.9 miles:** You'll cross a creek. Falls Lake Trail continues on the opposite side. A second trail heads upstream and runs into private property.

**2.4 miles:** Falls Lake Trail intersects a trail that goes right to the lake and left into private property.

**2.5 miles:** The trail emerges into a small clearing. Turn left to reach Possum Track Road.

**2.6 miles:** You'll reach Possum Track Road. Turn left. The trail continues 10 yards ahead on the right.

## Neuse Bend Point Section (3)

**Length:** 2.9 miles
**Difficulty:** Moderate
**Blazes:** White
**Surface:** Natural
**Bicycles:** No
**Directions:** To reach the trailhead from Raleigh, take Falls of the Neuse Road north to Raven Ridge Road, turn left, and drive 3 miles to the intersection with Possum Track Road (SR 2062). The northern trailhead for the Honeycutt Creek section is 1.5 miles to the right at the dead end of Possum Track Road.

From Durham, go east on NC 98 for 1.6 miles from the intersection with NC 50. Turn right on Six Forks Road (SR 1005), drive 3.1 miles to Possum Track Road (SR 2002), turn left, and go 3.9 miles to where the road dead-ends. Note: You'll need to bear right at Bayleaf Church to continue on Possum Track Road.

This rolling woodland section of trail runs from the dead end of Possum Track Road to another point on the same road. It offers no lake views.

**0.3 mile:** The trail crosses a paved road.

**0.6 mile:** You'll cross a dirt road.

**1.2 miles:** You'll cross a wooden bridge over a creek. Soon, you'll have your first views of the lake since the trailhead.

**2.3 miles:** The trail crosses a creek, then turns right to run parallel to it.

**2.5 miles:** You'll cross a creek via a wooden bridge.

**2.9 miles:** The trail emerges onto Possum Track Road.

## Cedar Creek Section (4)

**Length:** 2.8 miles
**Difficulty:** Easy to moderate
**Blazes:** White
**Surface:** Natural
**Bicycles:** No
**Directions:** If you are coming from the trailhead on Possum Track Road, turn right and go 0.2 mile across the bridge. The next trailhead is on the same side of the road.

From Durham, go east on NC 98 for 1.6 miles from the intersection with NC 50. Turn right on Six Forks Road (SR 1005), drive 3.1 miles to Possum Track Road (SR 2002), turn left, and go 2.1 miles to the trailhead on the left just before the bridge. Note: You'll need to bear right at Bayleaf Church to continue on Possum Track Road.

From Raleigh, take Six Forks Road north to Bayleaf, turn right on Possum Track Road (SR 2002), and drive 2.1 miles to the trailhead on the left just before the bridge. Note: You'll need to bear right at Bayleaf Church to continue on Possum Track Road.

This section begins at Possum Track Road and runs to Bayleaf Church Road. Though much of the early part of the trail winds through a former clear-cut area, this is still one of the most beautiful and unique sections of Falls Lake Trail. In the spring when white dogwood blossoms still litter the path, pink and white mountain laurel begins to emerge all along the trail. You'll also encounter a beautiful stand of birches, some American holly groves, two creeks, and an old homesite. After about 1.5 miles, the trail skirts close enough to the shore to offer a good look at the lake.

### Mileposts

**0.4 mile:** The trail joins a larger logging road and winds through a clearing. Metal posts indicate the route.

**1.1 miles:** You'll cross a stream via a bridge.

**1.3 miles:** The trail crosses a wider trail, then forks. Take the right fork.

**1.5 miles:** A short trail to the lake forks right.

**1.7 miles:** The trail crosses a small seasonal creek.

**2.4 miles:** The trail crosses a bridge, then turns right.

**2.5 miles:** The trail crosses a small seasonal creek. Within 60 yards, a trail to the lake forks right. Falls Lake Trail continues left.

**2.8 miles:** The trail emerges at Bayleaf Church Road. It continues across the street. Walk straight across to the far section of the driveway loop. Just a few yards farther, the trail reenters the woods on the left.

## Loblolly Point Section (5)

**Length:** 1.2 miles
**Difficulty:** Easy to moderate
**Blazes:** White
**Surface:** Natural
**Bicycles:** No
**Directions:** From Raleigh, drive north on Six Forks Road, turn right on Possum Track Road (SR 2002), go 0.5 mile to Bayleaf Church Road (SR 2003), turn left, and drive 1 mile to the trailheads. The trailhead on the left takes you to Six Forks Road.

From Durham, go east on NC 98 for 1.6 miles from the intersection with NC 50. Turn right on Six Forks Road (SR 1005), drive 3.1 miles to Possum Track Road (SR

2002), turn left, go 0.5 mile to Bayleaf Church Road (SR 2003), turn left, and drive 1 mile to the trailheads. The trailhead on the left takes you to Six Forks Road.

This section goes from Bayleaf Church Road to Six Forks Road. It offers a few lake views, rolling hills, and a look at Lower Barton Creek, which is the dammed creek you cross between this section and the Blue Jay Point section.

## Mileposts

**130 yards:** You'll cross a small spring-fed creek.
**0.1 mile:** You'll cross a bridge over a creek.
**0.7 mile:** The trail crosses a rocky creek.
**1.1 miles:** You'll cross a rocky creek and a trail that heads right to the lake.
**1.2 miles:** The trail emerges at Six Forks Road. To continue on Falls Lake Trail, turn right and cross the bridge. The trail enters Blue Jay Point County Park. It is marked with a large wooden sign.

# Blue Jay Point Section (6)

**Length:** 3.4 miles
**Difficulty:** Moderate
**Blazes:** White
**Surface:** Natural
**Bicycles:** No
**Directions:** From Raleigh, take Six Forks Road north. The trailhead is on the right just beyond the first bridge over Falls Lake.

From Durham, go east on NC 98 for 1.6 miles past the intersection with NC 50 to Six Forks Road (SR 1005). Turn right on Six Forks and drive 1.6 miles to the trailhead, located on the left just before the second bridge over the lake.

This section of trail begins and ends on Six Forks

Road. Because it is easily accessed from the trails of Blue Jay Point County Park, this is the most visited section of Falls Lake Trail. The trail stays close to the shore for much of this route, providing many lake views. A profusion of wildflowers bloom here in spring. Benches are scattered along the trail within the county park's boundaries. Restrooms, water fountains, and vending machines are accessible by taking one of the trails heading to the parking lot.

## Mileposts

**75 yards:** You'll cross a bridge over a gully.

**0.1 mile:** You'll cross a small creek via a bridge.

**0.6 mile:** After some switchbacks, the trail crosses a bridge. Less than 100 yards later, it crosses another bridge.

**0.7 mile:** You'll cross Beaver Point Trail, the first trail in the Blue Jay Point County Park system. To the right, it heads to the lake. To the left, it heads to Azalea Loop Trail.

**1.0 mile:** You'll cross a creek via a bridge. Benches have been placed intermittently from here to the end of the trail.

**1.3 miles:** You'll cross the gravel Blue Jay Point Trail. To the right, it goes to the lake. To the left, it goes to playing fields.

**1.4 miles:** You'll cross a creek via a bridge. The trail forks. The right fork is Falls Lake Trail. The left fork is a red-blazed connector that follows a creek for just over 100 yards to one of the Blue Jay Point parking lots.

**1.5 miles:** The trail forks again. The right fork is Falls Lake Trail.

**1.6 miles:** The trail forks. To the left, Laurel Loop Trail heads to the playground. To the right Falls Lake Trail joins the yellow-blazed Laurel Loop. Go right. Forty yards later, the trail forks again. The right fork goes to the lakeshore. Continue left on Falls Lake Trail/Laurel Loop Trail.

**1.7 miles:** The two trails separate. Laurel Loop Trail forks to the left and Falls Lake Trail to the right.

**1.8 miles:** You'll cross a creek via a wooden bridge.

**1.9 miles:** You'll reach a T intersection and join the blue-blazed Sandy Point Trail. To the right, Sandy Point Trail heads to the lakeshore. Continue left on Falls Lake Trail and Sandy Point Trail.

**2.0 miles:** The trail intersects a driveway. Turn right and cross the driveway to continue on Falls Lake Trail.

**2.3 miles:** You'll cross two bridges over adjoining creeks.

**2.6 miles:** You'll cross a creek via a bridge. The trail forks 100 yards later. Falls Lake Trail continues straight ahead. To the right, a 200-yard trail leads to a scenic peninsula.

**2.7 miles:** You'll cross a creek via a bridge.

**3.1 miles:** You'll reach Six Forks Road. Turn right and cross the causeway to continue on Falls Lake Trail.

**3.4 miles:** You'll reenter the woods on a path to the right. (Note: the path here heads to the Barton Creek Boat Ramps' upper parking lot; it does not go along the lake shore.

## Upper Barton Creek Section (7)

**Length:** 2.3 miles
**Difficulty:** Easy
**Blazes:** White
**Surface:** Natural, asphalt, gravel
**Bicycles:** No
**Directions:** To reach the trailhead from Raleigh, take Six Forks Road north to the Upper Barton Creek Boat Ramps, located on the right. If you reach NC 98, you've gone too far.

From Durham, follow NC 98 for 1.6 miles past the intersection with NC 50, then turn right on Six Forks Road and go about 0.9 mile to the entrance to the Upper Barton Creek Boat Ramps, on the left.

This section of trail has a mixed surface. It sometimes travels on old roadbeds that can be exceptionally muddy in wet weather. You'll enjoy a couple of lake views near the beginning.

**0.0 mile:** If you're coming from the Blue Jay Point section, you'll begin at the first parking lot for the Upper Barton Creek Boat Ramps. After crossing the parking lot, you'll reenter the woods on an old roadbed.

**0.3 mile:** You'll cross a power cut.

**0.4 mile:** You'll cross two bridges.

**0.7 mile:** You'll cross a small seasonal creek. Bear right at the fork.

**0.8 mile:** You'll cross the power cut again and reenter the woods.

**1.0 mile:** After winding along the lakeshore, the trail turns right on a gravel road, then heads to the right along the power cut.

**1.7 miles:** You'll cross a creek.

**1.9 miles:** You'll cross a bridge.

**2.0 miles:** The trail turns right on an old road.

**2.1 miles:** The trail turns left onto a path.

**2.2 miles:** You'll emerge onto NC 98. To continue to the next section, head left along the road.

**2.3 miles:** When the guardrail ends, you'll need to cross NC 98; use extreme caution. You'll reenter the woods on a path to your right.

## Shinleaf Peninsula Section (8)

**Length:** 3.6 miles
**Difficulty:** Moderate
**Blazes:** White
**Surface:** Natural
**Bicycles:** No
**Directions:** From the intersection of NC 98 and NC 50, go east on NC 98 for 3.1 miles. The trailhead is on the left.

This section goes from NC 98 to New Light Road. If you hike only one section of Falls Lake Trail, make this it. This particularly beautiful part of the trail has rock outcroppings near streams and a deep ravine cut by a creek. You'll see laurel in the uplands, hundreds of ferns, and a few sizable beech trees in the bottoms. The trail passes through Shinleaf Recreation Area, which offers walk-in campsites, water, and restrooms. The Norwood family graveyard is on the trail just west of the Shinleaf parking lot.

## Mileposts

**0.1 mile:** The trail crosses a power cut.

**0.2 mile:** You'll cross an old road. The lakeshore is to your right. Although it's not visible from the trail, this section of the lake has a narrow sandy beach.

**0.3 mile:** You'll cross a seasonal creek via a bridge.

**0.5 mile:** You'll cross another seasonal creek via a bridge. About 100 yards later, you'll cross an old roadbed.

**0.7 mile:** You'll cross a seasonal creek via a bridge.

**0.8 mile:** You'll cross a creek.

**1.5 miles:** After crossing a creek, the trail descends two flights of wooden steps, then crosses a bridge over another creek.

**1.7 miles:** Falls Lake Trail continues straight ahead at the fork.

**1.8 miles:** You'll cross a small creek.

**2.3 miles:** You'll cross two creeks via a wooden bridge.

**2.7 miles:** You'll cross another creek.

**3.0 miles:** You'll emerge from the woods onto a gravel drive just off the Shinleaf Recreation Area parking lot. Turn left and cross the paved driveway to continue on the trail. Less than 75 yards after reentering the woods, you'll pass some graves. Just past the graves, the trail makes a 45-degree turn to the left.

**3.1 miles:** You'll cross a small creek.

**3.2 miles:** You'll cross a small seasonal creek.

**3.5 miles:** You'll cross an old roadbed.

**3.6 miles:** The trail ends at New Light Road. To continue on Falls Lake Trail, cross the road, turn right, and walk 0.1 mile to reenter the woods.

## Twin Creek Section (9)

**Length:** 0.5 mile
**Difficulty:** Easy to moderate
**Blazes:** White
**Surface:** Natural
**Bicycles:** No
**Map:** USGS Bayleaf
**Directions:** From the intersection of NC 50 and NC 98, go east on NC 98 for 1.6 miles to New Light Road (SR 1907). Turn left and drive 1 mile to the trailhead, located on the left. The trailhead is 0.3 mile beyond Shinleaf Recreation Area.

This short section of trail goes from New Light Road to Ghoston Road. It's a pleasant hike but doesn't warrant a visit by itself. The section has a couple of creeks, but the sound of traffic is persistent.

### Mileposts

**0.1 mile:** You'll cross a bridge.
**0.3 mile:** You'll cross another bridge.
**0.5 mile:** You'll reach Ghoston Road. To continue on Falls Lake Trail, cross the road and reenter the woods.

## Quail Roost Section (10)

**Length:** 2.7 miles one-way
**Difficulty:** Moderate
**Blazes:** White
**Surface:** Natural
**Bicycles:**: No
**Maps:** USGS Creedmoor, Bayleaf
**Directions:** From the intersection of NC 98 and NC 50, go east on NC 98 for 0.6 mile to Ghoston Road (SR 1908). Turn left and drive 0.8 mile to the trailhead, on the left. The trail will take you to NC 50.

This section goes from Ghoston Road to NC 50 and

the Falls Lake Information Center. Though it does not offer many views of the lake when the trees are in leaf— and what glimpses there are occur in the first mile—the trail is still appealing. At its best in the spring, it takes hikers through ferny bottom land and to a significant creek with a fine flat rock for picnicking. At times, it seems as if the trail parts a sea of chickweed.

## Mileposts

**0.4 mile:** You'll cross a creek over an earthen dam and pass a tiny pond.
**1.1 miles:** You'll cross a creek via a bridge.
**1.3 miles:** You'll pass a graveyard.
**1.5 miles:** You'll cross a clearing.
**1.6 miles:** The trail forks. Straight ahead is a road. Take the right fork to stay on Falls Lake Trail.
**1.7 miles:** The trail intersects a road and turns right.
**2.0 miles:** The trail forks. Take the left fork. A hundred yards later, it forks again. Falls Lake Trail continues right.
**2.1 miles:** The trail crosses a gravel road.
**2.3 miles:** You'll cross a paved road.
**2.5 miles:** You'll cross another paved road.
**2.7 miles:** You'll reach NC 50.

# Sandling Beach Recreation Area (fee area) ———

**Directions:** From Durham, go east on NC 98 (Wake Forest Road) to NC 50 (Creedmoor Road). Drive north on NC 50 for 4 miles.
From Raleigh, go north on NC 50 for 4 miles from the intersection with NC 98.

The many picnic tables and shelters and the absence of ramps for motorized boats define the character of this recreation area. The two hiking trails and the secluded picnic tables make peace and quiet a possibility even on weekends. Most of the shelters have restrooms, as does the beach, so if you like to hike but prefer to have a bathroom and a water fountain nearby, this is the place for you.

## Woodland Nature Trail

**Length:** 0.7 mile
**Difficulty:** Easy
**Blazes:** None
**Surface:** Natural
**Bicycles:** No

This loop interpretive trail has numbered observation stations.

## Lakeside Trail

**Length:** 1.7 miles
**Difficulty:** Easy
**Blazes:** None
**Surface:** Natural
**Bicycles:** No

This scenic trail will take you past several picnic shelters and innumerable secluded picnic tables. Views of the lake abound.

### Mileposts

**0.0 mile:** This trail is accessible from all the picnic shelters. Begin at the trailhead leading from the last parking lot, at the steps in the far left corner.
**0.1 mile:** You'll reach a fork. Take the right fork. The left fork goes 100 yards to a picnic shelter.
**0.3 mile:** You'll reach a fork. Take the right fork. The left fork goes 150 yards to a parking lot.
**0.5 mile:** You'll reach a parking lot. The trail continues on the other side of the shelter
**0.7 mile:** You'll cross a driveway.
**0.8 mile:** The trail reaches a sidewalk and continues on

N
W &#8596; E
S

Hwy 50

To Hwy 98
and Raleigh

Sandling Beach
Recreation Area

Falls
Lake

Woodland Nature Trail

| trail | |
| road | |
| creek | |

the other side, where it forks. The two paths rejoin near the restrooms adjacent to the swim beach.

**1.2 miles:** The trail forks again. The left branch passes picnic shelters. The right hugs the lakeshore.

**1.3 miles:** The trails rejoin.

**1.7 miles:** The trail ends at the parking area for Picnic Shelter 1.


## Beaverdam Recreation Area (fee area) _____

**Maps:** USGS Creedmoor; photocopied maps are occasionally available from area bike shops; the trianglemtb.com website has a map.

**Directions:** See the directions to Beaverdam in the Falls Lake section on page 428. Once past the gatehouse, take the first left, then the next left. You'll see a signboard at the trailhead on the left. Park in either of the two parking lots on the right.

The mountain biking trails at Beaverdam are the result of an agreement between the North Carolina Division of Parks and Recreation and the North Raleigh Mountain Biking Association. These trails include the first single track to be opened in any North Carolina state park. They are a pleasure to ride. The obstacles are widely spaced and never more than moderately difficult, though the trails are new and additional obstacles and technical challenges may be added. The elevation changes are moderate, making these trails easier than those at New Light and a good place for newcomers to hone their skills and get in shape. The recreation area includes a swimming beach and picnic tables. All in all, Beaverdam is a great place to spend the day.

As is the case with other actively managed mountain biking trails in the area, Beaverdam is closed when conditions are wet. Please call the Falls Lake office at 919-676-1027 to see if the trails are open.

A fee is charged for access to the recreation area.

## Outer Loop

**Length:** 2.6 miles
**Difficulty:** Easy to moderate
**Blazes:** Green
**Surface:** Natural
**Bicycles:** Yes

Though this is the most difficult of the three loops at Beaverdam, it has only a few moderately difficult obstacles and hills. It is heavily shaded throughout. Glimpses of the lake during the first third of the ride add scenic appeal.

### Mileposts

**0.0 mile:** Head right from the trailhead at the driveway.
**0.2 mile:** You'll pass the return loop on the left. You'll then cross a bridge and bear right.
**2.2 miles:** You'll cross a bridge. The Inner Loop joins the trail from the left.
**2.4 miles:** Turn right at the T intersection to return to the parking lot. The Inner Loop is to the left.
**2.6 miles:** You'll return to the trailhead.

## Inner Loop

**Length:** 1.6 miles
**Difficulty:** Easy to moderate
**Blazes:** Yellow
**Surface:** Natural
**Bicycles:** Yes

This is a shorter, easier version of the Outer Loop without the lake views.

### Mileposts

**0.0 mile:** Head right from the trailhead at the driveway.
**0.2 mile:** You'll pass the return loop on the left, then cross

a bridge. Continue straight at the fork. To the right is the Outer Loop.

**1.4 miles:** The trail joins the Outer Loop near the bridge. After the bridge, turn right to return to the parking lot.

**1.6 miles:** You'll reach the trailhead.

## West Loop

**Length:** 2.5 miles
**Difficulty:** Easy to moderate
**Blazes:** Red
**Surface:** Natural
**Bicycles:** Yes

Glimpses of an open field add visual interest to this brief creek-side loop.

### Mileposts

**0.0 mile:** Head left from the trailhead at the driveway. The first 0.2 mile of the trail has two-way traffic.

**0.2 mile:** You'll cross the second of two bridges, then begin the one-way loop to the right.

**1.5 miles:** You'll cross two bridges.

**1.6 miles:** You'll cross a small boardwalk.

**2.0 miles:** You'll cross a service road. Cyclists must stay on the trail.

**2.3 miles:** You'll reach the end of the one-way loop. Cross the bridges to return to the parking area.

**2.5 miles:** You'll return to the trailhead.

# New Light Mountain Bike Trails

**Maps:** USGS Creedmoor; free photocopied trail maps are available from most Raleigh-area bike shops; a permanent map is posted at the parking area; an on-line map is available at www.trianglemtb.com.

*New Light Mountain Bike Trails*

**Directions:** From Raleigh, take NC 50 (Creedmoor Road) north to the intersection with NC 98. From Durham, take NC 98 (Wake Forest Highway) east to the intersection with NC 50. From the intersection of NC 50 and NC 98, head east on NC 98 for 1.6 miles to New Light Road (SR 1907). Turn left, then take the first left onto Old Weaver Trail. Drive 0.5 mile to the parking area on the left.

Area mountain bikers are fortunate to have the New Light trails, located just a few minutes north of Raleigh. Developed by the North Raleigh Mountain Bikers Association—the same group that created the trails at Crabtree Park and Beaverdam—these trails are full of twists and turns without feeling cramped. And they're numerous enough that overcrowding is rarely a problem, even on busy weekends. Bikers enjoy plenty of hills and obstacles, as well as views of Falls Lake and the forests lining it. Most of these trails are unsuitable for beginners. The trails at Beaverdam Recreation Area and Lake Crabtree County Park are more gratifying to novices.

The New Light trails are definitely at their best in summer. Long stretches of both the trails and the fire roads become a soupy mess in wet weather. Most importantly, because these trails are built on North Carolina Wildlife Resources Commission land, hunters have priority in season. The area is open to mountain bikers only on Sundays during hunting season. Any abuse of the privilege of riding these trails will result in their closure. Please don't spoil the fun for everyone!

As this guide was going to press, the governing authorities were negotiating with local mountain bike enthusiasts to create a lasting memorandum of agreement that will give mountain bikers a voice in future logging and use decisions at New Light. Consult www.trianglemtb.com for updated information.

The system encompasses 10 named trails, but it's not necessary to keep track of which one you're on. Each trail is marked with a sign, and many intersections have signs with arrows pointing out the shortest route back to the parking lot. The various single-track trailheads are all off double-track fire roads that extend from the parking area on Old Weaver Road.

Each time you reach an intersection in New Light, it marks the end of the trail you're currently on and the beginning of a new named trail. Rather than listing Mileposts for each loop, directions to each trailhead and the distance of the loops are given below.

## First Loop

**Length:** 2.4 miles
**Difficulty:** Moderate
**Blazes:** None
**Surface:** Natural
**Bicycles:** Yes
**Directions:** The trailhead to the right of the parking lot.

In combination with the double track leading back to the parking lot, this trail makes an excellent introduction to the area. Riders encounter a few creek crossings on bridges and moderate elevation gain and loss. The hills are more strenuous if you begin the ride at the trailhead nearest the parking lot.

The trail forks at the end of First Loop. You can keep right to return to the parking area or go left to access the Lake Downfall and Route 66 Trails.

## Lake Downfall Trail

**Length:** 0.6 mile
**Difficulty:** Easy
**Blazes:** None
**Surface:** Natural
**Bicycles:** Yes
**Directions:** Bear right at the first fork in the fire road. Bear right at the second fork and again at the third. The Lake Downfall trailhead is 0.1 mile after the third fork.

This short and easy (when dry) loop rewards riders with some lake views. It becomes a tire-sucking mess in wet weather.

## Route 66 Trail

**Length:** 1.4 miles
**Difficulty:** Moderate
**Blazes:** None
**Surface:** Natural
**Bicycles:** Yes
**Directions:** To reach the Route 66 trailhead, bear right at the first fork in the fire road. You'll reach the second fork after 0.6 mile. You can access one trailhead by going right for 0.4 mile, or you can continue straight at the fork (choose the middle path) for 0.2 mile.

This trail has rocks, roots, gullies, obstacles, and significant elevation changes.

## Sig's Loop

**Length:** 2.1 miles
**Difficulty:** Moderate to strenuous
**Blazes:** None
**Surface:** Natural
**Bicycles:** Yes
**Directions:** See directions for The Gauntlet below.

This challenging trail offers a couple of lake views and lots of fun! Most of the obstacles have trails built around them, for those who aren't feeling particularly ambitious.

## The Gauntlet

**Length:** 1.6 miles
**Difficulty:** Moderate to strenuous
**Blazes:** None
**Surface:** Natural
**Bicycles:** Yes
**Directions:** To reach the trailhead, take the right fork of the fire road. You'll reach the next fork after 0.6 mile. Take the far left fork. After 0.3 mile, the trailhead for The Gauntlet is on the left and the trailhead for Sig's Loop is on the right.

The Gauntlet will take you near the highest point in the New Light trails. It has many obstacles, including a rock outcropping near the summit and a death-defying hill that can be circumvented via a gentler route.

## Easy Street

**Length:** 0.7 mile
**Difficulty:** Strenuous
**Blazes:** None
**Surface:** Natural
**Bicycles:** Yes
**Directions:** There are two trailheads for this trail. The first is to the right off the fire road very near the parking area. To reach the second trailhead, take the right fork of the fire road 0.2 mile after the first right fork.

Contrary to its name, this trail is neither easy nor streetlike. It packs many tight turns and small obstacles into a short distance.

## Way In Way Out

**Length:** 1 mile
**Difficulty:** Moderate
**Blazes:** None
**Surface:** Natural
**Bicycles:** Yes
**Directions:** There are three trailheads for this trail. To reach the one closest to the parking area, follow the right fork of the fire road. The trailhead is 0.2 mile past the fork near Easy Street. To reach the other two trailheads, follow the left fork of the fire road. The first trailhead is on the left 0.25 mile past the fork. The second is on the left 0.8 mile past the fork.

This trail roughly parallels the left fork of the fire road. It makes for a fun, challenging alternative to Eastern Territories.

## Eastern Territories

This set of trails is comprised of Left Loop and Right Loop. Left Loop is accessible directly from the fire road. These trails are relatively easy for New Light, having few obstacles and long straightaways.

## Left Loop

**Length:** 1.9 miles
**Difficulty:** Easy to moderate
**Blazes:** None
**Surface:** Natural
**Bicycles:** Yes
**Directions:** To reach the trailhead, follow the left fork of the fire road. The first trailhead is on the left 0.3 mile after the fork. The second is on the left 0.8 mile after the fork.

## Right Loop

**Length:** 1.9 miles
**Difficulty:** Easy to moderate
**Blazes:** None
**Surface:** Natural
**Bicycles:** Yes
**Directions:** Follow the directions to the first trailhead for Left Loop. Follow Left Loop 0.6 mile to the trailhead for Right Loop.

# William B. Umstead State Park

**Address:** Park Office, 8801 Glenwood Avenue, Raleigh, NC 27612
**Telephone:** 919-571-4170
**Hours:** The gate is open from 8 A.M. to 6 P.M. from November to February; from 8 A.M. to 7 P.M. during March and October; from 8 A.M. to 8 P.M. during April, May, and September; and from 8 A.M. to 9 P.M. from June through August. The visitor center is open Monday through Friday from 8 A.M. to 5 P.M.
**Maps:** USGS Raleigh West, Cary; free park maps are available at the visitor center.
**Directions:** To reach the Crabtree Creek Section from I-40 East, take the I-540/US 70 exit (Exit 283). Go 4.3 miles and take Exit 4A (US 70 East). After 0.7 mile, you'll merge onto US 70 East. Drive 1 mile past the Angus Barn restaurant and turn right into the park entrance. The visitor center is 0.9 mile ahead on the right.

To reach the Reedy Creek Section, take I-40 to Harrison Avenue (Exit 287). Turn north onto Harrison Avenue and drive straight into the park.

In recent years, William B. Umstead State Park has come to be considered the central park of the Triangle. Its 5,500 protected acres are bordered by Raleigh-Durham International Airport, US 70, and I-40. Increasingly dense development has turned the park into an oasis of natural eastern Piedmont habitat.

*William B. Umstead State Park*

As the forests and creeks around the park have been disturbed by construction, the water quality of the park's streams has suffered. In 1999, William B. Umstead State Park was recognized as one of 52 urban parks in the nation seriously threatened by development. An organization called the Umstead Coalition acts as a watchdog group for the park and leads many guided hikes.

Unlike most parks in the state parks system, Umstead has no dominant geographic attraction. No mountain range, large lake, or river defines its character. Instead, it is typical of the second-growth forests in the area. There has been controversy in recent years about whether to keep Umstead's mission as it is—that is, to let it function as a preserve where nature has the land on its own terms. Continued management under existing priorities will give visitors an incredible opportunity to find peace on a secluded trail, to watch a beaver, or to look for tree frogs in their natural habitat.

The virgin trees in what would become William B. Umstead State Park were logged in the late 18th and 19th centuries. Prior to settlement, the land was home to a massive oak-hickory forest where bison, bobcats, and elk roamed. Now, the forests are in various stages of succession, the process by which fields return to woodland. Some forests consist mainly of tall pines. Others are dominated by hardwoods. There are pockets of laurel and rhodo-dendron as well.

The park has two particularly noteworthy areas. One is a 50-acre stand of possibly virgin Southern sugar maples and beeches growing along Crabtree Creek. This area has been recognized by the United States Department of the Interior in the National Registry of Natural Landmarks. Its official name is the Piedmont Beech Natural Area. Access to it is by permit only. The other is the Crabtree Slopes Natural Area, located on the south side of Crabtree Creek. Mountain laurel grows in abundance on these north-facing slopes.

Although some animals in Umstead may have suffered due to development around the park, beavers still inhabit the streams, as do a variety of fish, including green sunfish and largemouth bass. Several species of salamanders are present, including four-toed salamanders. Toads and frogs such as spring peepers can be heard. The park has a population of wild turkeys. Other birds include pine warblers, red-eyed vireos, and wood thrushes. Raccoons, opossums, foxes, squirrels, bobcats, and deer also make their home within the park's boundaries.

In the years before and during European settlement, Native Americans lived in this area, which was situated between two important trade routes. To the north lay the Occoneechee Trail (see the section on Eno River State Park) and to the south the Pee Dee Trail. The first European settlers arrived in this area after 1774, when land grants permitted homesteading in what would become Wake County.

William B. Umstead State Park's genesis came during the New Deal, when a federal agency called the Resettlement Administration purchased exhausted farmland along Sycamore Creek. The government intended to show that even land abused for many decades could eventually heal itself and become a valuable recreational resource. The families who lived within the new park's boundaries were paid for their land. The houses and farm buildings were demolished, though many of the foundations and chimneys remain. In 1938, the Civilian Conservation Corps (CCC) began constructing lakes, roads, camps, and picnic shelters. The architecture of many of the park's structures is typical of CCC projects of the period.

When World War II began, the federal government's attention was drawn elsewhere. In 1943, it sold about 5,000 acres to

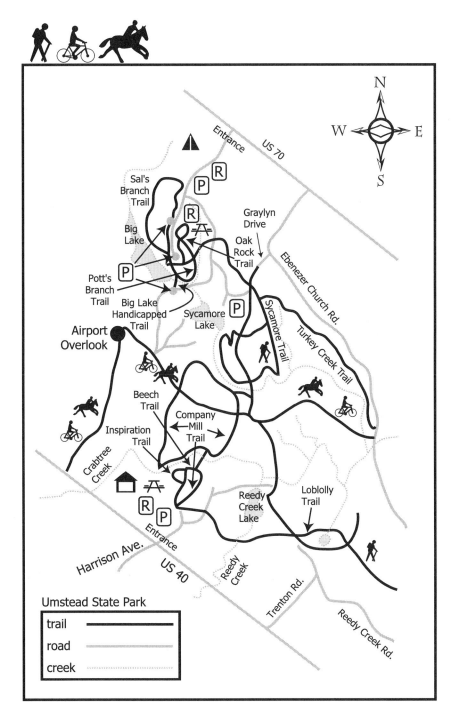

Umstead State Park

| trail | —————— |
| road | ~~~~~~~~~ |
| creek | ............ |

N
W
E
S

Entrance
US 70

Sal's
Branch
Trail

Big
Lake

R
P
R

Graylyn
Drive

Oak
Rock
Trail

Pott's
Branch
Trail

Big Lake
Handicapped
Trail

Sycamore
Lake

P

Ebenezer Church Rd.

Turkey Creek Trail

Sycamore Trail

Airport
Overlook

Beech
Trail

Company
Mill
Trail

Inspiration
Trail

Crabtree
Creek

R
P

Reedy
Creek
Lake

Loblolly
Trail

Harrison Ave.

Entrance

US 40

Reedy
Creek

Trenton Rd.

Reedy Creek Rd.

the state of North Carolina for one dollar. Crabtree Creek State Park was born. The following years saw more changes. Segregationists divided the park into two sections in 1950. Reedy Creek State Park, for black North Carolinians, was created from 1,234 acres, while Crabtree Creek State Park was open for whites only. In 1955, the name of the park was changed to honor former governor William B. Umstead, a conservationist who was a great friend to the state parks system. Finally, in 1966, the period of lawful segregation ended, and the Reedy Creek and Crabtree Creek Sections were united and opened to the use of all North Carolinians.

# Reedy Creek Section _____

## Company Mill Trail

**Length:** 5.2 miles
**Difficulty:** Easy to moderate
**Blazes:** Orange squares
**Surface:** Natural
**Bicycles:** No

This trail gets its name from the remains of a mill built by the Page family in the early 1800s. At the site, you can see what is left of the dam. The old millstone lies beside the trail. This vibrant mill was an economic and social center for the area in the 19th century. Now, the creek's many large, flat rocks make this a great spot for picnicking.

Company Mill Trail offers a chance to explore fern-lined creeks through bottom lands. Quartz sparkles on the trail as it ascends to the ridge line. Other highlights include a bridge across Crabtree Creek and piles of rock left by farmers in the 19th and early 20th centuries. You'll see spectacular pines, oaks with leaves as long as your forearm, and scrubby areas that have fallen victim to the Southern pine beetle.

**0.0 mile:** The trail begins behind the picnic shelter just inside the Reedy Creek entrance.

**0.3 mile:** You'll cross the creek. Continue straight over the bridge.

**0.6 mile:** You'll reach the steps to a bridge across Crabtree Creek. The remains of the mill are to the right after the bridge. Go left, heading upstream.

**0.9 mile:** You'll cross a bridge over a tributary of Crabtree Creek.

**2.1 miles:** You'll cross Bike and Bridle Trail.

**2.8 miles:** The trail reaches some switchbacks.

**3.2 miles:** You'll see the remnants of an old dam on the opposite side of the river. A hundred yards farther, you'll reach a junction with a spur trail leading to Sycamore Trail. Continue right.

**3.6 miles:** The trail intersects Bike and Bridle Trail. Turn right off the trail and walk 60 yards on the road, then turn left into the woods.

**4.5 miles:** You'll pass the Company Mill millstone. The remains of the dam are just upstream.

**4.6 miles:** You'll return to the metal bridge.

**5.2 miles:** You'll return to the shelter.

## Inspiration Trail

**Length:** 0.5 mile round-trip
**Difficulty:** Easy
**Blazes:** Blue diamonds
**Surface:** Natural
**Bicycles:** No

This nature trail has interpretive signs and several benches. Although this is a short, easy hike, the trail is rocky and uneven, and sturdy footwear is a good idea. The beautiful quartz-strewn path sparkles underfoot.

**0.0 mile:** Begin the trail just behind the picnic shelter on the north side of the parking area in the Reedy Creek Section.

**0.2 mile:** Follow the loop to the left.

**0.3 mile:** Keep right at the fork to return to the parking lot.

**0.5 mile:** You'll return to the picnic shelter.

## Loblolly Trail

**Length:** 2.6 miles, plus about 3.5 miles of city greenways beyond the park boundary (see page 261)
**Difficulty:** Moderate
**Blazes:** White
**Surface:** Natural
**Bicycles:** Yes

Loblolly Trail begins at the Reedy Creek parking lot in William B. Umstead State Park and ends in the vicinity of Old Trinity Road near Carter-Finley Stadium. Parking is also available at the RBC Center (see page 261). As with many trails in the Piedmont, Loblolly has a few rough spots where weather and pine beetles have left their mark. Its least scenic stretches within the park are between the Reedy Creek parking lot and the creek itself, but don't let this disenchant you with what is one of the most scenic trails in the park. Loblolly Trail offers bridged stream crossings, a sandy bank along Reedy Creek, and an opportunity to observe a still woodland pond. Those who prefer loop hikes will be pleased to learn that this trail crosses Bike and Bridle Trail twice.

Beyond the park boundary, the trail crosses Richland Creek, skirts the edge of a lake, and follows Richland Creek through the scenic Carl A. Schenck Memorial Forest, offering a view of I-40 before it ends near the RBC Center.

## Mileposts

**0.8 mile:** You'll cross a bridge over Reedy Creek.

**1.1 miles:** The trail climbs over a ridge to a second stream. Keep right at the fork immediately after the stream crossing.

**1.7 miles:** You'll cross Bike and Bridle Trail.

**2.1 miles:** You'll reach a pond. A trail circles the shore.

**2.5 miles:** You'll reach an intersection with Bike and Bridle Trail.

**2.6 miles:** The trail ends at the park boundary.

# Crabtree Creek Section

## Bike and Bridle Trail

**Length:** 14.1 miles, including the airport overlook spur
**Difficulty:** Moderate to strenuous
**Blazes:** Red circles
**Surface:** Gravel
**Bicycles:** Yes
**Directions:** Enter the Crabtree Creek Section off US 70. Stop at the visitor center and pick up a free map on your way in, then follow the road past the camping area.

This trail—really a gravel road that passes through the more secluded areas of the park—is perhaps the only state park trail with an airport overlook. The sound of air traffic is nearly constant. The views include the dam at the north end of Reedy Creek Lake.

Please exercise caution, as this trail is used by bicyclists and equestrians as well as hikers.

## Mileposts

**0.0 mile:** Begin at the horse trailer parking area in the Crabtree Creek section. To reach the parking area, follow the signs for the youth camp to Sycamore Road. The parking area is at the end of the road past the lodge.

**0.1 mile:** You'll reach an intersection with the main trail. Turn right. To the left, the trail continues for 0.3 mile before ending at Graylyn Road.

**0.9 mile:** You'll pass the first intersection with Sycamore Trail.

**1.3 miles:** After passing the second intersection with Sycamore Trail, you'll cross a stone bridge over Sycamore Creek. The first intersection with Company Mill Trail is just beyond the bridge.

**1.6 miles:** Bike and Bridle Trail forks left and right. Go right; the trail is an out-and-back hike, unless you form a loop using roads outside the park. If you decide to head left, skip to Milepost 7.3.

**1.7 miles:** You'll cross Company Mill Trail.

**2.4 miles:** You'll cross Company Mill Trail again.

**3.2 miles:** You'll reach the airport overlook. Bike and Bridle Trail turns left.

**4.4 miles:** You'll reach the end of this section of Bike and Bridle Trail, the park boundary, and Reedy Creek Park Road. Turn around and retrace your route to the airport overlook.

**5.6 miles:** Turn right back at the airport overlook.

**7.2 miles:** You'll return to the fork at Milepost 1.6. Keep right.

**7.3 miles:** The trail forks again into the two arms of the loop. Head left.

**8.8 miles:** After crossing Sycamore Creek, you'll reach the park boundary and Ebenezer Church Road. To continue the loop, turn right and ride beside the road for 0.5 mile until you reach the next leg of the trail.

**9.3 miles:** Turn right into the park.

**10.0 miles:** After making a sharp right turn, you'll cross Loblolly Trail.

**10.5 miles:** You'll pass a short dirt road that connects to Reedy Creek Road.

**10.9 miles:** You'll pass Loblolly Trail.

**11.5 miles:** You'll reach a fork. The left fork ends at the trailhead beside the ranger station. Go right.

**12.4 miles:** You'll return to the fork at Milepost 7.3. Follow the left fork around the loop.
**12.5 miles:** You'll return to the fork at Milepost 7.3. Follow the right fork.
**14.1 miles:** You'll return to the fork at Milepost 0.1. Turn left to return to the Crabtree Creek horse trailer parking area. The left fork leads to Graylyn Road.

## Turkey Creek Trail

**Length:** 2.4 miles
**Difficulty:** Moderate
**Blazes:** Red and silver reflectors
**Surface:** Crushed stone
**Bicycles:** Yes

This trail is one of the most appealing in the park, offering significant elevation changes, a rocky creek, and a few exceptional woodland views. Turkey Creek is a good trail for hikers, cyclists, and equestrians.

### Mileposts

**0.0 mile:** The trail begins 0.5 mile past the Graylyn Drive entrance off Ebenezer Church Road. The trailhead is on the left.
**0.5 mile:** You'll cross Turkey Creek via a bridge.
**2.4 miles:** You'll reach the end of the trail and Ebenezer Church Road.

## Sycamore Trail

**Length:** 6.5 miles
**Difficulty:** Moderate
**Blazes:** Blue triangles
**Surface:** Natural
**Bicycles:** No
**Directions:** To walk the entire trail, park in the lot for Big Lake. From the Crabtree Creek entrance, follow Umstead Parkway. When the road forks, bear right. Park in the

last parking lot. If you'd like to hike just the southern section, you can park at the horse trailer lot and begin at Milepost 1.4. If you want to hike only the lower section of Sycamore Trail, it can be accessed from the Bike and Bridle Trail parking lot. To reach that parking lot, turn off US 70 onto Umstead Parkway. A sign at the far end of the parking lot points toward Bike and Bridle Trail.

The northern end of this loop follows rolling terrain through stands of mature hardwoods and holly trees. The trail also passes an old homestead complete with a wisteria grove that is spectacular in late spring. But because wisteria is a highly invasive nonnative species that destroys native plants and trees, Umstead officials are working toward removing this plant from the park. The wisteria grove, located near the graveyard at the 1.4-mile mark, was a character in the Clyde Edgerton novel *Floatplane Notebooks*.

In addition to immortalized plants, the trail offers footbridges and lovely views of Sycamore Creek. If you fancy a back-country picnic, the southern end of the trail has boulders, small rapids, and a beautiful stone bridge at Milepost 4.5.

## Mileposts

**0.0 mile:** The trailhead is beside Shelter 1.
**0.3 mile:** You'll cross a bridge.
**0.4 mile:** You'll cross a stone bridge and a gravel road.
**0.8 mile:** You'll cross a road.
**1.4 miles:** You'll pass a power line and cross Bike and Bridle Trail.
**2.0 miles:** The loop begins. Go right.
**2.3 miles:** The trail reaches another intersection with Bike and Bridle Trail, then descends some switchbacks to Sycamore Creek.
**3.3 miles:** You'll cross Bike and Bridle Trail again.
**4.4 miles:** You'll cross a bridge.
**4.6 miles:** You'll return to the start of the loop. Keep left.

**5.2 miles:** You'll cross Bike and Bridle Trail.
**5.8 miles:** You'll cross a road.
**6.2 miles:** You'll cross a road.
**6.5 miles:** You'll return to the trailhead.

## Oak Rock Trail

**Length:** 0.6 mile
**Difficulty:** Easy
**Blazes:** White squares
**Surface:** Natural
**Bicycles:** No

You'll find some interpretive signs for unexpected trees along this nature trail, as well as the usual signs for white oaks and red maples. The trail provides access to a pleasant serpentine section of creek and a look at an enormous American beech. To reach the trailhead from the visitor center, continue straight on Umstead Parkway, keep right at the fork, and park in the first parking lot.

### Mileposts

**0.0 mile:** The trailhead is in the northern corner of the parking lot.
**0.3 mile:** You'll pass a stone CCC dam.
**0.6 mile:** You'll return to the parking lot.

## Pott's Branch Trail

**Length:** 1.3 miles round-trip
**Difficulty:** Easy to moderate
**Blazes:** Orange diamonds
**Surface:** Natural
**Bicycles:** No

Pott's Branch is an easy woodland trail that offers access to Big Lake and some creek-side strolling. The forest includes tall pines and bottom-land hardwoods. Highlights include the confluence of two small creeks and an old stone CCC dam. This walk is especially appealing in April when the dogwoods are still in flower and the laurel along the creek begins to bloom. To reach the trailhead from the visitor center in the Crabtree Creek section, continue on Umstead Parkway, keep right at the fork, and park in the farthest lot.

## Mileposts

**0.0 mile:** The trailhead for Pott's Branch and Sal's Branch is in the far right corner of the parking lot and is clearly marked. After 100 yards, Pott's Branch Trail heads left before the first stairstep.

**0.2 mile:** To the right is a short spur trail that follows Sycamore Creek as it flows between Big Lake and Sycamore Lake.

**0.6 mile:** You'll reach a bridge at the intersection with the blue-blazed Sycamore Trail. Pott's Branch Trail continues straight. You can head back to the parking lot by turning left on Sycamore Trail.

**0.8 mile:** You'll pass a CCC dam.

**0.9 mile:** Pott's Branch intersects a paved trail at a wheelchair-accessible observation deck.

**1.1 miles:** After the trail winds through a picnic area, you'll see the parking lot. Pott's Branch continues left and joins the paved trail.

**1.2 miles:** Sycamore Trail goes straight. Pott's Branch Trail continues right.

**1.3 miles:** You'll return to the parking lot. The trailhead where you began is directly ahead.

## Sal's Branch Trail

**Length:** 2.9 miles
**Difficulty:** Moderate
**Blazes:** Orange circles
**Surface:** Natural
**Bicycles:** No

Sal's Branch Trail offers numerous footbridges, ferny bottom lands, pine forests, and a brief view of Big Lake. You'll hear some traffic noise from US 70 at the northern end of the trail.

## Mileposts

**0.0 mile:** Begin at the trailhead, located at the edge of the woods behind the visitor center. The trail forks immediately after entering the woods. Head right. After 100 yards, you'll cross Bike and Bridle Trail before crossing several bridges.

**0.4 mile:** The spur trail to the campground is to the right.

**0.7 mile:** You'll cross a bridge.

**0.9 mile:** You'll cross another bridge.

**1.2 miles:** You'll cross a maintenance road.

**1.3 miles:** You'll cross a bridge.

**1.4 miles:** The trail emerges from the woods onto a dirt road above Big Lake.

**1.5 miles:** Turn left to reenter the woods and continue on Sal's Branch Trail.

**2.1 miles:** You'll cross a maintenance road.

**2.4 miles:** You'll cross a bridge.

**2.6 miles:** After crossing a bridge, you'll return to the first fork below the visitor center. The parking lot is to your right.

# Blue Jay Point County Park

Blue Jay Point County Park's chief draw is Falls Lake Trail. Directions to the trailhead and a trail description are on pages 196-98.

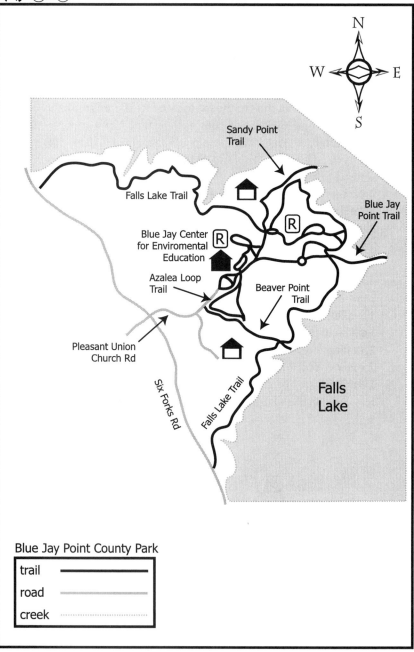

Sandy Point
Trail

Falls Lake Trail

Blue Jay
Point Trail

Blue Jay Center
for Enviromental
Education

Azalea Loop
Trail

Beaver Point
Trail

Pleasant Union
Church Rd

Six Forks Rd

Falls Lake Trail

Falls
Lake

N

W   E

S

Blue Jay Point County Park

| trail | ——————— |
| road | |
| creek | ·················· |

# Carl A. Schenck Memorial Forest

**Address:** Department of Forestry, College of Natural Resources, Campus Box 8002, Raleigh, NC 27695
**Telephone:** 919-515-2891
**Hours:** Sunrise to sunset
**Maps:** USGS Raleigh West
**Directions:** From I-40, take the Wade Avenue exit (Exit 289). Follow Wade Avenue to the Blue Ridge Road exit. Turn left on Blue Ridge Road, drive 0.5 mile to Reedy Creek Road, turn left, and go 0.9 mile to the sign for the forest. Turn left onto the gravel road and go 0.1 mile to the gate. Park on the side of the road without blocking the gate.

The 260-acre Carl A. Schenck Memorial Forest is owned and managed by North Carolina State University. The Department of Forestry uses the land as a living laboratory to study the benefits and consequences of various forest management techniques. The forest is dominated by loblolly pines, although you'll also find young hardwoods and acres of lush ferns in the bottom lands of Richland Creek and its tributaries. The forest's one loop trail, Frances Liles Interpretive Trail, will take you through pine forests of dramatically different characters. Some segments of the forest have been heavily managed by controlled burns to keep the understory open. Other sections have been allowed to undergo natural succession, and the understory is a tangled mass of competing flora. The forest also contains experimental pines—combinations of different species grafted together in an attempt to grow straighter trees for use as timber. Informational signs point out interesting aspects of the forest and its management.

Birders will find Schenck a delight, as its variety of forest and field habitats supports a diverse mix of avian life. To preserve the birds' presence, the university enforces a strict leash regulation for all dogs in the forest. Unleashed dogs have done significant harm to ground-nesting birds. Anyone walking an unleashed dog can expect a citation from police patrolling the forest to protect the birds.

Like its neighbor William B. Umstead State Park, Carl A. Schenck

Memorial Forest was the victim of the poor farming practices prevalent in the late 19th and early 20th centuries. Before the university acquired it in the late 1930s, the land was part of the state-run Camp Polk Prison Farm. Soil depletion and erosion had left the land in terrible condition in 1938 when the North Carolina Division of Forestry planted the now-towering loblollies that stand along the first section of Frances Liles Interpretive Trail.

Originally called Richland Creek Forest, this land was renamed Carl A. Schenck Memorial Forest in honor of Dr. Carl Alwin Schenck, the founder of the Biltmore Forest School, our nation's first school of forestry.

## Frances Liles Interpretive Trail

**Length:** 1.3 miles, plus 0.2 mile on a gravel road
**Difficulty:** Easy
**Blazes:** Yellow
**Surface:** Natural and gravel
**Bicycles:** No

This rewarding trail is named after Frances L. Liles, who worked as an administrative assistant in the North Carolina State University School of Forest Resources for 25 years.

### Mileposts

**0.0 mile:** Begin by walking down the gated gravel road. The trailhead is on the right about 100 feet from the gate.
**0.4 mile:** You'll cross a bridge.
**0.5 mile:** You'll cross a bridge.
**0.6 mile:** You'll cross another bridge.
**0.7 mile:** You'll cross a bridge.
**0.8 mile:** You'll reach an intersection with Loblolly Trail. Frances Liles Interpretive Trail continues left.
**1.1 miles:** The trail reaches a fork. Continue left.
**1.2 miles:** You'll reach the end of the trail. Turn left onto the gravel road to return to the parking area.
**1.4 miles:** You'll pass a picnic shelter.
**1.5 miles:** You'll return to the gate.

# Durant Nature Park

**Address:** 8305 Camp Durant Road, Raleigh, NC 27614
**Telephone:** 919-870-2871
**Hours:** 8 A.M. to sunset
**Maps:** See map of trails on page 260.
**Directions:** To reach the north entrance from US 1 (Capital Boulevard) north of Raleigh, turn onto Durant Road. After 1.1 miles, turn left on Camp Durant Road and drive to the parking lot. The northern trailheads for all three hiking trails are off this parking lot.

Durant Nature Park's primary mission is to serve as a local center for environmental education. Though the 4 miles of foot trails and the couple of miles of gravel road open to hikers and bicyclists are significantly less crowded than those of William B. Umstead State Park and Lake Crabtree Park, they do come with glimpses of commercial and residential areas. An old homestead and other evidence of the park's human history add a layer of interest to its recreational opportunities. The park's two small lakes and rock-strewn creeks add scenic appeal and provide homes for a variety of amphibians and fish. Beavers are also occasionally spotted in Durant.

## Border Trail

**Length:** 2.3 to 2.5 miles, which includes 1.9 miles for the trail plus the loop and 0.4 mile to 0.6 mile to return to your car
**Difficulty:** Easy
**Blazes:** Wooden blocks decorated by a pink lady's-slipper wildflower
**Surface:** Natural
**Bicycles:** No
**Directions:** The trailhead branches off the small road in the northwest corner of the parking lot, located on the right as you drive into the park.

As this trail's name suggests, a significant part of its length runs along the park's border. Views of suburbia abound on the northern half of the trail along Reedy Branch. That said, Border Trail offers plenty of chances to explore the scenic branch. It also has a bridged crossing of Simms Branch, views of Blind Water Lake, and an old farmhouse. Reedy Branch boasts an appealing rapid named Whale Rocks. The trail takes you past an amphitheater and the Ponderosa Farmstead to Beaver Pond Overlook on Blind Water Lake, where great birding opportunities abound.

## Mileposts

**0.0 mile:** Begin at the northern parking lot. After just a few yards on a dirt road, the path leading to Border Trail forks right.

**0.1 mile:** You'll reach a fork. Border Trail goes right.

**0.2 mile:** You'll reach Reedy Branch. Turn left at Secret Rock Falls. A city greenway is on the other side of the creek.

**0.6 mile:** Keep right at the fork.

**0.7 mile:** You'll cross a bridge.

**0.8 mile:** You'll cross Simms Branch via a bridge.

**0.9 mile:** You'll come to a T intersection. Follow the blazes to the right.

**1.0 mile:** You'll cross a bridge.

**1.2 miles:** You'll cross another bridge.

**1.3 miles:** You'll pass an amphitheater at the ruins of an old chimney shortly before coming to the Ponderosa Farmstead.

**1.4 miles:** You'll reach the Beaver Pond Overlook before crossing a creek. Border Trail joins one of the park's interior roads. From this point on, the road is gravel and is open to bikes.

**1.5 miles:** You'll reach a T intersection. To the left is Lakeside Trail; a left turn leads 0.4 mile on the gravel road back to the northern parking lot. Go right and follow the short loop back to the Ponderosa Farmstead.

**1.6 miles:** The road forks. Turn right. The left fork ends at the park boundary.

**1.9 miles:** You'll return to the fork near the Ponderosa Farmstead sign. The fork you took to start this small loop is on your right now. Continue straight to retrace your steps along Reedy Branch and back to the parking lot, or go right to the intersection near the dam and the Lakeside trailhead.

## Lakeside Trail

**Length:** 0.9 mile plus 0.4 mile to return to the parking lot
**Difficulty:** Easy
**Blazes:** Wood blocks with blue lakes
**Surface:** Gravel, asphalt, and natural
**Bicycles:** No
**Directions:** The trailhead branches off the small road in the northwest corner of the parking lot, located on your right as you drive into the park.

This trail takes you around the quiet shores of Blind Water Lake. It offers views of the lake and the attractive buildings along its shore.

### Mileposts

**0.0 mile:** Begin at the trailhead at the southern end of the dam on Blind Water Lake. You'll cross a stream after 100 yards.
**0.2 mile:** The trail turns left. To the right is an old barn roof.
**0.3 mile:** You'll reach a T intersection with a dirt trail within view of Sawmill Lake. Go right along the lakeshore.
**0.4 mile:** You'll cross a creek and then arrive at an intersection. Both forks head toward the main park road near the south parking lot. Go left on the gravel road. At the next intersection, which lies just over 100 yards ahead, you'll see the dam at the eastern edge of Sawmill Lake, picnic shelters, and a basketball court. The trail goes left across the dam.
**0.5 mile:** On the other side of the dam, turn left at the

intersection with the paved Lakeside Trail. The gravel road leads to the northern parking area.

**0.6 mile:** The trail intersects one of the gravel park roads just past the changing rooms. Continue straight along the shore. On the right after less than 100 yards is the turn-off to the training lodge; this road also goes 0.2 mile to the northern trailhead for Lakeside Trail and the northern parking lot.

**0.8 mile:** You'll cross a bridge just before reaching the log house and shelters that form the campsite.

**0.9 mile:** You'll cross a wooden bridge just below the dam for Blind Water Lake. At the top of the hill, you'll reach a T intersection with the gravel road leading over the dam. The trailhead you started on is 100 yards to the left. The northern parking lot is 0.4 mile to the right along the gravel road.

## Secret Creek Trail

**Length:** 0.5 mile
**Difficulty:** Easy
**Blazes:** Pairs of navy-blue footprints
**Surface:** Natural
**Bicycles:** No
**Directions:** The trailhead is beyond the southeast corner of the parking lot on the gated gravel road just past the park office. In all, this trail has three trailheads located on the east side of the main road leading south from the northern parking lot.

This short, woodsy trail has a scenic spot or two.

### Mileposts

**0.0 mile:** Begin beside the gate separating the northern parking lot from the main road.

**0.1 mile:** The trail forks. Secret Creek Trail goes right.

**0.5 mile:** The trail emerges from the woods between the restrooms and the Sweet Gum Shelter. A trailhead for Secret Creek is on the north side of the Sycamore Shelter.

# Lake Johnson Park

**Address:** 4601 Avent Ferry Road, Raleigh, NC 27606
**Telephone:** 919-233-2121
**Hours:** Sunrise to sunset
**Map:** USGS Raleigh West
**Directions:** From I-40/I-440, take the Gorman Street exit (Exit 295) and turn north on Gorman Street. Go 1.3 miles, turn left on Avent Ferry Road, and drive 1.7 miles to the small parking lot and boathouse on the left just before the bridge. An additional parking lot is across the lake.

The web of wooded trails surrounding scenic Lake Johnson includes a paved trail where pedestrians and cyclists can enjoy each other's company. A more solitary network of dirt trails goes from the lake to the paved trail and beyond, linking Lake Johnson Park to the neighborhoods surrounding it. The trails also connect with the city's greenways system, so the lake can serve as a stop on a longer adventure or as a destination in its own right. Lake Johnson's special attractions include a 1,000-foot boardwalk that spans the lake and connects the north shore and boathouse to the south shore and the boat rental and launch facility.

## Lake Johnson Trail, Paved Section

**Length:** 3 miles
**Difficulty:** Easy to moderate
**Blazes:** Signposts with mileage
**Surface:** Asphalt
**Bicycles:** Yes

This paved, wooded path is open to cyclists and pedestrians. It begins at the parking lot on the southern shore of the lake and winds around the eastern and northern shores before ending at the boathouse and boardwalk. The

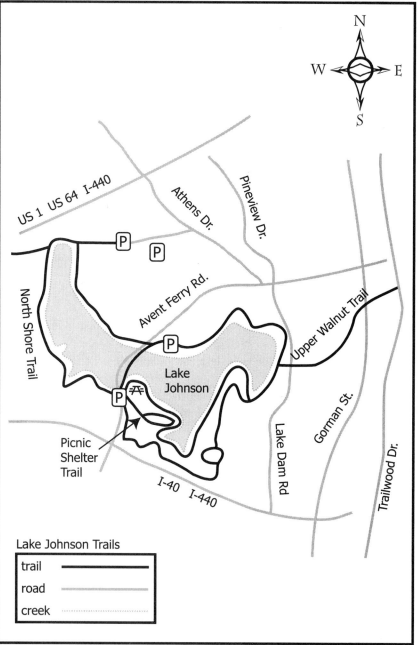

N
W —&#9673;&#8594; E
S

US 1  US 64  I-440

Athens Dr.

Pineview Dr.

P

P

North Shore Trail

Avent Ferry Rd.

Upper Walnut Trail

P

Lake Johnson

P

Picnic
Shelter
Trail

I-40  I-440

Lake Dam Rd

Gorman St.

Trailwood Dr.

Lake Johnson Trails

| | |
|---|---|
| trail | ─────── |
| road | ─────── |
| creek | ········ |

*Lake Johnson*

route offers ample shade and several lake views. A few branches of the trail are located in the south section of the park. The Mileposts below describe the longest possible (outermost) trail. Note that you'll intersect many green-blazed dirt trails. These are a network of shorter paths running from the lake up to the paved trail and beyond to the neighborhoods around the park.

## Mileposts

**0.0 mile:** Begin at the paved path at the south end of the southern parking lot. You'll reach a T intersection after 75 yards. Go right. A left turn leads toward the bridge over the lake.

**0.1 mile:** On the right is a short paved path to Avent Ferry Road.

**0.7 mile:** You'll reach another T intersection. You can go in either direction, since this is a loop that merges into a single trail. Head north at the next intersection to continue around the lake.

**1.7 miles:** The trail forks just before the bridge leading to the dam. The left fork continues across the dam and around the lake. The right fork leaves the Lake Johnson property and becomes Upper Walnut Trail. Go left.

**2.7 miles:** You'll reach the boathouse and boardwalk adjacent to Avent Ferry Road. The trail continues around the lake on the other side of Avent Ferry Road and eventually leads back to the southern parking lot (see North Shore Trail on page 241). For the shortest route to the southern parking lot, go 0.2 mile across the bridge.

**3.0 miles:** You'll reach the parking lot on the south side of the lake.

## Picnic Shelter Trail

**Length:** 0.3 mile
**Difficulty:** Easy
**Blazes:** None
**Surface:** Asphalt
**Bicycles:** Yes

This short, easy trail heads to one of the most scenic public picnic shelters in the Piedmont. Swimming is not allowed.

### Mileposts

**0.0 mile:** Begin at the south-shore parking lot and take the trail at the end of the lot farthest from the lake. After 75 yards, head left at the T intersection.
**0.1 mile:** You'll reach a second fork. Head left.
**0.2 mile:** You'll reach a T intersection. The picnic shelter is a few yards to the left, toward the lake.
**0.3 mile:** You'll arrive at the shelter.

## Lakeshore Trail

**Length:** 1.6 miles
**Difficulty:** Moderate to strenuous
**Blazes:** Two different blazes are used. You'll see green dots, but note that all the unpaved trails in the park are blazed green, so the trails you intersect that head up to the paved trail and beyond also have green blazes. The main trail around the lake is marked by white bars.
**Surface:** Natural
**Bicycles:** Yes

This trail is half a world away from the paved trail just a few feet up the hill. Narrow, winding, and lightly traveled, it's actually a network of trails, small loops, and forks that go back and forth between the lakeside trail and the paved path above. If you wish to take the most direct route, keep bearing left once you pass the picnic shelter.

This trail has wildlife and poison ivy. It is popular with mountain bikers, so hikers should keep their eyes open.

## Mileposts

**0.0 mile:** Begin at the paved path that starts at the south end of the southern parking lot. You'll reach a T intersection after 75 yards. Go right. A left turn leads toward the bridge over the lake.

**0.1 mile:** The trail goes right along the lakeshore and winds behind the picnic shelter. You'll follow the lakeshore from this point.

**0.5 mile:** The waterside trail intersects the paved path at the picnic shelter along the lakeshore. The white bar blazes begin here.

**1.6 miles:** You'll reach an intersection with the paved trail. If you continue left, you'll reach the dam at 1.85 miles.

## North Shore Trail

**Length:** 2 miles
**Difficulty:** Easy on north shore, moderate to strenuous on south shore
**Blazes:** Green
**Surface:** Wood chips, natural, and boardwalk
**Bicycles:** Yes

This trail begins as a wide, easy, mulch-lined greenway. After it crosses the bridge and the boardwalk behind Athens Drive High School, it becomes a network of thinner, more difficult, potentially more rewarding trails. A note to mountain bikers: The trails on the southern end of this network run through a marshy area and are frequently closed to mountain bikers. If conditions are soupy, stick to higher, drier ground.

## Mileposts

**0.2 mile:** A trail branches right to a neighborhood.
**0.3 mile:** A dirt-and-grass trail branches off to right and heads 0.3 mile to the back of the Lake Johnson pool. Continue straight.
**0.4 mile:** A trail branches right to a solitary picnic table.
**0.6 mile:** The dirt trail reaches a T intersection with a paved trail. To the left is a boardwalk. Cyclists should be careful at the boardwalk, since there are steps at the end of it. Go left. To the right, the trail goes 0.2 mile to a parking area off Athens Drive.
**0.9 mile:** A series of dirt trails branches right to an apartment complex.
**1.2 miles:** You'll cross a creek, where the trail forks. The left fork goes onto a peninsula. Follow the right fork, which continues around the lake. A couple of short loops diverge from the main trail, then rejoin it. None is longer than 0.3 mile.
**1.4 miles:** You'll cross a bridge.
**2.0 miles:** You'll reach Avent Ferry Road. The parking lot is across the street.

*Lake Lynn*

# Lake Lynn

**Directions, Address, and Telephone:** See Raleigh Bike Routes, page 327.
**Hours:** Sunrise to sunset
**Maps:** USGS Bayleaf, Raleigh West

## Lake Lynn Trail

**Length:** 2.2 miles
**Difficulty:** Easy
**Blazes:** Mileage markers
**Surface:** Asphalt
**Bicycles:** Yes
**Directions:** From I-540, take the US 70 East exit (Exit 4A). You'll intersect Aviation Parkway/Westgate Drive, then merge onto US 70 East. About 3.1 miles after the intersection with Aviation Parkway/Westgate Drive, turn left on Lynn Road. About 1.2 miles later, you'll pass the intersection with Leesville Road. The turnoff to the parking area is 0.1 mile ahead on the left.

Lake Lynn was created by damming Hare Snipe Creek. It is an ideal destination for lovers of walks amid

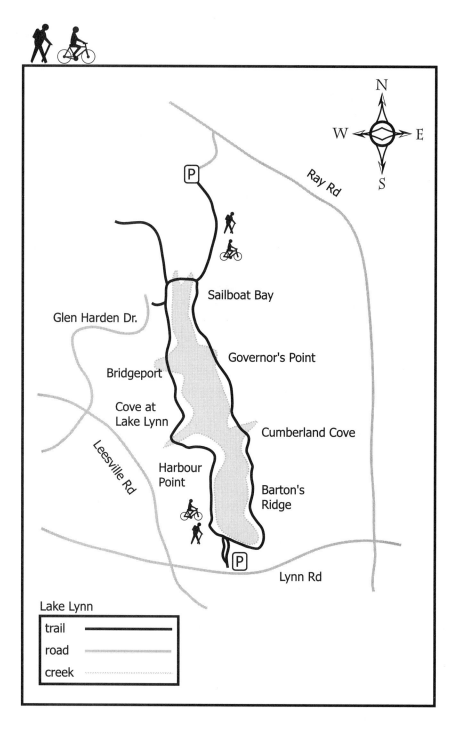

N
W   E
S

Ray Rd

P

Sailboat Bay

Glen Harden Dr.

Governor's Point

Bridgeport

Cove at
Lake Lynn

Cumberland Cove

Leesville Rd

Harbour
Point

Barton's
Ridge

P

Lynn Rd

Lake Lynn

| | |
|---|---|
| trail | |
| road | |
| creek | |

well-landscaped civilization. Though nothing about this trail is suggestive of a back-country experience, exceptional wildlife viewing opportunities are available for those who prefer not to get their feet wet. The wonderfully scenic trail that surrounds the lake is a mixture of winding pavement and boardwalks, including one that takes visitors through the marsh at the north end of the lake. Many birds frequent the marsh. Inquisitive ducks and geese may approach as you reach the water's edge.

Residential areas have been built on all but the north side of Lake Lynn. Many of these neighborhoods have incorporated their own landscaping with that of the park. An exercise trail with marked stations winds through one of the communities on the east side. A well-designed dock is on the west shore.

Lake Lynn is not the place to go to get away from your fellow humans. Even at midday during the week, plenty of friendly folks can be found walking, skating, and cycling around the lake. However, if you enjoy the company of your own species, if you prefer pavement to the mere possibility of poison ivy, and if you harbor a desire to see a duck fish for dinner, you'd be hard-pressed to find a more beautiful place in Raleigh.

## Mileposts

---

**0.0 mile:** The trail begins beside the dam at the south side of the lake. Head right. Less than 100 yards from the parking lot, the trail forks. Turn right and walk across the dam.

**0.2 mile:** The trail turns left and heads up the east shore.

**0.25 mile:** The trail forks. The right fork is one end of the 0.4-mile exercise trail.

**0.4 mile:** You'll reach the other end of the exercise trail beside the gazebo.

**0.5 mile:** You'll cross Hare Snipe Creek.

**1.1 miles:** The trail follows the bridge to the left. After just a few yards, you can continue across the lake or veer right and go 0.3 mile to Ray Road. Continue left.

**1.2 miles:** The trail forks. The right fork is a short trail into a residential area. The left fork is the continuation of Lake Lynn Trail.

**2.2 miles:** You'll complete the loop at the western edge of the dam near the parking area.

# North Carolina Museum of Art Park

**Address:** North Carolina Museum of Art, 2110 Blue Ridge Road, Raleigh, NC 27699
**Telephone:** 919-839-6262
**Hours:** The park closes at sunset.
**Directions:** From I-40, take the Wade Avenue exit (Exit 289). Follow Wade Avenue to the Blue Ridge Road exit. Turn left onto Blue Ridge Road, drive 0.5 mile to the entrance to the North Carolina Museum of Art, follow the signs to the parking lot, walk past the main entrance to the building, and continue up the hill toward Blue Ridge Road.

Here's your chance to see how a well-placed sculpture can add to a landscape. As you make your way past the museum's outdoor entertainment complex and around the curve into the meadow beyond, it becomes clear that Museum Park Trail is a great place to stroll.

At 163 acres, the museum has some space to work with, and its plans are ambitious. In addition to the existing paved trail, a natural-surface foot trail is planned that may ultimately cross the beltline via a pedestrian bridge to connect to North Carolina State University and to the west Raleigh greenways system. The North Carolina Department of Transportation has begun construction of a greenway to connect Museum Park Trail to William B. Umstead State Park and the Cary greenways system. When this work is completed, North Carolina Museum of Art Park will be a hub connecting two of the Triangle's most extensive greenways systems.

The park's land is primarily pasture for grazing NCSU's cattle. A small stream, House Creek, runs through the wooded bottom land. Forest and wetlands restoration projects have the potential

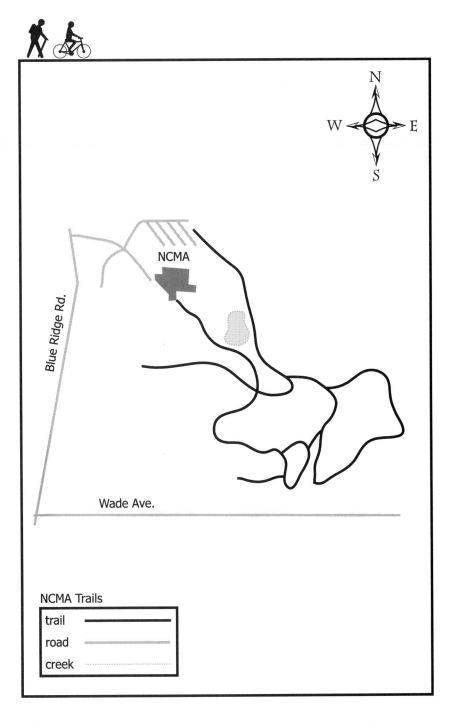

NCMA

Blue Ridge Rd.

Wade Ave.

NCMA Trails

| | |
|---|---|
| trail | —————— |
| road | —————— |
| creek | ·················· |

to transform the land into a beautiful natural area. The museum has teamed with ecologists at NCSU who oversee environmental management of the park. Plans are in the works to enhance the natural experience by using the foot trail as a setting for experimental sculpture.

## Museum Park Trail

**Length:** 0.9 mile
**Difficulty:** Easy
**Blazes:** Mileage markers
**Surface:** Asphalt
**Bicycles:** Yes

This trail is a great addition to the museum. The outdoor sculpture is reason enough to get out and stretch your legs. The 10-foot-wide paved trail is completely wheelchair accessible.

If you finish the trail and want to keep going, you can cross Blue Ridge Road near the museum entrance and walk 0.9 mile down Reedy Creek Road to Carl A. Schenck Memorial Forest. Cyclists might find Museum Park Trail a nice addition to William B. Umstead Park's Bike and Bridle Trail, 2.2 miles from the museum entrance on lightly traveled and largely unpaved Reedy Creek Road.

### Mileposts

**0.0 mile:** Begin at the upper visitor parking lot. Follow the sidewalk past the main entrance to the museum and then up the hill.

**0.2 mile:** On the left is the entrance to Museum Park Trail closest to Blue Ridge Road. The greenway continues straight ahead 100 yards to the intersection of Blue Ridge and Reedy Creek Roads. Continue left.

**0.8 mile:** You'll cross the driveway beside the lower parking lot and picnic area.

**0.9 mile:** The paved trail ends just below the upper parking lot.

*Raleigh Greenways*

# Raleigh Greenways

**Address:** Box 590, Raleigh, NC 27602
**Telephone:** 919-890-3285
**Maps:** A free color map of the city giving general location information for the greenways system is available from the Raleigh Parks and Recreation Department. You can call the office or pick one up in the Municipal Building downtown. The USGS maps needed to view the entire system include Cary, Raleigh East, Raleigh West, and Wake Forest.

## Crabtree and Leadmine Greenways

The greenways along Crabtree and Leadmine Creeks in north Raleigh offer a taste of what the future could hold if Triangle cities continue their pursuit of a comprehensive system of interconnected greenways. Here, it is possible to enjoy a scenic, peaceful journey of several miles without sharing your space with motor vehicles. More importantly, these urban trails allow cyclists and pedestrians to get from neighborhoods inside the beltway west to the Crabtree Valley Mall area and beyond, or north past Shelley Lake as far as Sawmill Road—all without taking much of a risk of becoming roadkill. The greenways provide direct access to parks and residential neighborhoods. In addition, daily commuters can use them and help keep cars off Raleigh's clogged thoroughfares. Some trails, such as the new Crabtree Valley Trail, which crosses US 70, make it possible to use human power to access places that were previously difficult to negotiate without a motor vehicle.

## North Hills Trail

**Length:** 1 mile
**Difficulty:** Easy down, moderate up
**Surface:** Asphalt
**Bicycles:** Yes
**Directions:** The most convenient entrance to North Hills Trail is through North Hills Park near the tennis courts. The park is immediately north of I-440. To reach it, take the Six Forks Road/North Hills exit (Exit 8) off I-440. Take the first left after the mall onto Lassiter Mill Road, drive 0.3 mile, and turn right on Currituck Road. You'll see a sign for North Hills Park on the left.

North Hills Trail provides access to Alleghany Trail and Ironwood Trail (which, in turn, leads to the Shelley Lake trails). It travels through woods and along the banks of both Crabtree Creek and Leadmine Creek and offers a look at their confluence. Once you get down to the creek, the trail is flat, but getting back up the hill will certainly get your heart pumping.

## Alleghany Trail

**Length:** 2.4 miles
**Difficulty:** Easy
**Surface:** Asphalt
**Bicycles:** Yes

Alleghany Trail passes through pleasant neighborhoods and Drewry Hills Park as it follows Crabtree Creek from North Hills Trail to Anderson Drive near the intersection with Oxford Road. You can continue on Fallon Creek Trail across Anderson Drive to Kiwanis Park.

This trail is worth a visit even if you aren't on your way somewhere else. In addition to a lovely, tree-lined urban trail system, Alleghany provides access to the Lassiter Mill site, the preserved millstone, and the Great Falls of Crabtree (relative to the size of Crabtree Creek, the falls actually do qualify as "great"). In 1908, Cornelius Jesse Lassiter bought this land and put up a gristmill that, like the old pump station in Eno River State Park, was a popular place for summer fun in the days before air conditioning. This was also the site of the last steel-truss bridge in Wake County. The bridge was removed in 1984.

## Crabtree Valley Trail

**Length:** 1 mile
**Difficulty:** Easy
**Surface:** Asphalt
**Bicycles:** Yes

This greenway provides access to Crabtree Valley Mall. By the time this guide is available, the trail will be extended. The new Crabtree-Oak Park Trail will follow Crabtree Creek for another 1.5 miles. In the near future, the proposed Crabtree Duraleigh Trail will extend west to Ebenezer Church Road, making a greenway link possible between Raleigh proper and the William B. Umstead State Park trails.

## Fallon Creek Trail

**Length:** 0.5 mile
**Difficulty:** Easy
**Surface:** Asphalt
**Bicycles:** Yes
**Directions:** Parking is available on Noble Road near the intersection with Hawes Court.

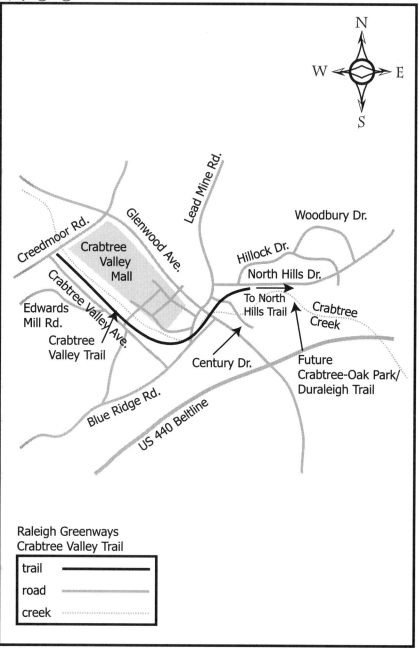

Woodbury Dr.

Hillock Dr.

North Hills Dr.

Crabtree Creek

Lead Mine Rd.

Glenwood Ave.

Creedmoor Rd.

Crabtree Valley Mall

Crabtree Valley Ave.

Edwards Mill Rd.

Crabtree Valley Trail

To North Hills Trail

Century Dr.

Future Crabtree-Oak Park/ Duraleigh Trail

Blue Ridge Rd.

US 440 Beltline

N
W E
S

Raleigh Greenways
Crabtree Valley Trail

| trail | ———— |
| road | ———— |
| creek | ·········· |

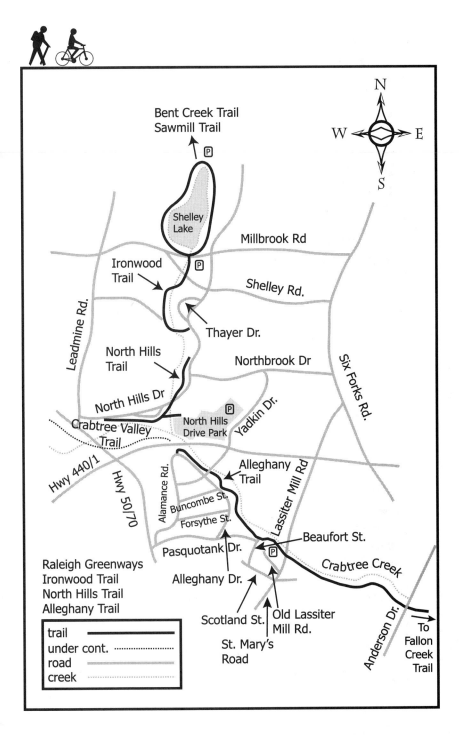

Bent Creek Trail
Sawmill Trail

N
W E
S

Shelley Lake

Millbrook Rd

Ironwood Trail

Shelley Rd.

Leadmine Rd.

Thayer Dr.

North Hills Trail

Northbrook Dr

Six Forks Rd.

North Hills Dr

Yadkin Dr.

Crabtree Valley Trail

North Hills Drive Park

Alleghany Trail

Lassiter Mill Rd

Hwy 440/1

Hwy 50/70

Alamance Rd.

Buncombe St.

Forsythe St.

Beaufort St.

Crabtree Creek

Pasquotank Dr.

Raleigh Greenways
Ironwood Trail
North Hills Trail
Alleghany Trail

Alleghany Dr.

Scotland St.

Old Lassiter Mill Rd.

St. Mary's Road

Anderson Dr.

To Fallon Creek Trail

| trail | ———— |
| under cont. | ·············· |
| road | ———— |
| creek | ············ |

This short paved trail goes across Fallon Creek and alongside Crabtree Creek. It passes a truly remarkable river birch near the bridge at the confluence of the two creeks. By the time this guide is available, the trail will continue southeast to Buckeye Trail and northwest to Alleghany Trail.

## Buckeye Trail

**Length:** 2.5 miles
**Difficulty:** Moderate
**Surface:** Asphalt
**Bicycles:** Yes
**Directions:** This greenway can be accessed from Milburnie Road west of the intersection with New Bern Avenue, from Crabtree Boulevard near the intersection with Raleigh Boulevard, or from the playground near Crabtree Boulevard and Culpepper Lane.

This appealing east Raleigh greenway meanders along Crabtree Creek. It offers great views of the creek and the bottom-land flood plains, a bluff-top walk, and one of the steepest hills of any greenway in the Triangle.

## Ironwood Trail

**Length:** 1.3 miles
**Difficulty:** Easy
**Surface:** Asphalt
**Bicycles:** Yes
**Directions:** From the north, Ironwood Trail is just off the parking lot for Shelley Lake. The trail has two additional entrances—one across North Hills Drive from the end of North Hills Trail and the other south of the intersection of North Hills Drive and Thayer Drive.

This quiet, wooded greenway offers two scenic bridges and views of Leadmine Creek. It connects North Hills Trail with the Shelley Lake trail system.

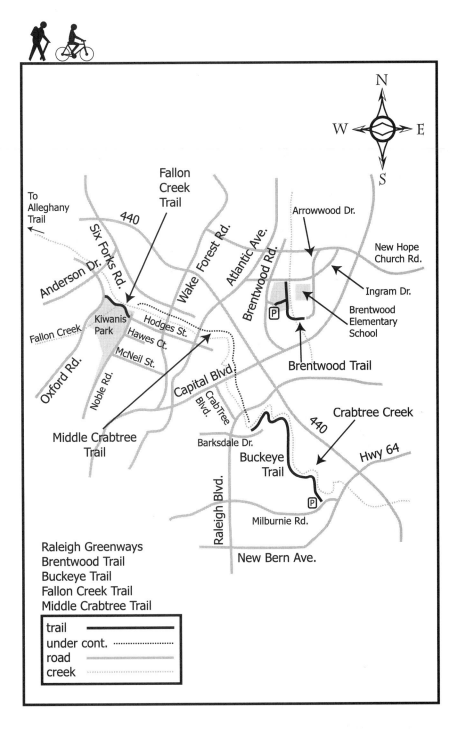

N
W ← → E
S

To Alleghany Trail ←

440

Six Forks Rd.

Anderson Dr.

Fallon Creek Trail

Wake Forest Rd.

Atlantic Ave.

Brentwood Rd.

Arrowwood Dr.

New Hope Church Rd.

Ingram Dr.

P

Brentwood Elementary School

Fallon Creek

Kiwanis Park

Hodges St.

Hawes Ct.

McNeil St.

Oxford Rd.

Noble Rd.

Capital Blvd.

CrabTree Blvd.

Brentwood Trail

Middle Crabtree Trail

Barksdale Dr.

Buckeye Trail

440

Crabtree Creek

Hwy 64

Raleigh Blvd.

P

Milburnie Rd.

New Bern Ave.

Raleigh Greenways
Brentwood Trail
Buckeye Trail
Fallon Creek Trail
Middle Crabtree Trail

| trail | ——— |
| under cont. | ········· |
| road | |
| creek | ········· |

## Shelley Lake Trail

**Length:** 3 miles
**Difficulty:** Easy
**Surface:** Asphalt
**Bicycles:** Yes
**Directions:** The parking lot for Shelley Lake Sertoma Park is on Millbrook Road 0.25 mile west of the intersection with North Hills Drive. Begin your walk at the intersection with Ironwood Trail in the southwest corner of the park, just past the parking lot below the dam.

This trail circles Shelley Lake in north Raleigh. Shelley Lake was created by damming Leadmine Creek. At the headwaters on the north end of the lake is a marshy area with many shoreline plants and an abundance of bird life to reward quiet observers. Those who prefer a loftier viewpoint will enjoy the wooden observation deck on the southwest shore. Boats are available to rent on weekends during the warm months.

With cooperation between the city of Raleigh and Wake County, the Shelley Lake Trail system could extend north to Falls Lake Trail. Citizen interest might someday extend Falls Lake Trail west to Eno River State Park in Durham.

## Lake Park Trail

**Length:** 0.6 mile
**Difficulty:** Easy
**Surface:** Natural
**Bicycles:** Yes

This natural-surface trail visits a particularly scenic spot on the creek that features flat rocks and long, gentle falls.

## Bent Creek Trail

**Length:** 1.3 miles

**Difficulty:** Easy
**Surface:** Asphalt
**Bicycles:** Yes
**Directions:** Bent Creek Trail may be accessed from Shelley Lake Trail. It crosses North Hills Drive just north of the intersection with North Cliff Drive. The northern terminus is at the intersection of Bent Creek and Longstreet Drives.

This paved trail passes some scenic spots along Leadmine Creek, including a fine grove of river birch trees on either side of Lynn Road. A short dirt section of trail follows the bank of the creek between North Hills Drive and Lynn Road.

## Snelling Branch Trail

**Length:** 0.7 mile
**Difficulty:** Easy
**Surface:** Asphalt
**Bicycles:** Yes
**Directions:** Access is from Shelley Lake Trail, Optimist Park, and Dixon Drive.

This greenway follows Snelling Branch. A playground is located at the entrance on Dixon Drive.

## Sawmill Trail

**Length:** 0.9 mile
**Difficulty:** Easy
**Surface:** Natural
**Bicycles:** Yes
**Directions:** This trail can be accessed from Bent Creek Trail or Sawmill Road just west of Brandywine Court.

This dirt trail follows a tributary of Leadmine Creek. Quite scenic in spots, it includes three creek crossings via bridges.

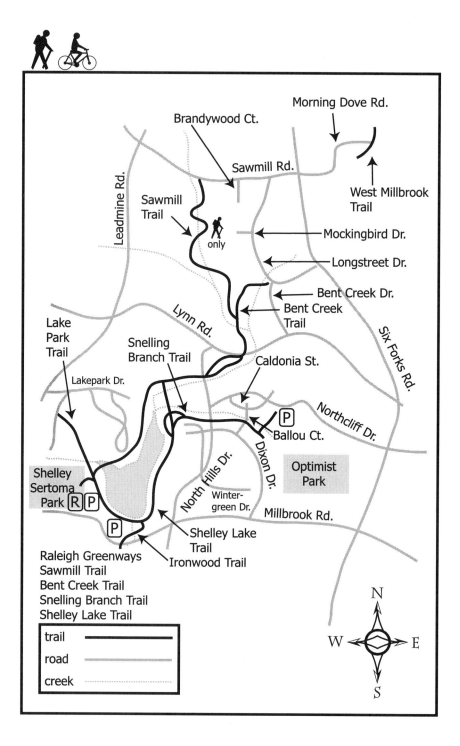

Morning Dove Rd.

Brandywood Ct.

Sawmill Rd.

Leadmine Rd.

Sawmill
Trail

only

West Millbrook
Trail

Mockingbird Dr.

Longstreet Dr.

Bent Creek Dr.

Bent Creek
Trail

Lynn Rd.

Lake
Park
Trail

Snelling
Branch Trail

Caldonia St.

Six Forks Rd.

Lakepark Dr.

Northcliff Dr.

P

Ballou Ct.

Shelley
Sertoma
Park    R  P

North Hills Dr.

Dixon Dr.

Optimist
Park

P

Winter-
green Dr.

Millbrook Rd.

Shelley Lake
Trail

Ironwood Trail

Raleigh Greenways
Sawmill Trail
Bent Creek Trail
Snelling Branch Trail
Shelley Lake Trail

| trail | ——— |
| road | ——— |
| creek | ········ |

N
W    E
S

## Durant Trail

**Length:** 1.1 miles
**Difficulty:** Easy
**Surface:** Asphalt and gravel
**Bicycles:** Yes
**Directions:** The eastern terminus is on Cub Trail about a block south of the intersection with Durant Road. Durant Nature Park has plenty of parking. From the northern parking lot, the greenway intersects Camp Durant Road just down the hill beside the creek.

This pleasant paved trail offers woods, a creek, and an uninterrupted look at suburbia. It winds back and forth across Reedy Branch along the edge of Durant Nature Park from Hiking Trail Road to the Windsor Forest neighborhood, where it meets a short private paved trail. Durant Trail is well used by area families and offers good access to the creek.

## Falls River Trail

**Length:** 1.1 miles
**Difficulty:** Easy
**Surface:** Asphalt
**Bicycles:** Yes
**Directions:** This greenway crosses Falls River Avenue at its intersection with Summerton Drive.

Falls River Trail is sandwiched between a small creek and the back of a row of houses.

## Upper Walnut Trail

**Length:** 1.1 miles
**Difficulty:** Easy
**Surface:** Asphalt
**Bicycles:** Yes
**Directions:** See map of and directions to Lake Johnson Park on pages 237-42. Parking is available on Lake Dam Road just below the Lake Johnson dam.

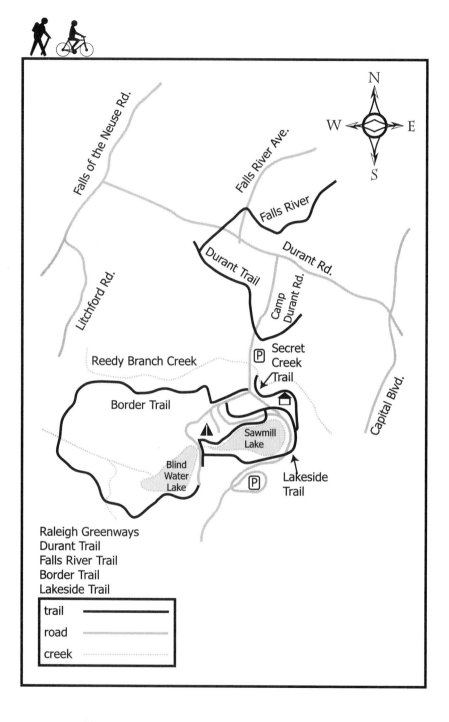

Raleigh Greenways
Durant Trail
Falls River Trail
Border Trail
Lakeside Trail

| trail | ——————— |
| road | ——————— |
| creek | ·················· |

This paved trail passes through a flood plain where mature hardwoods provide ample shade, wooden bridges offer views, and spring wildflowers combine with the sound of Walnut Creek to create a thoroughly enjoyable greenway experience.

## Neuse River Trail

**Length:** 4 miles
**Difficulty:** Moderate
**Surface:** Dirt, gravel, and pavement
**Bicycles:** Yes
**Directions:** From the intersection of US 64 and New Hope Church Road, head north on New Hope Church Road for 1 mile. Turn right on Southall Road, drive 0.8 mile, turn right on Castlebrook Drive, go 0.5 mile, turn right on Abington Drive, and continue to the parking lot. Parking is also available on Rogers Lane south from US 64 to Anderson Point Park.

This trail is on the eastern edge of Raleigh in an area that is experiencing rapid development. It is one of Raleigh's most interesting greenways because the Neuse River is visible for most of the trail's length. Other than the wooded 0.25 mile at its northern end and a short section that runs through a marsh, the trail itself is an unremarkable dirt road. However, the river and marsh—full of birds, frogs, salamanders, and solitude—are worth the trip. When plans to extend this trail are completed, it will offer nearly uninterrupted access to the river.

## Loblolly Trail

**Length:** 6 miles
**Difficulty:** Easy
**Blazes:** White in William B. Umstead State Park, yellow in Carl A. Schenck Memorial Forest
**Surface:** Natural
**Bicycles:** No
**Directions:** Ample parking is available near the RBC Center. From Wade Avenue, take the Edwards Mill Road exit.

*Jordan Lake*

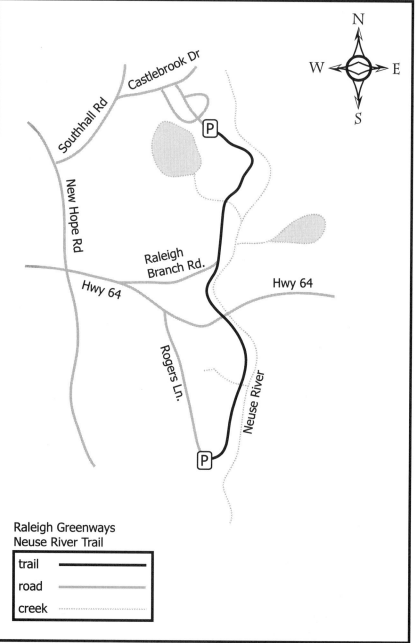

Southhall Rd

Castlebrook Dr

New Hope Rd

P

Raleigh
Branch Rd.

Hwy 64

Hwy 64

Rogers Ln.

Neuse River

P

N
W E
S

Raleigh Greenways
Neuse River Trail

| trail | |
|---|---|
| road | |
| creek | |

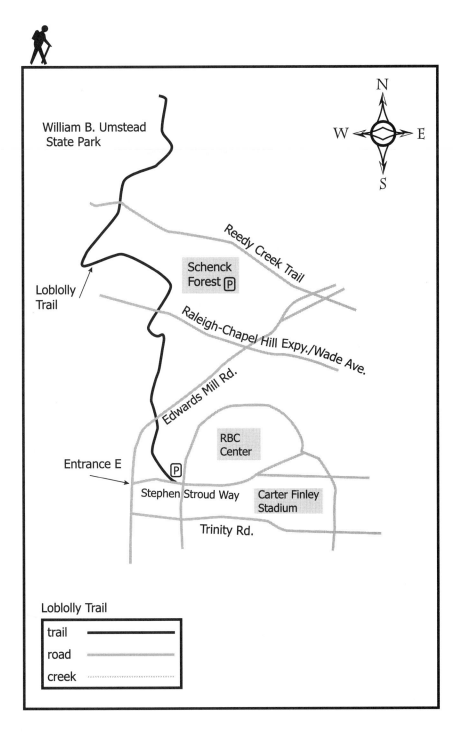

William B. Umstead
State Park

N
W    E
S

Reedy Creek Trail

Schenck
Forest P

Loblolly
Trail

Raleigh-Chapel Hill Expy./Wade Ave.

Edwards Mill Rd.

RBC
Center

Entrance E

P

Stephen Stroud Way

Carter Finley
Stadium

Trinity Rd.

Loblolly Trail

| trail | ———— |
| road | ~~~~~ |
| creek | ........... |

*Loblolly Trail*

Follow Edwards Mill to the RBC Center's Entrance E (Stephen Stroud Way), located across from Cardinal Gibbons High School. After turning onto Stephen Stroud Way, take the first left into the greenway parking area.

This 6-mile wooded trail extends from the RBC Center through Carl A. Schenck Memorial Forest and into the heart of William B. Umstead State Park. For hikers, this is as good as urban greenways get.

## Brentwood Trail

**Length:** 0.8 mile
**Difficulty:** Easy
**Surface:** Asphalt
**Bicycles:** Yes
**Directions:** Parking is available at the Brentwood Swim Club lot on Vinson Court. From Capital Boulevard, take Brentwood Drive to Vinson Court, located on the right.

Most of this brief trail is a paved path through Brentwood Park. It provides access to Brentwood Elementary School. The highlight is a short but pretty walk along Marsh Creek though a mature bottom-land forest.

## Beaver Dam Trail

**Length:** 1.4 miles
**Difficulty:** Easy
**Surface:** Dirt with a short paved section near Lake Boone Trail
**Bicycles:** Yes
**Directions:** The trailhead is in west Raleigh between Wade Avenue and Lake Boone Trail in the University Park area. The most convenient parking is near Hymettus Woods Park.

This greenway is really a neighborhood walk on the green space along Beaver Dam Creek between Nottingham Drive and Banbury Road. A few bridges add interest. Picnic tables have been placed here and there.

## Gardner Street Trail

**Length:** 0.7 mile
**Difficulty:** Easy
**Surface:** Dirt, gravel, and sidewalks
**Bicycles:** Yes
**Directions:** The entrance to Jaycee Park is on Wade Avenue just east of the intersection with Gardner Street. Begin at the Jaycee parking lot. Follow the sand path past the community center and turn right before the bridge. Don't be confused by the loop exercise trails. Just keep to the right for the most direct path to the greenway proper.

This greenway includes neighborhood sidewalks and a creek-side path through ivy-carpeted glades. It passes a small waterfall on Beaver Dam Branch in Jaycee Park. The rest of the trail is a pleasant walk to the Raleigh Little Theater and Rose Garden.

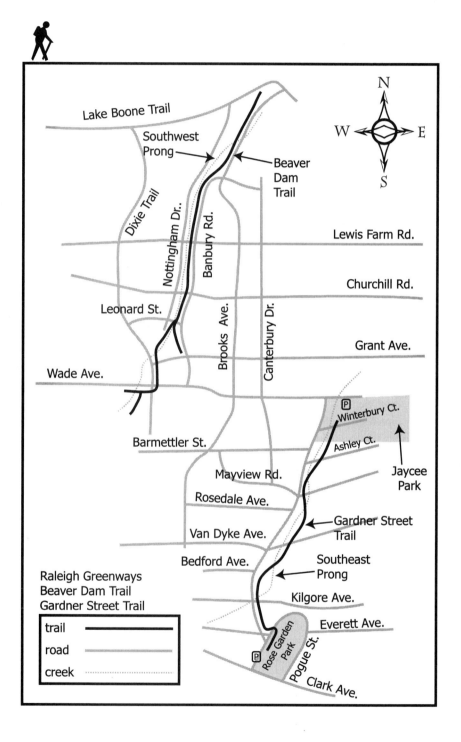

N

W E

S

Lake Boone Trail

Southwest Prong

Beaver Dam Trail

Dixie Trail

Nottingham Dr..

Banbury Rd.

Lewis Farm Rd.

Churchill Rd.

Leonard St.

Brooks Ave.

Canterbury Dr.

Grant Ave.

Wade Ave.

P Winterbury Ct.

Ashley Ct.

Jaycee Park

Barmettler St.

Mayview Rd.

Rosedale Ave.

Gardner Street Trail

Van Dyke Ave.

Southeast Prong

Bedford Ave.

Kilgore Ave.

Everett Ave.

Raleigh Greenways
Beaver Dam Trail
Gardner Street Trail

| trail | |
|---|---|
| road | |
| creek | |

Rose Garden Park

P

Pogue St.

Clark Ave.

## Little Rock Trail

**Length:** 0.9 mile
**Difficulty:** Easy
**Surface:** Asphalt
**Bicycles:** Yes
**Directions:** Access and parking are available at Chavis Park, located at the intersection of Chavis Way and East Lenoir Street.

Houses are visible along most of the length of Little Rock Trail, which winds through Chavis Park along Garner Branch. A wooded section near Bragg Street, a couple of bridge crossings, and a carousel add to the scenery. You can even watch the creek from a small rock outcropping known as, you guessed it, Little Rock.

## Rocky Branch Trail

**Length:** 1.5 miles
**Difficulty:** Easy
**Surface:** Asphalt
**Bicycles:** Yes
**Directions:** If you're driving to the greenway, you can park in the Pullen Park lot and cross Western Boulevard to Bilyeu Street. Use extreme caution, as there is no crosswalk. The Pullen Park lot closest to the greenway is located at the intersection of Western Boulevard and Ashe Avenue. Parking is also available on Boylan Avenue just south of Western Boulevard.

This trail runs along Rocky Branch and busy Western Boulevard in west Raleigh. It has appeal as a commuting route for pedestrians and eastbound cyclists from West Cabarrus Street to the bike lanes on Ashe Avenue. Westbound cyclists can use the paved path that runs along the north side of Western Boulevard. By the time it reaches Washington Elementary School, Rocky Branch Trail is more peaceful. A planned extension will link Rocky Branch with Lower Walnut Creek Trail. With Pullen Park at one

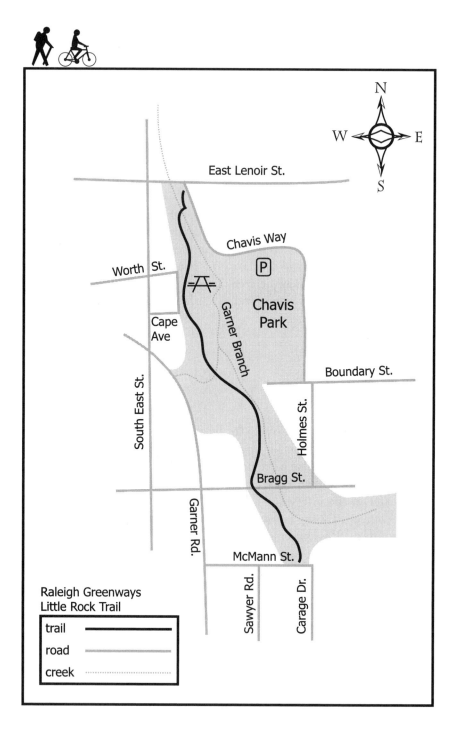

N
W E
S

East Lenoir St.

Chavis Way

Worth St.

P

Chavis Park

Cape Ave

Garner Branch

Boundary St.

South East St.

Holmes St.

Bragg St.

Garner Rd.

McMann St.

Raleigh Greenways
Little Rock Trail

Sawyer Rd.

Carage Dr.

| trail | ▬▬▬ |
| road | |
| creek | ⋯⋯⋯ |

end and some of Raleigh's most beautiful wetlands at the other, these greenways will form one of the most rewarding routes in the city.

## Lower Walnut Creek Trail

**Length:** 2.1 miles
**Difficulty:** Easy
**Surface:** Asphalt and boardwalks
**Bicycles:** Yes
**Directions:** One of the easiest access points is from Apollo Heights Park on Lunar Drive. From Martin Luther King Jr. Boulevard, turn south on Grantland Drive, drive 0.3 mile, and turn left on Lunar Drive. Parking is also available on Rose Lane.

You wouldn't think this greenway was possible if you didn't see it. Lower Walnut Creek Trail is lined with lush, open wetlands crowded with birds and other critters and beautiful bottom-land forests along the sandy, serpentine banks of Walnut Creek. And it's all inside the beltline! Boardwalks protect the marshy areas, and an observation deck gives you a chance to stop and watch the birds. Currently, the greenway ends at Garner Road, but note that future construction will continue it to Hammond Road, where it will fork. The future right fork will join Rocky Branch Trail. The future left fork will continue inside the beltline to the vicinity of The Farmers' Market on Lake Wheeler Road.

# Town of Apex

**Address:** Director of Parks, Recreation, and Cultural Resources, 237 North Salem Street, Apex, NC 27502
**Telephone:** 919-249-3419

As this guide was going to press, the town of Apex had plans to connect several short neighborhood greenways to form a longer

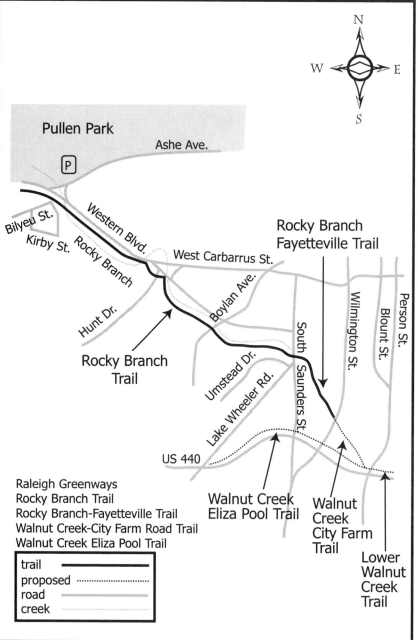

Pullen Park

Ashe Ave.

N
W      E
S

Bilyeu St.
Kirby St.
Western Blvd.
Rocky Branch

West Carbarrus St.

Rocky Branch
Fayetteville Trail

Hunt Dr.

Boylan Ave.

Rocky Branch
Trail

Umstead Dr.

Lake Wheeler Rd.

South Saunders St.

Wilmington St.

Blount St.

Person St.

US 440

Walnut Creek
Eliza Pool Trail

Walnut
Creek
City Farm
Trail

Lower
Walnut
Creek
Trail

Raleigh Greenways
Rocky Branch Trail
Rocky Branch-Fayetteville Trail
Walnut Creek-City Farm Road Trail
Walnut Creek Eliza Pool Trail

| | |
|---|---|
| trail | ———— |
| proposed | ············ |
| road | ———— |
| creek | ············ |

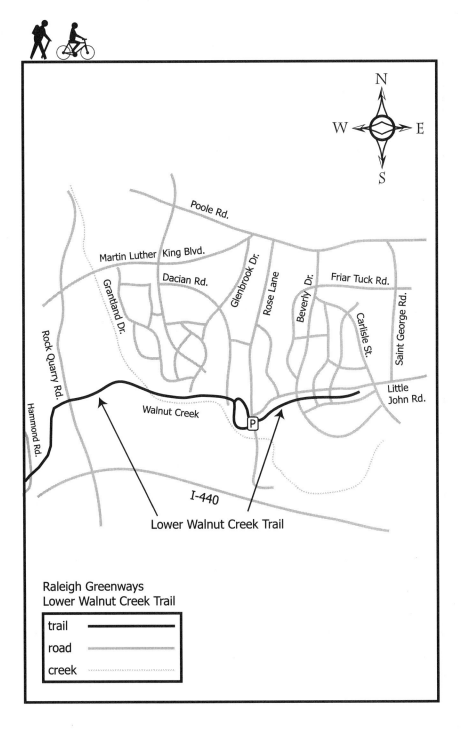

N
W        E
S

Poole Rd.

Martin Luther King Blvd.

Grantland Dr.

Dacian Rd.

Glenbrook Dr.

Rose Lane

Beverly Dr.

Friar Tuck Rd.

Carlisle St.

Saint George Rd.

Rock Quarry Rd.

Hammond Rd.

Walnut Creek

Little John Rd.

P

I-440

Lower Walnut Creek Trail

Raleigh Greenways
Lower Walnut Creek Trail

| trail | ——— |
| road | ········ |
| creek | ········ |

I-40

Lake
Crabtree

Old Reedy
Creek Rd.

N
W E
S

Weston Pkwy

North Cary Park →

Cary Pkwy

Homestead Dr.

Chamnes Dr.

W. Dynasty Dr.

N. Harrison Ave.

Maynard Rd.

Godbold
Park

Cary Greenways
Black Creek Trail

| | |
|---|---|
| trail | ———— |
| road | ———— |
| creek | ·········· |

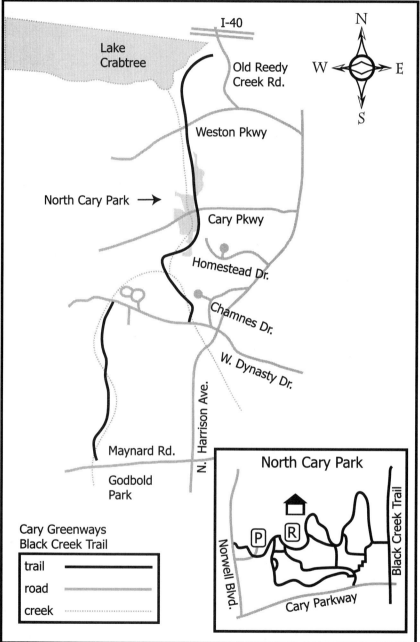

North Cary Park

P   R

Norwell Blvd.

Black Creek Trail

Cary Parkway

system, to be called the Beaver Creek Greenway. This greenway will link the downtown historic district to a proposed nature park. A second system of trails and sidewalks, the Haddon Hall Greenway, will link the Haddon Hall subdivision to downtown.

# Town of Cary

## Cary Greenways

**Address:** Cary Parks, Recreation, and Cultural Resources Department, P.O. Box 8005, Cary, NC 27512
**Telephone:** 919-469-4061
**Maps:** USGS Cary; free maps are available from the town of Cary.

In the near term, Cary's greenways will be of interest mainly to people who live and work nearby. One particularly appealing stretch that warrants a separate trip is Black Creek Greenway. Its 3.5-mile length isn't enough to draw cyclists on its own, but it's a good walk, particularly if you have a stroller to push. Cyclists as well as pedestrians might want to add a trip down Black Creek Greenway to an exploration of Lake Crabtree County Park or William B. Umstead State Park.

The future will bring an extension of White Oak Creek Greenway to American Tobacco Trail, opening the exciting possibility of a relatively safe cycling commute from Cary to Research Triangle Park or Durham. Future links between White Oak Creek Greenway and Black Creek Greenway would make an off-road excursion from William B. Umstead State Park to downtown Durham possible.

### Annie Jones Park Trails
**Length:** 1.25 miles combined
**Difficulty:** Easy
**Surface:** Asphalt and natural
**Bicycles:** Yes
**Directions:** From the intersection of Tarbert Drive and Cary

Parkway, drive north on Tarbert for 0.3 mile to the park entrance, located on the left. The paved greenway on the other side of the playground is McCloud Court Trail. From the parking lot, go right to access McCloud Court Trail or left across Tarbert Drive to access the other three trails. Coatbridge Trail heads into the woods beside the ball field.

These trails form an attractive, easy suburban walk. Although McCloud Court Trail and Coatbridge Trail are named, you don't need to keep track of which trail is which as you walk here.

## Black Creek Trail

**Length:** 3.5 miles
**Difficulty:** Easy
**Surface:** Asphalt
**Bicycles:** Yes
**Directions:** Take the Harrison Avenue exit (Exit 287) off I-40. Go south on Harrison Avenue for 0.3 mile, turn right on Weston Parkway, drive 0.6 mile, and turn right on Old Reedy Creek Road, where the pavement ends. The greenway entrance is 0.6 mile ahead on the left. A map is posted.

Black Creek Trail is the longest of Cary's greenways. It begins on the shore of Lake Crabtree and meanders along the bank of Black Creek. One highlight is a lakeside observation deck where you can watch herons fish. Beyond the lake are several benches and a few wooden bridges at points where the trail crosses Black Creek. Although thousands of residents and workers are close by, it's possible to find solitude during the week. This trail may be of particular interest to those attempting to string together a long walk or mountain bike ride. A sidewalk connector on West Dynasty Drive joins the northern and southern sections of the greenway. The northern terminus of the trail, located beside Lake Crabtree, intersects

*Black Creek Trail*

the trail system of Lake Crabtree County Park, which has trails open to walkers and bikers. If you're on your bike, you can continue heading east on Old Reedy Creek Road for 0.6 mile to the boundary of William B. Umstead State Park and an entrance to Bike and Bridle Trail (see the section covering the state park). No parking for cars is available on Old Reedy Creek Road at the state park boundary.

## Oxxford Hunt Greenway

**Length:** 1.5 miles
**Difficulty:** Easy
**Surface:** Gravel
**Bicycles:** Yes
**Directions:** See the directions for Bond Park on page 280. Go to the end of the Bond Park entrance road. The greenway begins on the left side of the road near the boathouse.

This greenway begins in Bond Park and extends to Old Apex Road. Outside the park, it follows a tributary of Crabtree Creek and skirts a pond. The walk along the creek and through local subdivisions is pleasant, but as with many urban greenways, Oxxford Hunt is appreciated most by those able to walk to it from home. The sections of the greenway within the park are part of the blue-blazed trail that circles Bond Lake. The sections outside the park are private but open to the public. Because the surface is gravel, this trail is not suitable for strollers or skates. It's not bad for bikes but not particularly interesting either.

## Parkway Greenway

**Length:** 0.8 mile
**Difficulty:** Easy
**Surface:** Asphalt
**Bicycles:** Yes
**Directions:** See the directions for Bond Park on page 280. From the parking lot by the Bond Park boathouse, follow the trail for 0.2 mile past the amphitheater and the volleyball courts and over the dam to the steps at the far end. The greenway begins at the bottom.

This greenway starts at the base of the Bond Park Dam and ends on Cary Parkway. At the Bond Park end, the wooded, scenic trail follows a tributary of Coles Branch. Closer to Cary Parkway, it is bordered by private residences on one side and the YMCA Park on the other.

## Symphony Lake Trail

**Length:** 1.2 miles
**Difficulty:** Easy
**Surface:** Asphalt
**Bicycles:** Yes
**Directions:** From the intersection of US 64 and US 1, follow Tryon Road for 0.3 mile to Regency Parkway and turn right. Drive 0.5 mile on Regency Parkway and follow the right fork to the parking area near the lake. Begin at the east side of the creek near the parking lot and walk straight down to the lake.

Walking this trail is a pleasant in-town experience.

An easy, scenic, paved loop trail surrounds Symphony Lake, which gets its name from the performance facility. Corporate buildings overlook the lake.

## Hinshaw Trail

**Length:** 0.8 mile
**Difficulty:** Easy
**Surface:** Asphalt
**Bicycles:** Yes
**Directions:** Take the Southeast Cary Parkway exit off US 1, then take the first left onto Thurston Drive. Parking is available at Kids Together Park and MacDonald Woods Park.

This wooded greenway follows Lynn's Branch from Greenwood Circle to Kids Together Park on Thurston Drive. Houses and backyards are numerous, but the serpentine shape of the creek adds character. Some short, unpaved spur trails lead to quiet portions of the creek.

## White Oak Trail

**Length:** 1 mile
**Difficulty:** Easy
**Surface:** Asphalt
**Bicycles:** Yes
**Directions:** White Oak Park is located at the intersection of Jenkins Carpenter Road and Park Village Drive. From the park, you can head west along a creek toward NC 55 or east toward Park Village Drive. Parking is available at White Oak Park and Davis Drive Park.

Aside from residents of the surrounding neighborhoods, this wide, relatively flat trail may appeal to novice rollerbladers and stroller pushers.

# Swift Creek Trail

**Length:** 0.9 mile
**Difficulty:** Easy
**Surface:** Asphalt
**Bicycles:** Yes
**Directions:** The easiest access point is Ritter Park. The entrance to the park is on West Lochmere Drive. Go 0.2 mile west of the intersection with Kildaire Farm Road and park in the first lot on the left. The trail is at the far end of the lot.

Swift Creek Trail runs along the bank of Swift Creek across from Hemlock Bluffs Nature Preserve. Although the preserve offers more of a backwoods, secluded experience, Swift Creek Trail has much to recommend it. First, it's paved, so rollerbladers, cyclists, and stroller pushers can enjoy it. Second, the greenway is interesting in itself, as this was the first in the nation constructed entirely from recycled materials. The asphalt pavement was made out of old rubber tires, asphalt shingles, and recycled pavement. Even the signs, posts, and benches had a previous life that has been renewed here, instead of ending in a landfill. Signs along the trail give details about the construction process and materials.

Although Swift Creek Trail is short, a much longer walk is possible. At its eastern end, the trail joins a private greenway that runs along Loch Highlands Drive to Penny Road. At its western terminus, Swift Creek Trail is only 0.2 mile from the 1.2-mile Symphony Lake Trail. If you've come off Swift Creek Trail, turn left and walk 0.2 mile on the sidewalk. Symphony Lake Trail circles the small lake located across Regency Parkway.

# Pirates Cove Trail

**Length:** 0.7 mile
**Difficulty:** Easy
**Surface:** Gravel and natural
**Bicycles:** Yes

**Directions:** Take East Maynard Road to Seabrook Avenue. Head around the circle, then continue straight another 0.1 mile to the dead end.

The crushed-gravel and dirt surface of this short trail keeps wheeled traffic to a minimum and creates a relatively quiet stroll along the west bank of Speight Branch. The short spur trails leading to the creek's edge and the towering hardwoods make this a brief, easy, and appealing walk in the woods.

## Higgins Trail

**Length:** 0.4 mile
**Difficulty:** Easy
**Surface:** Gravel
**Bicycles:** Yes
**Directions:** From the intersection of Maynard Road and West Chatham Street, head north on West Chatham, then take the first right onto Danforth Drive. Follow Danforth to the greenway entrance, located on the right.

This nondescript but not unpleasant trail has a 20-station workout course.

## Panther Creek Greenway

**Length:** 2 miles
**Difficulty:** Easy
**Surface:** Asphalt
**Bicycles:** Yes
**Directions:** From the intersection of US 64 and NC 55, take NC 55 West for 4.9 miles to Carpenter Fire Station Road. Turn left, drive 1.3 miles to Cary Glen Boulevard and the Cary Park entrance, turn left, and proceed 0.7 mile to the greenway intersection. No public parking is available at present.

Boasting lakeshore on one side and the new urban

development of Cary Park on the other, this greenway is a great amenity for locals but doesn't warrant a special trip.

*Bond Park*

# Bond Park

**Telephone:** 919-469-4100

**Hours:** November through March, 9 A.M. to sunset; April and May, September and October, 9 A.M. to sunset, Monday through Friday, 8 A.M. to sunset on weekends and holidays; June and August, 9 A.M. to sunset, Monday through Friday; 7 A.M. to sunset on Saturday and holidays; 8 A.M. to sunset on Sundays

**Maps:** USGS Cary; a free trail map is available at the community center and the boathouse.

**Directions:** From I-40, take the Davis Drive exit (Exit 280) and go south on Davis for 7.8 miles to High House Road. Turn left and drive 1.6 miles to Bond Park Road, the second entrance road on the right. This entrance is 0.5 mile west of the intersection of High House Road and Cary Parkway.

Fred G. Bond Metro Park, as it is officially known, offers a variety of outings for Cary residents. At 310 acres, it is the largest municipal park in Wake County. In addition to athletic fields and two picnic shelters available for rent, the park offers 5 miles of nature trails open to pedestrians and cyclists, as well as the 42-

acre Bond Lake. During boathouse hours, a fee is charged to use the boat-launch ramp on the lake. The park rents sailboats, canoes, pedal boats, kayaks, and johnboats from April to October. Another attraction is the challenge course, where, for a reasonable fee, groups of at least eight people can spend a day working on individual and interpersonal skills with a trained leader. The park's trails are crowded on the weekends and before and after work hours on weekdays. They are well marked with color-coded signposts and are easy to follow.

For those who are fond of urban outings that include a walk in the woods, Bond Park is worth a special trip. All the amenities of Cary are nearby, including numerous restaurants and shopping centers. If you don't live in Cary but would like to spend a quiet day in the woods, you'll find more solitude in nearby Lake Crabtree County Park or William B. Umstead State Park.

## Red-Blazed Trail

**Length:** 1.8 miles
**Difficulty:** Easy
**Blazes:** Red
**Surface:** Dirt and wood chips
**Bicycles:** Yes
**Directions:** This loop begins at the boathouse and heads south on Oxxford Hunt Greenway before circling playing fields 1 and 2. After crossing Bond Park Drive, it joins Green-Blazed Trail past the community center.

## Green-Blazed Trail

**Length:** 1.1 miles
**Difficulty:** Easy
**Blazes:** Green
**Surface:** Dirt and wood chips
**Bicycles:** Yes

## Lake Trail

**Length:** 2 miles
**Difficulty:** Easy

**Blazes:** Blue
**Surface:** Gravel and dirt
**Bicycles:** Yes

This is the most scenic of the Bond Park trails because of its proximity to the lake. It offers a chance to see birds, turtles, and other lake-side fauna. Although the path is wooded, decks and yards come within a few feet of it in places. Despite the proliferation of joggers, this trail has some interesting single-track sections.

## Hemlock Bluffs Nature Preserve

**Address:** 2626 Kildaire Farm Road, Cary, NC 27511
**Telephone:** 919-387-5980
**Preserve hours:** 9 A.M. to sunset
**Nature Center hours:** 10 A.M. to 5 P.M.
**Maps:** USGS Cary; a free map is available in the Stevens Nature Center.
**Directions:** From the intersection of US 64 and US 1, follow Tryon Road for 0.8 mile to Kildaire Farm Road, turn right, and drive 1.4 miles to the entrance. The trailheads are on the far side of the Stevens Nature Center. All are well marked and easy to follow. The free *Hemlock Bluffs Trail Guide*, available in the wooden box affixed to a post near the entrance trail, contains a printed map. A signboard with a map is located near the trailheads.

Hemlock Bluffs Nature Preserve consists of about 150 acres of relatively unspoiled forest situated between the south bank of Swift Creek and Kildaire Farm Road. It owes both its name and its unique beauty to the hemlocks that shield it from the surrounding city. The hemlocks here are rare. This site is over 200 miles east of and a few thousand feet lower than the typical North Carolina hemlock habitat in the Appalachian Mountains. Scientists believe that about 10,000 years ago, before the end of the last Ice Age, many species now living in the North Carolina mountains and more northern climates covered the Piedmont. The hemlocks

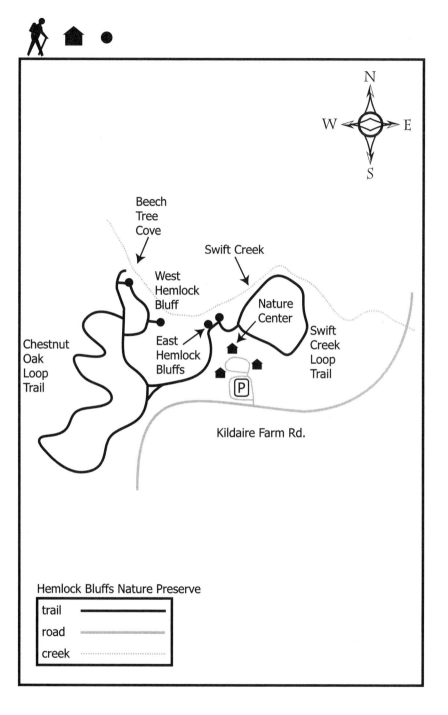

Beech
Tree
Cove

Swift Creek

West
Hemlock
Bluff

Nature
Center

East
Hemlock
Bluffs

Swift
Creek
Loop
Trail

Chestnut
Oak
Loop
Trail

P

Kildaire Farm Rd.

N

W    E

S

Hemlock Bluffs Nature Preserve

| trail | ———————— |
| road | ············ |
| creek | ·············· |

on the north-facing bluffs of the nature preserve are an anoma-
lous leftover from that ancient time.

The hemlocks and Swift Creek can be viewed from five decks
built atop the bluffs. The views are most expansive in winter.
Spring brings a variety of wildflowers to the bluffs. The park provides free written guides for both of its trails that describe the
scenery at numbered locations.

This preserve is worth a visit for both ecological and aesthetic
reasons, particularly if you're after a short walk and don't mind
the presence of other people. If you want a more solitary experience, your best bet is Chestnut Oak Loop Trail. It's the longest
walk, and most people stick to the trails leading to the bluffs and
the shorter Swift Creek Loop Trail.

## Swift Creek Loop Trail

**Length:** 0.6 mile
**Difficulty:** Easy
**Surface:** Natural and boardwalk
**Bicycles:** Bikes are allowed on the dirt path.

This is the most interesting trail in the preserve. Part
dirt path and part boardwalk, it takes you down the north
face of one of the bluffs via a set of steps and through the
rich bottom land surrounding Swift Creek.

### Mileposts

**0.0 mile:** Begin by turning right at the signboard. After
100 yards, you'll reach a turnoff to the left leading to a
viewing area and the decks of East Hemlock Bluff. Continue straight down the steps. At the bottom, you can go
left or right. Follow the trail to the right.
**0.4 mile:** You'll reach a fork. Keep right. The left fork is a
maintenance road.
**0.6 mile:** You'll return to the first fork.

## Chestnut Oak Loop Trail

**Length:** 1 mile
**Difficulty:** Easy to moderate
**Blazes:** Chestnut Oak Loop Trail has red blazes; the connector trail has yellow blazes.
**Surface:** Natural
**Bicycles:** No

Chestnut Oak Loop Trail is longer and slightly more challenging than Swift Creek Loop Trail. It passes through rolling terrain.

### Mileposts

**0.0 mile:** Begin at the signboard behind the Stevens Nature Center. Turn left at the signboard.
**0.1 mile:** You'll reach a fork. The bluffs and the northern trailhead for Chestnut Oak Loop Trail are to the right. To the left is the southern terminus of Chestnut Oak Loop Trail. Go right.
**0.2 mile:** You'll reach a second fork. Following the path straight ahead leads a few yards to the northern terminus of Chestnut Oak Loop Trail. A right turn leads past West Hemlock Bluff and Beech Tree Cove. Go right.
**0.3 mile:** You'll reach the turnoff to West Hemlock Bluff and the viewing deck, located a few yards to the right. Continue left toward Beech Tree Cove.
**0.4 mile:** You'll reach a second deck and a short spur to Beech Tree Cove. Continue left.
**0.5 mile:** You'll reach a fork. The right branch will take you on Chestnut Oak Loop Trail. Heading straight will lead you to a left turn toward the Stevens Nature Center. Go right.
**0.8 mile:** You'll reach a fork. The left fork leads to West Hemlock Bluff. Continue straight to return to the nature center.
**1.0 mile:** You'll reach the nature center.

# Swift Creek Bluffs

**Directions:** From I-40, take the Gorman Street exit (Exit 295) and head south on Gorman. Turn right on Tryon Road, go 2.1 miles, turn left on Holly Springs Road, and drive 2.3 miles to the Swift Creek bridge. Swift Creek Bluffs is on the right just beyond the bridge, adjacent to a town of Cary lift station. Park in the gravel lot.

**Maps:** USGS Apex

**Hours:** Sunrise to sunset

**Contact information:** See White Pines Nature Preserve on page 19.

This 23-acre tract is owned and managed by the Triangle Land Conservancy (see Appendix 2 for contact information). Thanks to its 100-foot bluff rising above the south bank of Swift Creek, this area is as dramatic as Hemlock Bluffs, which lies about 1.5 miles upstream. As with Hemlock Bluffs, the north-facing hillsides are home to many species more commonly associated with the mountains.

## Swift Creek Bluffs Trail

**Length:** 1 mile

**Difficulty:** Easy to moderate

**Blazes:** None

**Surface:** Natural

**Bicycles:** No

# State and Locally Designated Road Biking Routes

# Chatham County

**Address:** Office of Pedestrian and Bicycle Transportation, North Carolina Department of Transportation, P.O. Box 25201, Raleigh, NC 27611
**Telephone:** 919-733-2804
**Map:** An excellent map complete with historical information is available for free from the Office of Pedestrian and Bicycle Transportation.

Escaping city traffic to pedal over the rolling hills of the rural Piedmont is a great way to leave your stress behind. Chatham County is a fine place for that kind of bike ride. Thanks to the efforts of the North Carolina Department of Transportation and the county, it's easy to experience Chatham by bicycle. Cyclists enjoy a wonderful variety of scenery, from farms to old churches to quaint towns filled with traditional North Carolina architecture. Several of the bike routes described below also pass access points for Jordan Lake, which offers amenities including swimming and camping.

Residents of Orange County can take an interesting weekend trip by beginning in Chapel Hill and riding Chatham County Route 3 and Chatham County Route 5 to Siler City, where the Bed and Breakfast at Laurel Ridge offers accommodations within a short walk of the Deep River; call the Chatham County Chamber of Commerce at 919-742-3333 for more information. If you want to take a different route back, follow Chatham County Route 4 south out of Siler City, take the Bonlee-Route 3 Connector east to Chatham County Route 3, and bike Route 3 north back to Orange County.

## Chatham County Route 3

**Length:** 38.1 miles
**Difficulty:** Moderate

Chatham County Route 3 begins south of Chapel Hill at the Orange County line, where Meechum Road becomes Poythress Road. The northern end of the route boasts some steep hills. It also includes expanding suburbs and the rush-hour traffic they bring. The route passes the gracious, old Mann's Chapel Methodist Church. Those interested in avoiding traffic may wish to use Lamont Norwood Road as an alternative to Mann's Chapel Road. It's slightly less developed.

As the route winds southwest, it crosses the Haw River in the town of Bynum. Sleepy Bynum was once a hopping mill town with a general store and a theater. It is now the home of the annual Haw River Festival finale and well-known artist Clyde Jones. The old Bynum Bridge, built in 1922, is closed to motor vehicle use. The south side of the river is the site of the Haw River Canoe Access Point, developed by the Carolina Canoe Club and owned by Chatham County.

Beyond Bynum, Route 3 follows US 15/US 501 for 0.5 mile. This is one of the most dangerous sections of the ride. Once off US 15/US 501, the route heads toward Pittsboro. Downtown Pittsboro is 0.5 mile off US 64 and is well worth seeing, though caution is again in order. The Chatham County Courthouse dates to 1881 and, thanks to a restoration, still looks as it did when it was built. Listed on the National Register of Historic Places, it houses the Chatham Historical Museum, which is open on Fridays from 10 A.M. to 2 P.M.

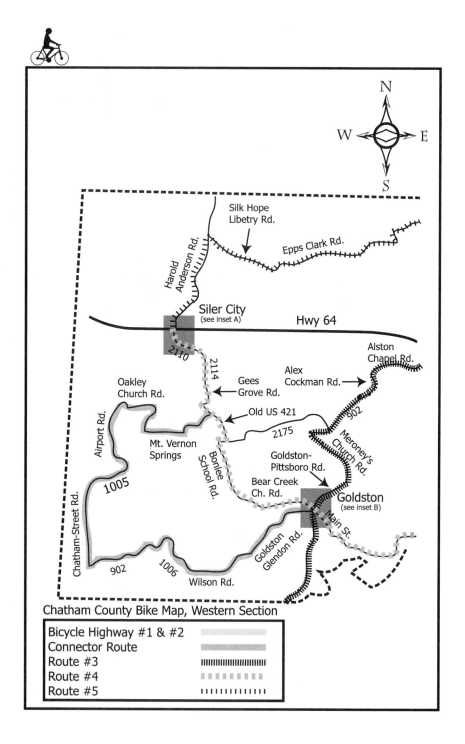

Chatham County Bike Map, Western Section

| | |
|---|---|
| Bicycle Highway #1 & #2 | |
| Connector Route | |
| Route #3 | |
| Route #4 | |
| Route #5 | |

Map labels:

N
W E
S

Silk Hope Libetry Rd.

Epps Clark Rd.

Harold Anderson Rd.

Siler City
(see inset A)

Hwy 64

2110

2114

Alston Chapel Rd.

Alex Cockman Rd.

Oakley Church Rd.

Gees Grove Rd.

Old US 421

902

Airport Rd.

Mt. Vernon Springs

2175

Meroney's Church Rd.

Goldston-Pittsboro Rd.

Bonlee School Rd.

Bear Creek Ch. Rd.

Chatham-Street Rd.

1005

Goldston
(see inset B)

Main St.

902

1006

Wilson Rd.

Goldston Glendon Rd.

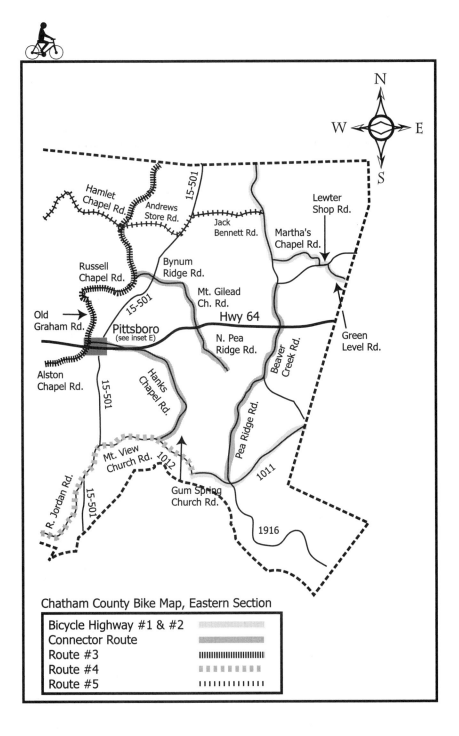

Chatham County Bike Map, Eastern Section

| | |
|---|---|
| Bicycle Highway #1 & #2 | |
| Connector Route | |
| Route #3 | |
| Route #4 | |
| Route #5 | |

Past Pittsboro, this is a delightful ride. Cyclists enjoy light traffic and great rural sights like the Rocky River, deep woods, open pastures, and bales of hay strewn across fields. The scenery is a notch grander than on many other bike routes in the Triangle. You'll find some friendly country stores as the route continues past Meroney Methodist Church and through Goldston before heading to Carbonton and the Moore County line. At the end of the route are a convenience store and seafood restaurant where cyclists can fuel up before continuing south on the Moore County bicycle routes, which are beyond the scope of this guide.

### Highlights and Services

**14.7 miles:** A diner and gas station are at the intersection with US 64. The county courthouse, restaurants, antique shops, and an ice-cream shop are in historic downtown Pittsboro, located 0.5 mile to the left.
**15.0 miles:** You'll cross Robeson Creek.
**21.6 miles:** You'll cross Landrum Creek.
**22.8 miles:** You'll cross the Rocky River.
**28.9 miles:** You'll cross Bear Creek.
**30.9 miles:** A country store is on the left.

## Chatham County Route 4

**Length:** 38.7 miles
**Difficulty:** Moderate

This route begins in Siler City at the intersection of Old US 421 and US 64 and ends in Moncure. Daytime parking is available at Bray Park on Alston Bridge Road. Among the route's highlights is Mount Vernon Springs, a popular resort from 1881 to 1920. The resort is long since gone, but the two springs remain—as a pair of pipes emerging from the ground, that is. The springs were named "Health" and "Beauty," after the specific benefits said to come to visitors partaking of the waters.

Beyond the springs, the route passes through the towns of Goldston and Gulf. Gulf Presbyterian Church is definitely worth seeing. Four miles east of Gulf at S. R. 2153, the route skirts Deep River Park, the site of the Deep River Camelback Truss Bridge. The bridge, built in 1908, is listed on the National Register of Historic Places. It is a wonderful place to picnic. The route also passes near the site of the Wilcox Iron Works, an important source of munitions during the American Revolution.

The route continues near the southern border of Chatham County to its terminus at Moncure. The roads here are relatively quiet compared to northern Chatham, though there is a stint on NC 87 that can see heavy traffic.

## Highlights and Services

**1.5 miles:** Bray Park is on the left.

**6.7 miles:** Mount Vernon Springs Road is on the left. You'll soon pass the historic Ore House and a marker for the Wilcox Iron Works.

**7.7 miles:** You'll cross Tick Creek.

**12.2 miles:** You'll cross Bear Creek.

**24.3 miles:** You'll pass Deep River Park, home of the Deep River Camelback Truss Bridge. The park has picnic tables and a lovely view of the river but no water or restrooms.

**26.0 miles:** You'll cross Georges Creek.

**30.3 miles:** You'll cross the Rocky River.

**36.8 miles:** The Chatham County Connector heads left on Gum Springs Road (SR 1943). Follow it if you're headed to Pittsboro.

**38.3 miles:** You'll cross US 1. A store is located at the intersection.

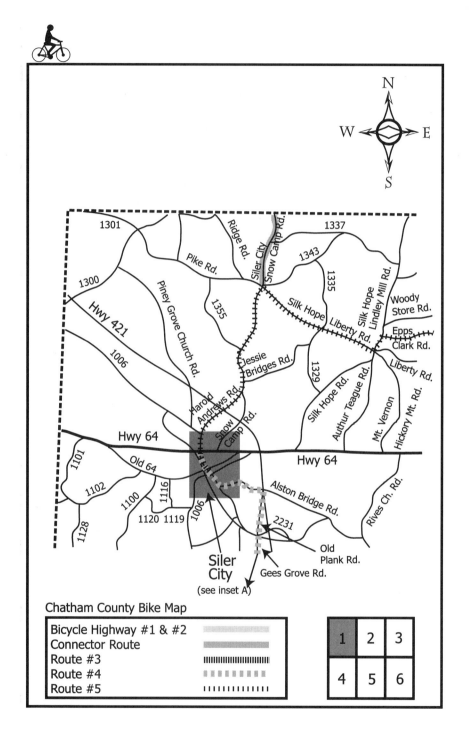

N
W E
S

1301
Pike Rd.
Ridge Rd.
Siler City
Snow Camp Rd.
1337
1343
1335
Silk Hope Lindley Mill Rd.
Woody Store Rd.
1300
Hwy 421
Piney Grove Church Rd.
1355
Silk Hope Liberty Rd.
Epps Clark Rd.
1006
Jessie Bridges Rd.
1329
Liberty Rd.
Harold Andrews Rd.
Silk Hope Rd.
Authur Teague Rd.
Mt. Vernon
Hickory Mt. Rd.
Hwy 64
Snow Camp Rd.
Hwy 64
1101
Old 64
1102
1100
1116
Alston Bridge Rd.
Rives Ch. Rd.
1128
1120  1119
1006
2231
Old Plank Rd.
**Siler City**
(see inset A)
Gees Grove Rd.

## Chatham County Bike Map

| | |
|---|---|
| Bicycle Highway #1 & #2 | |
| Connector Route | |
| Route #3 | |
| Route #4 | |
| Route #5 | |

| 1 | 2 | 3 |
|---|---|---|
| 4 | 5 | 6 |

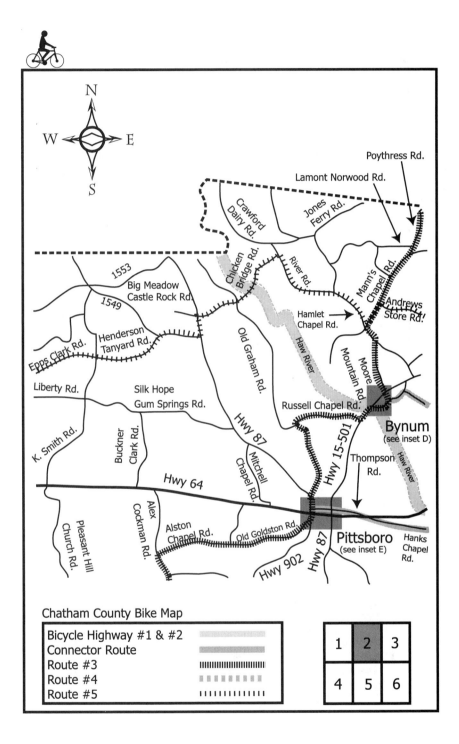

Chatham County Bike Map

| Bicycle Highway #1 & #2 | |
| Connector Route | |
| Route #3 | |
| Route #4 | |
| Route #5 | |

| 1 | 2 | 3 |
|---|---|---|
| 4 | 5 | 6 |

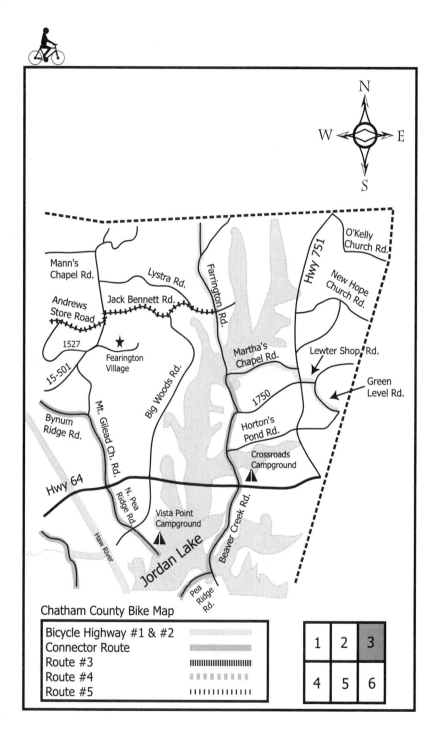

N
W E
S

Mann's Chapel Rd.

Lystra Rd.

Farrington Rd.

Hwy 751

O'Kelly Church Rd.

New Hope Church Rd.

Andrews Store Road

Jack Bennett Rd.

1527

15-501

Fearington Village

Big Woods Rd.

Martha's Chapel Rd.

Lewter Shop Rd.

1750

Green Level Rd.

Bynum Ridge Rd.

Mt. Gilead Ch. Rd.

Horton's Pond Rd.

Crossroads Campground

Hwy 64

N. Pea Ridge Rd.

Haw River

Vista Point Campground

Jordan Lake

Beaver Creek Rd.

Pea Ridge Rd.

Chatham County Bike Map

| | |
|---|---|
| Bicycle Highway #1 & #2 | ▬▬▬▬ |
| Connector Route | ▬▬▬▬ |
| Route #3 | ▮▮▮▮▮▮▮▮ |
| Route #4 | ▬ ▬ ▬ ▬ |
| Route #5 | ׀׀׀׀׀׀׀׀ |

| 1 | 2 | 3 |
|---|---|---|
| 4 | 5 | 6 |

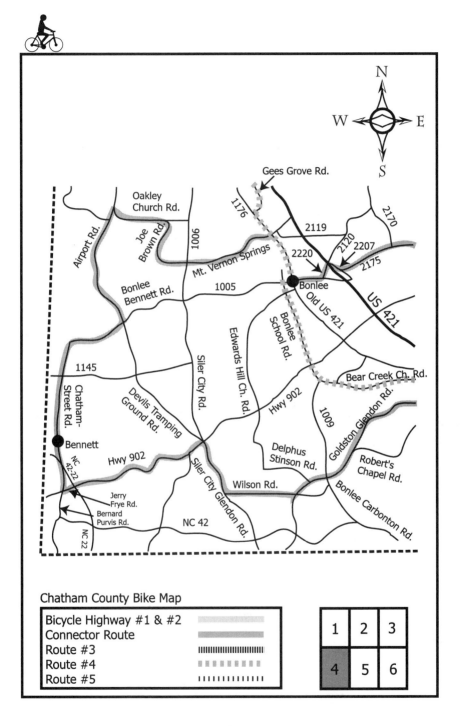

Gees Grove Rd.

Oakley
Church Rd.

1176

Airport Rd.

Joe Brown Rd.

1006

2119

2170

Mt. Vernon Springs

2220

2120

2207

2175

Bonlee
Bennett Rd.

1005

Bonlee

Old US 421

US 421

1145

Siler City Rd.

Edwards Hill Ch. Rd.

Bonlee School Rd.

Bear Creek Ch. Rd.

Chatham-Street Rd.

Devils Tramping Ground Rd.

Hwy 902

1009

Goldston Glendon Rd.

Bennett

NC 42-22

Hwy 902

Siler City Glendon Rd.

Delphus Stinson Rd.

Robert's Chapel Rd.

Jerry Frye Rd.

Bernard Purvis Rd.

NC 22

Wilson Rd.

NC 42

Bonlee Carbonton Rd.

Chatham County Bike Map

| Bicycle Highway #1 & #2 | |
| Connector Route | |
| Route #3 | |
| Route #4 | |
| Route #5 | |

| 1 | 2 | 3 |
|---|---|---|
| 4 | 5 | 6 |

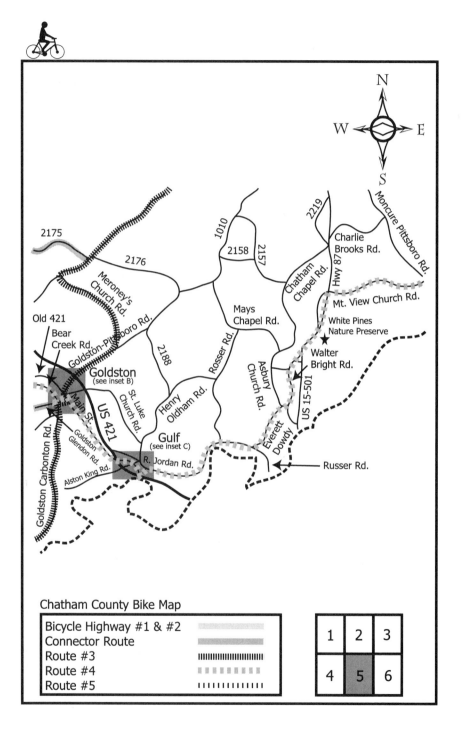

N
W E
S

2175

2176

Meroney's Church Rd.

1010

2158

2157

2219

Charlie Brooks Rd.

Moncure Pittsboro Rd.

Chatham Chapel Rd.

Hwy 87

Mt. View Church Rd.

Goldston-Pittsboro Rd.

Mays Chapel Rd.

White Pines Nature Preserve

Old 421

Bear Creek Rd.

Goldston
(see inset B)

2188

St. Luke Church Rd.

Rosser Rd.

Henry Oldham Rd.

Asbury Church Rd.

Walter Bright Rd.

US 15-501

Main St.

US 421

Goldston Carbonton Rd.

Goldston Glendon Rd.

Gulf
(see inset C)

R. Jordan Rd.

Everett Dowdy

Russer Rd.

Alston King Rd.

Chatham County Bike Map

| Bicycle Highway #1 & #2 | |
| Connector Route | |
| Route #3 | |
| Route #4 | |
| Route #5 | |

| 1 | 2 | 3 |
| 4 | 5 | 6 |

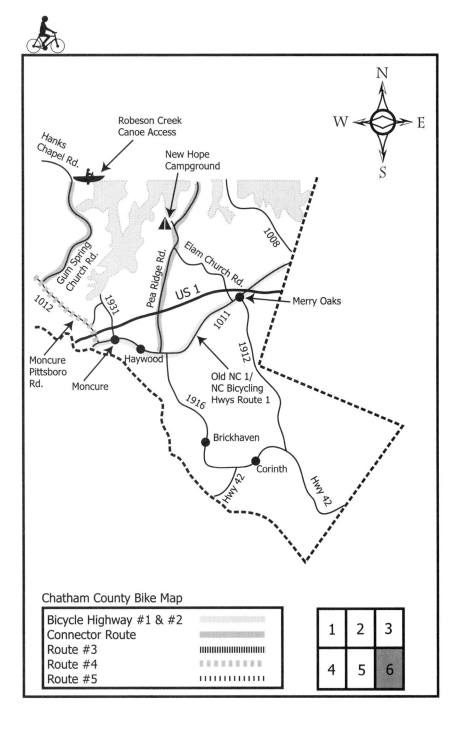

Robeson Creek
Canoe Access

Hanks
Chapel Rd.

New Hope
Campground

N
W ⟵⊙⟶ E
S

1008

Gum Spring Church Rd.

Pea Ridge Rd.

Elam Church Rd.

US 1

1012

1931

1011

Merry Oaks

Moncure
Pittsboro
Rd.

Moncure

Haywood

1912

1916

Old NC 1/
NC Bicycling
Hwys Route 1

Brickhaven

Corinth

Hwy 42

Hwy 42

Chatham County Bike Map

| Bicycle Highway #1 & #2 | |
|---|---|
| Connector Route | |
| Route #3 | ▐▐▐▐▐▐▐▐▐▐▐▐▐▐▐ |
| Route #4 | ▪ ▪ ▪ ▪ ▪ ▪ ▪ ▪ |
| Route #5 | ׀׀׀׀׀׀׀׀׀׀׀׀ |

| 1 | 2 | 3 |
|---|---|---|
| 4 | 5 | **6** |

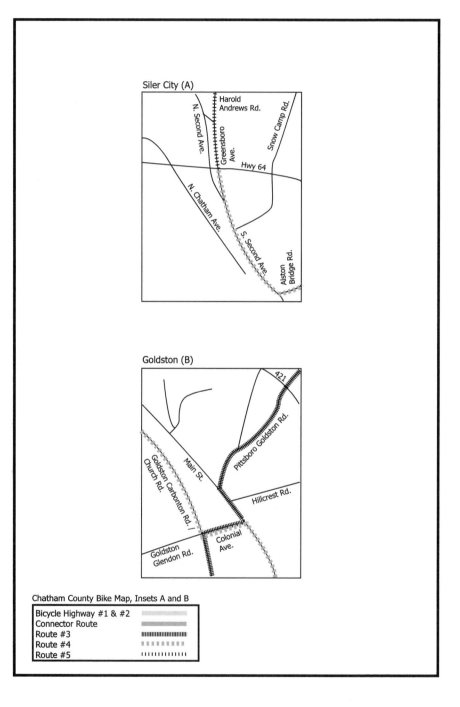

Siler City (A)

Harold Andrews Rd.

N. Second Ave.

Greensboro Ave.

Snow Camp Rd.

Hwy 64

N. Chatham Ave.

S. Second Ave.

Alston Bridge Rd.

Goldston (B)

421

Pittsboro Goldston Rd.

Goldston Carbonton Rd. / Church Rd.

Main St.

Hillcrest Rd.

Goldston Glendon Rd.

Colonial Ave.

Chatham County Bike Map, Insets A and B

| Bicycle Highway #1 & #2 | |
| Connector Route | |
| Route #3 | |
| Route #4 | |
| Route #5 | |

## Gulf (C)

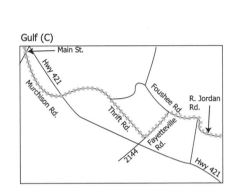

Main St.

Hwy 421

Murchison Rd.

Thrift Rd.

Foushee Rd.

R. Jordan Rd.

Fayetteville Rd.

2144

Hwy 421

## Bynum (D)

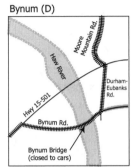

Moore Mountain Rd.

Haw River

Hwy 15-501

Durham-Eubanks Rd.

Bynum Rd.

Bynum Bridge (closed to cars)

## Pittsboro (E)

Old Graham Rd.

Graham Rd.

Hwy 15-501

Thompson St.

W. Salisbury St.

Masonic St.

Old Goldston Road

Hwy 64

Hwy 64

Hwy 15-501

### Chatham County Bike Map, Insets C, D and E

| Bicycle Highway #1 & #2 | |
| Connector Route | |
| Route #3 | |
| Route #4 | |
| Route #5 | |

# Chatham County Route 5

**Length:** 37.1 miles
**Difficulty:** Moderate

Chatham County Route 5 begins near Jordan Lake at the intersection of Lystra Road and Mount Carmel Church Road and heads west all the way to Siler City and the western terminus of Chatham County Route 4. This entire route lies in northern Chatham County, an area that is experiencing tremendous growth. Although traffic is increasing along the entire route, the section that lies east of the Haw River is the most crowded. Weekdays during the middle of the day and the early hours on weekends are the best bets if you want a quiet ride.

The roads west of the Haw still have a rural feel. The scenery is idyllic, particularly between NC 87 and Silk Hope. Some beautiful barns and at least one historic homestead lie on this stretch, and lush farm fields and still ponds add to the character of the ride. NC 87 is the main route between Burlington and Siler City, so it sees significant but sporadic truck traffic.

Silk Hope is not a town with a main street, but rather a vast community boasting a combination of rolling hills, farms, and new residential neighborhoods. The crossroads is the site of the fire station, the local elementary school, and a store where you can refill your water bottles and buy a snack. At Silk Hope Community Center, you'll find a memorial to the 14 members of the army's Golden Knights parachute team who died in a plane crash nearby.

West of Silk Hope is more rolling farmland. The route passes a few antique shops and crosses the Rocky River before ending in Siler City. Siler City has some interesting Victorian houses and two WPA projects dating from the New Deal—city hall and a mural in the post office by New York artist Maxwell Starr.

**Highlights and Services**

---

**1.5 miles:** You'll cross Bush Creek.

**12.3 miles:** You'll cross Terrells Creek.

**15.1 miles:** You'll cross the Haw River.

**33.3 miles:** You'll pass historic Rocky River Church, founded in 1757.

**33.8 miles:** The Granary, a large antique shop, is 0.5 mile down the gravel road to your right.

**34.4 miles:** You'll cross the Rocky River.

# Chatham County Connector:
# Pittsboro to Chatham County Route 4 and Jordan Lake

**Length:** 10.1 miles
**Difficulty:** Easy

This is a great ride now that all of Hanks Chapel Road/Gum Springs Church Road is paved. The route passes through downtown Pittsboro, where a brief detour will reward you with antiques, ice cream, and the restored Chatham County Courthouse. The connector passes historic Saint Bartholomew's Episcopal Church, founded in 1832. A word of caution to those exploring Pittsboro: Do not attempt the traffic circle on your bike. Make like a pedestrian and *yield*. The short section on US 64 also requires extra caution. After that, traffic eases as the route approaches Jordan Lake and scenic Robeson Creek

The ride begins at the intersection of Old Graham Road and West Salisbury Street in Pittsboro. The intersection is 0.1 mile north of the junction of US 64 and Old Graham Road. Head east on West Salisbury. The middle section of the route has steep grades, leading to Robeson Creek.

**Highlights and Services**

---

**0.3 mile:** You'll pass Saint Bartholomew's Episcopal Church.

**0.5 mile:** You'll cross Hillsboro Road. The courthouse is to the right.

**5.0 miles:** You'll pass the Robeson Creek Canoe Access.

**5.3 miles:** You'll pass the Robeson Creek Boat Access.

**5.5 miles:** You'll cross Robeson Creek.

## Chatham County Connector: Intersection of Martha's Chapel Road and Farrington Road (Chatham County Route 2) to end of Pea Ridge Road (Chatham County Route 1)

**Length:** 14 miles

**Difficulty:** Easy to moderate

This ride begins within sight of Jordan Lake (see page 9). It provides access to the Crosswinds, Poplar Point, Ebenezer Church, and New Hope Overlook Recreation Areas. This is a great ride, especially during the cold seasons. On warm weekends, the roads can get crowded with cars and trucks and the boats they're towing. Beyond the lake, you'll encounter rolling hills and pass through the Moncure area before ending near Haywood. Pea Ridge Road takes you past New Elam Christian Church, founded in 1873.

### Highlights and Services

**3.0 miles:** You'll pass a fishing access area just before the bridge across the lake.

**3.4 miles:** You'll pass Crosswinds Marina, then Crosswinds Campground.

**4.2 miles:** You'll cross US 64. A convenience store is at the intersection.

**4.7 miles:** You'll pass Poplar Point Recreation Area.

**6.5 miles:** The entrance to Ebenezer Church Recreation Area is on the right.

**7.0 miles:** You'll pass the boat ramp entrance to Ebenezer.

**9.8 miles:** On the right is W. H. Jones Road (SR 1974), which leads to the New Hope Overlook boat ramp.

**12.8 miles:** You'll cross US 1. A small country store is on the left.

## Goldston-Bennett-Bonlee Loop
**Length:** 36.8 miles
**Difficulty:** Moderate

This loop through the southwestern corner of Chatham County is beautiful and quiet. Horse, dairy, and poultry farms line the route as it passes the towns of Goldston, Bennett, and Bonlee. If you wish to drive to the route, you can park in downtown Goldston or at Goldston Park. The route begins in Goldston at the intersection of Goldston-Carbonton Road and Goldston-Glendon Road.

### Highlights and Services

**7.5 miles:** You'll cross Indian Creek.
**24.6 miles:** You'll cross Little Brush Creek.
**27.1 miles:** You'll cross Little Brush Creek again.
**33.6 miles:** You'll pass historic Mount Vernon Springs Presbyterian Church, founded in 1885.
**35.9 miles:** You'll cross Tick Creek.

## Bonlee-Route 3 Connector
**Length:** 6.6 miles
**Difficulty:** Easy

This short jog will get you from Bonlee to Chatham County Route 3, where you can head south to Goldston or north to Pittsboro. Poultry farms constitute most of the scenery. The route begins at the crossroads in Bonlee. Head east on Elmer Moore Road (SR 2126).

## Connector from Chatham County Route 3 to Chatham County Route 4
**Length:** 6.5 miles
**Difficulty:** Easy

This short ride passes through rolling farm country.

If you're coming from Goldston on Chatham County Route 3, the connector begins 1.1 miles from the intersection of SR 902 and Meroney's Church Road. Turn left on McLaurin Road (SR 2175). If you're headed south on Chatham County Route 3 from Pittsboro, the intersection is 3.6 miles from the junction of Alex Cockman Road and SR 902. Turn right on McLaurin Road.

*Bentonville Battleground*

# Johnston County

## Bentonville Battleground Loop

**Address:** 5466 Harper House Road, Four Oaks, NC 27524

**Telephone:** 910-594-0789

**Website:** http://www.ah.dcr.state.nc.us/hs/bentonvi/bentonvi.htm

**Hours:** The roads are accessible at all hours. From April to October, the visitor center is open Monday through Saturday from 9 A.M. to 5 P.M. and Sunday from 1 P.M. to 5 P.M. From November to March, it is open Tuesday through Saturday from 10 A.M. to 4 P.M. and Sunday from 1 P.M. to 4 P.M. It is closed on holidays.

**Map:** A map showing the historical markers is available at the visitor center.

**Directions:** Take I-40 East out of Raleigh to the Newton Grove/NC 50/NC 55 exit (Exit 341). Follow NC 50/NC 55 east through Newton Grove. From the traffic circle in Newton Grove, go north on US 701 for 3.4 miles, turn right on Harper House Road (SR 1008), proceed 2.5 miles, turn left on Mill Creek Road, and turn left into the visitor center parking lot. If you want to ride past all the markers, take your bike back out the way you came in on Harper House Road. Two miles east of the visitor center is Marker 1, where General William T. Sherman and half his Union troops camped the night before the battle. Begin the route directly across the street from the Harper House at Marker 2.

**Length:** 14.4 miles
**Difficulty:** Easy

Bentonville Battleground State Historic Site includes a 14-mile driving tour that makes an interesting and easy bike ride, thanks to the relatively light traffic and flat terrain. A total of 29 historical markers point out earthworks, battle lines, graveyards, and other remnants of the Civil War fight that took place here. Most of the markers are far enough off the road that you can pause to read them and not risk being run down by motorists. While the history of Bentonville Battleground makes this ride well worth the effort, the scenery is also a draw. Eastern North Carolina's sandy soil and flat terrain make for some exceptionally lovely rural views.

The only road on this loop that sees occasional heavy traffic is Harper House Road (SR 1008), and only during rush hour. That said, caution is still warranted. Although traffic is lighter than in the Triangle proper, this is not a designated bike route, and there are no Share the Road signs or bike lanes. Shoulders are narrow or nonexistent, and what traffic there is moves at a fast pace.

The site has limited hours of operation, so be sure to finish your ride before it closes, or ask the attendant about parking outside the gates. Maps, brochures, and historical information are available at the visitor center.

The Battle of Bentonville took place just south of town in March 1865 in the final days of the Civil War. As Union general William T. Sherman marched north from Savannah, Georgia, on his way to meet the army of General Ulysses S. Grant in Virginia, the Confederacy

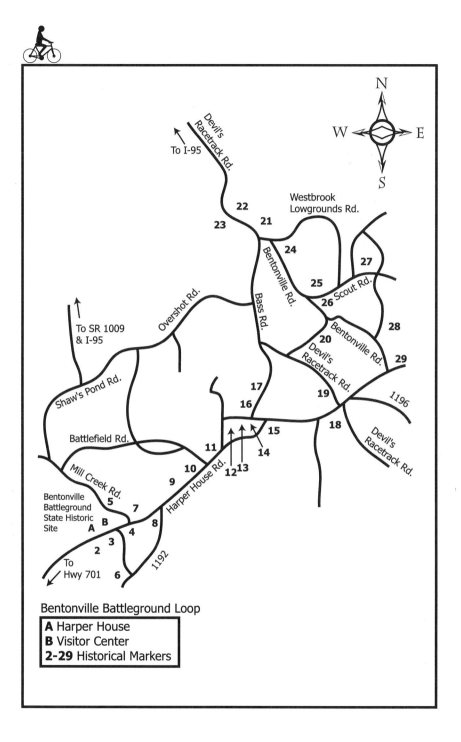

Bentonville Battleground Loop

**A** Harper House
**B** Visitor Center
**2-29** Historical Markers

made one final attempt to halt his progress. When poor road conditions forced Sherman to divide his army, the Confederates delayed half his troops in the Battle of Averasboro. Confederate general Joseph E. Johnston laid a trap for the other half of Sherman's forces as they approached Bentonville. After some initial success, the greatly outnumbered Confederates were eventually forced to abandon their assault. The three-day fight left more than 4,000 dead and was the largest battle ever fought in North Carolina. A little over a month later, General Johnston formally surrendered to General Sherman at Bennett Place in Durham, and the War Between the States finally ended.

# Raleigh

Overall, the 13 Raleigh bike routes provide a good means of exploring and getting around the Capital City. If you're interested in seeing Raleigh's neighborhoods, downtown, historic sites, and universities, traveling by bicycle will enable you to experience much more of your surroundings than driving a car. For those who work in the city, commuting by bike is a great way to get exercise and avoid the expense and hassle of parking. If you're not specifically interested in Raleigh, these routes are not the best bicycling the Triangle has to offer.

City biking is not for everyone. You should be comfortable riding with cars whose drivers may not be altogether welcoming. And be sure to learn about the special hazards of urban cycling, such as car doors that suddenly open in front of you, cars that edge out of their parking spaces just enough to see the road and take you

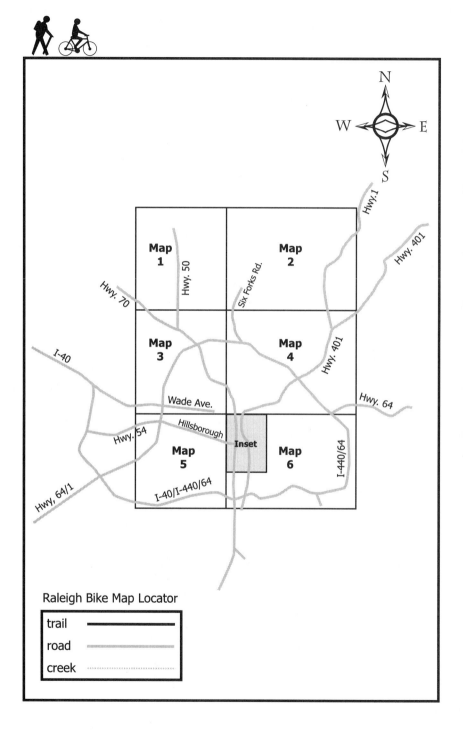

Raleigh Bike Map Locator

| trail | ——————— |
| road | ≈≈≈≈≈≈≈ |
| creek | ·············· |

out, and drivers who will cut you off to make right turns. Commuting by bicycle is a great way to get some exercise and stay healthy, but only if you don't get yourself killed in traffic!

Those who would love to see the city by bike but cannot stomach the cars might try riding just after sunrise on weekend mornings. The downtown routes are particularly appealing at those times. If you have doubts about your ability to ride any of the routes, try walking, driving, or bussing them first, or talk to someone at your local bike shop for advice. Finally, for security's sake, it's always a good idea to ride with a friend. If you're unfamiliar with the areas these bike routes pass through and would like to check with the Raleigh Police, the number is 919-890-3335.

If you're from out of town, you'll find plenty of city parks where you can leave your car while you pedal these routes. These are noted on the free map available from the city.

## Raleigh Bike Route 1

**Length:** 6.1 miles
**Difficulty:** Easy

**Directions:** From Wade Avenue/Raleigh-Chapel Hill Expressway, continue on Wade Avenue as it becomes a ramp and merges onto Capital Boulevard/U.S. 401 North. After 1.1 miles, turn right onto Dennis Avenue. Lions Park is 0.4 mile.

This loop begins at Lions Park and winds through a variety of residential neighborhoods. It gives riders access to historic Oakwood Cemetery and a tree-lined view of Crabtree Creek on Buckeye Greenway. Buckeye Greenway, the most pleasant part of the ride, has one respectable hill to get your blood pumping. Milburnie Road and Oakwood Avenue are heavily traveled during rush hour, and both crossings of Raleigh Boulevard are hazardous.

## Raleigh Bike Route 2

**Length:** 6.1 miles
**Difficulty:** Easy

**Directions:** For the best ride, begin at Shelley Lake Sertoma Park and take the Shelley Lake Trail and Snelling Branch Trail to Route 2. See page 256 for directions to Shelley Lake Sertoma Park and a description of the greenways.

Much of this short loop is along north Raleigh residential roads with light traffic. The route does not pass any parks but is within easy distance of both North Hills Park and Shelley Lake. The rides to Shelley Lake along the Ironwood Trail and Snelling Branch Trail make nice additions to the loop. (See pages 254 and 257 for these trails.) For the most scenic ride, leave the designated route at the entrance to Snelling Branch Greenway on Dixon. Shelley Lake Trail picks up at the other end of Snelling Branch. On the far side of Shelley Lake, you can get on Ironwood Trail and return to the designated route on North Hills Drive at the 4.3-mile mark. North Hills Road and Northbrook Drive are heavily traveled during rush hour, and both crossings of West Millbrook Road are hazardous.

## Raleigh Bike Route 3

**Length:** 5 miles
**Difficulty:** Easy

**Directions:** Take I-40 or I-440 to Wade Avenue (Exit 4). Approximately 0.4 mile past the intersection of I-40 and I-440, turn left onto Ridge Road. You can park at the swimming pool, which is about 0.8 mile ahead on the left next to Martin Middle School.

This loop is located northwest of downtown, just inside the beltline. It consists mostly of lightly traveled

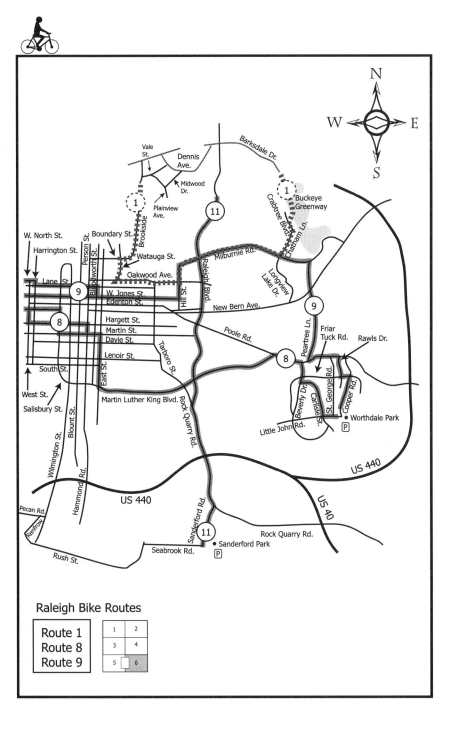

Raleigh Bike Routes

| Route 1 | | |
|---|---|---|
| Route 8 | | |
| Route 9 | | |

| 1 | 2 |
|---|---|
| 3 | 4 |
| 5 | 6 |

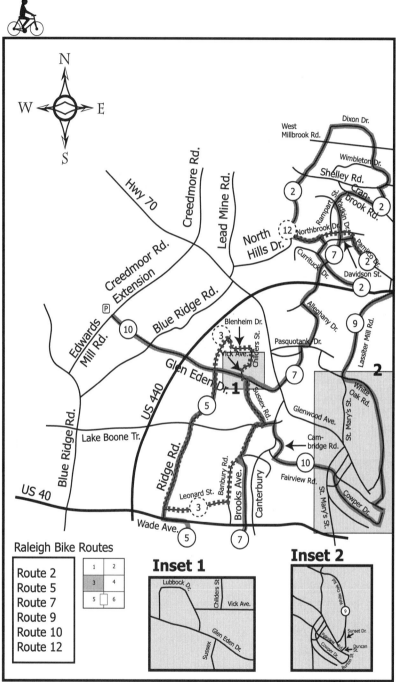

**Raleigh Bike Routes**

Route 2
Route 5
Route 7
Route 9
Route 10
Route 12

| 1 | 2 |
|---|---|
| 3 | 4 |
| 5 | 6 |

**Inset 1**

**Inset 2**

residential roads. Ridge Road is a bit busier than the others but has 2 miles of marked bicycle lanes that give cyclists some room to operate. The route passes alongside the same green space occupied by Beaver Dam Trail, see page 265. Glen Eden Drive and Lake Boone Trail are both heavily traveled during rush hour, and the crossing of Dixie Trail is hazardous.

## Raleigh Bike Route 4

**Length:** 5.7 miles
**Difficulty:** Easy

**Directions:** From I-40, take the Raleigh-Chapel Hill Expressway (Exit 289) toward Raleigh North/Raleigh East. Merge onto the expressway and travel 2.8 miles, then merge onto I-440 South/ U.S. 1 South, heading toward I-40 East/Hillsborough Street. Take the N.C. 54/Hillsborough Street exit (Exit 3). Take the slight left ramp, heading toward Meredith College. After 0.1 mile, turn left onto Hillsborough Street/N.C. 54. Travel 0.3 mile and turn right onto Beryl Road. Travel 0.1 mile and turn left onto Method Road. Method Park, where you can park, is at 514 Method Road.

This short, flat loop begins at Method Park and offers a good look at Dorton Arena, the south side of the state fairgrounds, and the bucolic scenery of the NCSU veterinary school. It also passes the NCSU Arboretum and four neighborhood parks. The roads are primarily lightly traveled residential streets. Method Road/Kent Road has the most traffic. The intersections at Western Boulevard and Blue Ridge Road are hazardous at all times.

## Raleigh Bike Route 5

**Length:** 5.3 miles
**Difficulty:** Easy to moderate

**Directions:** Park at Lake Johnson Park, which is described on page 237. Take the Lake Johnson Trail (page 237) or the Upper Walnut Trail (page 259) to the southern terminus of Route 5.

This north-south route begins just east of Lake Johnson in the southwest corner of the city and heads north past the western edge of NCSU and the eastern edge of Meredith College. The roads that comprise the route (Gorman Street, Wade Avenue, and Ridge Road) become clogged with cars during rush hour. Be particularly alert at the intersections along Wade Avenue, at the intersection of Gorman Street and Avent Ferry Road, and while riding past the parallel-parked cars on Gorman Street.

## Raleigh Bike Route 6

**Length:** 6.3 miles
**Difficulty:** Easy

**Directions:** From I-440, take the Rock Quarry Road exit (Exit 301). Turn south onto Rock Quarry Road and drive a little over a mile to the entrance to Sanderford Park. It is on the left, just before you reach Seabrook Road. Park near the eastern terminus of the route, which is located at the intersection of Seabrook and Sanderford Roads.

This east-west route passes through rapidly growing neighborhoods in south Raleigh just outside the beltline. Carolina Pines Park lies on the route, and Sanderford Park is just 0.1 mile north of its eastern terminus on Raleigh Bike Route 11. The roads are lightly traveled, though the intersections at Hammond Road, Wilmington Street, South Saunders Street, and Lake Wheeler Road can all be hazardous at times.

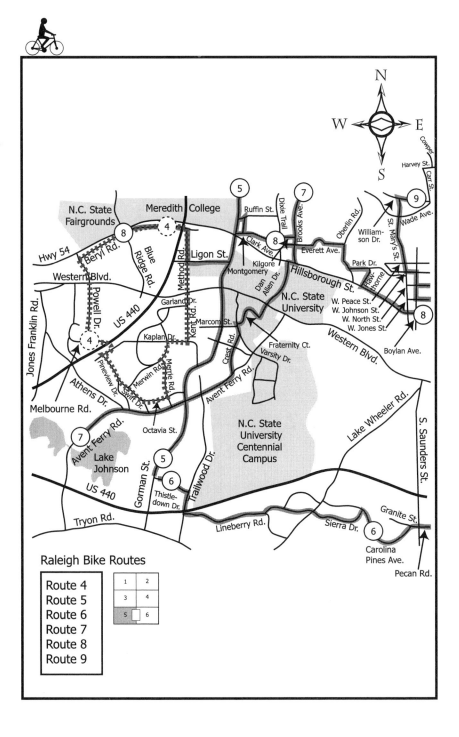

Raleigh Bike Routes

Route 4
Route 5
Route 6
Route 7
Route 8
Route 9

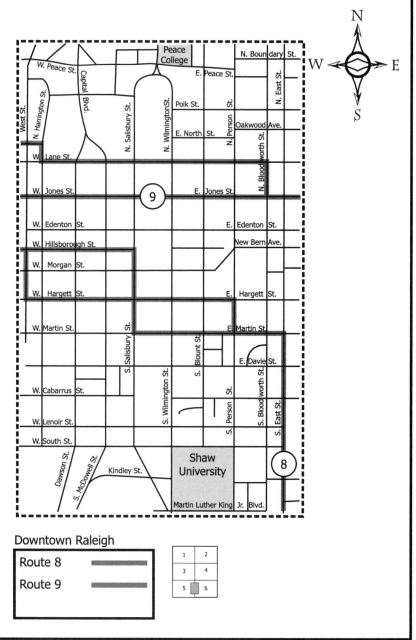

## Downtown Raleigh

| Route 8 | ▬▬▬▬▬ |
| --- | --- |
| Route 9 | ▬▬▬▬▬ |

| 1 | 2 |
| --- | --- |
| 3 | 4 |
| 5 | 6 |

## Raleigh Bike Route 7

**Length:** 8.7 miles
**Difficulty:** Easy

**Directions:** For directions to Lake Johnson Park, see Route 5 or page 237.

This north-south route begins at Lake Johnson, passes through NCSU, and follows Brooks Avenue through the quaint neighborhoods just north of the campus. Farther north, it sticks to residential roads before ending just north of the beltline in the North Hills neighborhood. Don't ride the southern half of this route unless you're comfortable with traffic. Avent Ferry Road is heavily traveled, as are all the roads on the NCSU campus. The intersections at Wade Avenue and Glenwood Avenue are hazardous.

## Raleigh Bike Route 8

**Length:** 9.3 miles
**Difficulty:** Easy

**Directions:** From I-440, take the Poole Road exit (Exit 15). Turn west and drive approximately 1.2 miles. Go past the shopping center and turn left at the light onto Sunnybrook Road. Worthdale Park, which is on the right before you cross Walnut Creek, is where you park to catch the eastern terminus of this route.

From the western edge of the city near the state fairgrounds, this east-west route passes through the neighborhoods north of NCSU and then the downtown warehouse district. A long stretch on Martin Luther King Boulevard leads to the southeast corner of the city and Worthdale Park. Many of the roads are busy. By far the best time to take this ride is an early morning during a spring weekend, when traffic is light and the flowering plants at the arboretum, the Little Theater Rose Garden, and King Gardens are in bloom.

## Raleigh Bike Route 9

**Length:** 12.4 miles
**Difficulty:** Moderate

**Directions:** See directions to Worthdale Park in Route 8.

This varied cross-town route shows Raleigh's different faces. From the southeast corner of the city near Worthdale Park, it heads north through old neighborhoods before going downtown. You'll ride past the fences surrounding Saint Augustine's College, through the historic Oakwood residential district, and past the Capital Area Visitors Center, where information about downtown attractions is available.

As the route leaves downtown and heads for north Raleigh, it passes through old "inside the beltline" neighborhoods like the tony Williamson Drive. Before moving north of the beltline, it crosses Crabtree Creek and goes past Lassiter Mill Greenway, which is well worth a brief detour. Beyond the beltline, it passes North Hills Mall and goes through more residential areas before ending at Cedar Hills Park, which boasts a disc golf course and other amenities.

Many of the roads on this route are busy, and all of the downtown intersections can be hazardous. Take special care in crossing New Bern Avenue, Glenwood Avenue, and Six Forks Road.

## Raleigh Bike Route 10

**Length:** 5.8 miles
**Difficulty:** Easy to moderate

**Directions:** From I-40, take the Raleigh-Chapel Hill

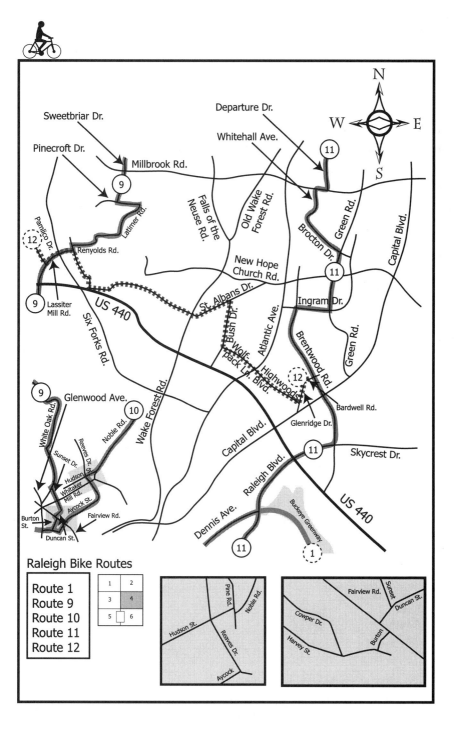

Raleigh Bike Routes

Route 1
Route 9
Route 10
Route 11
Route 12

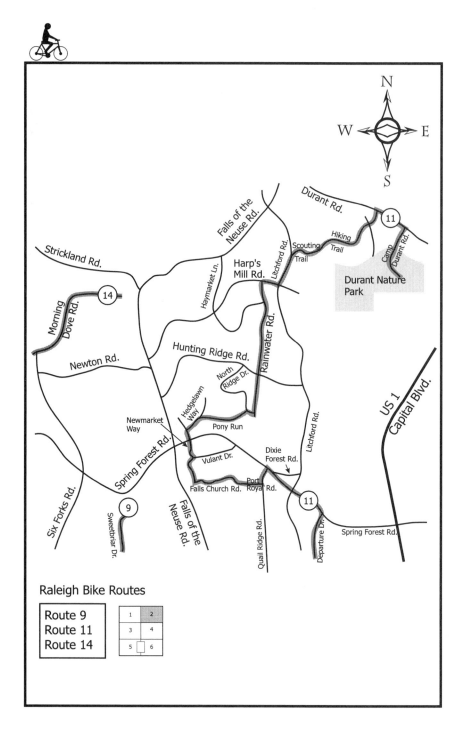

N
W &larr;&rarr; E
S

Durant Rd.

Falls of the Neuse Rd.

11

Strickland Rd.

Litchford Rd.

Scouting Trail

Hiking Trail

Harp's Mill Rd.

Camp Durant Rd.

Durant Nature Park

Haymarket Ln.

14

Morning Dove Rd.

Rainwater Rd.

Newton Rd.

Hunting Ridge Rd.

North Ridge Dr.

US 1 Capital Blvd.

Hedgelawn Way

Litchford Rd.

Newmarket Way

Pony Run

Spring Forest Rd.

Vulant Dr.

Dixie Forest Rd.

Six Forks Rd.

Falls Church Rd.

Port Royal Rd.

11

Sweetbriar Dr.

9

Falls of the Neuse Rd.

Quail Ridge Rd.

Departure Dr.

Spring Forest Rd.

Raleigh Bike Routes

| Route 9 |
| Route 11 |
| Route 14 |

| 1 | 2 |
| 3 | 4 |
| 5 | 6 |

Expressway (Exit 289), heading toward Raleigh North/ Raleigh East. Merge onto the expressway. Travel 1 mile and take the Edwards Mill Road exit. Turn slightly left onto Edwards Mill Road. Laurel Hills Park is located at 3808 Edwards Mill Road.

This east-west route goes from Laurel Hills Park in west Raleigh to Kiwanis Park and Fallon Creek Trail, see page 251. north of downtown. You'll have to negotiate a small commercial district around the intersection with Oberlin Road, but most of the route passes through residential areas.


## Raleigh Bike Route 11

**Length:** 16.2 miles
**Difficulty:** Moderate

**Directions:** Park at Sanderford Park. See Route 6 for directions.

This is the longest of Raleigh's bike routes and the most consistently dangerous. It begins in the southeast corner of the city at Sanderford Park and heads north along busy roads populated by relatively fast-moving vehicles. Traffic is constant until you get north of Capital Boulevard, where it starts to slacken a bit. You'll encounter several dangerous intersections. A particularly hazardous one is at Spring Forest Road, which you'll cross at 11.7 miles. You'll have to negotiate five lanes of traffic without the benefit of a light. Beyond Millbrook Exchange Park, the streets become quieter as you wind through the new neighborhoods around Durant Nature Park. This route crosses every other eastern Raleigh bike route. All in all, it's a reasonable ride for city commuters, but the southern half is not pleasant enough for a recreational ride and should be avoided by anyone not skilled in riding with traffic.

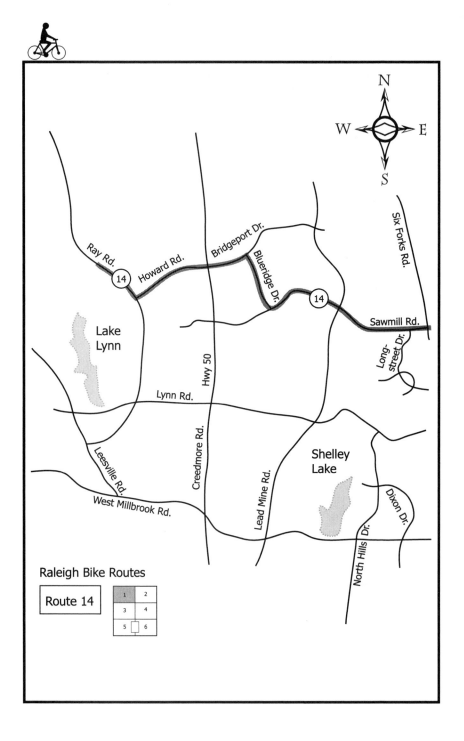

N
W    E
S

Six Forks Rd.

Ray Rd.

⑭ Howard Rd.

Bridgeport Dr.

Blueridge Dr.

⑭

Sawmill Rd.

Long-
street Dr.

Lake
Lynn

Hwy 50

Lynn Rd.

Creedmore Rd.

Leesville Rd.

West Millbrook Rd.

Lead Mine Rd.

Shelley
Lake

Dixon Dr.

North Hills Dr.

Raleigh Bike Routes

Route 14

| 1 | 2 |
| 3 | 4 |
| 5 | 6 |

## Raleigh Bike Route 12

**Length:** 5.4 miles
**Difficulty:** Easy

**Directions:** For directions, see the North Hills Trail on page 250 under the Leadmine Creek Greenway section.

This east-west route has its western terminus on North Hills Drive just north of Leadmine Creek Greenway. It passes through the North Hills neighborhood, then follows a long stretch of St. Albans Drive into northeast Raleigh before ending at the intersection with Raleigh Bike Route 11. Other than in the immediate vicinity of North Hills Mall, traffic along most of the route is light to moderate. You'll encounter dangerous intersections at Six Forks Road, Wake Forest Road, and Atlantic Avenue. Also, watch for the deep railroad tracks on Wolfpack Lane.

## Raleigh Bike Route 14

**Length:** 4.9 miles
**Difficulty:** Easy to moderate

**Directions:** From I-540, take the Leesville Road exit (Exit 7). Go 0.2 mile and turn right onto Leesville Road. Travel 0.2 mile and stay straight to go onto Strickland Road. Travel 1.3 miles and turn slightly right onto Ray Road. Lake Lynn Park is at 7921 Ray Road.

This east-west route goes from Lake Lynn Park in northwest Raleigh to Mourning Dove Road. You'll encounter moderate traffic. Due to its narrow shoulders and steady traffic, Ray Road is the worst stretch for cyclists.

# Carolina Connection (US Bike Route 1)

**Address:** Office of Pedestrian and Bicycle Transportation, North Carolina Department of Transportation, P.O. Box 25201, Raleigh, NC 27611
**Telephone:** 919-733-2804

The Carolina Connection travels through the Piedmont and Sandhills of North Carolina. This route is the North Carolina section of US Bike Route 1, which runs from Maine to Florida. The directional signs along US Bike Route 1 are black and white, rather than the usual green and white of the North Carolina Bicycling Highways. Like the rest of the bicycling highways, this route was originally laid out along lightly traveled rural back roads. Yes, that's right, High House Road and Aviation Parkway were rural roads once upon a time. Following the southern section of the route will take you along some of the most car-clogged, harrowing stretches of roadway in the state. It's possible to ride the route through Cary without getting killed—as my existence attests—but it's neither pleasant nor advisable unless you're comfortable with constant traffic and an almost total lack of shoulders. If you're interested in doing the southern section but don't like traffic, begin at one of the Jordan Lake recreation areas, map out your own course from Wilsonville, and connect with the route near Merry Oaks.

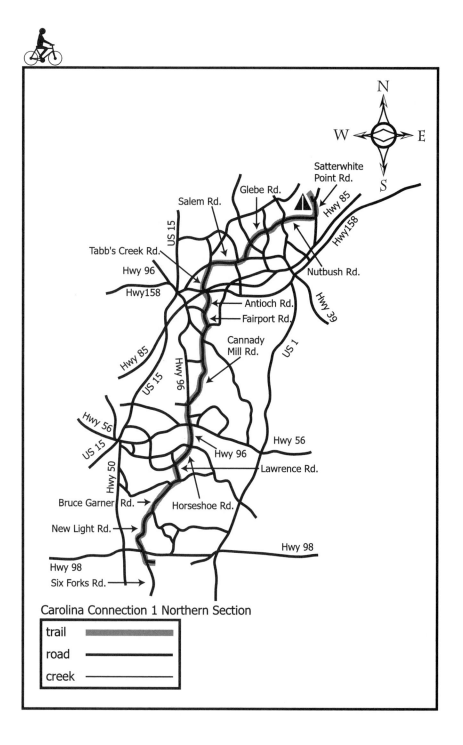

N

W ⬥ E

S

Satterwhite
Point Rd.

Glebe Rd.

Salem Rd.

US 15

Hwy 85

Hwy158

Tabb's Creek Rd.

Hwy 96

Hwy158

Nutbush Rd.

Antioch Rd.

Fairport Rd.

Hwy 39

Cannady
Mill Rd.

US 1

Hwy 85

Hwy 96

US 15

Hwy 56

US 15

Hwy 56

Hwy 96

Lawrence Rd.

Hwy 50

Bruce Garner Rd.

Horseshoe Rd.

New Light Rd.

Hwy 98

Hwy 98

Six Forks Rd.

Carolina Connection 1 Northern Section

| trail | ▬▬▬▬ |
|-------|------|
| road  | ———— |
| creek | ———— |

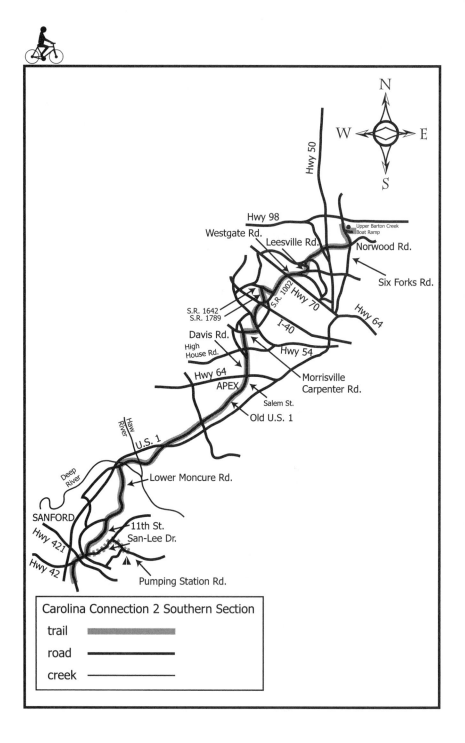

N
W — E
S

Hwy 50

Hwy 98

Westgate Rd.

Leesville Rd.

Upper Barton Creek
Boat Ramp

Norwood Rd.

Six Forks Rd.

S.R. 1002    Hwy 70

S.R. 1642
S.R. 1789

I-40

Davis Rd.

High
House Rd.

Hwy 54

Hwy 64

Hwy 64

APEX

Morrisville
Carpenter Rd.

Salem St.

Old U.S. 1

Haw
River

U.S. 1

Deep
River

Lower Moncure Rd.

SANFORD

Hwy 421

11th St.
San-Lee Dr.

Hwy 42

Pumping Station Rd.

Carolina Connection 2 Southern Section

trail

road

creek

Cary aside, this route has many attractions. The northern section will take you past Falls Lake in Wake County, then north through Granville County before turning east toward Kerr Lake just outside Oxford. Campgrounds are located at both ends of the northern section, so an out-and-back weekend tour is possible. Once you've cleared Cary, the southern section travels through Apex, then follows a pleasant path through rural Chatham County on its way to downtown Sanford. Campgrounds are also located at both ends of the southern section.

## Northern Section

**Length:** 45.5 miles
**Difficulty:** Easy to moderate
**Maps:** North Carolina DOT Bicycling Highway Maps C-4 and C-5; begin with C-4.

At the start of this route, you're likely to encounter trucks towing boats on the roads around Falls Lake. Sometimes, the drivers of these vehicles forget to allow for the width or length of their trailers when passing cyclists. The boat traffic is greatest on weekends in the warm months. Ride defensively. There is one short section on NC 158 that requires extra caution because of high-speed traffic.

Once you clear Falls Lake, this is a rural ride with sporadic evidence of suburbia. The terrain is gently rolling, and the road surfaces are almost all exceptionally smooth. The scenery consists mainly of fields and woods broken by small houses, trailers, and occasional farmhouses and Neo-Colonial contemporary homes. The route crosses the Tar River at a scenic spot and passes through the quaint community of Wilton.

The section from Fairport Road north goes through the community of Dickerson and near Oxford. A few stretches of road pass through residential areas with moderate traffic, though nothing compared to the stretch in Cary. The scenery includes tobacco fields and cornfields that are pleasantly interrupted by Georgian farmhouses and horse pastures. Just prior to reaching the Vance

County line, you'll see the 1860-vintage Salem United Methodist Church on the left.

### Highlights and Services

**1.2 miles:** You'll pass Shinleaf Recreation Area.

**1.5 miles:** You'll cross Falls Lake.

**2.6 miles:** You'll pass Holly Point Recreation Area.

**7.4 miles:** A store is on the right.

**9.8 miles:** You'll cross Smith Creek.

**14.7 miles:** A small grocery store and a grill are located at the intersection of NC 96 and NC 56 at Wilton.

**18.8 miles:** You'll cross the Tar River.

**23.1 miles:** You'll pass the Granville County Livestock Arena.

**24.4 miles:** You'll pass through Dickerson.

**26.8 miles:** A volunteer fire department is on the left.

**33.7 miles:** You'll reach the Vance County line.

**39.6 miles:** La Grange Plantation Inn Bed-and-Breakfast, built around 1771, is on the left.

**39.7 miles:** You'll pass the entrance to Nutbush Recreation Area.

**40.5 miles:** You'll cross a finger of Kerr Lake.

## Southern Section

**Length:** Depends on rerouting; see below.
**Difficulty:** Easy
**Maps:** North Carolina DOT Bicycling Highways Maps C-4, C-3, and C-2; begin with C-4.

As this guide was going to press, the southern section of the route was being rerouted between the intersection of Westgate Road and US 70 and the intersection of NC 54 and Morrisville Carpenter Drive. An alternate starting place is downtown Apex.

This section begins in Cary, takes you down Main Street in Apex, and passes through the rural communities of Friendship and New Hill. The ride along Old US 1 loosely parallels the Norfolk & Southern Railroad line. Once you leave Wake County and head into Chatham County, you'll pass through the rural communities of New Hill, Merry Oaks, Haywood, and Moncure. There's plenty to look at as the route crosses the Haw and Deep Rivers. South of Moncure, the route dips into Lee County and continues south of Sanford through the Sandhills, which are beyond the scope of this guide. In Sanford, it passes through downtown, where small businesses, restaurants, and a bike shop line the streets. Traffic can be heavy, but posted speed limits in the downtown are relatively low. If you'd like to spend the night in the area, San-Lee Environmental Education and Recreation Park is a good place to camp.

## Highlights and Services

**3.5 miles:** You'll reach the intersection of High House Road and Davis Drive in Cary, where you'll find restaurants, a hotel, shops, grocery stores, etc.
**6.9 miles:** A store is on the right.
**14.2 miles:** You'll pass through New Hill.
**16.8 miles:** You'll pass through Bonsal.
**19.1 miles:** A store is on the right.
**19.4 miles:** You'll pass Merry Oaks Baptist Church.
**22.9 miles:** You'll cross the Haw River.
**24.1 miles:** A store is on the right.
**25.0 miles:** You'll cross the Deep River.
**29.1 miles:** You'll cross Roberts Creek.
**33.9 miles:** You'll cross Lick Creek.

# Cape Fear Run

**Address:** Office of Pedestrian and Bicycle Transportation, North Carolina Department of Transportation, P.O. Box 25201, Raleigh, NC 27611
**Telephone:** 919-733-2804
**Length:** 52.2 miles
**Difficulty:** Easy to moderate
**Maps:** North Carolina DOT Bicycling Highways Maps E-1 and E-2; begin with E-1.

The Cape Fear Run, otherwise known as Route 5, begins in Apex at the intersection of Salem Street and Center Street (SR 1010). The intersection lies along US Bicycling Route 1. From Apex, the route heads southeast out of the Triangle toward its terminus in Wilmington. The section of the Cape Fear Run described below goes as far south as the town of Wade.

Apex is a former railroad town named for its status as the highest point on the Chatham Railroad between Richmond, Virginia, and Jacksonville, Florida. It sits atop the crest that divides two river basins. Locals are fond of saying that rain falling on one side of the street flows to the Neuse, while rain falling on the other side flows to the Cape Fear.

Beyond Apex, the route passes through the growing communities of Holly Springs and Fuquay-Varina and skirts the edge of Cary. New subdivisions with large homes and small trees rise above the odd trailer and farmhouse. Open spaces are rapidly disappearing, and traffic is a constant, even on weekdays. On the upside, there are shoulders for most of this first section, and plenty

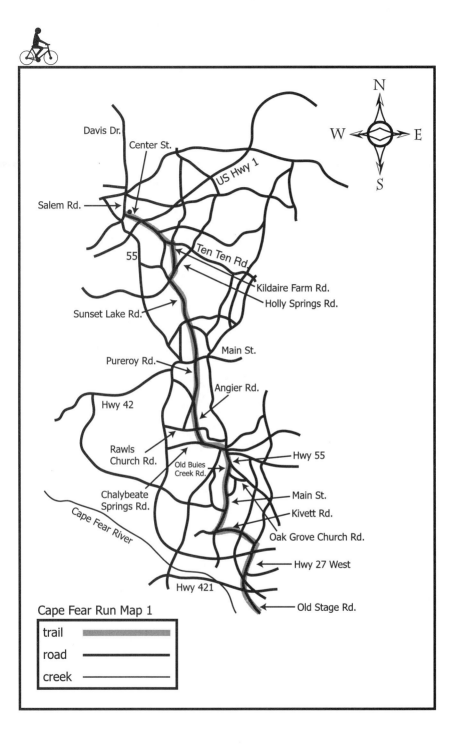

N
W ⊕ E
S

Davis Dr.
Center St.
US Hwy 1
Salem Rd.
55
Ten Ten Rd.
Kildaire Farm Rd.
Holly Springs Rd.
Sunset Lake Rd.
Main St.
Pureroy Rd.
Angier Rd.
Hwy 42
Rawls
Church Rd.
Old Buies
Creek Rd.
Hwy 55
Chalybeate
Springs Rd.
Main St.
Kivett Rd.
Cape Fear River
Oak Grove Church Rd.
Hwy 27 West
Hwy 421
Old Stage Rd.

Cape Fear Run Map 1

| trail | |
|-------|--|
| road | |
| creek | |

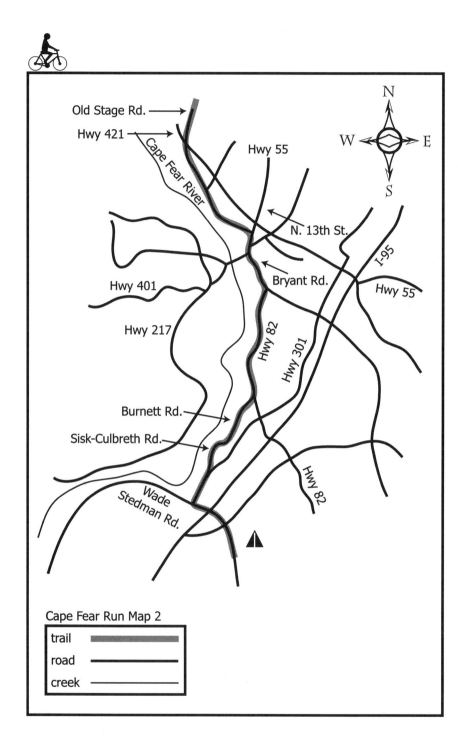

Old Stage Rd.

Hwy 421

Cape Fear River

Hwy 55

N. 13th St.

Bryant Rd.

I-95

Hwy 401

Hwy 217

Hwy 55

Hwy 82

Hwy 301

Burnett Rd.

Sisk-Culbreth Rd.

Hwy 82

Wade Stedman Rd.

N
W  E
S

Cape Fear Run Map 2

| trail | |
| road | |
| creek | |

of services are available. Gently rolling hills make for a moderate ride during the first 15 miles.

Beyond Fuquay-Varina, the traffic is lighter but still plentiful as the scenery takes a turn for the pastoral. The town of Angier is an appealing spot where you can get a decent cup of coffee and a snack. Once you've cleared Angier, the traffic of the Triangle is behind you. If you ride in summer, you can watch tobacco and vegetables grow. If you're out during the fall, the cotton fields may just be in bloom. The route takes you through the town of Buies Creek, where the clay hills of the Piedmont give way to the sandy flats of the coastal plain, making your pedaling a bit easier.

The last sizable town you'll pass through is Erwin, where traffic picks up again but is still lighter than in the Triangle proper. The final attraction on this section before the Cumberland County line is the Averasboro Battleground. The museum, the battlefields, the historical markers, and the privately owned antebellum house that once served as a Confederate hospital are all on the bike route.

Although you can't see the Cape Fear River from the roads that make up the Cape Fear Run, the route roughly parallels the river past Buies Creek. If you'd like to get a glimpse of the Cape Fear, the easiest place to do so is Erwin. As you pass through town on NC 82, look for NC 217 West. The river is 1 mile off the route.

If you'd like a shorter ride that passes some interesting sights, the public parking lot at the Averasboro Battleground is a good starting point. The roads through that area are flat, traffic is relatively light, and the riding is pleasant and easy.

## Highlights and Services

**9.7 miles:** A convenience store is on the right.

**11.3 miles:** You'll cross Terrible Creek.

**18.4 miles:** You'll make the first of two crossings of Neills Creek.

**26.2 miles:** You'll cross the northern extreme of the Black River.

**29.3 miles:** You'll cross Buies Creek.

**32.8 miles:** You'll cross Thornton's Creek.

**35.7 miles:** You'll cross Juniper Creek.

**41.8 miles:** You'll pass a home that served as a Confederate hospital. Other sites associated with the Averasboro Battlefield are well marked and clearly visible from the road.

**43.3 miles:** You'll reach the Cumberland County line.

**51.7 miles:** Stores are located on either side of I-95.

**52.2 miles:** You'll reach the KOA campground in Wade; to contact the campground, call 910-484-5500.

*North Carolina Bicycling Highway Route 2*

# North Carolina Bicycling Highway Route 2 (Mountains-to-Sea Route)

**Address:** Office of Pedestrian and Bicycle Transportation, North Carolina Department of Transportation, P.O. Box 25201, Raleigh, NC 27611
**Telephone:** 919-733-2804

This ride begins in the western North Carolina town of Murphy and winds 700 miles across the state before ending at the coastal town of Manteo. On its way from west to east, it passes through the Triangle counties of Alamance, Orange, Chatham, Wake, and Franklin. The Triangle section is as varied as the state's bicycling highways get. It takes you down meandering country roads with expansive views of fields, pastures, and farmhouses. It also includes congested roads where traffic is fast and often dangerous. Needless to say, the views along the busy sections are not the most appealing, if you dare to take your eyes off the road. If you're determined to peddle every mile of Route 2 through the Triangle, it is possible to survive, as I can attest. Your odds will be substantially increased if you pick an off-peak time, such as just after sunrise on a weekend morning. As described below, Route 2 is divided into three sections. Each section is from 30 to 35 miles long and offers public parking at one or both ends.

## Western Section: Jordan Lake to Snow Camp

**Length:** 31 miles
**Difficulty:** Moderate
**Map:** North Carolina DOT Bicycling Highway Map A-10

This section starts in Chatham County at the Fearrington Point Boat Ramps on Jordan Lake. To begin the route, turn left out of the boat-ramp driveway onto Farrington Point Road. The route will take you through the growing southern end of Chapel Hill and into downtown Carrboro before heading into the countryside at the western extreme of the Triangle. The section between Old Farrington Road and US 15/US 501 is heavily traveled, particularly during rush hour and on weekends, but it's a pleasant ride during off-peak times. Traffic close to Chapel Hill can be unbearable during rush hour, but once you've crossed US 15/US 501, the posted speed limits are relatively low. The most dangerous stretch of the ride is probably the hill leading to downtown Carrboro. This narrow, steep section of road has no bike lanes and constant traffic at peak times. The best time to ride it is early on a weekend or at midday during the week.

Route 2 gets more pleasant as you head west out of Carrboro, thanks in part to the town's designated bike lanes. After that, the shoulders range from measly to nonexistent, so you shouldn't ride this section unless you're comfortable sharing the road with cars. Traffic is heavy on Jones Ferry Road. Cyclists should be particularly cautious from NC 54 Bypass to the turn onto Old Greensboro Highway. This section of road is narrow and winding and sees lots of traffic. Old Greensboro Highway is less congested. In fact, the farther you get from Carrboro, the fewer cars you'll encounter. Still, the route demands caution, as the traffic travels at high speed and there are many blind curves.

Beyond the Haw River, the ride gets better and better. Traffic lessens, and the route passes some interesting sights. On the route is a Friends meeting house organized in the late 1700s that is a great place for a picnic. Although development is ongoing, the rolling hills and farms of the rural Piedmont still dominate the scenery. The route passes through the town of Snow Camp, where, in summer, an outdoor drama tells stories of this area's Quaker history.

## Highlights and Services

**1.2 miles:** You'll pass a store.

**9.6 miles:** The route heads left on Main Street in downtown Carrboro. Many services are located to the right. A bike shop is on the route just beyond this intersection.

**10.5 miles:** You'll pass under NC 54. Fast-food restaurants and a grocery store are to the right.

**11.1 miles:** You'll cross University Lake.

**12.3 miles:** You'll cross Phils Creek.

**20.6 miles:** You'll enter Alamance County and cross the Haw River.

**23.6 miles:** You'll cross NC 87. Stores are located to the left and right.

**24.7 miles:** You'll pass the historic Spring Friends Meeting House.

## Central Section: Falls Lake to Jordan Lake

**Length:** 35.1 miles
**Difficulty:** Easy to moderate
**Maps:** North Carolina DOT Bicycling Highway Maps A-10 and A-11

This section of Route 2 contains roads like Aviation Parkway and Davis Drive, familiar to anyone who tunes in to Triangle traffic reports. Bicycling during peak traffic on the section that goes from Cary through the Leesville area is nothing short of suicidal. That said, you'll see the occasional stunned Mountains-to-Sea tourist with fully loaded panniers whose North Carolina DOT maps give no warning of an ill-timed ride on Davis Drive. From Cary to the Leesville area, the shoulders are frequently nonexistent and the drivers are aggressive and harried.

Some sections are reasonably safe except during the busiest hours. The roads from Jordan Lake to the edge of Cary's intense development and those in the vicinity of Falls Lake can be pleasant, though occasionally crowded.

Just east of Jordan Lake, the route passes the exceptionally beautiful Martha's Chapel and takes you through the quiet community of Green Level, where you'll see an old-fashioned country store and horses grazing in pastures. I'm not aware of another stretch of road in the state that can rival the variety of architectural styles exhibited by the residences of the appealingly eclectic Green Level. Route 2 then passes through Cary, goes through Morrisville, crosses Lake Crabtree, and skirts the edge of RDU International Airport on its way to Leesville. North of Leesville, the traffic goes from murderous to merely dangerous. The ride becomes decidedly more pleasant on Six Forks Road. Beyond Six Forks is Falls Lake. Although NC 98 is busy, it has an adequate shoulder.

## Highlights and Services

**0.6 mile:** You'll cross Jordan Lake.
**3.9 miles:** You'll cross a tributary of Crabtree Creek.
**5.1 miles:** You'll pass the Green Level Equestrian Center.
**8.2 miles:** You'll pass the Green Level Country Store.
**8.5 miles:** You'll cross Bachelor Branch.
**10.2 miles:** You'll pass a shopping center.
**11.5 miles:** You'll pass another shopping center.
**17.3 miles:** You'll cross Lake Crabtree.
**17.6 miles:** The entrance to Lake Crabtree County Park is on the right.
**29.8 miles:** You'll cross NC 50 (Creedmoor Road) and pass convenience and grocery stores.
**31.4 miles:** You'll cross Upper Barton Creek.

**33.9 miles:** You'll cross Falls Lake.

**34.2 miles:** You'll pass Pleasant Union Church Road (SR 1847), which is the turnoff to Blue Jay Point County Park.

**34.6 miles:** You'll pass a fishing access area.

**34.8 miles:** You'll cross Falls Lake.

## Eastern Section: Falls Lake to Nash County

**Length:** 35.4 miles

**Difficulty:** Easy to moderate

**Maps:** North Carolina DOT Bicycling Highway Maps A-11 and A-12

This section begins at the Upper Barton Creek Boat Ramps, where you can park for free. You'll cross Falls Lake before heading out of Wake County and through Franklin County. The route passes through the small town of Youngsville, then meanders past tobacco fields, cornfields, and the occasional farm pond. Just beyond Youngsville, it passes the headwaters of the Little River, although they aren't visible from the road.

The riding along this stretch of well-maintained roads is mostly pleasant and significantly less harrowing than the Central Section of Route 2. The rural area has seen development, but the new neighborhoods and accompanying traffic are occasional instead of constant. The route flattens out a bit as it heads east. The rolling hills are perceptibly more gentle than those on the Western Section of Route 2.

### Highlights and Services

**2.2 miles:** You'll cross Falls Lake.

**3.3 miles:** You'll pass a store.

**12.7 miles:** You'll cross Horse Creek.

**17.3 miles:** You'll pass a country store offering gem mining.

**23.6 miles:** You'll pass another store.

**24.5 miles:** You'll pass a store.

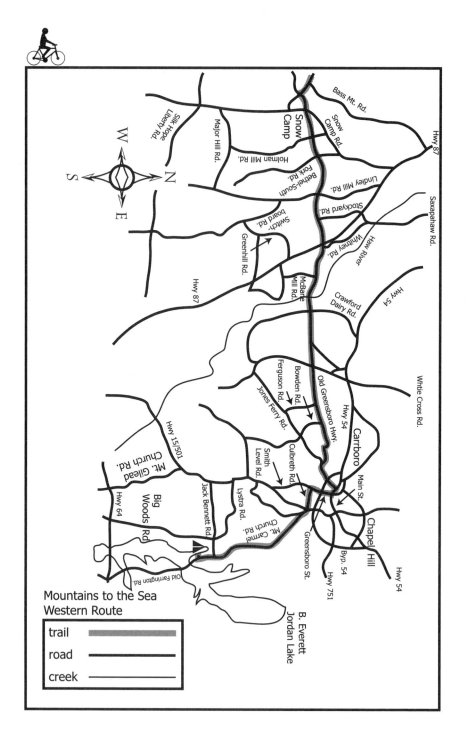

Mountains to the Sea
Western Route

| trail | ████████ |
| road | ─────── |
| creek | ─────── |

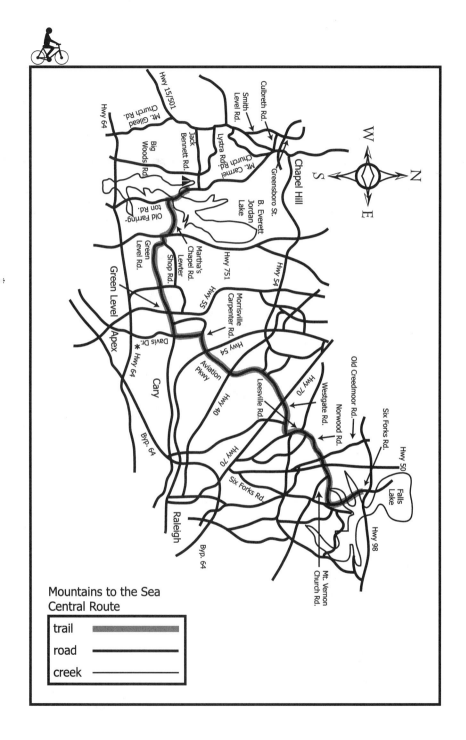

Mountains to the Sea
Central Route

| | |
|---|---|
| trail | |
| road | |
| creek | |

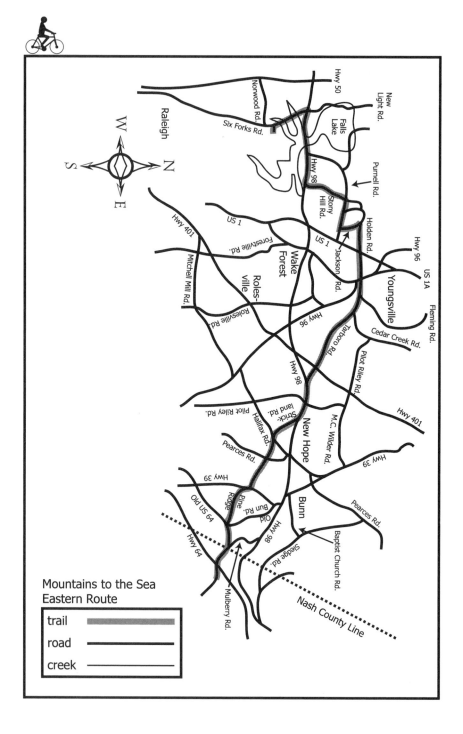

Raleigh

Hwy 50

New Light Rd.

Norwood Rd.

Six Forks Rd.

Falls Lake

Hwy 98

Purnell Rd.

Stony Hill Rd.

Holden Rd.

US 1

US 1

Hwy 96

US 1A

Hwy 401

Forestville Rd.

Wake Forest

Jackson Rd.

Youngsville

Mitchell Mill Rd.

Roles-ville

Hwy 96

Tarboro Rd.

Cedar Creek Rd.

Fleming Rd.

Rolesville Rd.

Hwy 98

Pilot Riley Rd.

Hwy 401

Pilot Riley Rd.

Strick-land Rd.

Halifax Rd.

New Hope

M.C. Wilder Rd.

Pearces Rd.

Hwy 39

Hwy 39

Old US 64

Pine Ridge Rd.

Old Bun Rd.

Hwy 98

Bunn

Pearces Rd.

Hwy 64

Sledge Rd.

Baptist Church Rd.

Mulberry Rd.

Nash County Line

## Mountains to the Sea
## Eastern Route

| trail | ▬▬▬▬▬▬▬ |
| road | ———— |
| creek | ———— |

# North Line Trace

**Address:** For information and maps, contact the Office of Pedestrian and Bicycle Transportation, North Carolina Department of Transportation, P.O. Box 25201, Raleigh, NC 27611 (919-733-2804). For information about the Kerr Lake campgrounds, contact the Nutbush Bridge and Satterwhite Point Recreation Areas, 6254 Satterwhite Point Road, Henderson, NC 27536 (252-438-7791). For information about Hyco Lake Recreation Area, contact the Person-Caswell Lake Authority by calling 336-599-4343.
**Length:** 63 miles
**Difficulty:** Moderate

North Line Trace ranks with the best road biking anywhere. The trace has particular appeal for weekend bicycle tourists, thanks to the accommodations at both ends of the route through the Triangle area. Hyco Lake Recreation Area and its campground lie on the western edge of Person County. At the eastern end, the Kerr Lake area has campgrounds. An out-and-back tour from either end is a great way to spend a weekend.

The route boasts rolling hills, smooth roads, light traffic, and bucolic scenery including lovely creeks and the Tar River. It passes through Person County, Granville County, and the western edge of Vance County near Kerr Lake. It also visits downtown Roxboro.

You can begin the route at the Caswell County-Person County line near the Hyco Reservoir, where you'll find parking, camping, picnicking, fishing, and boating. Start your ride by heading east on Kelly Brewer Road (SR 1313).

## Highlights and Services

**1.2 miles:** You'll cross the Hyco Reservoir.

**1.4 miles:** You'll pass the CP&L Hyco Lake Recreation Area.

**3.4 miles:** You'll cross the reservoir again.

**13.3 miles:** You'll pass a store.

**17.1 miles:** You'll cross Marlowe Creek.

**18.6 miles:** You'll cross Mill Creek.

**21.6 miles:** You'll pass a store.

**23.8 miles:** You'll pass a volunteer fire department.

**25.0 miles:** You'll cross the Tar River.

**26.7 miles:** You'll pass through the community of Denny's Store.

**30.6 miles:** You'll cross Shelton Creek.

**32.0 miles:** You'll pass through Goshen and cross Fox Creek.

**36.4 miles:** You'll cross Grassy Creek.

**41.3 miles:** You'll cross Mountain Creek.

**43.9 miles:** You'll cross Grassy Creek.

**48.2 miles:** You'll cross Gills Creek.

**49.9 miles:** You'll cross Michael Creek.

**50.2 miles:** You'll reach the Vance County-Granville County line.

**58.6 miles:** You'll pass a historic residence.

**58.7 miles:** The entrance to Nutbush Recreation Area is on the left.

**59.5 miles:** You'll cross Kerr Lake.

**63.0 miles:** You'll enter Satterwhite Point Recreation Area.

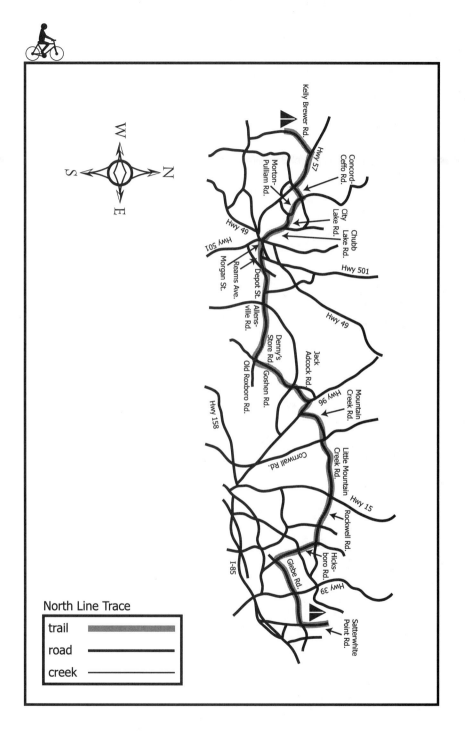

North Line Trace

| trail | |
|-------|--|
| road | |
| creek | |

# Triangle
# Paddling

*Cape Fear River Basin*

# Cape Fear River Basin

The uppermost streams of the Cape Fear River Basin begin west of the Triangle, near Greensboro and High Point. These streams form the Haw and Deep Rivers, which flow through the western and southern reaches of the Triangle and give us some of our best whitewater and flat-water paddling opportunities. The rivers and lakes of the Cape Fear River Basin, including Jordan Lake, supply many residents with drinking water, as well as the promise of a great day of paddling.

Population has taken a toll on the waters of the Cape Fear system. More than a quarter of all North Carolinians live on land drained by the Cape Fear River Basin, which contains the largest number of stream miles of any basin in the state. Fortunately, the Cape Fear River Basin has not suffered the same fate as the Neuse River Basin, which also drains much of the Triangle. The disastrous impact of industrialized hog production brought the Neuse River to national prominence in the 1990s. Although the Cape Fear River Basin—the most industrialized river system in the state—has thus far avoided such massive pollution, it faces a variety of ongoing threats. The chief threat is from sedimentation and runoff due to urban sprawl. And it's not only our local creeks, rivers, and lakes that suffer. As sediment eventually settles in the flat landscape of the coastal plain, the tiny organisms at the bottom of the food chain ingest toxins and in turn become poisonous to the fish that feed on them. And those fish become toxic to the larger organisms—including humans—that eat them.

As citizens and leaders have become aware of the threats that face the Cape Fear, many have tried to take action on the river's behalf. Education is probably the basin's best hope. The Triangle's development has brought many benefits, but the way we develop has consequences that can undermine our quality of life. Solutions encompass everything from budgeting for adequate wastewater facilities to leaving a buffer of natural vegetation alongside creeks and rivers to filter out sediment. Involvement with organizations like the Triangle Land Conservancy is another great way to reverse the trends that threaten the Cape Fear and other Triangle river basins. To date, the conservancy has directly protected or assisted in the protection of more than 2,100 acres along the Deep River and more than 1,200 acres along the Haw River. It has also helped add a 105-acre tract to Raven Rock State Park and protected several hundred more acres on other streams in the Cape Fear River Basin. If we are careful as individuals and demand that our leadership foster good stewardship, future generations of Triangle residents will be able to enjoy clean water.

# Haw River

**Maps:** USGS Mebane, Saxapahaw, White Cross, Silk Hope, Bynum, Farrington, New Hope Dam

The Haw River begins in Guilford County and winds through Rockingham, Alamance, Orange, and Chatham Counties before emptying into Jordan Lake. Downstream from the lake, it flows another 7 miles before joining the Deep River and becoming the Cape Fear.

Aside from being a place of beauty, the Haw River is *the* place to go in the Triangle for white water. Although the Cape Fear is the best river for summer rapids, the Haw boasts consistent water

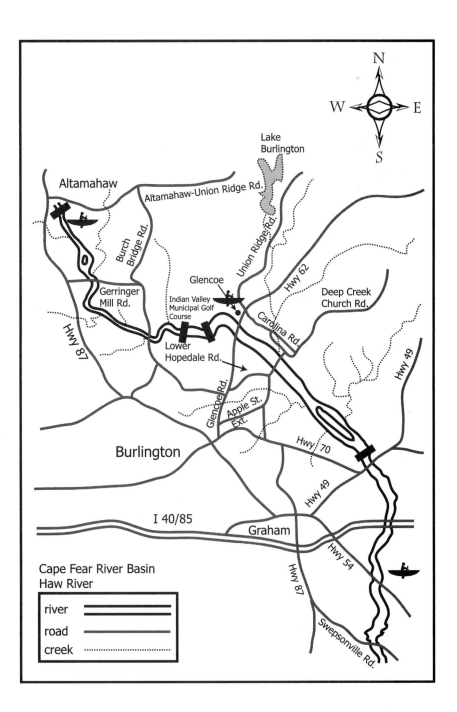

N
W E
S

Lake
Burlington

Altamahaw

Altamahaw-Union Ridge Rd.

Burch
Bridge Rd.

Union Ridge Rd.

Glencoe

Hwy 62

Gerringer
Mill Rd.

Indian Valley
Municipal Golf
Course

Deep Creek
Church Rd.

Hwy 87

Lower
Hopedale Rd.

Cardina Rd.

Glencoe Rd.

Apple St.
Ext.

Hwy 49

Burlington

Hwy 70

Hwy 49

I 40/85

Graham

Hwy 49

Hwy 87

Hwy 54

Cape Fear River Basin
Haw River

| | |
|---|---|
| river | |
| road | |
| creek | |

Swepsonville Rd.

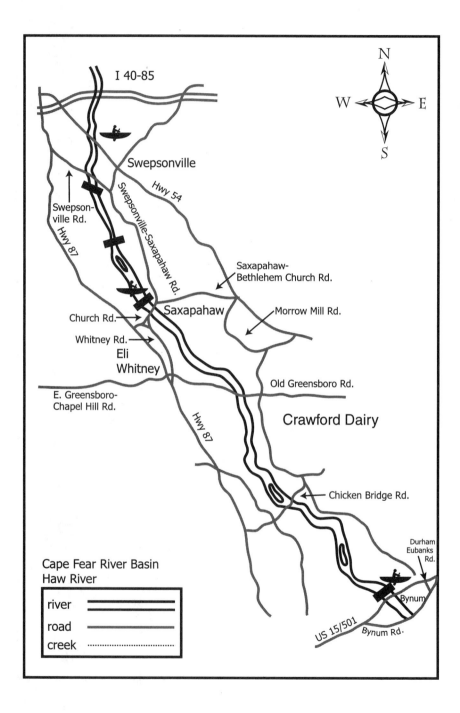

I 40-85

Swepsonville

Hwy 54

Swepson-
ville Rd.

Hwy 87

Swepsonville-Saxapahaw Rd.

Saxapahaw-
Bethlehem Church Rd.

Morrow Mill Rd.

Church Rd.

Saxapahaw

Whitney Rd.

Eli
Whitney

Old Greensboro Rd.

E. Greensboro-
Chapel Hill Rd.

Crawford Dairy

Hwy 87

Chicken Bridge Rd.

Durham
Eubanks
Rd.

Cape Fear River Basin
Haw River

| river | ═══════════ |
| road | ─────────── |
| creek | ·············· |

Bynum

US 15/501

Bynum Rd.

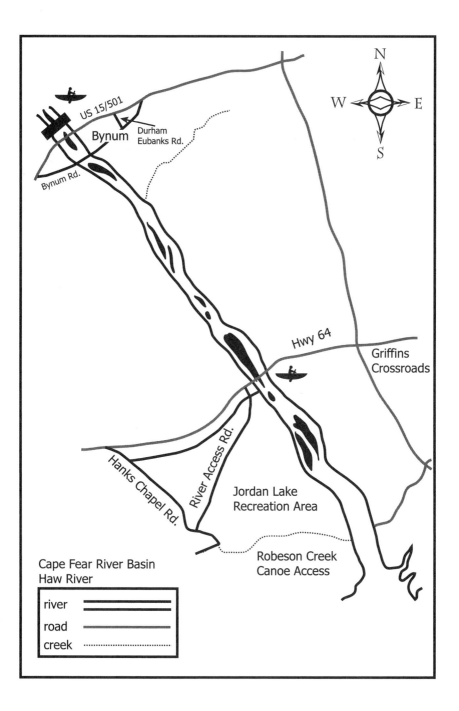

US 15/501

Bynum

Durham
Eubanks Rd.

Bynum Rd.

Hwy 64

Griffins
Crossroads

Hanks Chapel Rd.

River Access Rd.

Jordan Lake
Recreation Area

Robeson Creek
Canoe Access

Cape Fear River Basin
Haw River

| | |
|---|---|
| river | |
| road | |
| creek | |

N

W        E

S

levels and rapids relative to most other local rivers. It is surprisingly wild for most of its run through the Triangle. Although much of the Haw can be run by supervised beginners and intermediate paddlers, this is not a river to take lightly. A number of drownings have occurred, and even expert paddlers have gotten into trouble at high water. Know the river and your abilities before attempting a run. Newcomers to whitewater paddling should join experienced members of the Carolina Canoe Club.

The Haw River gets its name from a tribe of Alamance County Native Americans alternately called the Saxapahaw, Sissepahaw, or Shoccoree. Like other rivers in the Piedmont, the Haw saw settlement by Europeans in the first half of the 18th century. Small gristmills began appearing in the 1700s. By the late 1800s, the Haw was powering textile businesses. For almost two centuries, it has been dammed and used as a power source and as a dumping ground by mills and textile plants. Before the federal government passed the Clean Water Act in 1972, many mills and municipalities polluted the Haw with impunity. Since that time, dumping pollutants into the river has been regulated but not eliminated. Most current-day pollution in the Triangle takes the form of sedimentation and chemical runoff caused by development, as well as discharge from wastewater treatment facilities. Treated effluent from communities from Greensboro to Swepsonville is dumped in the Haw each year.

Concern about the river's health has grown over the years. In 1982, a group of folks formed the Haw River Assembly to protect the river and to educate those living in the watershed. The group's efforts center around monitoring water quality and hosting the annual Haw River Festival. Since local resident Louise Omoto Kessel proposed the festival in 1989, members of the assembly have devoted from a week to a month each year to forming a troop of traveling educators. They set up camp along the river and teach children about this valuable natural resource.

While the Haw River Assembly has been crucial in improving the quality of life along the Haw, environmental activists have not been the river's only caretakers. Glen Raven, Inc., a textile company in Altamahaw, is a sponsor of the new Haw River Trail project, setting aside hundreds of acres of land as a riparian buffer to protect water quality. Other goals of the project are to develop a public boating access point and hiking trails. Private citizens of Alamance County have donated land and funds to ensure the opening of six public access points along the Haw. Haw River Trail will be a series of as many as 11 developed put-ins along the river as it passes through Alamance County and possibly Chatham County. The Alamance County Parks and Recreation Department is in the process of beginning a canoe rental program. By the time this guide is in print, rental boats should be available. Contact the department for updated information.

## Haw River, Section 1:
## Altamahaw to Glencoe

**Length:** 8.2 miles
**Time:** 5 hours
**Levels and Difficulties:**

Minimum = 2.5 feet (class 1-2)
Median = 4 feet (class 1-2+); the section has one class-2+ rapid that can be avoided.
Maximum = No specific information is available.

**Maps:** USGS Ossipee, Lake Burlington
**Gauge:** USGS Haw River at Haw River
**Put-In:** The put-in is at the bottom of the dirt access road on the north side of the bridge. Don't be fooled by the stairs that wrap beneath the bridge. That is not the put-in. The dirt access road leads to a sandy path that ends near a small, sandy island. Cross the island and put in downstream of the dam and upstream of the bridge; be sure to stay off the dam. Glen Raven has plans to build a permanent parking area. In the meantime, park in the grassy area across the street. Don't block the dam access road.
**Takeout:** The takeout is river left before the NC 62 bridge at Glencoe.
**Directions to the Takeout:** From I-85, take Exit 143 and follow NC 62 North through Burlington. After 6.3 miles, turn left on River Road (SR 1600) at the sign for the

*Haw River*

Glencoe Historic District. Take an immediate left into the dirt parking area.

**Directions from the Takeout to the Put-In:** Turn right out of the parking area, then right on NC 62. Drive 0.6 mile to Old Glencoe Road (SR 1545), turn right, go 2.1 miles to Burch Bridge Road (SR 1530), turn right, proceed 2.4 miles to Gerringer Mill Road (SR 1530), and turn left. Drive 1.7 miles to NC 87, turn right, and go 2.2 miles to the bridge. On the left immediately after the bridge is a gravel road where you can unload. You can park in the grassy field across the street at the intersection of NC 87 and Altamahaw-Union Ridge Road (SR 1002).

This section begins near the historic dam above Glen Raven Mill. Aside from the one notable exception mentioned above, it consists of a series of small rapids and riffles at normal water levels. The roads described in the directions for this section are not a designated bike route, but with the exception of NC 87 and all roads during rush hour, a bike shuttle is possible.

## Major Rapids and Hazards

After the second bridge, you can either keep right of the island or go left to run a narrow class-2+ chute with a tight turn. Be sure to scout this hazard, as fallen trees can cause extreme danger in high water. As of this writing, one tree had fallen across the river. At low water, it is barely possible to paddle beneath this tree.

A 2-foot dam spans the river at the golf course. Portage right.

After the golf course, you'll reach an 8-foot dam. Portage right.


## Haw River, Section 2:
## NC 62 bridge at Glencoe to Graham access at NC 54 in Alamance County

**Length:** 5.8 miles
**Time:** 4 hours
**Levels and Difficulties:**

Minimum = 2 feet (class 1-2)
Median = 4 feet (class 1-2+)
Maximum = No specific information is available.

**Maps:** USGS Lake Burlington, Burlington, Mebane
**Gauge:** USGS Haw River at Haw River
**Put-In:** As of this writing, the final location of the parking area for the put-in was undecided. The easiest place to launch is from the bottom of the steep dirt road between NC 62 and the entrance to Glencoe Mill.
**Takeout:** A developed canoe access point with parking, the takeout is river right and is clearly visible from the water.
**Directions to the Takeout::** From I-85, take Exit 148, drive 1.5 miles east on NC 54, turn right on Cooper Road, and make an immediate left into the parking area.
**Directions from the Takeout to the Put-In:** Return to I-85. Get on I-85 West, then take Exit 143 for NC 62 North. See the directions to the Section 1 takeout above.

This section has the most consistent white water in Alamance County. You'll encounter frequent small rapids, including a rock garden near the put-in and several river-wide ledges. The initial rapids are usually paddled river right. A play spot known locally as Carolina Falls is off the main river to the right.

As for the scenery, there's quite a bit of development along the banks, but little of it is visible in the summer months. One of the most interesting spots on this stretch is the put-in at Glencoe. The mill and the small community around it are listed on the National Register of Historic Places. North Carolina Preservation is helping to find new owners for the historic structures. That organization also sponsors the put-in at Glencoe.

### Major Rapids and Hazards

You'll have to deal with one dam. This collapsed structure at 4.5 miles in the town of Haw River can be run on the left side at some water levels. Scout carefully before attempting this obstacle to be certain it is within your capabilities. Wooden and metal spikes protruding from the dam could cause you and your boat significant damage. Portage if in doubt.

Carolina Falls is reached via a branch to the left off the main body of the Haw. Three branches flow to the falls, but the first is blocked by fallen trees. Take either of the next two. Below the falls are more small rapids and a rock garden.

## Haw River, Section 3:
## Graham access (NC 54 bridge) in Alamance County to Jordan River access near Saxapahaw Dam

**Length:** 7.7 miles
**Time:** 4 hours
**Levels and Difficulties:** See Section 2 for levels; the difficulty is class 1-2.
**Maps:** USGS Mebane, Saxapahaw
**Gauge:** USGS Haw River at Haw River
**Put-In:** The put-in is at Graham's developed canoe access.
**Takeout:** The takeout is river left upstream of the

Saxapahaw Dam at the Boy Scout dock. Red-lettered signs indicate the mandatory takeout. Under no circumstances should anyone paddle downstream of the takeout point. Follow the trail right to the gate, then out to the road. The Jordan River access parking area is to the right. Do not block the gate with your vehicle.

**Directions to the Takeout:** From I-85, take Exit 148 and follow NC 54 East for 3.5 miles to NC 119 (Swepsonville Road). Turn right, drive 1.1 miles into Swepsonville, turn left on Swepsonville-Saxapahaw Road (SR 2158), and go 6.4 miles to Church Road. The parking area for the Jordan River access is on the right. The takeout is just upstream (see above). To reach the trail from the takeout, retrace your route on Swepsonville-Saxapahaw Road for 0.1 mile and turn left on the unnamed gravel road. Follow it for 0.1 mile to the gate to load. Do not block the gate across the road or the one across the path to the dam.

**Directions from the Takeout to the Put-In::** Retrace your route to NC 54, head west for 2 miles, turn left on Cooper Road, and take an immediate left into the parking lot for the Graham access.

You'll note significant development and a golf course on the upper portion of this run. Summer leaves hide almost all of the buildings. The last few miles of this stretch are on a lake backed up by the dam in Saxapahaw.

It is possible to use a bike shuttle to travel the roads described in the directions above. NC 54 has high-speed traffic but wide shoulders. Swepsonville-Saxapahaw Road has significant rush-hour traffic and no shoulders.

### Major Rapids and Hazards

Several small rapids are located near the put-in. You'll also have to contend with two dams. You can portage on the right before the wooden ruins of the old dam at Swepsonville. Watch for the protruding wooden and metal spikes, which could cause significant damage to you and your boat.

Do not approach the 8-foot dam downstream, and use extra caution in high water. You can portage this second dam on the left over the poison-ivy-covered wall or around the wheelhouse gate. At the time of this writing, the unpleasant portage around this second dam made this the least appealing stretch of the river. Organizers of Haw River Trail are lobbying to breach the dam, which would greatly improve the recreational potential of this section.

## Haw River, Section 4:
## Saxapahaw to Old Greensboro Highway

**Length:** 5.5 miles

**Time:** 3 hours

**Levels and Difficulties:** Parts of this section are passable year-round, but if the upstream gauge reads much less than 3 feet, you might end up carrying your boat through ankle-deep water. This is particularly true where islands divide the river during the final mile. For levels, see Section 2. The difficulty is class 1-2.

**Map:** USGS Saxapahaw

**Gauge:** USGS Haw River at Haw River

**Put-In:** The put-in is at the Jordan River canoe access at the Saxapahaw Community Center. A steep, rocky slope with a metal handrail will take you to the bank.

**Takeout:** The takeout is river right before the bridge. No developed access is available.

**Directions to the Takeout:** From NC 54 west of Carrboro, take the Jones Ferry Road exit. Follow Jones Ferry Road (SR 1005) west for 0.9 mile to Old Greensboro Highway (SR 1005), turn right, and go 9.7 miles to the bridge.

**Directions to the Takeout to the Put-In:** Continue west on Old Greensboro Highway for 3 miles to NC 87 North, turn right, and drive 2.6 miles to Church Road (SR 2171), which crosses the Haw River below Saxapahaw Dam after 1.1 miles. Immediately after crossing the bridge, turn left into the parking area for the community center and the Jordan River access.

# Haw River, Section 5:
# Old Greensboro Highway to Chicken Bridge

**Length:** 5.6 miles

**Time:** 3 hours

**Levels and Difficulties:** For levels, see Section 1. The difficulty is class 1-2.

**Maps:** USGS Saxapahaw, White Cross, Bynum

**Gauge:** USGS Haw River at Haw River

**Put-In:** The put-in is river right on the west side of the bridge.

**Takeout:** The takeout is on the left past the islands and Chicken Bridge. The clear trail makes for an easy carry back to the gravel parking lot beside the bridge.

**Directions to the Takeout:** From NC 54 west of Carrboro, take the Jones Ferry Road exit. Follow Jones Ferry Road (SR 1005/SR 1942) for 7.3 miles to Crawford Dairy Road (SR 1539/SR 1956), turn right, drive 1.6 miles to Chicken Bridge Road (SR 1545), turn left, and go 1.3 miles to the bridge. A gravel parking area is above the takeout on the left side of the road before the bridge.

**Directions from the Takeout to the Put-In:** Return to Crawford Dairy Road. Turn left, drive 4.5 miles to Old Greensboro Highway, turn left, and go 1.1 miles to the bridge.

Sections 5 and 6 comprise the most scenic and remote stretch of the Haw in Alamance County. The pristine setting and the absence of portage make these the most appealing of the class 1-2 sections. You'll also enjoy plenty of wildlife, including herons, hawks, muskrats, and beavers. You can combine the two sections and make a great day of it.

The roads described in the directions above make for a great bike shuttle. Old Greensboro Highway is part of the Mountains-to-Sea bike route. But be aware that this road sees high-speed commuter traffic and has no shoulders.

# Haw River, Section 6:
## Chicken Bridge Road to Bynum Dam and the US 15/US 501 Bridge

**Length:** 6.6 miles
**Time:** 2 to 3 hours
**Levels:**

Minimum = 4-5 feet
Median = 5-6 feet
Maximum = 6-8 feet

**Difficulties:** Class 1-2+
**Map:** USGS Bynum
**Gauge:** USGS Haw River near Bynum
**Put-In:** The put-in is river left downstream of Chicken Bridge. The clear trail makes for an easy carry back to the gravel parking lot beside the bridge.
**Takeout:** The takeout is on the far left at the small lake just above the dam. Don't try to venture a peek over the dam, as there's a drop of 20-plus feet. As this guide was going to press, construction of a new bridge had partially disrupted the parking area at US 15/US 501.
**Directions to the Takeout:** Follow US 15/US 501 about 10 miles south from Chapel Hill to the bridge.
**Directions from the Takeout to the Put-In:** From the bridge, go north on US 15/US 501 for 0.2 mile to Moore Mountain Road (SR 1524), turn left, proceed 2 miles to Hamlets Chapel Road (SR 1525), turn left, go 2.3 miles to River Road, turn left, drive 2.9 miles to Chicken Bridge Road (SR 1545), turn left, and go 1.1 miles to the bridge.

This section and the section downstream are the two most popular portions of the Haw among experienced paddlers. Both lie in Chatham County. They have better water quality and offer a more remote feel than many of the sections upstream. Neither section is appropriate for inexperienced or novice paddlers. This section can be a good one for beginning whitewater paddlers who have received professional instruction and are looking to hone their skills.

far left for Crystal Falls Chute, a class-2 double-drop ledge. Just prior to entering the falls, a small rivulet to the right leads to a blind-drop class 2-+ ledge.

After Crystal Falls Chute, start moving river right. In another mile, you'll enter C-Turn Drop, a series of technical class 1-2 rapids leading to a quick move to the far left and back to the right. Make sure to line up for this double drop or you may be thrown into the island or the protruding rocks. You may sneak through this rapid straight down the center-right.

You'll reach the takeout after 0.5 mile of flat water.

## Haw River, Section 8:
## US 64 river right to canoe access area

**Length:** 1.5 miles
**Time:** 1 hour plus surfing
**Levels and Difficulties:** The paddler's gauge is given below.

0 foot = 4.7 (class 2)
1 foot = 5.9 (class 3-)
2 feet = 7.1 (class 3)
3 feet = 8.3 (class 3+)
4 feet = 9.5 (class 4)
5+ feet = Expert boaters only; this is full-on flood stage

**Map:** USGS Merry Oaks
**Gauge:** USGS Haw River near Bynum or paddler's gauge
**Put-In:** The put-in is at a developed access area.
**Takeout:** The takeout is also at a developed access area.
**Directions to the Takeout:** From US 64 about 2.4 miles east of the intersection with US 15/US 501 and about 2 miles west of Jordan Lake, turn south on Foxfire Trace (SR 1991). Go 0.6 mile to Dee Ferrell Road (SR 1944), turn left, go 0.7 mile to Hanks Chapel Road (SR 1943), turn left, and proceed 1 mile to the Robeson Creek Canoe Access, on the left. The ramp is 0.9 mile down the gravel driveway.
**Directions from the Takeout to the Put-In:** Return to Hanks Chapel Road and turn right. Drive 1 mile to Dee Ferrell

Road, turn right, then take the next right onto Foxfire Trace. Drive 0.5 mile to River Access Road (SR 1992), located on the right.

This section, known locally as the Lower Haw, is one of the most popular whitewater playgrounds in the Piedmont. This stretch of river has an exceptional drop in elevation because it runs over the fall line separating the Piedmont from the coastal plain. As the descriptions below attest, this section includes huge rapids at high-water levels, when rescue becomes extremely difficult and dangerous. Thin trails from the put-in to the takeout make it possible for nonexperts to watch the action from the banks. When unseasonably wet weather arrives during the warm months—particularly following a hurricane—the river is often crowded with boaters lined up for the best play spots.

As described above, the roads between the takeout and the put-in make for a short, easy bike shuttle.

## Major Rapids and Hazards

Lunch Stop is a class-2 rapid about 100 yards from the put-in at river right, where the water constricts to a narrow channel. Good nose-surfing can be had in depths of up to 2 feet. Over 2 feet, the rapid washes out, though an ender hole is located directly below it.

Ocean Boulevard/Joshua's Ledge is a class-2 rapid (class 3 over 2 feet). Past Lunch Stop, take an immediate left around the small island to enter a 200-yard series of wave trains with excellent ferrying and eddying possibilities. If you choose to stay river left, in 100 yards you'll reach a ledge with a pinning hydraulic at 3 feet. It makes for excellent side-surfing at 1-2 feet.

Proceed river right after Ocean Boulevard for a good technical class-2 drop, the entrance of which contains a 360 hole that is truculent at 2-plus feet. In another 100 yards, you'll enter the granddaddy rapid, the class-3 Gabriel's Bend. If you're having difficulty at this stage, remember that the farther left you stay on the river, the easier the rapids and drops. At 3-plus feet, Gabriel's Bend has some vicious holes. Try to stay slightly left of center for the cleanest run of about 100 yards. For daredevils, the trick is to see how many eddies you can catch to the bottom. Twenty are considered excellent, 15 advanced, 10 intermediate, etc. The bottom two holes contain the most diversified playability.

Moose Jaw is the only blind drop in the river. It's a mere class 3 if you know it well. If you don't, you may need to buy a new canoe afterward or roll your kayak, for the center rock at the middle of the drop can be difficult to avoid. A good deal of first aid has been administered because of this rock, so be certain to scout. You can run far right for a technical 3 C-turn or move three drops over for the Maze, a technical class 2. You'll encounter class-1 rapids until the takeout, located 0.5 mile down at river right.

# Deep River

**Maps:** USGS Goldston, Colon, Merry Oaks, Moncure, Cokesbury

The Deep is a great river for history buffs, novice paddlers, and anyone who wants to spend a quiet day keeping up with a heron. The Deep and the Neuse are the only two local rivers that can usually be run in the summer. Not surprisingly, the Deep feels more remote than the Neuse. Sycamores, not subdivisions, line its banks, and most of the noises you'll hear are from splashing fish. A few small rock outcroppings make good picnic spots, and the trees growing out over the water offer welcome shade in the summer.

Thanks to the tireless efforts of the Triangle Land Conservancy (TLC) and its supporters, the land along the Deep is being spared from development. To date, the TLC has protected 2,100 acres from the House in the Horseshoe in Moore County to the Cape Fear River at Raven Rock State Park in Harnett County. The TLC worked to create the McIver Landing Canoe Access in

Gulf. (See Appendix 2 for more information on the TLC.) The state of North Carolina sees great potential along the wooded banks of the Deep. The Deep River corridor is one of 47 sites identified for possible future state parks.

The few rapids on the river are relatively easy, and most can be readily scouted. But you needn't tackle the mighty Deep on your own. A local guide service, Rock Rest Adventures, runs tours, clinics, and a shuttle-and-rental service called the Deep River Canoe Outpost (see Appendix 2).

If boating is not your bag, you can still check out the Deep at several locations. Deep River Park is perhaps the most rewarding.

Like most local rivers, the Deep was a site of early development. The land around the Deep was hunting ground for the Catawba, Wacksaw, and Sopone Indian tribes. The first Europeans came around 1750 from Virginia and eastern North Carolina. The presence of limestone and iron ore attracted some hardy souls who began commercial operations. Local ironworks turned out munitions during both the Revolutionary War and the Civil War. The Deep River Iron Furnace, located on the south side of the river close to the US 421 bridge, began operations in 1773. The Endor Iron Furnace, located about 1.5 miles upstream of US 15/US 501, operated throughout the Civil War and is on land now protected by the TLC.

Coal was discovered along the Deep in the 1850s, and mining operations began promptly. There was once talk of the now-quiet town of Gulf—named after a deep spot in the river—becoming the Pittsburgh of the South. The Civil War interrupted those ambitions, although the Egypt Coal Mine operated until 1928.

One site of historical significance is the Lockville Dam, located just upstream of US 1. During the Revolutionary War, British general Charles Cornwallis camped along the Deep near where the dam now stands (see Sections 3 and 4 below).

Anyone interested in further exploring the history and lore of the Deep River should get a copy of *A History of the House in the Horseshoe: Her People and Her Deep River Neighbors*, written by George Wilcox, a descendant of John Wilcox, who arrived in 1768 and operated the Deep River Iron Furnace.

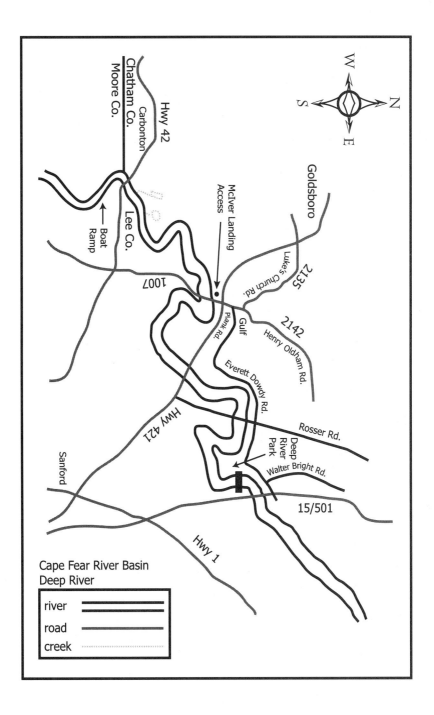

Cape Fear River Basin
Deep River

| river | ═══════ |
| road | ─────── |
| creek | ········ |

## Deep River, Section 1:
## Carbonton boat ramp to Deep River Park

**Length:** 12.9 miles

**Time:** 4 hours

**Levels and Difficulties:** Specific information on levels is not available. This section is deep enough to run at any level. The difficulty rating is class 1-2.

**Gauge:** USGS Deep River Moncure

**Maps:** USGS Goldston, Colon

**Put-In:** The boating access for this section includes a boat ramp and parking.

**Takeout:** Deep River Park has developed access. The takeout is river left just downstream of the old bridge. It consists of a set of steep steps from the river to the parking area.

**Directions to the Takeout:** From Chapel Hill and points north, take US 15/US 501 South through Pittsboro. About 8 miles south of the traffic circle, turn right on Walter Bright Road (SR 2217). Go 1.8 miles, turn right on Everette Dowdy Road (SR 2145), drive 3.1 miles, then turn left into the parking area for Deep River Park. From Raleigh and points east, follow US 64 West to US 15/US 501 South, then follow the directions above.

**Directions from the Takeout to the Put-In:** Continue west on Everette Dowdy Road for 3.1 miles into the community of Gulf; note that the name changes to R. Jordan Road. Turn left onto Plank Road (SR 1007) at the lovely Gulf Presbyterian Church. Follow Plank Road for 4.1 miles to NC 42 (Carbonton Road), turn right, and go 3 miles to the wildlife access area, located on the left.

This is an almost exclusively flat, scenic stretch of river. The roads described above can make a very pleasant bike shuttle except for a hazardous crossing of US 421. Anyone looking for a shorter paddle can put in or take out at the McIver Landing Canoe Access in Gulf, located downstream of the Plank Road Bridge.

The rapid just before the takeout at Deep River Park is difficult to see on approach because of an overhanging willow's low branches. It can easily be scouted if necessary.

A dam is located just below the put-in. You can portage left, struggle up a steep bank, and carry down the steep rocks. There is an easier put-in, but the takeout is strewn with huge rocks and is quite difficult.

## Deep River, Section 2:
## Deep River Park to US 15/US 501

**Length:** 5.7 miles

**Time:** 2.5 hours

**Levels and Difficulties:** Specific information on levels is not available. This class-1 section can be run year-round.

**Gauge:** USGS Deep River near Moncure

**Map:** USGS Colon

**Put-In:** Deep River Park has a developed canoe access. You'll have to perform a steep carry down a set of stairs.

**Takeout:** The takeout is river right at the US 15/US 501 bridge. You'll have a short, steep carry unless you park at the top of the hill.

**Directions to the Takeout:** From Chapel Hill and points north, follow US 15/US 501 a little over 9 miles south from the traffic circle in Pittsboro. From Raleigh and points east, take US 1 to US 15/US 501. Go north on US 15/US 501 for about 3 miles to the bridge. On the south side of the bridge is a rough dirt access road that goes down to the bank. This road is impassable in wet weather.

**Directions from the Takeout to the Put-In:** Go north on US 15/US 501 for 0.3 mile, then turn left on Walter Bright Road (SR 2217). After 0.9 mile, turn left on Everette Dowdy Road (SR 2145) and drive 3.1 miles to Deep River Park, on the left.

This is a short, quiet section.

# Deep River, Section 3:
# US 15/US 501 to the US 1 bridge

**Length:** 7.5 miles

**Time:** 3 hours

**Levels and Difficulties:** Specific information on levels is not available. This class 1-2 section is deep enough to run at any level.

**Gauge:** USGS Deep River near Moncure

**Maps:** USGS Colon, Merry Oaks, Moncure

**Put-In:** The put-in is difficult and steep. An alternative put-in/takeout is at White Pines Nature Preserve. It involves a long but beautiful carry. See page 19 for a trail description.

**Takeout:** The takeout is at the US 1 bridge before the Lockville Dam. You'll have to portage up the 3-foot bank lined with sharp rocks.

**Directions to the Takeout:** The US 1 bridge is immediately north of Exit 78 (Deep River Road). On the southwest side of the bridge is a rough, deeply rutted dirt road leading down to the bank.

**Directions from the Takeout to the Put-In:** Follow Deep River Road (SR 1466) south for 7.4 miles to US 15/US 501/NC 87. Turn right on US 15/US 501 and go north for 1.6 miles to the access road on the left just before the bridge. A rough dirt road leads beneath the bridge to the bank.

On this section, you'll pass the Triangle Land Conservancy's first acquisition: White Pines Nature Preserve (see page 19), located at the confluence of the Rocky and Deep Rivers.

### Major Rapids and Hazards

Downstream of the confluence of the Rocky and Deep Rivers are three rapids that are easily run under normal conditions. The takeout for this trip is before the Lockville Dam. It requires a difficult portage.

# Deep River, Section 4:
# US 1 bridge to Buckhorn Dam

**Length:** 8 miles

**Time:** 3.5 hours

**Levels and Difficulties:** Specific information on levels is not available. This class-1 section can be run year-round.

**Maps:** USGS Moncure, Cokesbury; also see Cape Fear River Basin map on page 381.

**Gauge:** USGS Deep River near Moncure

**Put-In:** A dirt road below the US 1 bridge serves as the put-in. The banks are about 3 feet tall and are lined with sharp rocks.

**Takeout:** The takeout is river left in a swampy area off the main river well above Buckhorn Dam. The banks are thick with poison ivy in the summer.

**Directions to the Takeout:** From Chapel Hill and points north, follow US 15/US 501 South through Pittsboro. About 1.1 miles past the traffic circle, turn left on Pittsboro-Moncure Road (SR 1012). Go to the T intersection with US 1 (approximately 7.5 miles). Turn left (west) on Old US 1 (SR 1011), drive 2.1 miles to Corinth Road (SR 1916), turn right, proceed 5.5 miles to Buckhorn Road (SR 1921), turn right, and drive 2.3 miles to the dam. From Raleigh and points east, take US 1 to Exit 79, turn left onto Moncure-Pittsboro Road and proceed to Old US 1. Follow directions above from Old US 1.

**Directions from the Takeout to the Put-In:** Retrace your route to US 1. The US 1 bridge is immediately north of where you'll enter the road, but you'll need to go to the next exit and turn around to get to the right side of the divided highway. The bridge is just north of Exit 78. On the southwest side of the bridge is a rough, deeply rutted dirt road leading down to the bank.

This section begins on the Deep River just upstream from where the Deep and the Haw join to form the Cape Fear. It is also Section 1 of the Cape Fear River run. Comprised almost exclusively of flat water backed up by the dam, it can be run year-round. While not a draw for the whitewater set, this last section of the Deep and first section of the Cape Fear is quite scenic and historic. After putting in on the Deep, you'll immediately pass the ruins of a bridge built by British troops under General Cornwallis during the Revolutionary War. The Haw comes in from the left to join the Deep, and then you're on the Cape Fear, the major highway of the late 18th century.

After passing under a railroad bridge and cruising by McKay Island, you'll cross under the NC 42 bridge before approaching Buckhorn Dam. The bridge has a boating access area and is a good alternate takeout. It's also a good place to begin an overnight trip to Raven Rock State Park.

### Major Rapids and Hazards

Buckhorn Dam is a major hazard and should be avoided. On the NC 42 bridge is a sign warning you that the dam is 2 miles ahead. Another warning sign marks the dam itself. As you approach the dam, you can paddle to a swampy area on the left to take out. Make sure you've got long pants and shoes for protection from the poison-ivy jungle. Do not attempt to go over the dam in your boat. You won't survive it.

# Cape Fear River

**Maps:** USGS Moncure, Cokesbury, Mamers, Lillington, Coats, Erwin

The Cape Fear begins its journey to the Atlantic in southeastern Chatham County where the Haw and Deep Rivers join. The spot where the two meet, Mermaid Point, inspired a local legend. The story goes that the mermaids who swam the Atlantic sometimes traveled upstream on the Cape Fear to rinse the salt from their long hair. They made their way to a spit of sand that once lay just downstream of the point of land, where they would climb from the water to dry out, sing, and rest before beginning their 199-mile return trip to the ocean. At present, Mermaid Point is not visible due to inundation by Buckhorn Dam.

Although you may not encounter any mermaids, there are other reasons to take a trip down the Cape Fear. Paddling enthusiasts count on the Cape Fear as the only year-round whitewater river close to the Triangle. And those who prefer to leave their white knuckles in the car can enjoy the flat-water section behind Buckhorn Dam. The Cape Fear is also one of the few rivers in the Piedmont where paddlers can camp. See Section 2 below for details about one of the greatest overnight trips the Triangle has to offer. Although stretches of the river have been marred by development and industry, plenty of natural beauty remains. Efforts are under way to protect the land along the Cape Fear and the Deep as far downstream as Raven Rock State Park.

The Cape Fear was the site of some of the earliest settlement and development in the Piedmont. The settlement of the upper Cape Fear began in the late 1600s and early 1700s. The early European immigrants made their homes in the area just outside the scope of this guide—downstream of the lower Little River in Cumberland County. Significant European settlement began upstream in the wake of a survey conducted by Lord Granville in 1746. Once the Crown figured out the lay of the land, it began issuing grants along the Cape Fear and its tributaries. As soon as Europeans settled along the Cape Fear, they began to make "improvements" to the river. There were few roads and no highways in the area. Water was the major source of power and means of transportation. Dams were built to use the power of the river to operate mills. Repeated attempts were made to build a series of locks and dams that would open the upper Cape Fear to navigation, so goods could be transported to and from Wilmington and the Atlantic. Buckhorn Dam is still intact, stretching from the shore in Chatham County to the one in Lee County. Built in the first decade of the 20th century, it generated electrical power until CP&L (now Progress Energy) pulled its plug in 1962.

Any paddler or armchair adventurer with an interest in the history of the Cape Fear should be sure to get a copy of John

Hairr's guide, *From Mermaid's Point to Raccoon Falls: A Guide to the Upper Cape Fear River.*

## Cape Fear River, Section 1:
## US 1 bridge over the Deep River to Buckhorn Dam

This is also Section 4 of the Deep River run. See page 377 on the Deep River for details.

## Cape Fear River, Section 2:
## Buckhorn Dam at the end of Buckhorn Road to the wildlife access area on Wildlife Road east of Lillington in Harnett County

**Length:** 16 miles
**Time:** 10 hours
**Levels and Difficulties:**

Minimum = 1-2 feet (class 1-2)
Median = 2-3 feet (class 2)
Maximum = 3-5 feet (class 2-3)

**Maps:** USGS Cokesbury, Mamers, Lillington
**Gauge:** USGS Cape Fear River near Lillington
**Put-In:** The put-in is at Buckhorn Dam, where a trail takes you well below the dam.
**Takeout:** An easy-access boat ramp serves as the takeout.
**Directions to the Takeout:** From Raleigh, take US 401 South to Lillington. US 401, US 421, and NC 210 run conjunctively as you cross the Cape Fear and begin driving on Lillington's Main Street. From Chapel Hill, take US 15/US 501 South to US 421 in Sanford. Follow US 421 South into Lillington. At the intersection with US 401/NC 210, turn right onto Main Street. From Durham, follow NC 55 South to Fuquay-Varina, then go south on US 401 to Lillington. Upon arriving in Lillington from any of the above cities, proceed south on Main Street. Five blocks (0.4 mile) after US 421 and US 401 diverge at the intersection of Main and Front Streets, turn left on McNeill Street. As you leave town, the name changes to Ross Road (SR 2016). After 2.3 miles, turn left on Wildlife Road. It is 0.7 mile to the ramp.

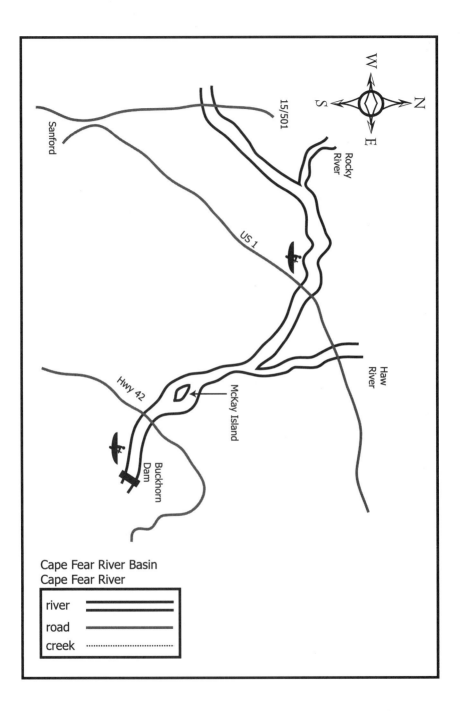

Cape Fear River Basin
Cape Fear River

| river | |
|-------|--|
| road | |
| creek | |

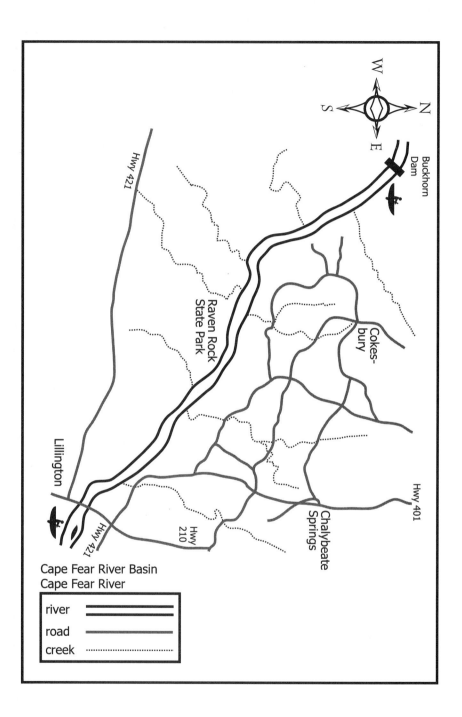

Cape Fear River Basin
Cape Fear River

| river | ━━━━━━ |
| road  | ━━━━━━ |
| creek | ·············· |

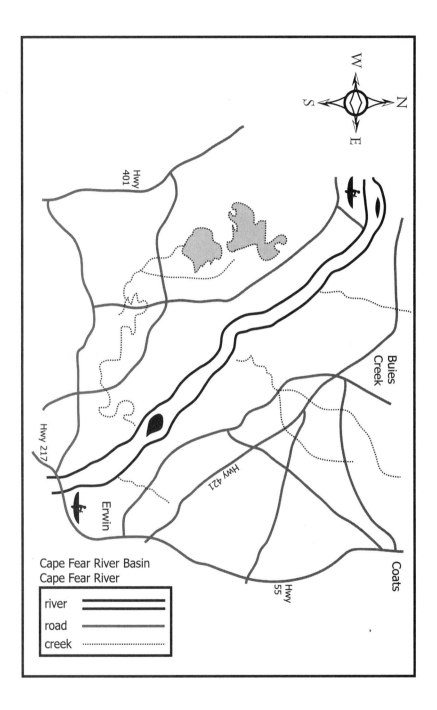

Cape Fear River Basin
Cape Fear River

| | |
|---|---|
| river | |
| road | |
| creek | |

Hwy 401

Hwy 217

Hwy 421

Hwy 55

Erwin

Buies Creek

Coats

N
S
E
W

**Directions from the Takeout to the Put-In:** Return to the intersection of Main and Front Streets in Lillington. Turn left on Front (US 421). Drive north on US 421 for 13.5 miles to Seminole Road (SR1280/SR 1579), turn right, go 4.5 miles to NC 42 (Avents Ferry Road), and turn right. After 8 miles, you'll pass the wildlife access area on your left. To reach Buckhorn Dam, continue on NC 42 East for 2 miles, then turn right on Buckhorn Road and drive to the dam.

This stretch of river is one of the most underrated recreational opportunities within easy driving distance of the Triangle. While it won't do for whitewater paddlers whose sole desire is to play in foaming, frothing rapids, it's a great paddle for those looking to get out on a river for a couple days of leisurely paddling and a night of prime camping. Raven Rock State Park is located roughly halfway between the put-in and the takeout, so you can follow a day of moderate paddling with a night under the stars. The park provides places to lash your boat, and the canoe campground is a short walk from the river's edge. Campers can register and pay at the canoe campground. This trip is particularly appealing in the spring, when the rhododendron on Raven Rock blooms. Paddlers should be competent to handle class 2-3 water. At high-water levels, the rock garden just below Buckhorn Dam becomes class 3-plus. If you want a slightly longer paddle and don't mind portaging around the dam, you can put in upstream at the boating access area on NC 42.

## Major Rapids and Hazards

Buckhorn Dam, located at the put-in, is a major hazard that should be avoided.

Buckhorn Falls, the rock garden just below the put-in, is a class-3 rapid above 4 feet of water.

Lanier Falls is a class-2 ledge just above the boundary of Raven Rock State Park.

Fishtraps is a class-2 rapid. The line is left to right between two islands at mile 6.

Rock Cliffs is a mild rapid. Within 0.5 mile, you'll reach a canoe camping area. If you want to portage out, you'll do so over a 2.2-mile trail to the nearest accessible park road.

## Cape Fear River, Section 3:
## Wildlife access area to NC 217 bridge near Erwin Road

**Length:** 8 miles
**Time:** 2 to 3 hours
**Levels and Difficulties:**

Minimum = 2-3 feet (class 1-2)
Median = 3-4 feet (class 2)
Maximum = 4-6 feet (class 2-3)

**Maps:** USGS Lillington, Erwin
**Gauge:** USGS Cape Fear River near Lillington
**Put-In:** The put-in is an easy-access boat ramp.
**Takeout:** You have two painful choices: river left, which entails a short but strenuous 50-yard pull up the bank; river right before the bridge, which entails a long, gradual pull up a dirt path. Avoid the private property river right after the last rapid.
**Directions to the Takeout:** From Raleigh, take US 401 South to US 421, then follow US 421 South to NC 217. After passing through Erwin on NC 217 South, you'll reach the bridge. From Durham, take NC 55 South to NC 217. After passing through Erwin on NC 217, you'll reach the bridge. From Chapel Hill, take I-40 West to NC 55, then go south on NC 55 to NC 217. After passing through Erwin on NC 217, you'll reach the bridge.
**Directions from the Takeout to the Put-In:** Continue on NC 217 South for 0.1 mile to Bunnlevel-Erwin Road (SR 1779), turn right, go 1.6 miles to Titan Roberts Road (SR 2016), turn right, drive 2.6 miles to Ross Road (SR 2016), turn right, proceed 4.1 miles to Wildlife Road (SR 2069), turn right, and go 0.7 mile to the boat ramp.

This section is often the only local option for whitewater enthusiasts seeking healthy rapids in the dog days of summer. Because the Cape Fear is dam-controlled, this is the one local whitewater river that runs year-round. Unfortunately, the admission for paddling the class 1-2 rapids is 4 miles of flat water. Nonetheless, this is a good route for teaching paddlers. Ironically, often after a good rain, the river drops to low levels until days later, when the upstream spillage from Jordan Lake is released.

You won't need your camera for this trip. Gravel pits, a golf-course housing development, a water-filtration plant, overhead electric lines, litter along the banks and at the takeout, and a new river-side housing complex all make for a less-than-pristine paddling environment.

## Major Rapids and Hazards

Island Narrows Rapid is located 6 miles down, where a huge boulder separates two chutes. The left chute has an eddy line that is excellent for practicing ferrying and peel-outs. Be prepared to roll at levels of 5-plus feet. On several ledges, you'll need to scout to find the best surfing holes.

Located a mile from the takeout is an ender hole at 5-plus feet. The lack of gradient is often compensated for by the high volume of water.

*Neuse River*

# Neuse River Basin

The headwaters of the Neuse bubble out of the ground in Person and Orange Counties. These small streams become the Eno and Flat Rivers before they join in Falls Lake to form the Neuse River. The Neuse then flows south and east through Wake County and the eastern Triangle on its way to Pamlico Sound. At 2 million years of age and counting, the Neuse is one of the world's oldest rivers. It is also one of only three river basins contained entirely within the borders of North Carolina. The Neuse has plenty of neighbors, as it drains lands that hold one-sixth of the state's population. Most of those people live in the Triangle. Farther east, the basin consists largely of agricultural land until it nears the city of New Bern.

In the Triangle, the rivers of the basin provide a terrific recreational resource as well as drinking water. Paddling on these rivers is one of the best ways to cool off and enjoy the natural beauty that remains amidst our rapidly growing cities.

Both the population centers and the agricultural operations along the Neuse—particularly those involving intensive livestock farming—have created problems with water quality. In the 1990s, the river made national news as enormous fish kills clogged the lower reaches of the basin. In 1996, following a Pulitzer Prize-winning series of stories in the *Raleigh News and Observer* about hog farming, the North Carolina Division of Environmental Management proposed the first restrictions on these massive operations. North Carolina enacted what came to be called the Neuse Rules in 1998.

The state also took aim at pollution in the Triangle. Nitrogen contributes to huge algal blooms both locally and downstream. The algae reduce the amount of dissolved oxygen in the water and choke aquatic life. We in the Triangle are responsible for a large proportion of the nitrogen that pollutes the Neuse. The more gasoline we burn, the more fertilizer we use, and the more toilets we flush, the more we contribute to the problem. Driving efficient vehicles, making certain our wastewater facilities are sufficient for the populations they serve, and taking care about what we put on our lawns are all steps we can take to improve the health of the Neuse and all of our waterways.

A third significant source of pollution in the Neuse and other Triangle rivers is sedimentation. Silt and sediment from development and urban storm drains cause problems for the Neuse River Basin's creeks in the Triangle. Aquatic life can't survive in sediment-filled waters. Urban runoff also carries toxic heavy metals into the rivers we depend upon for drinking water. Studies are under way to find better ways to control sediment, but one solution is clear. A buffer of trees as narrow as 50 feet can filter out up to 90 percent of sediments resulting from nearby development. Such a buffer also enhances the aesthetic appeal of a day on the river. Restrictions protecting these riparian buffers are good not just for the creatures living in the state's rivers but for all of us who drink their waters.

# Eno River

The Eno is one of the most beautiful little rivers in the state, and there's no better way to experience it than by boat. Like many area rivers, most of the Eno cannot be run for much of the year because of low water levels. Winter and spring are most likely to yield adequate depths for getting over the rocks and through the rapids.

Unlike other local rivers, the Eno is remarkably clean—for now. If you're new to paddling and spend at least part of every expedition in the water, this is a great comfort. The Eno is a good river for intermediate paddlers because of its moderately difficult class 2-3 rapids, which are relatively easy to scout and portage if you decide you're not up to them. Thanks to the presence of Eno River State Park, the river's scenery will be protected in perpetuity. Well-maintained trails line the banks in many places. During the weekends, friendly hikers are often there to cheer paddlers on.

If you prefer to conserve your adrenaline, or if you're a beginner, the section from Few's Ford to the Pleasant Green Road Access and the sections below West Point have no significant rapids and are good for novices. Paddlers must use caution at the takeout below the Pleasant Green dam and should call the park for updated information about possible removal of the dam. The first and last sections described below have consistently adequate water levels and can be paddled upstream and back down, so no shuttle is necessary. For general information about paddling the Eno, call the Eno River State Park office at 919-393-1686. Be aware that Eno River State Park and West Point on the Eno have specific hours of operation. Be sure to have your shuttle car out of the gated parking lots before closing.

For information on the history of the Eno River, see page 63.

## Eno River, Section 1:
## US 70 to Few's Ford Access off Cole Mill Road

**Length:** 5.5 miles
**Time:** 3 to 3.5 hours
**Levels and Difficulties:**

Minimum = 3.5-4.5 feet (class 2+)
Median = 4.5-5.5 feet (class 3)
Maximum = 5.5-7 feet (class 3+)

**Map:** USGS Hillsborough
**Gauge:** USGS Eno River near Hillsborough
**Put-In:** Begin on US 70 Bypass on the east side of Hillsborough. No parking or access is available at the US 70 bridge, but there is room to park off the road at the intersection with Riverside Drive just past the bridge. The put-in is not easy.

**Takeout:** The takeout is at Cole Mill Road (SR 1569) at Few's Ford Access in Eno River State Park. You may put in anywhere in the park, but the easiest access is near the Piper-Cox House. Turn into the second parking area on the right. Look for the canoe sign.

**Directions to the Takeout:** See the directions to Few's Ford Access on page 67 in the Eno River State Park section. Traditionally, paddlers have launched at the end of the gravel road off the parking lot after the park office. Renovations to the parking area and some of the buildings could change this. Speak to the ranger in the park office to see where you should take out.

**Directions from the Takeout to the Put-In:** After leaving the state park, turn right on Pleasant Green Road. Drive 2.3 miles to US 70, turn right, and go 4.2 miles to the bridge over the Eno. You'll find room to park on the far side of the bridge near the intersection with Riverside Drive (SR 1706).

This especially beautiful stretch of river winds through what is known as the Eno Wilderness. It gives paddlers a real back-country feel. The scenery alone is well worth the trip. The rapids along this section include the ledge with the largest drop on the Eno. However, it requires a 3.5-foot minimum, or nearly 0.5 foot more of water than the lower sections.

### Major Rapids and Hazards

You'll encounter steady rapids for the first 1.5 miles.

Berry's Mill and Holden's Mill are class-2 broken dams.

Frank's Ledge is a huge, river-wide ledge that should be scouted and possibly portaged. It is usually run center-left and rates class 3-plus in high water.

About 100 feet below Frank's Ledge is a class-2 rapid called Rock Jumble.

The last rapid is Few's Mill Ledge, which rates class 2-3, depending on the water level.

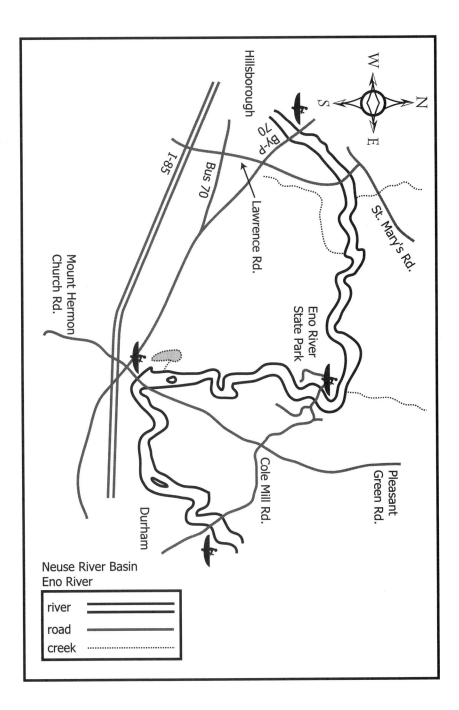

Neuse River Basin
Eno River

| | |
|---|---|
| river | ═══════ |
| road | ───────── |
| creek | ············· |

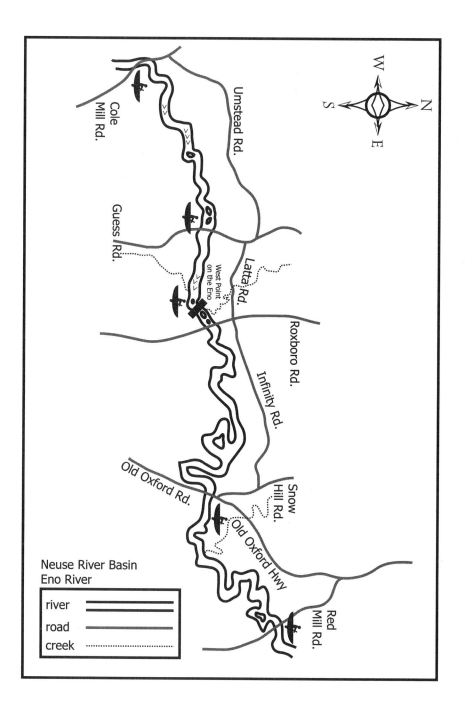

Cole Mill Rd.

Guess Rd.

Umstead Rd.

Latta Rd.

West Point on the Eno

Roxboro Rd.

Infinity Rd.

Snow Hill Rd.

Old Oxford Rd.

Old Oxford Hwy

Red Mill Rd.

W N S E

Neuse River Basin
Eno River

river
road
creek

## Eno River, Section 2: Few's Ford Access
## off Cole Mill Road to Pleasant Green Road Access

**Length:** 3 miles

**Time:** 1.5 to 2 hours

**Levels and Difficulties:** Specific information on levels is not available. Except for the rapids below the put-in, this mostly flat-water section can be run year-round. Its difficulty is class 1 under normal conditions.

**Map:** USGS Hillsborough

**Gauge:** USGS Eno River near Hillsborough

**Put-In:** The put-in is at Few's Ford Access of Eno River State Park at Cole Mill Road (SR 1569). Beginning here and continuing to West Point, all the put-ins and take-outs offer parking areas maintained by the state park. You can put in at the end of the gravel road off the second parking area on the right.

**Takeout:** The takeout is above the Duke Power dam at Pleasant Green Road (SR 1567). This is the Pleasant Green Road Access in Eno River State Park.

**Directions to the Takeout:** From I-85, take Exit 170 and follow Business 70 West for approximately 0.2 mile to Pleasant Green Road (SR 1567). Turn right and drive 0.5 mile to the access.

**Directions from the Takeout to the Put-In:** Turn left out of Pleasant Green Road Access and go 1.9 miles to the intersection with Cole Mill Road. Turn left and drive into Few's Ford Access. Turn into the second parking area on the right, just past the park office.

As this guide was going to press, discussions were being held about the possible removal of the Pleasant Green dam. Removing the dam would completely alter the character of this section of river and leave all descriptions in this guide inaccurate. Call the park for updated information.

This section is almost all flat water, except for a few small rapids right after the put-in. You'll find some development along the banks but also many secluded, scenic spots. The section ends at the Duke Power dam. Keep clear of the dam, particularly in high water! Under no circumstances should you attempt to run this dangerous obstacle. Two signs announce the dam's presence, as does a natural landmark. Stoney Creek enters the Eno on the right just upstream of the dam. It's a pretty little creek and a clear indication that it's time to pull over. If you continue, the portage on the right to the bottom of the dam is relatively easy, although the steps to reach the put-in are too narrow to accommodate large canoes.

It's possible to paddle this section as an out-and-back trip with no shuttle.

### Major Rapids and Hazards

The Duke Power dam, located near the takeout, should not be approached under any circumstances.

## Eno River, Section 3: Duke Power dam at Pleasant Green Road to Cole Mill Road

**Length:** 3.6 miles
**Time:** 1 to 2 hours
**Levels and Difficulties:**

Minimum = 3-4 feet (class 1-2)
Median = 4-5 feet (class 2+)
Maximum = 5-7 feet (class 2-3)

**Maps:** USGS Hillsborough, Northwest Durham
**Gauge:** USGS Eno River near Durham
**Put-In:** The put-in is at the Duke Power dam at Pleasant Green Road (SR 1567) at the Pleasant Green Road Access of Eno River State Park. The put-in is marked by a canoe-launch sign.
**Takeout:** The takeout is at Cole Mill Road (SR 1401/ SR 1569) at the Cole Mill Access of Eno River State Park.
**Directions to the Takeout:** Follow the directions to the Cole Mill Access in the section on Eno River State Park on page 63.
**Directions from the Takeout to the Put-In:** Leave the state park

and return to the intersection with Cole Mill Road. Turn left on Cole Mill Road, drive 1.1 miles to Pleasant Green Road, turn left, and go 1.9 miles to the Pleasant Green Road Access, located on the right immediately after the bridge.

This beautiful stretch passes through the rocky scenery of Cabe Gorge. You're likely to see hikers. Most of the numerous rapids are small ledges followed by pools of flat water. The few major rapids are noted below. Three mill sites lie along this section. One, John Cabe's mill, includes ruins. The one place where it's easy to get yourself in trouble is the put-in. Be certain you put in well below the old Duke Power dam to avoid the hydraulic just below the dam. Narrow steps lead down the hill to a point downstream where it's safer to launch. Because the land along this stretch of river is part of Eno River State Park, it's possible to run the river and then stash and lock your canoe and hike back to the put-in.

### Major Rapids and Hazards

The Duke Power dam may be back-endered by expert kayakers. It requires levels of 5 feet (class 4-5). Nonexperts should stay clear of the dam.

After 1-plus mile, you'll reach the class-2 Cabes Mill Rapid.

After 2 miles, you'll reach Drowning-Horse Pool, a class-2 rapid with a surf hole. There is no hole at 5-plus feet.

The class 2-3 Bobbit's Hole offers narrows with surfing at 5-plus feet.

## Eno River, Section 4:
## Cole Mill Road to Guess Road

**Length:** 4.9 miles for Sections 4 and 5 together, 3.2 miles with a takeout on Guess Road
**Time:** 2 to 3 hours
**Levels and Difficulties:**

Minimum = 3-4 feet (class 2+)
Median = 4-5 feet (class 2-3)
Maximum = 5-7 feet (class 3+)

**Map:** USGS Northwest Durham
**Gauge:** USGS Eno River near Durham
**Put-In:** The put-in is at the Eno River State Park parking lot off Cole Mill Road (SR 1401) about 0.5 mile north of the river.
**Takeout:** The takeout is at Guess Road (SR 1003), but there is no good access. This takeout is not recommended.
**Directions to the Takeout:** It is recommended that you use the West Point takeout described in Section 5. (See page 57 for directions to the takeout.)

It's best to run Sections 4 and 5 together and avoid the nasty put-in/takeout experience that awaits you at the Guess Road bridge. Construction on Guess Road will leave this bridge inaccessible for years to come.

This scenic section has more small rapids than the previous one and a couple of historic sites as well. The old Durham Pump Station and a few hiking trails line the banks. You'll also see the Guess-Geer Mill complex. The old supply dam has been breached, forcing the river to the right. This rapid is quite significant at certain water levels. The Guess Road bridge is just below these falls.

### Major Rapids and Hazards

The breached dam at the Guess-Geer Mill complex is located at 3.1 miles, just above the Guess Road bridge.

# Eno River, Section 5:
# Guess Road to West Point on the Eno
**Length:** 1.7 miles
**Time:** 1 hour
**Levels and Difficulties:**

Minimum = 3-4 feet (class 2+)

*West Point on the Eno*

Median = 4-5 feet (class 2-3)
Maximum = 5-7 feet (class 3+)

**Map:** USGS Northwest Durham
**Gauge:** USGS Eno River near Durham
**Put-In:** The put-in at Guess Road (SR 1003) offers no good access. This put-in is not recommended.
**Takeout:** The takeout is at West Point Park, located just south of the river off Roxboro Road (US 501). Guess Road is not recommended as a takeout because of traffic congestion and a steep ascent complete with poison ivy. The takeout is river right well above the dam.
**Directions to the Takeout:** See the directions in the West Point on the Eno section on page 57.
**Directions from the Takeout to the Put-In:** Turn left out of West Point Park, drive 0.7 mile to Latta Road, turn left, go 1.3 miles to Guess Road, turn right, and proceed 0.2 mile to Umstead Road. Turn left on Umstead, drive 3.6 miles to Cole Mill Road, cross Cole Mill onto Old Cole Mill Road, and continue through the gates of the state park.

It is best to run this as an extension of Section 4 to avoid the nasty put-in at Guess Road. This is a very short run with more frequent rapids than the previous two sections. The last significant rapid is a ledge that extends the entire width of the river. Beyond that point, the water gets slower and deeper as you come up behind the dam at West Point on the Eno. Be extremely cautious in approaching the dam. Stay well away from it. Takeout is river right, where you can pick up the path leading to the parking area.

This is the most challenging section of the Eno from a whitewater standpoint.

### Major Rapids and Hazards

You'll encounter a class-2 broken dam.

Pump-Station Rapid rates class 3-plus at 5-plus feet. This is the most technical rapid on the river. Beware of cross-currents and thick eddy lines. The safest route after bearing right around the broken dam is to cut back to the center and brace for high wave action.

You'll encounter a technical sneak at river right. River left has a very tricky eddy line. The best surfing rapids (pirouettes and ender holes) are left and center.

Outer-Loop Rapid is located just below Guess Road, where the river channels to the right into a mini-flume caused by bridge construction. At high water levels, you can sneak right through the rock garden. Otherwise, brace and run through the left chute. This is a technical class-3 rapid.

Sennett's Hole is a class-2 rapid. The rock garden is a technical class 3.

You'll reach the West Point dam at the end of your trip. Pull over to river right for takeout well in advance of the dam. You do not want to be swept into this class 5-6 debris-riddled hydraulic!

## Eno River, Section 6:
## West Point Park to Penny's Bend Nature Preserve
**Length:** 3.6 miles
**Time:** 1.5 hours
**Levels and Difficulties:** Specific information on levels is not available. This flat-water section may be run year-round.

It rates class 1 under normal conditions.

**Maps:** USGS Northwest Durham, Northeast Durham

**Gauge:** USGS Eno River near Durham

**Put-In:** The put-in is below the West Point dam in West Point Park.

**Takeout:** The takeout is river left at the steps in Penny's Bend Nature Preserve off Snow Hill Road (SR 1639).

**Directions to the Takeout:** See the directions in the section on Penny's Bend Nature Preserve on page 94.

**Directions from the Takeout to the Put-In:** From the Penny's Bend parking lot, turn left on Snow Hill Road and drive 0.8 mile to Infinity Road (SR 1639). Turn left, go 2.9 miles to US 501 (Roxboro Road), turn left, and drive 0.7 mile to the West Point entrance, on the right.

The Eno's character changes considerably in this section. This is perhaps the least appealing stretch because of development along the river. The significant exception is the last 0.5 mile of river, known as Penny's Bend. Still, this is a suitable place for a beginner, as the underlying geology has changed from the Carolina Slate Belt to the sandier, flatter Triassic Basin. There are no rapids on this stretch, which can easily be combined with the section below for a longer outing. Under normal conditions, the only significant obstacles are uprooted trees.

## Eno River, Section 7:
## Penny's Bend to the Eno River Boat Ramps

**Length:** 3.5 miles

**Time:** 1.5 hours

**Levels and Difficulties:** Specific information on levels is not available. This flat-water lake section can be run year-round. It rates class 1 under normal conditions.

**Map:** USGS Northeast Durham

**Gauge:** USGS Eno River near Durham

**Put-In:** The put-in is at Penny's Bend Nature Preserve.

**Takeout:** The takeout is a developed boat ramp. After you pass under the Red Mill Road bridge, be on the lookout for the takeout river left.

**Directions to the Takeout:** From I-85 north of Durham, take the Red Mill Road exit (Exit 182), turn north on Red Mill Road, drive 3.9 miles to Teknika Parkway, turn right, go 0.2 mile, and turn right on Rodolphe Drive. Proceed to where the road ends, then turn left into the parking area for the Eno River Boat Ramps.

**Directions from the Takeout to the Put-In:** Return to Rodolphe Drive, turn left on Teknika Parkway, drive 0.9 mile to Old Oxford Highway, turn left, go 1.9 miles to Snow Hill Road, turn right, and take an immediate left into Penny's Bend.

This section will take you to a point very near the confluence of the Flat and Eno Rivers, where the two streams join to form the Neuse. That said, this section is technically a lake paddle. Its entire length lies within Falls Lake State Recreation Area. This is a great section for sea kayakers, paddling novices, or anyone looking for a flat-water paddle with scenic appeal and wildlife. An added benefit is that it is possible to launch from the takeout, do an out-and-back, and skip the shuttle. Strong paddlers may be able to fight the flow and make it all the way upstream to Penny's Bend.

# Flat River

Although the Flat River is less celebrated and less protected than its neighbor the Eno, it is no less appealing, thanks to its rich scenery and great biodiversity. The river begins in Person County and winds southeast before joining the Eno in Falls Lake to form the Neuse. Don't use the northernmost bridge across the Flat in Person County without permission, as it requires a walk across private property. Instead, head south, where two put-ins offer access to very different but equally beautiful sections of water. Aside from a difficult final rapid, the biggest challenge in canoeing the Flat is finding a day when the water is running high enough that your boat won't scrape all the way down.

In addition to being a great local resource for recreational paddlers, the Flat is a barometer of the state of environmental affairs in the Triangle. Biologists list several rare or threatened species among the Flat's residents, including eight or more species of mussels, a mayfly, and the Neuse River waterdog. As clean and rich as the Eno, the Flat is unprotected. Threats to this local treasure come in two forms. First, there is no open-space plan for the Flat, leaving the city of Durham free to pursue plans to inundate a pristine gorge section of the river in an expansion of Lake Michie. A second area of concern is the increasing rate of development in Person County, which threatens to undermine the Flat's exceptional water quality and rich aquatic habitat before Durham's plan to flood the river is realized. Eno River State Park exists today because a small group of concerned citizens made it happen. If the same protection cannot be won for the Flat, the Triangle may lose one of the most vibrant and beautiful remnants of its rich natural heritage.

The most prominent family to live in the vicinity of the Flat River was the Mangums (see the section on Hill Forest on page 88). As tensions mounted between the North and the South prior to the Civil War, the local people prepared for violence. A militia unit named the Flat River Guards was raised in 1860. The Flat River Guards eventually joined the Sixth Regiment of North Carolina Infantry. It was with this regiment that the son of Judge William Preston Mangum marched off to Manassas in 1861. The younger Mangum died of wounds received in that battle.

A 19th-century family named Crabtree had a home and a gristmill on the Flat. The ruins of both are still visible.

## Flat River, Section 1:
## Red Mountain Road to SR 1614 in Hill Forest

**Length:** 2 miles

**Time:** 1 to 1.5 hours

**Levels and Difficulties:** This flat-water section can be run with a 2-foot minimum.

**Map:** USGS Rougemont

**Gauge:** Flat River near Bahama

**Put-In:** The put-in is at Red Mountain Road.

**Takeout:** The takeout is at a low bridge with very little traffic at SR 1614 in Hill Forest. Parking is available up the hill near the gates of the Slocum Forestry Camp (see the section on Hill Forest on page 88).

**Directions to the Takeout:** See the directions for Hill Forest on page 88.

**Directions from the Takeout to the Put-In:** Drive out of Hill Forest the way you came in. When you reach Moores Mill Road, turn left and go 0.2 mile to US 501. Turn right onto US 501 North, drive 2 miles to Red Mountain Road, turn right, and go 2.3 miles to the bridge. No developed access or parking is available here.

This section begins at the bridge on Red Mountain Road and goes to the bridge in Hill Forest. Under normal conditions, it's easy flat water with only a few riffles but an abundance of beautiful trees and very little development. Several sandy banks are ideal for picnicking. Since most of this section winds through Hill Forest, you can even stop and go for a hike.

## Flat River, Section 2:
## SR 1614 in Hill Forest to Lake Michie

**Length:** 4 miles; 3 miles of white water
**Time:** 2 hours
**Levels and Difficulties:**

Minimum = 2-3 feet (class 2)
Median = 3-4 feet (class 2+)
Maximum = 4-5 feet (class 3)

**Maps:** USGS Rougemont, Lake Michie
**Gauge:** Flat River near Bahama
**Put-In:** The put-in is at SR 1614 in Hill Forest (see above).
**Takeout:** The takeout is river left near the bridge at the park above Lake Michie.
**Directions to the Takeout:** See the directions for Lake Michie on page 436.
**Directions from the Takeout to the Put-In:** From the parking area at Lake Michie, return to US 501. Turn right onto

US 501 North, drive 3.3 miles to Moores Mill Road, turn right, go 0.2 mile, turn right into Hill Forest, and drive 1.1 miles to the bridge. Parking is available up the hill near Slocum Forestry Camp.

This section of the Flat has more white water and more visual appeal than the previous one. It winds past several small bluffs and numerous boulders. The final and most difficult rapid is at the remains of a dam about 3.5 miles below the put-in. You can portage left over the rocky bank, but be sure to watch for poison ivy. Beyond this last rapid, the river deepens into flat water backed up by Lake Michie.

At the takeout, you'll be on the property surrounding Lake Michie, which is owned and managed by the city of Durham. You must obtain a permit to take out above the lake. A sign at Lake Michie details the regulations. Permits can be obtained from the offices at Lake Michie (see page 436), Little River, or the Durham Parks and Recreation Department. No privately owned boats are permitted on the lake at any time.

## Major Rapids and Hazards

At 1.5 miles, you'll reach Round-the-Bend. Run left of center for some surfing.

At 2.2 miles, you'll reach Island Rapid. Run left of the center rock for good surfing.

At 3 miles, you'll reach Gauging Station Rapid. Run right of the center rock for the best surfing.

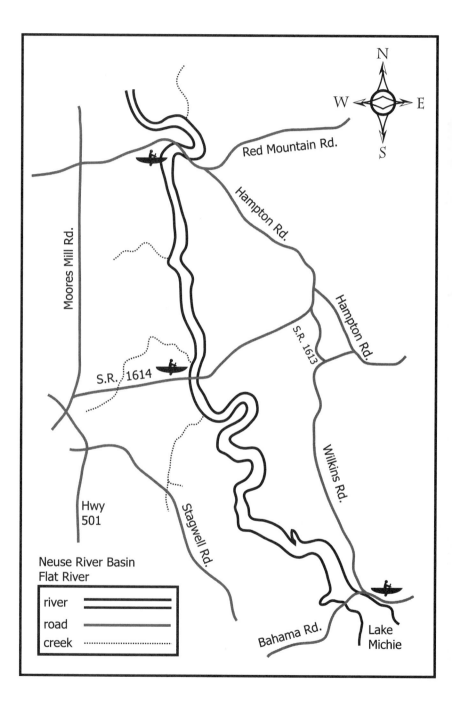

N
W &harr; E
S

Red Mountain Rd.

Hampton Rd.

Hampton Rd.

Moores Mill Rd.

S.R. 1613

S.R. 1614

Wilkins Rd.

Hwy
501

Stagwell Rd.

Bahama Rd.

Lake
Michie

Neuse River Basin
Flat River

| river | ——— |
| road | ——— |
| creek | ········ |

# Neuse River

The Neuse River begins in northeastern Durham County where the Flat and Eno Rivers join at an area now submerged beneath Falls Lake. Beyond the lake, the Neuse flows through eastern Wake County and Johnston County before leaving the Triangle. The population within the Neuse River Basin is growing rapidly. The river has been listed among the 20 most threatened in the United States. In the Triangle, the Neuse is a freshwater river, but it becomes brackish near New Bern before finally emptying into Pamlico Sound. One of the Neuse's claims to fame is that it has the widest mouth of any river in the continental United States.

Fed by water released from Falls Lake, the Neuse offers paddlers the gift of dependability. It can be run year-round except in times of extended drought.

Paddling the Neuse is a rewarding experience, despite the development along its shores. Several stretches have wooded banks. Paddling these spots with the gridlock of rush-hour traffic close by is a lesson in itself. The paddler occupies another world, in which the water is the only thing rushing and the loudest noises come as a turtle plops off a log or a great blue heron retreats from your approach.

The city of Raleigh is well aware of the precious resource in its midst. The Neuse River Master Plan is an evolving attempt to protect the river while developing recreational areas and nature preserves. The plan is available on the web at www.treklite.com/neuse/.

The developed parking areas at put-ins and takeouts make the river accessible for boaters who don't relish a harrowing climb up a poison-ivy-covered hill. At the time of this writing, there were six developed put-ins/takeouts: one at Falls Dam, one off Old Milburnie Road, one at Anderson Point Park off Rogers Road, one on Elizabeth Drive off Buffaloe Road, one on Poole Road, and one at Smithfield Commons.

When explorer John Lawson visited the Neuse on his 1701 trip through the Piedmont, he remarked on the strength of the rapids at the falls (see page 66). As it passes east of downtown

*Neuse River*

Raleigh, the Neuse flows over the fall zone between the Piedmont and the coastal plain. To early European settlers, the rapids of the fall zone were both a barrier preventing transportation of goods upstream and a means of powering mills. The rapids thus made the Neuse a magnet for commercial activity and settlement in Wake County. Before European settlers began using the river, Native Americans had lived in the basin for an estimated 14,000 years. But the river's history didn't begin there. Experts believe the Neuse to be over 2 million years old, making it one of the oldest rivers in the United States.

Unfortunately, the recent history of the Neuse has been characterized by abuse and neglect. Unlike downstream communities that must contend with huge hog farms and their associated waste, the booming development in the Triangle has created the equally serious problem of stream sedimentation. Another development-related problem has occurred because the urban population has grown faster than wastewater-treatment capacity. The communities along the river are aware of the pollution problems they face. This is another issue in which citizen involvement can help a great deal. Organizations such as the Neuse River Foundation (see Appendix 2) are actively working to clean up the Neuse and protect it from further degradation.

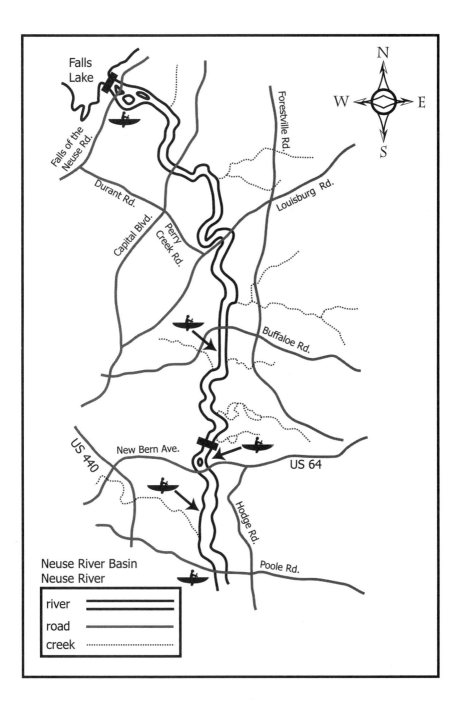

Falls
Lake

Falls of the
Neuse Rd.

Durant Rd.

Capital Blvd.

Perry
Creek Rd.

Forestville Rd.

Louisburg Rd.

Buffaloe Rd.

US 440

New Bern Ave.

US 64

Hodge Rd.

Poole Rd.

Neuse River Basin
Neuse River

N
W        E
S

| river | ═══════ |
| road | ──────── |
| creek | ·············· |

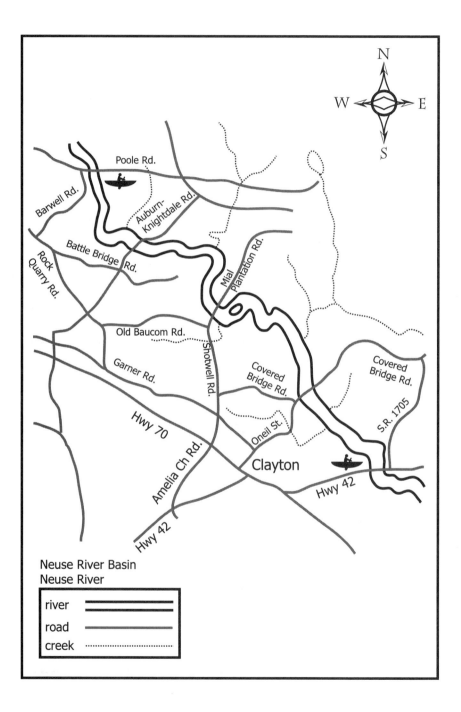

N
W E
S

Poole Rd.

Barwell Rd.

Auburn-
Knightdale Rd.

Rock
Quarry Rd.

Battle Bridge Rd.

Mial
Plantation Rd.

Old Baucom Rd.

Shotwell Rd.

Garner Rd.

Covered
Bridge Rd.

Covered
Bridge Rd.

S.R. 1705

Hwy 70

Oneil St.

Amelia Ch Rd.

Clayton

Hwy 42

Hwy 42

Neuse River Basin
Neuse River

| river | ═══ |
| road | ── |
| creek | ········ |

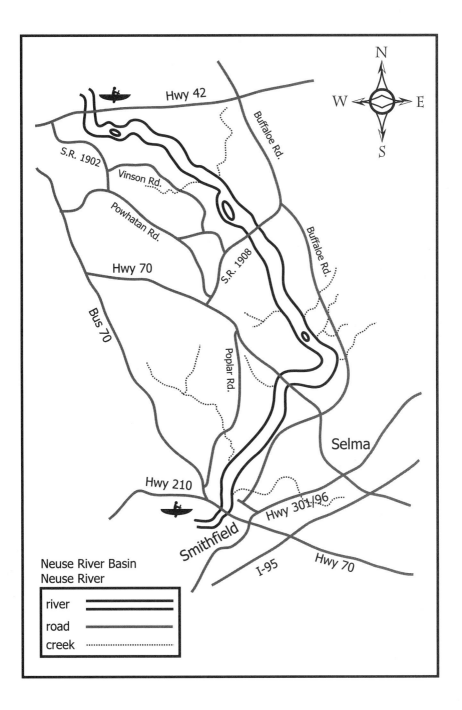

Hwy 42

S.R. 1902

Vinson Rd.

Buffaloe Rd.

Powhatan Rd.

Hwy 70

Buffaloe Rd.

S.R. 1908

Bus 70

Poplar Rd.

Selma

Hwy 210

Hwy 301/96

Smithfield

I-95

Hwy 70

Neuse River Basin
Neuse River

| river | |
| road | |
| creek | |

## Neuse River, Section 1:
## Falls of the Neuse Road to Buffaloe Road Canoe Access Area

**Length:** 10 miles
**Time:** 4.5 to 5 hours
**Levels and Difficulties:**

Minimum = 2-3 feet (class 1-2)
Median = 3-4 feet (class 2+)
Maximum = 4-5 feet (class 3+)

**Maps:** USGS Wake Forest, Raleigh East
**Gauge:** Neuse River at Falls of the Neuse
**Put-In:** You have some choices of put-ins and takeouts for this first section. Play-boaters can put in at the bridge, play to their hearts' content in the rapids, and take out at the canoe access parking lot on the right. Less experienced paddlers can put in at the canoe access area just downstream of the bridge.
**Takeout:** At the Raleigh Parks and Recreation Department's Buffalo Road Access Area, you can take out just downstream of the Buffaloe Road bridge at river right at the dam warning sign.
**Directions to the Takeout:** From the Raleigh Beltline (I-440), take Exit 11 and go north on US 1 (Capital Boulevard) for about 2 miles to Buffaloe Road. Turn right on Buffaloe Road, go about 3.1 miles to Elizabeth Drive, turn right, and drive 0.2 mile to the access.
**Directions from the Takeout to the Put-In:** Return to Buffaloe Road, turn right, and drive east for 0.9 mile to Forestville Road (SR 2049). Turn left, go 3.7 miles to Louisburg Road (US 401), turn left, drive 2.3 miles to Perry Creek Road (SR 2006), proceed 1.6 miles, cross US 1, and continue straight on Durant Road (SR 2006) for 2.5 miles. Note: The US 1 bridge over the Neuse is to the right. After 2.5 miles on Durant Road, turn right on Falls of the Neuse Road, go 2.6 miles, and turn left into the parking area for Tailrace Fishing Area before you cross the bridge. Note: The second canoe access area is on the right before the bridge. Get: Outdoors (see Appendix 2),

an excellent source of gear and information, is located just above Tailrace.

If you're strictly in search of play-boating—with no shuttling involved—you may have found your Shangri-la. You can spend hours in the rapids at the bridge. If you're not a member of the whitewater crowd, you can skip almost all of the rapids if the river level is low enough. Once you get downstream of the rapids below the dam, the river is slow moving at normal levels, but river-wide strainers are possible, as trees have fallen into the water. The scenery is surprisingly good considering the development surrounding the river. Be aware that water is sometimes released from the dam to lower the level of Falls Lake. If you're on the river when this happens, the water level will change immediately and drastically. Contact the Army Corps of Engineers for information about releases; see the section on Falls Lake State Recreation Area on page 428.

## Major Rapids and Hazards

The rapids on this section are class 1 to class 3-plus, depending entirely on the water level.

You'll encounter two ledges immediately below the dam. You may not paddle down the Dam Release Rapids, but only up to them from the put-in, located near the gravel walkway from the parking lot and the restrooms. Depending on the water level, these are the section's most challenging set of play rapids. At 4 to 5 feet, large holes develop for 360s, pirouettes, and retendos. At lower levels, nose- and side-surfs are negotiable.

About 100 yards below the Dam Release Rapids, just above the bridge, are the Bridge Holes, two beginner surfing holes, one river right and the second river center. Proceed to the far river right.

About 50 yards below the bridge is Fisherman's Ledge, a 3-foot ledge that is sticky at low levels. If you wish to run downriver, bear far right to avoid the hydraulic. Otherwise, either drop down into the hole for a wild side-surf—especially with a right-paddle lean—or go right to the bank eddy. Directly below this hole is a diagonal ender ledge at levels over 4. Otherwise, it provides for some neat 360s.

Fisherman's Ledge is a small drop that encompasses three-fourths of the river and includes a nice escape. The biggest obstacles are the fishermen casting out for dinner—which could include your boat, your paddle, or you. Three to 4 feet is the ideal level for surfing.

You'll encounter a few minor rapids—major, if you pin a strainer—before you reach the parking lot.

## Neuse River, Section 2:
## Buffaloe Road Access Area to
## Milburnie Dam Access Area off Loch Raven Parkway

**Length:** 4.5 miles
**Time:** 2.5 to 3 hours
**Levels and Difficulties:**

Minimum = 2-3 feet (class 1-2)
Median = 3-4 feet (class 2+)
Maximum = 4-5 feet (class 3+)

**Map:** USGS Raleigh East
**Gauge:** Neuse River at Falls of the Neuse
**Put-In:** The put-in is at the Raleigh Parks and Recreation Department's Buffaloe Road Access Area.
**Takeout:** The takeout is river left at the Raleigh Parks and Recreation Department's Milburnie Dam Access Area. If the water is low to normal—that is, no water is going over the dam but just to the intakes—it is possible to take out at river left a short distance above the dam on an old road that ends in the river. This road is on city property and goes around the long wing of the dam.
**Directions to the Takeout:** From the Raleigh Beltline (I-440), take Exit 13, go east on US 64 for about 2.8 miles to Old

Milburnie Road (SR 2217), turn left, drive 0.1 mile to Loch Raven Parkway, turn left, and take the first right onto the gravel road to the canoe access area.

**Directions from the Takeout to the Put-In:** Return to Old Milburnie Road, turn left, drive 2.6 miles, turn left on Forestville Road (SR 2049), and go 1.2 miles. Turn left on Buffaloe Road (SR 2215), go 1.2 miles to Elizabeth Drive, turn left, and drive 0.2 mile to the access area.

Although there are developed canoe access sites at both ends of the run, the city of Raleigh prefers that paddlers skip this section and put in at Milburnie Dam Access Area. Milburnie Dam is a dangerous obstacle. If you paddle this section, you'll need to take out well above the dam for a long, poison-ivy-filled carry.

### Major Rapids and Hazards

Milburnie Dam is the only major hazard on this section.

## Neuse River, Section 3:
## Milburnie Dam Access Area to Anderson Point Access Area

**Length:** 1.5 miles
**Time:** 1 hour
**Levels and Difficulties:**

Minimum = 1.25 feet (class 1); this section may generally be run year-round.
Median = 3 feet (class 1-2)
Maximum = 4-5 feet (class 1); at higher water levels, all the rapids wash out.

**Map:** USGS Raleigh East
**Gauge:** Neuse River at Falls of the Neuse
**Put-In:** The put-in is at the Raleigh Parks and Recreation Department's Milburnie Dam Access Area.
**Takeout:** The takeout is river right immediately upstream

of the railroad trestle at the Raleigh Parks and Recreation Department's Anderson Point Access Area.

**Directions to the Takeout:** From I-440, take Exit 13B, go east on US 64 for 2.1 miles, turn right on Rogers Road (you'll see a sign for Anderson Point Park), and drive 1.2 miles to the parking lot on the left. On the far side of the parking lot is a gravel drive leading down to the riverbank.

**Directions from the Takeout to the Put-In:** Return to US 64, turn right, and drive east for 0.9 mile to Old Milburnie Road (SR 2217). Turn left on Old Milburnie Road, go 0.1 mile to Loch Raven Parkway, turn left, and take the first right onto the gravel road leading to the access area.

This section is comprised largely of flat stretches punctuated by small class-1 rapids, most of them upstream of the US 64 bridge.

### Major Rapids and Hazards

This section has the potential for river-wide strainers.

## Neuse River, Section 4:
## Anderson Point Access Area to Poole Road Access Area

**Length:** 2 miles
**Time:** 1 hour
**Levels and Difficulties:**

Minimum = Specific information is unavailable. This section can generally be run year-round.
Median = 3 feet (class 1-2)
Maximum = Specific information is unavailable.

**Map:** USGS Raleigh East
**Gauge:** Neuse River at Falls of the Neuse
**Put-In:** The put-in is at the Raleigh Parks and Recreation Department's Anderson Point Access Area.
**Takeout:** The takeout is river right upstream of the bridge

at the Raleigh Parks and Recreation Department's Poole Road Access Area.

**Directions to the Takeout:** From the Raleigh Beltline, take Exit 15 and go east on Poole Road for 2.5 miles to the access area, located on the left just before the bridge.

**Directions from the Takeout to the Put-In:** Turn right out of the access area and drive 1.6 miles to New Hope Road. Turn right on New Hope, go 2.4 miles, turn right on US 64 East, go 0.9 mile, turn right on Rogers Lane (you'll see a sign for Anderson Point Park), and go 1.2 miles to the parking lot on the left. On the far side of the parking lot is a gravel drive leading down to the riverbank.

This section is comprised largely of flat stretches punctuated by small rapids. It also has Gunnison Rapid, the most significant rapid below the falls. Beginning paddlers can sometimes receive expert instruction on this rapid from the Raleigh Parks and Recreation Department's Adventure Program.

### Major Rapids and Hazards

Gunnison Rapid is a class-2 boulder field about 0.75 mile below the railroad bridge and 0.5 mile below the confluence with Crabtree Creek. It is generally run in the center to the left of the boulder field but should be scouted by those unfamiliar with it. It can become difficult or dangerous at high water levels.

## Neuse River, Section 5:
## Poole Road Access Area to NC 42 bridge outside Clayton

**Length:** 14.5 miles
**Time:** 6 hours
**Levels and Difficulties:** Specific information on levels is unavailable. This class 1-2 section may generally be run year-round.
**Maps:** USGS Raleigh East, Garner, Clayton
**Gauge:** USGS at NC 42 bridge

**Put-In:** The put-in is at the Raleigh Parks and Recreation Department's Poole Road Access Area, which has a ramp.
**Takeout:** The takeout is river left immediately before the NC 42 bridge. A dirt road leads to Castleberry Road.
**Directions to the Takeout:** From I-40 south of Raleigh, take Exit 306 and drive east on US 70 to Clayton. NC 42 briefly joins US 70 in Clayton. When NC 42 and US 70 divide, turn left on NC 42 and drive east for 2.3 miles to the bridge. Immediately after crossing the bridge, turn left on Castleberry Road (SR 1705). Near the intersection of NC 42 and Castleberry Road, a rough dirt road leads past the wastewater pump station down to the bank. Do not leave your vehicle where it might block access to the gates or the river.
**Directions from the Takeout to the Put-In:** Return to US 70 and turn right. Go 7 miles west on US 70, turn right on Auburn-Knightdale Road (SR 2555), drive 5.6 miles, turn left on Grasshopper Road (SR 2511), proceed 0.8 mile, and turn left on Poole Road (SR 1007). The access area is 2.2 miles ahead on the right, just beyond the bridge.

This flat-water section has only a few small rapids and one significant ledge. The varied scenery includes some beautifully isolated stretches interspersed with development.

### Major Rapids and Hazards

About 0.5 mile below Poole Road is a ledge that approaches class 2 in high water.

# Neuse River, Section 6:
# NC 42 bridge to Smithfield Commons

**Length:** 12 miles
**Time:** 5 to 6 hours
**Levels and Difficulties:** Specific information on levels is not available. This section—class 1 under normal conditions—can be run year-round.

**Maps:** USGS Clayton, Flowers, Selma
**Gauge:** USGS at NC 42 bridge
**Put-In:** The put-in is at the NC 42 bridge.
**Takeout:** The takeout is river left at Smithfield Commons off North Front Street in Smithfield.
**Directions to the Takeout::** From I-40 south of Raleigh, take Exit 306, go east on US 70 for about 11.5 miles, and exit onto US 70 Business, following the signs for Smithfield. After 7.2 miles on US 70 Business, you'll reach a bridge. Turn left on Front Street immediately after the bridge and drive 0.1 mile to the parking area for Smithfield Commons and the boat ramp. The ramp is at the far end of the parking area.
**Directions from the Takeout to the Put-In:** Return to US 70 Business and turn right to head west. Drive 10.3 miles, turn right on NC 42 East, go 2.2 miles, and turn left on Castleberry Road (SR 1705) immediately after the bridge. Near the intersection of NC 42 and Castleberry Road, a rough dirt road leads past the wastewater pump station to the bank. Do not leave your vehicle where it might block access to the gates or the river.

This section is characterized by scenery that is sometimes pristine and other times far from it. You'll have a pleasant run through coastal-plain land that is clearly different from the rolling hills of the western Triangle. When you're ready to get off the river, you'll find downtown Smithfield quite pleasant to explore. And don't forget that the town is famous for both the Ava Gardner Museum (www.avagardner.org) and barbecue!

# Little River

From their beginnings in northern Orange County, the North and South Forks of the Little River flow east to their confluence just across the line in Durham County on their way to joining the Neuse in Falls Lake. The development that has overtaken much of Orange and Durham Counties has so far left the Little River relatively unscathed. It remains one of North Carolina's cleanest streams. The state's Natural Heritage Program has identified five species of freshwater mussels living in the Little—a sure sign of a healthy river. Residents of the Bull City are fortunate to have such a relatively pristine resource, as the Little River reservoirs provide a significant part of Durham's drinking water. Of course, the booming growth south of the Little has increased pressure to develop its riparian forests. Efforts are currently under way to preserve this beautiful waterway to ensure continued water quality, a corridor for wildlife, and recreation for residents. For further information, see the section on Little River Regional Park on page 93.

## Little River, Section 1:
## South Lowell Road to Johnson Mill Road

**Length:** 2.7 miles
**Time:** 1 to 2 hours
**Levels and Difficulties:**

Minimum = 3-4 feet (class 2-)
Median = 4-5 feet (class 2+)
Maximum = 5-6 feet (class 3+); beware of the danger of being swept past the bridge.

**Map:** USGS Rougemont
**Gauge:** USGS Little River near Orange Factory
**Put-In:** The put-in is on the North Fork at South Lowell Road (SR 1461).
**Takeout:** The takeout is at Johnson Mill Road (SR 1461).
**Directions to the Takeout:** From I-85 in northern Durham, take Exit 176 and go north on US 501. Turn left at the intersection with Mason Road, drive 1.1 miles to Johnson Mill Road, turn right, and go 1.4 miles to the bridge.
**Directions from the Takeout to the Put-In:** Continue north on Johnson Mill Road for 1.1 miles to Lowell Road (SR 1454). Turn left and drive 1.1 miles to the bridge.

On this section, you'll have an eerie feeling that civilization is nearby. You'll travel through a beautiful mini-gorge for the first half of the trip—until the North and South Forks merge. At that point, recreation cabins start to appear. Get river right in plenty of time before the bridge. You don't want to be swept under the bridge into a class 3-4 gorge!

### Major Rapids and Hazards

Flush Rapid is the final and biggest rapid before the bridge. Stay in control, and stay river right to the bridge.

You'll encounter some downed trees and some technical S-turns in high water.

## Little River, Section 2:
## Johnson Mill Road bridge to US 501 bridge
**Length:** 1 mile, the last 0.25 mile of which is in a reservoir
**Time:** 15 minutes if flushed out or swimming; 1 hour at surfing levels
**Levels and Difficulties:**

Minimum = 2.3-3 feet (class 3-, though some local
   experts rate it technically class 4)
Median = 3-4 feet (class 3+, though some local experts
   rate it technically class 4)
Maximum = 4-6 feet (class 4-5)

**Map:** USGS Rougemont
**Gauge:** USGS Little River near Orange Factory
**Put-In:** The put-in is at the Johnson Mill Road bridge.
**Takeout:** The takeout is river right before the US 501 bridge.
**Directions to the Takeout:** From I-85 in northern Durham, take Exit 176 and go north on US 501 to the bridge over the western end of Little River Lake. At the time of this writing, the city of Durham had plans to develop a canoe access site for the upstream portion of the river. Note that no paddling is allowed on Little River Lake. Contact the Durham Parks and Recreation Department for the status of this project.

**Directions from the Takeout to the Put-In:** Drive south on US 501 for 2.5 miles to Mason Road, turn right, go 1.1 miles to Johnson Mill Road, turn right, and proceed 1.4 miles to the bridge.

This section is best known for its nonstop whitewater action. At the right water level, the only problem with the run is its short length. The action starts as soon as you put in and doesn't stop until you reach the lake. The gorge has great scenery as well—if you have the time to see it—including huge cliffs at river left and lots of boulders.

A permit is required to run the lower gorge section and to take out before the bridge at US 501 (Roxboro Road). Permits can be obtained at the boathouses at Little River Lake (919-477-7889) and Lake Michie, from Orange Factory, and through the Durham Parks and Recreation Department.

## Major Rapids and Hazards

Diagonal Boof is located about 500 yards down. Be sure to eddy river left before the drop. You'll need to boof right into a diagonal chute to avert the boulder. You'll find an excellent cartwheel hole at 4-plus feet.

Another 300 yards down is Mini-Over-the-Rocks, a rapid similar to those on the Nolichucky River. The center is clogged. Look for diagonal currents. Brace or sneak far right, where there's surfing galore!

Another 200 yards down is Wild Ledges, which has the biggest drop on this section, depending on where you choose to run. Eddy above to determine your course.

Pretender, the final rapid, looks ferocious but is straightforward. Eddy out behind the center rock for nose-surfing.

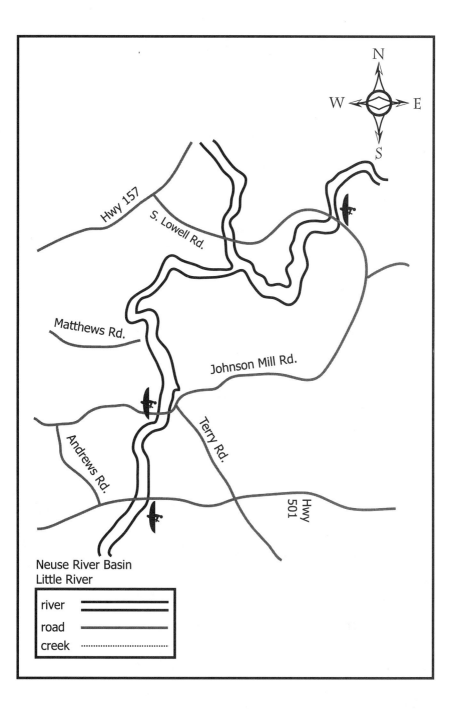

N
W E
S

Hwy 157

S. Lowell Rd.

Matthews Rd.

Johnson Mill Rd.

Andrews Rd.

Terry Rd.

Hwy 501

Neuse River Basin
Little River

| | |
|---|---|
| river | |
| road | |
| creek | |

*Jordan Lake*

# Jordan Lake State Recreation Area

**Telephone:** For the state parks office, call 919-362-0586. For the Army Corps of Engineers Office, call 919-542-2227. To report wildlife violations, call 800-662-7173. To get wind-speed information from the Sailor's Hotline, call 919-387-5969.

**Hours:** From November to February, the recreation area is open from 8 A.M. to 6 P.M. During March and October, it is open from 8 A.M. to 7 P.M. During April and September, it is open from 8 A.M. to 8 P.M. From May to August, it is open from 8 A.M. to 9 P.M.

**Map:** A free map is available from the park office and online at www.ils.unc.edu/parkproject/visit/jord/section.html.

**Fees:** Day-use fees are charged from Memorial Day through Labor Day and on weekends during the spring and fall. Additional fees are charged for camping and reserving picnic shelters.

**Directions:** All of the major recreation areas are clearly marked with brown signs. Many have signs on US 64 pointing you in the right direction.

Jordan Lake is managed by a group of agencies that includes the Army Corps of Engineers, the North Carolina state parks, the North Carolina Wildlife Resources Commission, the North Carolina Division of Forest Resources, and private concessionaires. Rules vary depending upon where you are, but most of the developed sites are run by the North Carolina state parks. Be sure you know the rules that govern the recreation areas you visit. When in doubt, use the contact numbers listed above.

Jordan Lake State Recreation Area encompasses just under 47,000 acres of lake and land. Recreational access is available at 12 separate areas. The lower sections of Jordan Lake—near where the Haw River feeds into it—are especially popular with flat-water paddlers. The lake there is narrow and has many shaded coves to explore.

Three of the developed areas have public swim beaches: Ebenezer, Parker's Creek, and Seaforth. All of these have showers and changing areas. Three areas have beaches open only to campers: Poplar Point, Vista Point, and Crosswinds. The beaches, which consist of trucked-in sand and roped-off areas of the lake, can get crowded on warm weekends. Lifeguards are on duty at state park areas only on certain days—usually busy summer weekends and holidays—so be careful. Water depths vary from one area to another. Use extra caution when supervising kids.

The most popular activity on Jordan Lake is boating. Motorboats and Jet-Skis set the tone many days of the year. Twelve recreation areas have boat ramps. Robeson Creek, a canoe launch area, is probably the best place to head if you're a canoeist or kayaker who prefers to keep motorized companions at a minimum. One annual spectacle worth seeing is the holiday boat parade, which usually takes place the weekend after Thanksgiving. Boats decked out in lights and playing Christmas songs float past Seaforth Recreation Area.

Jordan Lake is one of the few places in the Triangle where you can pitch a tent or plug in your RV after a day of paddling. Five areas offer tent and/or trailer camping: New Hope Overlook, Poplar Point, Crosswinds, Vista Point, and Parker's Creek.

No introduction to Jordan Lake is complete without a mention of the eagles and other birds. The wildlife observation deck south of Northeast Creek is a spectacular location for birding.

The bald eagles return year after year. Information about the birds and scheduled activities such as an eagle count is available from the local chapter of the Audubon Society (see Appendix 2). Visitors are sometimes rewarded with glimpses of beavers and the occasional river otter.

The Army Corps of Engineers began constructing dams here in 1974. The Haw River and New Hope Creek were both dammed to form the lake. The dams marked the completion of a project begun after a hurricane in 1945 caused major flooding in the Cape Fear River Basin. The project was not without controversy, as white water paddlers lost some of the most popular and challenging rapids in the Piedmont.

The stated missions of the lake include flood control, water supply, water-quality conservation, outdoor recreation, and fish and wildlife conservation.

## Crosswinds Campground _____

**Maps:** USGS Green Level, New Hill
**Directions:** From Raleigh, drive west on US 64 to the intersection with Farrington Point Road and Beaver Dam Road at Wilsonville. Turn right on Farrington Point Road and go 0.5 mile to the campground.

From Chapel Hill, take US 15/US 501 South out of town. After crossing the NC 54 overpass, turn left on Mount Carmel Church Road (SR 1008). Crosswinds Campground is about 12 miles ahead.

From Durham, follow NC 751 South to US 64. Turn right on US 64 and go west to the intersection with Farrington Point Road and Beaver Dam Road in Wilsonville. Turn right on Farrington Point Road and drive 0.5 mile to the campground.

Crosswinds Campground is open seasonally. The facilities include two boat ramps that are open seasonally, a campground, a dump station, restrooms with hot showers, a beach, a telephone, and a trail. All facilities are open to campers only.

# Parker's Creek Recreation Area ——————

**Maps:** USGS Farrington
**Directions:** From Raleigh, drive west on US 64 to Wilsonville. Continue 2.4 miles on US 64 to Parker's Creek, on the right.

From Chapel Hill, take US 15/US 501 South out of town. After the NC 54 overpass, turn left on Mount Carmel Church Road (SR 1008). After 12.5 miles, you will intersect US 64 at Wilsonville. Turn right on US 64 West. Parker's Creek is on the right after 2.4 miles.

From Durham, follow NC 751 South to US 64. Turn right on US 64 West to reach Wilsonville. Parker's Creek is on the right after 2.4 miles on US 64 from Wilsonville.

Parker's Creek has two boat ramps available to campers only. It also offers 256 campsites, each with a picnic table, a grill, and a lantern holder.


# Poplar Point Recreation Area ——————

**Maps:** USGS New Hill, Merry Oaks
**Directions:** From Raleigh, follow US 64 West to the intersection with Farrington Point Road and Beaver Dam Road in Wilsonville. Turn left on Beaver Dam Road (SR 1008). Poplar Point is on the right after 0.6 mile.

From Chapel Hill, take US 15/US 501 South out of town. After the NC 54 overpass, turn left on Mount Carmel Church Road (SR 1008). After 12.5 miles, you will intersect US 64 at Wilsonville. Poplar Point is straight ahead.

From Durham, go south on NC 751 to US 64. Turn right on US 64 West to reach the intersection with Farrington Point Road and Beaver Dam Road in Wilsonville. Turn left on Beaver Dam Road. Poplar Point is 0.6 mile ahead on the right.

This area is the best place at Jordan Lake for solo campers and single parents. The facilities are open only to registered campers, so new people aren't coming and going all day. The facilities include four boat ramps and 580 campsites, each with a picnic table, a grill, and a trash receptacle. A dump station and bathrooms with hot showers are also available for campers.

## Seaforth Recreation Area

**Maps:** USGS Merry Oaks
**Directions:** From Raleigh, go west on US 64 to the intersection with Farrington Point Road and Beaver Dam Road in Wilsonville. Continue on US 64. Seaforth is on the left after 2.4 miles.

From Chapel Hill, go south on US 15/US 501. After the NC 54 overpass, turn left on Mount Carmel Church Road (SR 1008). After 12.5 miles, you will intersect US 64 at Wilsonville. Turn right on US 64 West. Seaforth will be on your left.

From Durham, go south on NC 751 to US 64. Turn right on US 64 West and drive to the intersection with Farrington Point Road and Beaver Dam Road in Wilsonville. Continue on US 64. Seaforth is on the left after 2.4 miles.

The facilities here include six boat ramps, a picnic area, restrooms, a swimming beach, and Pond Trail (see page 16).

## Vista Point Recreation Area

**Maps:** USGS Merry Oaks
**Directions:** From Raleigh, go west on US 64 to the intersection with Farrington Point Road and Beaver Dam Road in Wilsonville. Continue on US 64 for 3.4 miles, then turn left on North Pea Ridge Road (SR 1700) at Griffins Crossroads. It is 2.5 miles to Vista Point.

From Chapel Hill, go south on US 15/US 501. After the NC 54 overpass, turn left on Mount Carmel Church Road (SR 1008). After 12.5 miles, you'll intersect US 64 at Wilsonville. Turn right on US 64 West. Turn left on North Pea Ridge Road at Griffins

Crossroads. It is 2.5 miles on North Pea Ridge Road to Vista Point.

From Durham, go south on NC 751 to US 64. Turn right and drive west on US 64 to the intersection with Farrington Point Road and Beaver Dam Road in Wilsonville. Continue on US 64 for 3.4 miles, then turn left on North Pea Ridge Road. It is 2.5 miles to Vista Point.

This popular spot among sailors has a beach for launching windsurfers and sailboats as well as canoes and kayaks. It also offers two group campsites with picnic tables and grills. Swimming and hot showers are available for campers.

# Robeson Creek Recreation Area ─────────────

**Maps:** USGS Merry Oaks

**Directions:** From Raleigh, go west on US 64 for 5.7 miles past Wilsonville. Turn left onto Dee Farrell Road (SR1944). Drive 0.7 mile to Hanks Chapel Road, where you turn left. Drive 1 mile to the Robeson Creek Canoe Access on the left.

From Chapel Hill, go south on US 15/501. After the NC 54 overpass, turn left on Mount Carmel Church Road (SR 1008). After 12.5 miles, you will intersect US 64 at Wilsonville. Follow directions from Wilsonville in the Raleigh directions above.

From Durham, go south on NC 751 to US 64. Turn right onto US 64 West and drive to the intersection with Farrington Point Road and Beaverdam Road inWilsonville. Follow directions from Wilsonville in the Raleigh directions above.

# Falls Lake State Recreation Area

**Address:** 13304 Creedmoor Road, Wake Forest, NC 27578; the address for the Army Corps of Engineers is 11405 Falls of the Neuse Road, Wake Forest, NC 27587.
**Telephone:** 919-676-1027 (park office) or 919-846-9332 (Army Corps of Engineers)
**Hours:** The hours vary according to the individual access points.
**Map:** A free map is available from the Falls Lake Information Center and online at www.ils.unc.edu/parkproject/visit/fala/section.html.
**Fees:** Day-use fees are charged from Memorial Day through Labor Day and on weekends during the spring and fall. Additional fees are charged for camping and reserving picnic shelters.
**Directions:** To reach the information center, follow NC 98 (Wake Forest Road) to NC 50, then go north on NC 50 for 1.8 miles.

Like Jordan Lake, Falls Lake is managed by a group of agencies that includes the Army Corps of Engineers, North Carolina's state parks, the North Carolina Wildlife Resources Commission, the North Carolina Division of Forest Resources, and private concessionaires. Rules vary from agency to agency, so be sure you're aware of those that govern the recreation areas you visit.

Falls Lake State Recreation Area includes a 12,000-acre lake and 26,000 acres of surrounding woodlands. The 22-mile-long lake extends upstream from the Neuse River dam in Wake County to the confluence of the Eno and Flat Rivers in Durham County. Like Jordan Lake, Falls Lake owes its existence to a need for flood control, drinking water, conservation, and recreation.

Several sites along the lake's shores have been developed for recreational use. Ten have boat ramps; four have beaches with trucked-in sand and roped-off swimming areas; six have picnic tables and/or shelters; and four have campgrounds. Many of these sites are populated by motorboats and Jet-Skis, which means they aren't the most peaceful places for contemplating natural beauty. Holly Point is particularly busy. Sandling Beach, Beaverdam, and Shinleaf are relatively quiet; Beaverdam is the best bet of the three. An additional draw at Beaverdam is the annual series of canoe races held there. Information and schedules are available from the park and in the *Falls Lake Guide*, published each spring and available free from many locations around the Triangle.

The best chance for a quiet, solitary visit is between late fall and early spring, when the hordes of people and bugs have retreated from the cold weather. During summer, lots of folks enjoy the water and the programs offered by the Falls Lake staff. These include family nature programs announced in local periodicals.

The Falls Lake property encompasses a variety of wildlife habitats, including upland and lowland forests, marshlands, and the lake itself. If you're quiet and observant, you might spot deer, quail, rabbits, wild turkeys, bluebirds, red-tailed hawks, and beavers. Birders often sight bald eagles and have even caught glimpses of the rare and endangered red-cockaded woodpecker. The birding here is particularly good because the lake's numerous shallows attract shorebirds. Falls Lake has more remote areas than does Jordan Lake. Beaverdam is a particularly good place for birding and general wildlife viewing. Many of the wildlife habitats are actively managed by the Army Corps of Engineers. The lake is kept stocked with a healthy population of fish.

Falls Lake was created in 1981 when the Army Corps of Engineers dammed the Neuse River. The mandate for the lake came out of the same flood-control legislation that authorized Jordan Lake. Twenty-two miles of the Neuse were flooded by the lake, including the Falls of the Neuse, which dropped 30 feet over the course of a mile.

Archaeological study in the Falls Lake area has revealed that humans have inhabited the area for at least 9,000 years. Adschusheer, the Native American village visited by British explorer John Lawson in 1701 (see page 66), is believed to have been within the Falls Lake property in the vicinity of the Eno River. More recently, 19th-century politician and militia leader James Mangum built his house near what was then Beaverdam Creek. Now, this privately owned site is across the lake from Beaverdam Recreation Area. Several mill sites dating from the 1800s are located around the lake. History buffs should also note that Stagville Plantation, now an antebellum museum open to the public, lies between the Little and Flat Rivers near the northwest end of the lake, off Old Oxford Highway north of Durham.

*Beaverdam*

## Beaverdam Recreation Area ——————————————

**Maps:** USGS Creedmoor
**Directions:** From Durham, take NC 98 East (Wake Forest Road) to NC 50 (Creedmoor Road), then go north on NC 50 for 4 miles.
From Raleigh, drive north on NC 50 for 4 miles past the intersection with NC 98.

The lack of motorboat traffic here makes this the most peaceful day-use recreation area on the lake. It offers plenty of opportunities for birders and other wildlife watchers, plus both sheltered and unsheltered picnic tables with a good view of the lake. Canoeists and other paddlers can gain access to the main body of Falls Lake by portaging the dam.

## Holly Point Recreation Area_____

**Maps:** USGS Creedmoor
**Directions:** From the intersection of NC 98 (Wake Forest Road) and NC 50 (Creedmoor Road) east of Durham and north of Raleigh, drive east on NC 98 for 1.6 miles to New Light Road (SR 1907). Turn left on New Light Road and go 2 miles north to the recreation area.

The sandy beach and boat dock at Holly Point overlook a narrow strip of the lake, which adds to the recreation area's scenic appeal at quiet times and its bustle on busy days. The vast majority of the boat traffic is motorized. The 158 campsites are well spaced and heavily shaded. Centrally located mulch toilets and a bathhouse with showers are available. The boat launch is open to campers only.

## Rollingview Recreation Area_____

**Maps:** USGS NW Durham, Creedmoor
**Directions:** From Durham, go east on NC 98 (Wake Forest Road) to Baptist Road (SR 1807), turn left, and drive 4 miles to the entrance. From Raleigh, take NC 50 (Creedmoor Road) to NC 98, go west toward Durham on NC 98 for 5.9 miles to Baptist Road, turn right, and drive 4 miles to the entrance.

This area attracts a crowd in good weather. If you're after a full-service campground with complete amenities, Rollingview will meet your needs.

# Shinleaf Recreation Area _____

**Maps:** USGS Creedmoor, Bayleaf
**Directions::** From the intersection of NC 98 (Wake Forest Road) and NC 50 (Creedmoor Road) east of Durham and north of Raleigh, go east on NC 98 for 1.6 miles to New Light Road (SR 1907), turn left, and drive 0.6 mile to the entrance, on the right.

The relatively private wooded campsites and the proximity of Falls Lake Trail give visitors to this area an opportunity that's rare so close to Raleigh and Durham—an extended hike followed by a night under the stars.

# Eno Boat Ramps _____

**Maps:** USGS NW Durham
**Directions:** Follow I-85 north from Durham to the Red Mill Road exit (Exit 182). Head north on Red Mill Road for 3.5 miles to Teknika Parkway, turn right, drive 0.2 mile to Akzo Boulevard, turn right, and go 0.5 mile to the Eno Boat Ramps.

This area offers workers in the nearby Treyburn office complex a peek at a narrow finger of the lake and puts an after-work paddle within their reach. The gravel road and the lack of traffic make for a relatively peaceful lunchtime run.

*Cane Creek Reservoir*

# Cane Creek Reservoir

**Address:** OWASA, 400 Jones Ferry Road, Carrboro, NC 27510
**Telephone:** 919-942-5790
**Hours::** The reservoir is open from late March to mid-November. Call for days and hours.
**Map:** USGS Cane Creek
**Fees::** Fees are charged for lake use and boat rentals.
**Directions:** From I-40, take the NC 54 West exit (Exit 273B). Drive 3.1 miles to the US 15/US 501 South/NC 54 West exit toward Carrboro. Follow South Fordham Boulevard, which becomes NC 54 West. Look for Carrboro Plaza on your left. About 8.5 miles after passing Carrboro Plaza, the entrance to Cane Creek Reservoir will be on your right just beyond the intersection with Stanford Road.

The 540-acre Cane Creek Reservoir was built in 1989 by the Orange Water and Sewer Authority. It serves as one of the two major water sources for the Chapel Hill-Carrboro area and as a recreational resource for flat-water paddlers. Canoes and rowboats are available for rent. The reservoir tends to be quieter than University Lake and is particularly beautiful in the autumn.

# University Lake

**Address:** 400 South Old Fayetteville Road, Carrboro, NC 27510
**Telephone:** 919-942-8007
**Hours:** The lake is open from late March to mid-November. Call for days and hours.
**Map:** USGS Chapel Hill
**Directions:** From I-40, take the NC 54 West exit (Exit 273B). Drive 3.1 miles to the US 15/US 501 South/NC 54 West exit toward Carrboro, then follow South Fordham Boulevard (NC 54 West) to the Jones Ferry Road exit. Turn left on Jones Ferry Road, go 0.3 mile, turn right on Old Fayetteville Road, and drive to the entrance gate.

This 213-acre lake was built in 1932 by the University of North Carolina at Chapel Hill to serve as a water supply for the university and the surrounding communities. Operated by the Orange Water and Sewer Authority since its construction, it is an easy bike ride from most neighborhoods in Chapel Hill and Carrboro. In addition to the usual assortment of fish and wildlife in the Triangle, adult bald eagles have been spotted over University Lake on more than one occasion. Fees are charged for lake use and boat rentals.

# Lake Wheeler Park

**Address:** 6404 Lake Wheeler Road, Raleigh, NC 27603
**Telephone:** 919-662-5704 or 919-662-5712
**Hours:** The park is open from dawn to dusk seven days a week year-round; it may remain open longer for special facility rentals. It is closed Christmas, Thanksgiving, New Year's, and Martin Luther King, Jr., Day.
**Map:** USGS Lake Wheeler
**Directions:** From I-40, take the Lake Wheeler Road exit (Exit 297) and go 4.7 miles south to the park entrance, located on the right.

The 800-acre Lake Wheeler Park is comprised of 650 acres of water and 150 acres of land. It was constructed in 1956 by the Army Corps of Engineers to serve as a water supply for Raleigh. This well-used lake is one of the Capital City's premier recreation destinations. In 1998, the city expanded park operations by constructing the Waterfront Program Center. In 2000, it added a low-profile launching dock to make life easier for paddlers and sailors. In 2001, it took the welcome step of banning Jet-Skis from Lake Wheeler. Although motorized boats do frequent the lake, it's still one of the best places to paddle in flat water in the Raleigh area. No-wake periods are enforced on Tuesdays, Thursdays, and Saturdays from opening time until 11 A.M. Fees are charged for all private boat launches regardless of type of craft; seasonal passes are available. Visitors can rent nonmotorized boats. From April through October, the park hosts monthly evening waterfront concerts. In addition, a variety of programming is offered revolving around water-based and nature subjects.

# Lake Michie

**Address:** 2303 Bahama Road, Bahama, NC 27503
**Telephone:** 919-560-4355; for camping reservations, call 919-560-4358.
**Hours:** Between March 1 and June 30, the lake is open daily from sunrise to sunset.
**Map:** USGS Bahama
**Directions:** From US 15/US 501, take the Roxboro Road exit (Exit 177). Go north on Roxboro Road (US 501) for 10 miles, turn right on Bahama Road, and drive 3.5 miles to the lake's entrance.

Known as one of the best fishing holes in the Triangle, Lake Michie is worth a visit for its natural beauty. This 550-acre lake was built in 1925 under the direction of John Michie, then superintendent of Durham's waterworks. A trip to Lake Michie needn't end at sunset, as you can spend a night in one of the primitive campsites. If you happen to be here during rowing season, you might awaken to the sound of a coxswain on one of Duke's rowing squads. Be sure to check out Spruce Pine Lodge while you're here. Park access is free, but fees are charged for boating, fishing, and camping.

# Appendix 1
# ACTIVITIES

## Mountain Biking

American Tobacco Trail, Durham County, 3.1 miles of double-track

American Tobacco Trail, Wake County, 5.5 miles

Beaver Dam Trails, Falls Lake State Recreation Area, Wake County, 6.7 miles

Bond Park, Cary, 4 miles of mixed trails

Chapel Hill Greenways, 3.1 miles

Duke Forest, Blackwood Division, Orange County, 1.1 miles

Duke Forest, Durham Division, Durham County, 14.2 miles

Duke Forest, Eno Division, Orange County, 3.6 miles

Duke Forest, Hillsboro Division, Orange County, 0.6 mile

Duke Forest, Korstian Division, Orange and Durham Counties, 8 miles

Eagle Spur, Durham County, 2.2 miles of double-track

Harris Lake County Park, Wake County, 6.8 miles

Hill Forest, Durham County, 10.3 miles

Lake Crabtree County Park, Wake County, 4.5 miles

Lake Johnson Park, Raleigh, 3.6 miles

Legend Park, Clayton, 4.5 miles

Little River Regional Park and Natural Area, 4 miles

New Light Mountain Bike Trails, Wake County, 13.6 miles

Raleigh Greenways, 4.9 miles of mixed trails

San-Lee Environmental Education and Recreation Park, Lee

County, 4.5 miles
Southern Community Park, Chapel Hill, 1.5 miles
William B. Umstead State Park, Cary, 16.5 miles

## Hiking

American Tobacco Trail, Wake County, 5.5 miles
Blue Jay Point County Park, Wake County, 5 miles
Bond Park, Cary, 4 miles
Carl A. Schenck Memorial Forest, 1.5 miles
Cary Greenways, 14 miles
Cedar Falls Park, Chapel Hill, 1.4 miles
Chapel Hill Greenways, 6.2 miles
Clemmons State Educational Forest, Johnston County, 3.2 miles
Duke Forest, Blackwood Division, Orange County, 1.1 miles
Duke Forest, Durham Division, Durham County, 14.2 miles
Duke Forest, Eno Division, Orange County, 3.6 miles
Duke Forest, Hillsboro Division, Orange County, 0.6 mile
Duke Forest, Korstian Division, Orange and Durham Counties, 8
    miles
Durant Nature Park, Raleigh, 3.7 miles
Durham Greenways, 15.8 miles
Eagle Spur, Durham County, 2.2 miles
Eno River State Park, Cabe Lands Access, Durham County, 1.2
    miles
Eno River State Park, Cole Mill Access, Durham and Orange
    Counties, 5.7 miles
Eno River State Park, Few's Ford Access, Durham and Orange
    Counties, 11.5 miles
Eno River State Park, Pump Station Access, Durham County, 3.8
    miles
Falls Lake Trail State Park, Wake County, 25.5 miles
Harris Lake County Park, Wake County, 5 miles
Hemlock Bluffs Nature Preserve, Cary, 1.6 miles
Hill Forest, Durham County, 10.3 miles
Johnston Mill Nature Preserve, Orange County, 1.9 miles
Jordan Lake Educational State Forest, Chatham County, 2.25 miles

Jordan Lake State Recreation Area, Chatham County, 10.8 miles
Lake Crabtree County Park, Wake County, 6.1 miles
Lake Johnson, Raleigh, 6.8 miles
Lake Lynn Park, Raleigh, 2.2 miles
Little River Regional Park and Natural Area, 4 miles
Mason Farm Biological Preserve, Chapel Hill, 1.7 miles
North Carolina Botanical Gardens, Chapel Hill, 1.5 miles
North Carolina Museum of Art Park, Raleigh, 0.9 mile
Occoneechee Mountain State Natural Area, Orange County, 2.2
    miles
Penny's Bend Nature Preserve, Durham County, 2.5 miles
Raleigh Greenways, 35.9 miles
Raven Rock State Park, Harnett County, 18.4 miles
San-Lee Environmental Education and Recreation Park, Lee
    County, 2.7 miles
Southern Community Park, Chapel Hill, 1.5 miles
THANKS Trail, Pittsboro, 0.9 mile
West Point on the Eno, Durham, 3.3 miles
White Pines Nature Preserve, Chatham County, 1.7 miles
William B. Umstead State Park, Cary, 38.3 miles

## Road Biking

Cape Fear Run, 95.5 miles
Chatham County, 188 miles
Johnston County, 14.4 miles
North Carolina Bicycling Highway Route 2 (Mountains-to-Sea
    Route), 101.5 miles

## Flat-Water Paddling

Cane Creek Reservoir, Orange County
Eno River, Sections 2, 6, and 7, Durham County
Falls Lake State Recreation Area, Beaverdam Recreation Area,
    Wake County

Harris Lake County Park, Wake County
Jordan Lake State Recreation Area, Roberson Creek Canoe
    Access
Lake Crabtree, Cary
Lake Johnson, Raleigh
Lake Wheeler Park, Wake County
University Lake, Chapel Hill

## Whitewater Paddling

Cape Fear River, Chatham and Harnett Counties
Deep River, Chatham and Lee Counties
Eno River, Orange and Durham Counties
Flat River, Durham County
Haw River, Alamance, Orange, and Chatham Counties
Little River, Orange and Durham Counties
Neuse River, Raleigh and Wake County

## Equestrian

American Tobacco Trail, Wake County, 5.5 miles
Duke Forest
Raven Rock State Park, Harnett County, 7 miles
William B. Umstead State Park, 16.5 miles

## Camping

Several camping options are available at Jordan Lake State
Recreation Area. Call 919-362-0586 for information.

Crosswinds Recreation Area has RV and tent sites, 129 with
water and electrical hookups. All sites have grills and picnic tables.
Showers are available.

New Hope Overlook has 24 primitive walk-in sites, each with
a picnic table, a grill, and a lantern post.

Parker's Creek has 250 sites with grills and picnic tables, 150 with water and electrical hookups. The six group sites have drinking water and restrooms. Showers are available.

Poplar Point Recreation Area has 580 sites with grills and picnic tables, 361 of them with water and electrical hookups. Showers are available.

Vista Point Recreation Area has RV sites and five group sites, all with water and electrical hookups.

Reservations are required for primitive group camping at Durant Nature Park. Call 919-870-2871.

Visitors to Eno River State Park can camp at Few's Ford Access Area. Few's Ford has five primitive backpack sites with tent pads and pit toilets; these sites are available on a first-come, first-served basis. Reservations are required for the access area's group site, which has benches, a fire pit, and a pit toilet.

Campers have several options at Falls Lake State Recreation Area. Call 919-676-1027 for information.

B. W. Wells Group Camp has 14 group sites. Reservations are required. Showers are available.

Holly Point Recreation Area has 153 campsites with grills and picnic tables, 89 of them with water and electrical hookups. Showers are available.

Rollingview Access Area has 115 campsites with grills and picnic tables, 80 of them with water and electrical hookups. Showers are available. Reservations are required for the group camp.

Shinleaf Recreation Area offers walk-in sites.

Hyco Lake Recreation Area has 60 campsites with picnic

tables, grills, and water and electrical hookups. Showers are available. For information, call 336-599-4343.

🚶🚶

Campers have two options at Kerr Lake State Recreation Area.
Nutbush Recreation Area has 103 campsites, 60 of them with hookups. Most sites have a picnic table and a fire ring.
Satterwhite Point Recreation Area has 119 campsites, 60 of them with hookups. Most sites have a picnic table and a fire ring.

🚶🚶

For information about the KOA campground in Wade, call 800-562-5350.

🚶🚶

Lake Michie offers primitive sites with grills and picnic tables.

🚶🚶

Raven Rock State Park has five backpack camping sites with a tent pad, a fire ring, and a vault toilet; the sites are available on a first-come, first-served basis. The park's six canoe camping sites have fire rings and a vault toilet; the sites are available on a first-come, first-served basis. The park's five group campsites have fire rings and a vault toilet; reservations are required. For information about camping at Raven Rock, call 910-893-4888.

🚶🚶

William B. Umstead State Park has 28 campsites with picnic tables and grills. Showers are available; the sites are offered on a first-come, first-served basis. Reservations are required for the park's group camp. For information about camping at the park, call 919-571-4170.

# Appendix 2
# TRIANGLE ORGANIZATIONS

Audubon Society, New Hope
  Chapter
P.O. Box 2693
Chapel Hill, NC 27515
919-403-8345

Audubon Society, Wake
  County Chapter
P.O. Box 12452
Raleigh, NC 27605

Carolina Butterfly Society
4209 Bramlet Place
Greensboro, NC 27407
burnetted@aol.com

Ducks Unlimited, Central
  Region
Regional Director, David
  Schuessler
6716 Ridgecroft Lane
Raleigh, NC 27615
910-847-0116
dschuessler@ducks.org

Ellerbee Creek Watershed
  Association
www.ellerbeecreek.org

Eno River Association
4409 Guess Road
Durham, NC 27712
www.enoriver.org

Haw River Assembly
P.O. Box 187
Bynum, NC 27228
919-542-5790

Nature Conservancy, North
  Carolina Chapter
4705 University Drive,
  Suite 290
Durham, NC 27707
919-403-8558

Neuse River Foundation,
  Upper Neuse River
  Chapter
112 South Blount Street
Raleigh, NC 27601
919-856-1180

North Carolina Sierra Club
112 South Blount Street
Raleigh, NC 27601
919-833-8467
www.sierraclub.org/
  sierra-nc.asp

Pamlico-Tar River Foundation
P.O. Box 1854
Washington, NC 27889
252-946-7211
www.ptrf.org

Sierra Club, Capital Group
P.O. Box 6076
Raleigh, NC 27628

Sierra Club, Headwaters
    Group
1422 Vanguard Place
Durham, NC 27713

Sierra Club, Orange-Chatham
    Group
P.O. Box 1303
Chapel Hill, NC 27514

Tar River Land Conservancy
123 North Main Street
P.O. Box 1161
Louisburg, NC 27549
919-496-5902
www.tarriver.org

Triangle Greenways Council
P.O. Box 14671
Research Triangle Park, NC
    27709-4671
www.trianglegreenways.com

Triangle Land Conservancy
P.O. Box 13031
Research Triangle Park, NC
    27709
919-833-3662
www.tlc-nc.org

Umstead Coalition
P.O. Box 10654
Raleigh, NC 27605-0654
http://umsteadcoalition.org

## Recreational Organizations

Backwoods Orienteering Club
www.treklite.com/bok

Capital Cycling Club
www.capcycling.org

Carolina Canoe Club
Membership Chairman
P.O. Box 368
Paw Creek, NC 28130
www.carolinacanoeclub.com

Carolina Sailing Club
919-782-6308
www.carolinasailingclub.org

Carolina Tarwheels
P.O. Box 111
Durham, NC 27702
www.tarwheels.org

Duke University Outing Club
Intramural Athletics
Box 90548
Durham, NC 27708-0548

Durham-Orange Mountain
    Bike Organization
    (DOMBO)
P.O. Box 2741
Chapel Hill, NC 27514
www.dombo-nc.org

North Carolina Bicycle Club
P.O. Box 32031
Raleigh, NC 27622
www.ncbikeclub.org

North Carolina Fats Mountain
Bike Club
P.O. Box 37725
Raleigh, NC 27627

North Carolina State University Outing Club
CB 8111
Raleigh, NC 27695

Raleigh Ski and Outing Club
P.O. Box 10364
Raleigh, NC 27605
919-847-RSOC

Triangle Boardsailing Club
P.O. Box 662
Cary, NC 27513
www.jollyroger.com/windsurf

Triangle Fly Fishers
www.triangleflyfishers.org

Triangle Mountain Biking
www.trianglemtb.com

University of North Carolina
at Chapel Hill Outing Club
203 Woollen Gym, CB 8605
Chapel Hill, NC 27599-8605

## Guide Services

Frog Hollow Outdoors
919-949-4315
www.froghollowoutdoors.com

Get: Outdoors
Falls of the Neuse Dam
9745 Fonville Road
Wake Forest, NC 27587
888-794-4459

## Public Transportation

Capital Area Transit
1430 South Blount Street
Raleigh, NC 27603
919-828-7228
www.raleigh-nc.org/transit/

Chapel Hill Transit
1089 Airport Road
Chapel Hill, NC 27516
919-968-2796
www.townofchapelhill.org/
transit

Durham Area Transit Authority
224 North Hoover Road
Durham, NC 27703
919-683-DATA
www.ci.durham.nc.us/
departments/works/data.cfm

Triangle Transit Authority
P.O. Box 13787
Research Triangle Park, NC
27709
919-549-9999
www.ridetta.org

# Index